Lucy Aikin, William Ellery Channing

Correspondence of William Ellery Channing and Lucy Aikin

1826-1842

Lucy Aikin, William Ellery Channing

Correspondence of William Ellery Channing and Lucy Aikin
1826-1842

ISBN/EAN: 9783744664295

Printed in Europe, USA, Canada, Australia, Japan

Cover: Foto ©ninafisch / pixelio.de

More available books at **www.hansebooks.com**

CORRESPONDENCE

OF

WILLIAM ELLERY CHANNING, D.D.

AND

LUCY AIKIN.

CORRESPONDENCE

OF

WILLIAM ELLERY CHANNING, D.D.,

AND

LUCY AIKIN,

FROM 1826 TO 1842.

EDITED BY

ANNA LETITIA LE BRETON.

BOSTON:
ROBERTS BROTHERS.
1874.

CAMBRIDGE:
PRESSWORK BY JOHN WILSON AND SON.

PREFACE.

In the year 1826, the Rev. Dr. Channing sent to Miss Aikin his work on the Character and Writings of Milton, which he had published in the United States. She wrote her acknowledgments to the author, whom she had met at her aunt Mrs. Barbauld's house in Stoke Newington while he was on a short visit to this country. Thus began a correspondence which continued for nearly twenty years, and ended only with his death.

The letters, at first somewhat formal, gradually ripen into expressions of warm friendship and the freest communication of the sentiments of the writers on subjects of the deepest interest in politics, theology, literature, the state of society, and the manners and condition of the people of their two countries. Although the greater period over which this correspondence extends, from 1826 to 1842, is within the personal recollection of those only who have arrived at mature age, the traditions of the stirring times of the first Reform Bill, of the accession of Her present Majesty, and of the other great events of the last half-century, are still fresh in the memory of most, and many questions then agitating the minds of the people both of this country and of the United States have not lost their interest or received their solution; while the social and religious topics treated in these letters possess a value for all time.

An agreement was made between the writers that the whole of the correspondence should belong to the survivor; and after the decease of Dr. Channing, the letters were given by Miss Aikin to her niece, the editor, in whose family she passed the last twenty years of her life.

In 1864, a Memoir of Lucy Aikin was published, to which were appended some of her letters to Dr. Channing. The editor having been pressed with entreaties from numerous friends and admirers of Dr. Channing to publish his part of the correspondence, has now the satisfaction of being able to complete the work by the addition of such a selection from his letters as, it is trusted, will be of general interest.

HAMPSTEAD, May, 1874.

P.S. After the correspondence had been printed and the publication announced, the editor was favoured with a letter from the Rev. W. H. Channing, the nephew and biographer of the late Dr. Channing. She gladly avails herself of the privilege of making known to her readers this valuable and interesting communication.

To Mrs. LE BRETON.

Kensington, April, 1874.

My dear Madam,—The friends of Dr. Channing will deem it a privilege to read the letters in which he so frankly opened his mind to Miss Aikin; for few of his writings give a truer portrait of his habits of life and thought. These letters are rich in singularly faithful sketches of autobiography—in fresh and fervent discussions of grand political, social and religious problems—in literary, personal and historical criticisms—in magnanimous sympathy for the people, the poor, the downcast, the undeveloped—in large and lofty aspirations towards a really new era of Christian society—in undaunted hope for the sure, however gradual, advancement of universal humanity—in serene trust in the continual guidance, illumination, influence and help of the Heavenly Father, bestowed alike on persons and the race.

For many years, indeed, Dr. Channing regarded Miss Aikin as one of his most confidential European friends; and he wrote to her in consequence with the undisguised freedom of familiar intercourse. He valued her letters very highly for the liberal information given in them, as to all movements in the world of letters, of politics and of religion around her—as to leading persons, new books and rising authors—and as to the tendencies of the times. And so heartily did he enjoy the originality, brightness, spirit, wit and shrewd sagacity with which Miss Aikin's opinions were declared, that, in the hope of inciting her to full response, he seems often to have suggested to her his rising thoughts, as if in half soliloquy. A crowning charm of these letters, therefore, will be found in their straightforward directness and simple sincerity. The writer's convictions are affirmed modestly, yet with utmost candour—decidedly, yet with desire to be set right where he may have erred. Apparently he felt sometimes, however, that he had been unguarded in disclosing his mental processes during the formation of a judgment. "This is strong language," he writes on one occasion, "and I have thrown it off very much as earnest people talk, who venture on hyperbole, and neglect to modify, in their zeal to make an impression. You must not take me to the letter."

It becomes a duty, therefore, which should be conscientiously fulfilled, to put on record Dr. Channing's own estimate of the worth of his portion of this correspondence. It is to be found in the following passage from a letter to Miss Aikin written in 1839:

"I wrote to you in my last that I could return your letters to me, so that I might have a right to reclaim my own. But the pleasure, which your last letter gave me, has left me no

PREFACE. ix

heart to execute my purpose. Still I wish for my own, not because they are good or bad enough to deserve a moment's thought, but simply because I was often conscious, after sending them away, that I had given utterance to crude notions, according little with my deliberate judgment. I therefore wish to guard against the possibility of their being published. It may be less troublesome to you to burn them than to return them, though I might be amused by them, as representing past states of mind. But this is of no moment. Do what will trouble you least."

Such an explicit statement of Dr. Channing's wishes as to the final disposal to be made of these letters might seem, at first sight, to serve as an injunction against printing any portions of them. But Miss Aikin evidently did not herself interpret the passage so strictly ; for in her letter to Dr. Channing's family, conveying this extract, she wrote :

"There are many letters, or parts of letters, to which certainly the sole objection that he mentions does not apply, and which I shall willingly transcribe for you..... And I would gladly append to them any notes, derived from my own share of the correspondence, which might be required for the elucidation of his. I am, indeed, aware that without such elucidation some papers would be obscure, and therefore liable perhaps to wrong construction. Without publishing, you may well desire to retain in your family these beautiful effusions of his bright and benevolent spirit."

a

The publication of this correspondence, then, consisting as it does of selected letters and parts of letters, may be considered as the fulfilment of Miss Aikin's purpose in regard to her honoured friend; and as such it is heartily welcomed by,

Yours sincerely,

WILLIAM HENRY CHANNING.

P.S. In this letter my purpose is to assume, personally, the responsibility for publishing these extracts from Dr. Channing's letters. His daughter and son gave, indeed, their general consent that selected parts of the correspondence should be printed. But as they have not been here to overlook the proofs, I alone should be held answerable for the publication.

W. H. C.

CONTENTS.

1826.   PAGE

To DR. CHANNING, July 9. Thanking him for a copy of his "Remarks on Milton"—Criticism of Milton, Prynne, Johnson—Liberty and Necessity 1

1827.

To MISS AIKIN, Feb. 27. Thanks for Miss Aikin's "Life and Works of Mrs. Barbauld"—His visit to her—Miss Sedgwick 4

To DR. CHANNING, May 1. Thanks for Sermon from him—Mrs. Barbauld's "Hymns for Children"—Unitarianism and Trinitarianism —His works reprinted in England—Professor Sedgwick 6

To MISS AIKIN, Nov. 1. True views of Religion—It should not be the property of the clerical profession—State of religious opinion in America—Lingard's History, what is its authority ? 9

To MISS AIKIN, Dec. 13. Introducing Mr. Jared Sparks—Remarks on Church Establishment—Miss A.'s "History of Charles I."— Exhorts her to be impartial 11

1828.

To MISS AIKIN, April 27. Introducing Professor and Mrs. Norton— Remarks on Lingard's "History of England"—State of the Church in Henry the Eighth's reign 12

To DR. CHANNING, May 28. Thanks for "Remarks on Napoleon"— Ill health—Unable to continue Charles I.—Importance of impartiality in writing on his times—Criticism on Bonaparte—Mr. Malthus, a student at Warrington Academy, his opinion of Unitarianism —Mr. Sparks, his difficulties at the State-Paper Office—Professor Smyth, of Cambridge.. 14

To DR. CHANNING, June 12. Sends "Lesson-book for Children"— Mr. Sparks—Repeal of Test Act, her opinion of—Lingard's History 18

	PAGE
To Dr. Channing, Aug. 12. Her opinion of his Sermon and his further remarks on Napoleon—Mr. and Mrs. Norton—The Reformation—Hallam's "Constitutional History"—His birth and education—Causes of the acceptance of the Reformation in England—Guizot's "English Revolution"	19
To Miss Aikin, Nov. 29. Little books not received—Remarks on Reformation under Henry VIII.—Aristocratic principles in England—Interest in the well-being of England	23
To Miss Aikin, Aug. 29. Sympathy with her illness—Wishes more information and opinion on the Puritans	25
To Dr. Channing, Dec. 26. The old Puritans—Free Dissenters—Evangelical doctrines—Moral and political state of England—Her opinion of his last work	27

1829.

	PAGE
To Miss Aikin, Mar. 30. Introducing Mr. and Mrs. Ware—Wishes the union of the good of all countries—American Puritans—Miss Aikin's translation of "Life of Zwinglius"	32
To Dr. Channing, June 12. Mr. and Mrs. Ware—Her sympathy with Americans—Zwingle—Fenelon—Doctrine of Original Sin—Charles Butler's "Life of Fenelon"	33
To Miss Aikin, Aug. 2. Religious faith—Hallam's "Constitutional History"—High-church—Toryism	36
To Dr. Channing, Oct. 8. Hallam—Toryism—High-church—Lord Eliot—Lady Fanshaw—Kantianism—Suspected Unitarianism at Oxford	38
To Miss Aikin, Dec. 31. Popery—Dr. Whately—Metaphysics—"Essays on the Formation of Opinion" and on "Pursuit of Truth"	42

1830.

	PAGE
To Dr. Channing, June 1. Remarks on Dr. C. in the "Edinburgh Review"—William Hazlitt—Metaphysics—Mr. Benson—Mr. Bailey, of Sheffield—James Montgomery	44
To Dr. Channing, June 7. Mr. Goodhue—Mrs. Joanna Baillie—Professor Smyth—Mr. Whishaw—Mr. Richmond—English society—Dr. C.'s "Means and Ends of a National Literature"—Rev. Mr. Somerville—Mrs. Somerville—Mr. Rogers	47
To Miss Aikin, Oct. 21. French Revolution of 1830—Reception of that event in England—Walpole's Letters—William Burns	51

To Dr. Channing, Dec. 14. W. Burns—Revolutions on the Continent—State of England—Jefferson's "Correspondence"—Sir J. Mackintosh—Lord Brougham—Religion in France—Horace Walpole 55

1831.

To Miss Aikin, Mar. 4. West Indies—Miss Emily Taylor—State of England—Southey—Brougham—"Edinburgh Review" 60

To Dr. Channing, May 1. Miss Taylor—Reform Bill—The King—"Life of Dr. Currie"—Berkeley—Price—Priestley—France—Lord J. Russell—Wordsworth 64

To Miss Aikin, June 22. Return to Boston—Beauty of the Tropics—Reform Bill 70

To Dr. Channing, June 28. Reform—Mr. Beverley—Marquis of Londonderry—Rammohun Roy—Godwin's "Thoughts on Man"—Paul Louis Courier—Belief in a future state—M. Vincent—Millenarians 74

To Miss Aikin, July 14. Introducing Mrs. Farrar—Price—Priestley—Dr. Wm. King, of Brighton 80

To Miss Aikin, Aug. 27. Elective franchise—Slavery—English Church reform—No mention of *priest* in New Testament—Godwin—Belief in a future state—Reception of his writings in France—Miss Mitford 82

To Dr. Channing, Sept. 6. Rammohun Roy—Dr. Boott—Mrs. Joanna Baillie—Classes in England—Mr. Pitt—Hannah More—Visiting the poor—West Indies—South coast of England—Proposed journey into Kent—King opens New London Bridge—Old Bridge... 86

To Dr. Channing, Oct. 23. Priestley—Mr. A. Aikin—Doctrine of Necessity—Dr. King—Miss Mitford—Disappointed of Kentish journey—Rejection of Reform Bill—Slavery—Bishop Hobart—Mr. Whishaw—Religion in France—English Bishops..................... 92

To Miss Aikin, Nov. 20. Rejection of Reform Bill—Aristocracy—Sir James Mackintosh—"History of England"—Visiting the poor—Godwin 99

To Dr. Channing, Dec. 8. Gratitude for effect of his writings—Approach of cholera—Spirit of aristocracy—Church patronage—State of religion in Italy—Rammohun Roy—Dr. Wallich—Mrs. Farrar... 104

To Miss Aikin, Dec. 29. Dr. Priestley—Condition of England—Slavery—Reform and Revolution 110

1832.

To Dr. Channing, Feb. 22. Condition of the poorer classes in England—Reform Bill—Difference between French and English mobs—Gibbon Wakefield—Mr. Pitt—Pauperism—Missions to the poor—Cholera—Priestley—Sir J. Mackintosh's "Essay"—Mr. Rees—Sismondi's Italian Republics—Ireland—The Farrars 114

To Miss Aikin, Feb. 23. Remarks on the moral and religious state of society—House of Lords and the Reform Bill—Improvement in France—Centennial anniversary of Washington—His character..... 122

To Dr. Channing, April 7. Effects of his writings on women—Joanna Baillie—Mrs. Somerville—Mrs. Marcet—Mrs. E. Romilly—Madame De la Rive—Condition and rights of women—France—Italy 125

To Miss Aikin, June 9. Weak health—Longing for a better climate—Return of the Farrars—Visiting the poor—Sir J. Mackintosh—Thanks for his book—Second reading of Reform Bill in the House of Lords—"Foreign Quarterly" 131

To Dr. Channing, July 15. Recovered health—Passing of Reform Bill—"Penny Magazine"—Acting beneficially on the poor—Death of Sir J. Mackintosh—Hartley's system—Sir J. Eliot—Hampden—Spirit of aristocracy—Pride of birth—"Life of Wiclif," by Le Bas—Theological library.. 136

To Miss Aikin, Aug. 26. Cholera in Boston—Good regulations—English climate, a strong inducement to visit it—Reform Bill—Aristocracy—Bishops—Pride of birth 142

To Dr. Channing, Oct. 15. Asks advice for a subject for a future work—Miss Martineau—Dr. Bathurst, Bishop of Norwich—Sydney Smith—Baron Mazeres—Cholera—Translation of Hindoo Veds—Bryant 146

To Dr. Channing, Nov. 19. Alarmed for his health—Entreats him to come to England—Lord Denman—His obligations to Mrs. Barbauld—Hallam—Possible war with Holland—Miss Martineau 152

1833.

To Miss Aikin, Jan. 3. State of health—Le Bas' "Life of Wiclif"—Scott's novels—Sir J. Mackintosh—Dr. Spurzheim—Miss Martineau—Threatening of civil war 156

To Miss Aikin, Jan. 12. Thanks for her interest in his illness—Bryant—American politics 160

To DR. CHANNING, Feb. 10. London University school—Hampstead—Sir James Mackintosh—Robert Hall—Macaulay's article on Lord Mahon's History—Ireland—"Useful Knowledge" and "Penny Magazine"—Mr. Tagart's "Life of Captain Heywood"—English reprint of Dr. C.'s book—Spurzheim—Miss Martineau—Joanna Baillie—Byron—Scott 163

To MISS AIKIN, May 30. East wind at Boston—Reform—Ireland—Slavery—North and South—Haughtiness of England—Captain Basil Hall—Miss Martineau's "Tales"... 169

To DR. CHANNING, June 13. Completion of "History of Charles I."—His sermons on "Self-denial" and "Immortality of Man"—Mr. Roscoe's Life—James Montgomery—Review of Miss Martineau in "Edinburgh" and "Quarterly" Reviews—Proposed review of Miss Aikin in "Edinburgh"—Duke of Wellington—House of Lords—Improvement in London—British Museum 173

To MISS AIKIN, Aug. 30. Congratulations on the completion of her work—His own works—Mr. Roscoe—Abolition of slavery in England—Sismondi sends "Silvio Pellico"—Mrs. Jameson's "Characteristics of Women" 179

To DR. CHANNING, Oct. 23. Review of Roscoe's Life, by Miss A.—Dr. Tuckerman—Rammohun Roy—Journey to Sandgate—Henry Bulwer Lytton's "England and the English"—Aristocracy—Robert Hall—Paris—Mr. Phillips—Dr. Tuckerman 183

To MISS AIKIN, Dec. 28. Thanks for her work, "Charles I."—Remarks on it—Rammohun Roy—Woman—Henry Bulwer Lytton—Slave emancipation—Dumont's "Life of Bentham" 190

1834.

To DR. CHANNING, Feb. 2. Charles I.—Plans for future writing—Slavery—William Smith—Dr. Lushington—Rammohun Roy—Bentham—State of literature—Politics of England—Dr. Tuckerman... 194

To MISS AIKIN, April. Proposes a subject for work—"Quarterly Review"—Bulwer's "England"—Guizot—Gibbon—Milman—"Godolphin"—Condition of England, also of United States 201

To MISS AIKIN, May 5. State of religion in England—Expected visit of Miss Martineau—American society—Women in Hindostan 204

To DR. CHANNING, May 29. Dr. Tuckerman—Mr. Phillips—Mr. (Dr.) Dewey—"Godolphin"—Condition of society—Church reform—Sismondi—Mrs. (Lady) Coltman 209

CONTENTS.

PAGE

To Dr. Channing, June 19. Similarity of manners in descendants of Presbyterians in United States and in England—Religion in England—Politics—Diffusion of literature—Anecdote in illustration —Archbishop Whately 216

To Miss Aikin, Aug. Proposes to her to write essays—Aristocracy in England—Trades' unions—Bryant—Names of parties in America 222

To Dr. Channing, Oct. 19. Spirit of aristocracy—Trades' unions— The Church—Histories of England—Hume—Lingard—Dr. Andrews —Turner—Bryant—Coleridge—Burning of the Houses of Parliament 227

1835.

To Miss Aikin, Jan. 5. State of health—Bulwer's novels—Henry Taylor—Philip Van Artevelde—Form of dialogue recommended— Style—Lake poets—C. Lamb—Byron—Tory ministry—Prospects of religion in England—Wishes to make inquiries in Dorsetshire about his family.. 233

To Dr. Channing, Mar. 10. Removing to another house—Improved prospect—Duke of Sussex—Rev. Joseph Hunter—Pedigree of Channings—Pedigree of Queen Elizabeth—English style—Southey— Lamb—Van Artevelde—Henry Taylor—Politics—Lord Brougham— Dr. Tuckerman 237

To Dr. Channing, May 13. Change of ministry — Wordsworth's poems—James Montgomery's poems—Thanks for sermon on "War" —Channing family.. 244

To Miss Aikin, June 22. House-building—Influence of beautiful scenery—Duke of Sussex—Van Artevelde—English politics—Social condition of America.. 247

To Dr. Channing, Sept. 13. Removing, not building — Remarks occasioned by his last letter—Orange association—Duke of Cumberland—Ill health—Low spirits—Hopeless illness of dear young friend —Beneficial influence on her of Dr. Channing's views—"Mackintosh's Memoirs"—Coleridge's "Table-Talk" 253

1836.

To Dr. Channing, Jan. 17. Joanna Baillie's dramas—State of the poor improving—Fire at New York—Severe winter 259

To Miss Aikin, Mar. 12. Excuses for silence—Great prosperity of America—Mrs. J. Baillie—Miss Martineau—"Cours de Droit Naturel," by Jouffroy—Peace and war................................. 263

To Miss Aikin, May 10. Miss Martineau—Mrs. Trollope's "Paris" —State of France—Society in Paris 266

CONTENTS. xvii

To Dr. Channing, June 12. Miss Martineau—Von Raumer's "England"—Germany—Rev. W. H. Channing—Ill health—Hartley ... 269

To Miss Aikin, Nov. 21. Thoughts in sickness—Alleviations—Spirit of trade, in France, in America—Lamartine—English Church—Election of President 273

To Dr. Channing, Dec. 10. Ireland—Coleridge's "Literary Remains"—Miss Martineau—Miss Tuckerman—Tasso—Don Quixote 276

1837.

To Dr. Channing, Feb. 12. Thanks for letter and sermon—Dr. Hopkins—English Church—Mr. Gannett—Prior's "Life of Goldsmith"—French novels—Influenza 281

To Miss Aikin, April 1. Pleasure in her improved health—His own state—German literature—Goldsmith and Addison's style—Mr. Norton's "Genuineness of the Gospels" 287

To Dr. Channing, April 23. Influenza—Greenacre's murder—Humanity of English mobs—Sermon of Dr. Channing's preached in Hampstead church—Power and privilege of a good pastor—Comparison of the effects of reading and writing—Public affairs—Bishop of Norwich (Bathurst)—Lockhart's "Life of Scott"—Character—Effect upon literature by diffusion of knowledge and mechanics' institute—Young ladies—Duke of Sussex wishes for Dr. Channing's last sermon 290

To Miss Aikin, Sept. 8. Duke of Sussex—Admiration of English country-houses—Miss Martineau—Remarks on good temper, in England and in America—Sir W. Scott—Politics—Means of preserving health 296

To Dr. Channing, Oct. 14. Miss Martineau—Female suffrage—English tempers—Duke of Sussex—Aristocracy—Titles—Religious movement—Lord Melbourne—Power of the Queen—State of country—Defence of Miss Martineau—Mr. Hallam 299

1838.

To Miss Aikin, Feb. 7. Asks opinion of Miller's "Philosophy of History"—Of Alison's "French Revolution"—Carlyle's "History"—Doubts her assertion of English humanity—"History of Ferdinand and Isabella"—Bancroft's "History of America"—*Holy* and *wholly*, how pronounced in England 303

PAGE

To DR. CHANNING, April 18. Complication with Canada—English humanity—Laws regarding women—State of women—Influence of the clergy on them—Carlyle—"Miller" and "Alison"—*Holy* and *wholly*—Equality of mankind impossible—Thanks for "Temperance" and "Texas".. 305

To DR. CHANNING, July 16. Rev. Mr. Gannett—The Queen—Thoughts of new work—Addison—Biography of Wilberforce, of Hannah More—Remarks on coronation 313

To MISS AIKIN, Aug. 24. Coronation—Loyalty—Aristocracy—Addison—Style—Visit to Mr. Wilberforce 317

To DR. CHANNING, Nov. 16. Prescott's "Ferdinand and Isabella"—English style—Scotch style—Blair—Robertson—Hume—Burns—Walter Scott—Charles Lamb—Dryden—Cowley—Addison—Defence of the aristocracy 320

1839.

To MISS AIKIN, Jan. 15. Aristocracy—Literary society in London—New sect at Oxford—Dr. Maltby, Bishop of Durham—Mr. Prescott 325

To MISS AIKIN, Feb. 1837 (misplaced). Her ill health—Coleridge's "Remains"—Don Quixote—Coleridge's invectives against Unitarians 328

To DR. CHANNING, Mar. 23. Dr. Pusey—Dr. Hampden—Origin and progress of High-church views—Bishop of Durham (Dr. Maltby)—The Unitarian sect—Society—Inequality of property—Thanks for address to the Franklin Society—Criticism—Bishop of London's society for education under Church control—Collecting materials for "Life of Addison" 331

To MISS AIKIN, April 28. Delight in spring—English Platonists—Hallam's "Literature of Middle Ages"—Luther 337

To MISS AIKIN, May 10. Sends tracts on "Slavery" and "War"—Evils of slavery—English Church—Rumours of war between England and America—Powell on "Tradition"—"Guesses at Truth"—"Quarterly Review"—Lord Brougham's review of Channing in the "Edinburgh" 340

To DR. CHANNING, June 19. Severe illness—Resignation—Criticisms on "War" and "Slavery"—Her views on war—Utilitarian philosophy—Whewell and Sedgwick on Paley—Activity of the clergy—Theological literature—Luther's "Table-Talk"—Mr. Rogers—Fine passage in "Texas" 345

To MISS AIKIN, Sept. 11. Congratulations on her recovery—His love of life—Present happiness—Retrospect of life—Lord Brougham ... 350

1840.

To Dr. Channing, Mar. 2. Letter lost at post-office—Penny post—Good effects—National education—Consequences of Reform Bill—Peaceable adjustment of dispute between England and America—Professor Smyth's lectures on "Modern History"—Precarious state of her brother—The Farrars 353

To Dr. Channing, May 16. Thanks for new works—Visiting the poor—Friend's remarks on his sermon—Goodness of Providence—Recovery of her brother—"Life of Sir Samuel Romilly"—The Puseyites—Church-rates—Body of Napoleon brought to Paris—Stability of the ministry—O'Connell 357

To Miss Aikin, July 18. Reply to her friend's criticism—A passage in his sermon on Dr. Follen—Anxiety to finish a work in hand—Remarks on her last letter—Professor Smyth—Character of Isabella of Castile—Carlyle—"Transcendental school"—Inspiration of Christ 363

To Dr. Channing, Oct. 11. Friend's apology—Goodness of God—Carlyle—Mysticism—National education—Strength of the Liberal ministry—Isabella of Castile—Ranke's "History of the Popes"—Wishes to know the subject of his proposed work—Visit to a friend near Southampton—New Forest—Review of Carlyle in the "Quarterly" 368

1841.

To Miss Aikin, Jan. 1. English victory in Syria—Chinese war—Remarks on war—Thinks her too severe on Carlyle—Mysticism ... 374

To Dr. Channing, Feb. 7. "Emancipation"—Slave-grown sugar—India — Peace and war — Milman's "History of Christianity"—Speculations on the origin of man—Professor Smyth's "Lectures"—Mr. Whishaw—Miss Strickland's "Queens of England" 376

To Miss Aikin, April 14. Thanks for letters—Languid health—Free-trade—Origin of the human race—Rumours of war 382

To Dr. Channing, June 12. Free-trade—Corn-laws—Despondent feelings on the state of the country as to religious freedom—Origin of man—Carlyle—France—Tory ministry 385

To Dr. Channing, June 30. Thanks for "Memoirs of Dr. Tuckerman"—Lancaster—Bell—Lord Brougham—National education—Visiting the poor 389

To Miss Aikin, July 10. English Church and Dissent—Wesley...... 400

To Dr. Channing, Aug. 6. Answer to preceding—Remarks on "Address on Home Mission Report"—Dissent—Progress of the race 404

|PAGE
To MISS AIKIN, Dec. 15. His illness—Unable to answer her last letter—Milman's "History of Christianity"—English Church—Miss Mitford's "Village"—"Charles O'Malley"........................... 408

1842.

To DR. CHANNING, Jan. 10. Acknowledges a sermon—Dr. Milman—Visit to Bath—Addison—Miss Sedgwick—German literature—William Taylor—Mrs. Austin—State of England—Her colonies—Mrs. Carter's "Dialogue between Body and Soul" 411

To MISS AIKIN, June 12. His illness through the winter—Pleasure in beautiful country in sickness—Miss Sedgwick—Beauty of American women—Superiority to English women 417

To DR. CHANNING, Aug. 9. English and American women—Thanks for "Duty of the Free States"—"Life of Oliver Heywood"—Mr. Savage—Addison—Unpublished letters of his time.................... 420

CORRESPONDENCE.

TO DR. CHANNING.

Hampstead, July 9, 1826.

I FEAR, Sir, I must have appeared negligent and ungrateful in not sooner returning you my thanks for a copy of your excellent remarks on the character and writings of Milton; but since I received them, which is about a fortnight, this is my first opportunity of writing. Accept my most cordial acknowledgments of the justice and honour you have done to that great and injured character—that true servant of God, that sublime teacher of the noblest truths to man.

From my earliest youth I have been an assiduous and reverential student of his poetical works, that inestimable storehouse of instruction and delight, that fount of inspiration; lately I have re-perused them with a more direct reference to the circumstances of the times and the character and situation of the author, and I am thus enabled to give my deliberate testimony to the soundness, and at the same time the novelty and originality, of your observations. In a short fragment of observations on Milton, which I found among Mrs. Barbauld's papers, was an expression of surprise that his ardent attachment to liberty so seldom breaks forth in his verse; but your remark that it was principally the freedom of the mind to which he paid homage, well explains this circumstance. He deeply felt that "who loves that must first be wise and good," and to make men so, he accounted the first and most important service to be rendered them. What you say of the futility of looking back to the Primitive Church for authority, is excellent, and so far as I know, entirely new; the notion of a progressive Christianity is very strikingly expressed, I remember, in that pamphlet of Mr. Wakefield's on Public Worship, which I think was considerably misconceived by my aunt, and therefore misrepresented in her answer. It is manifest that Christianity can only be permanent for the future, has only been so through past ages, by silently adapting itself to the manners and sentiments of different times and countries; even the Church of Rome is far from being now what it was in the tenth century. I was surprised on first looking into the Puritanical writers, particularly Prynne, to find how much he relied on the authority of the Fathers, and even of some of the early Popes; and I inquired how and when it was that those writers had lost their authority with modern English theologians, even those of High-church principles; an intelligent friend answered me, "Ever since Middleton gave them an incurable wound." On this subject Milton did not advance beyond his age. You have certainly not given Johnson more reprehension than he richly deserved for his outrages against one so inestimably his superior. My dear father made many efforts to counteract the effects of his prejudice and bigotry in this and many other instances; he was once engaged in the office of re-editing Johnson's Poets, with corrections and additions, and I always regretted that the failure of a bookseller interrupted this design; he published Milton, however, with some spirited remarks on his former editor. In this country, where Tory and High-church principles are still lamentably prevalent, it is impossible to estimate the mischief, as I should call it, which Johnson has effected, by lending the sanction of his authority to popular prejudices. I know no other example of powers so vigorous, self-devoted to the drudgery of forging chains and riveting fetters on the human mind.

The great questions on Liberty and Necessity, Matter and Spirit, have evidently much employed your thoughts, and I cannot but wish that they may employ your pen; the first especially is a theme of vital interest, and one on which there is the strangest contrariety between the results of our reasoning, and in some degree of our experience—for we witness the apparently irresistible sway of external motives in many instances—and a certain internal conviction which ought perhaps to be of still higher authority with us. I recollect that when I had the pleasure of seeing you at Newington, we spoke of the neglect into which metaphysical science had fallen among us, and certainly very little appears to be written on these subjects; nevertheless, they must always, I conceive, occupy a portion of the meditations of every inquiring mind, and I believe it will always be in the power of an original and able writer on them to attract considerable attention. The general progress of light and knowledge, too, reflects in various ways upon these pursuits, and makes it right that the standard works should at least be from time to time re-examined; it appears to me that Locke himself requires modernizing in several parts of his subject. Your glimpses of the advancement of the human mind are wonderfully cheering and animating, and who shall presume, even in thought, to set limits to its high career in a land where you already possess that prime boon which the learned and enlightened Selden vainly sighed for, "freedom in everything"? Here it may still be the work of ages to liberate the mind from bondage, for that great engine of civil and intellectual tyranny, a State religion, stands, and is likely to stand; but with you liberty is its birthright. It ought to be a cause of thanksgiving to every lover of man and his best interest to think that there is in the world such a temple of freedom erected. May God prosper it!

    Believe me, Sir, with high esteem,
       Very sincerely yours,
         Lucy Aikin.

To Miss Aikin.

Boston, February 27, 1827.

I owe you many thanks for your repeated attentions, although I must seem to you anything but grateful. Your letter acknowledging the reception of my " Remarks on Milton" was peculiarly gratifying to me. There was one passage in it which you probably wrote without thinking of the pleasure I was to derive from it. I refer to that in which you give your " testimony to the *soundness* of my remarks." Truth, I hope, is supremely dear to me; and I had been disturbed by occasional apprehensions lest my admiration of the man, joined with my distance from his age and country, had betrayed me into some false views. Your testimony gave me relief. I trust that you will give to the world the results of your researches into the age of Milton.

But let me turn from myself. I thank you, as thousands have done, for your tribute to the memory of Mrs. Barbauld, and I am peculiarly indebted to you for the present of her works. I can remember Mrs. Barbauld's poetry from early life, and I owe to her more than delight. Some of her pieces, we may suppose, she will recollect for ever with pleasure, for they have lifted many minds to that pure world in which she has found rest. Much of the prose volume was new to me, and I felt that she had not received the praise due to her in this species of composition. I was struck with the felicity of the style, and the freshness and animation, and frequently the originality, of her thoughts. I remember my short interview with her with much pleasure. Perhaps I never saw a person of her age who had preserved so much of youth; on whom time had laid so gentle a hand. Her countenance had nothing of the rigidity and hard lines of advanced life, but responded to the mind like a young woman's. I carry it with me as one of the treasures of memory.

I am happy to learn that you correspond with my friend Miss Sedgwick. She is the delight of those who best know her. I am very desirous that the intercourse between the intellectual of our two countries should be increased. England is hardly just as yet to the American mind, and I grieve for this, not because I want you to flatter us, but because the two great *free* nations of the world, on whom the cause of human improvement chiefly rests, ought to be joined by sympathy and mutual interest and respect. It will always give me great pleasure to hear from you; and if I can in any way serve you, I beg you to write to me as to a friend.

Very respectfully your friend,
W. E. CHANNING.

To Dr. Channing.

Hampstead, May 1, 1827.

I have many acknowledgments to return you, Sir, for a letter so truly acceptable to me, in various respects, as that with which you have favoured me. Since its date I have also received from you a dedication sermon, which I have read and re-read with increasing admiration and satisfaction. Of all the products of my aunt Barbauld's fine genius, which you have commemorated in a manner most gratifying to my feelings, there is none which during my whole life I have prized so highly as her "Hymns for Children," by which, with the most delightful allurements of style, the infant mind is insensibly led to look up through all which it beholds, whether of animated or inanimate, physical or moral nature, to the infinitely wise and beneficent Cause of all. To a spirit early and deeply imbued with this general religion, particular systems have something of low and narrow, from which it recoils with a sense of disappointment or disgust, ready to ask, like Lucan's Cato at the Temple of Jupiter Ammon, whether the universal deity,

Steriles ne elegit arenas,
Ut caneret paucis, mersitque hoc pulvere verum ?

But such spirits your views of Unitarianism are well calculated to conciliate, by showing it in strong and lovely contrast to those systems which you well describe as "shut up in a few texts," and insulated alike from all which nature teaches of a God, and from all the lights which the cultivated intellect is now deriving from reason and philosophy.

Your remarks on the influence of Trinitarianism in "shutting the mind against improving views from the universe," open up a long train of interesting reflections, which I should be glad to see you pursue much further. It has often grieved me to observe how extensively this popular system of theology operates to degrade and distort men's moral sentiments and their views of human life. Certainly the deity of that system is not *good;* he is jealous of that love of happiness which he has himself implanted in the human bosom instinctively, and hence endless contrarieties between the language of its followers and their feelings—between their system and their intimate convictions. Men are supposed to be called upon, not in time of persecution alone, but universally, to choose between this world and another, to renounce the enjoyments of the present life, and to count sorrows and privations as the only wholesome food of souls. But this is hard doctrine, and its most obvious effect is to prompt a very offensive species of *canting,* which prevails at present in this country to such a degree as to afflict and perplex all who are inclined to hope well of the progress of human improvement. To him who regards the Deity as truly *one,* and unchangeable through all ages, there is no such contrariety—this world, the present life, are parts of God's space and God's time; His goodness is here, and will be everywhere for ever; and He has not written one thing on man's heart, and another in a book of laws for his guidance.

Pray go on to give us more of the products of your acute, enlightened and pious mind, and your most eloquent and masterly pen. Bear in mind that you are writing for England as much as for America. The fifth edition of your discourse on the ordination of Mr. Sparks, printed at Liverpool, a Liverpool edition of your "Duties of Children," and a Bristol one of your "Discourse on the Evidences," all lie before me. Your remarks on Milton, and this last discourse, have also been reprinted, and so will everything be that you write; but if you would give us a *volume*, it would draw more attention and produce more effect than many tracts, because it would be noticed in reviews, circulated in book societies, and displayed on library shelves. Oh! that you would give us a system of morals according to your own views; this would be a treasure to the present and following generations. In your noble country, where all faiths stand on equal ground, you write both without the fears and without the exasperation of a sect struggling to erect itself beneath the frown of an imperious Establishment, a circumstance which gives you a superiority *here* more felt than expressed. I find in it an additional reason for joining you in the wish that the intellectual intercourse of our two countries should be continually extended, and that the utmost cordiality of feeling should exist between the friends of light and knowledge in both. I rejoice to hear of all your advances, and inquire eagerly after all your literary novelties, and so do many of my friends; and now that our administration has happily ceased to be *Tory*, it will be less than it has been a fashion to undervalue your efforts. My New York correspondent is not Miss Sedgwick, but her very intelligent brother, Mr. H. D. Sedgwick; but I imagine that writing to either is writing to both. Nothing will give me more gratification than to hear from you as often as your important avocations will admit. The state of America is a peculiarly interesting subject to many of my friends, and one on which it is difficult here to gain authentic information: we want to hear towards what form of religious sentiment your people most incline, and whether the absence of an Establishment leaves in fact any considerable number destitute of religious worship—in short, how this great experiment turns out.

Believe me yours, with great esteem,
LUCY AIKIN.

To MISS AIKIN.

Boston, November 1, 1827.

Your letter of May last, my dear Miss Aikin, gave me great pleasure, peculiar pleasure. Your favourable opinion of the sermon I sent you was the more welcome, because that production has drawn upon me more angry criticism than anything I have published. Your remarks, and many other circumstances, show me that it is accomplishing its end. I feel very deeply how much religion is obstructed by low and false views of it, and if I can remove them in any degree, I shall think myself living for some purpose. The religious principle is, without doubt, the noblest tendency of our minds. Its office is to connect us with the Supreme Mind, and I do mourn when I see it, as I often see it, perverted by wrong conceptions of its Object, breaking the spirit, and making men abject in speech and conduct. I do not know how greater good can be done than by showing men the sublime purpose for which the capacity of religion was given; how it accords with reason and conscience; how it strengthens, in particular, the loftier principles and virtues, and gives the mind an impulse towards perfection. I want that the subject should be taken out of the hands of the *canting*, who have disgusted you so much. How is it that men of intellect and sensibility should give up the noblest subject in the universe to technical theologians, who are degrading it by their narrow and mechanical mode of handling it? It sometimes amazes me that Religion, the science which treats of our highest relations and of the ultimate purpose of our being, should have fallen into disrepute; that it should be suffered to be the property of the clerical profession; and that the noblest minds should either not think of it, or should satisfy themselves with the tame conceptions of their inferiors. I know no subject of such universal interest, so little technical and positive, so worthy of vigorous and enlarged minds; and until such minds regard it as their noblest province, and resist the usurpations of those who now make it a monopoly, I despair of any great progress of society in that class of thoughts, feelings and virtues, which constitutes the elevation of our nature.

You are anxious to know something about the state of religious opinion here; how the current sets; how we get on without a religious Establishment. We agree a good deal with England.

There is with us, as with you, a degree of combination among the sects who hold the antiquated theology against the spirit of improvement. Perhaps one peculiarity of our country is, that these sects are striving to withstand the progress of better opinions by what are called *revivals*, by which you are to understand unusual *excitements*, seizing at once on a considerable portion of a congregation, produced chiefly by terror and by a machinery too complicated to be described in a short letter, but which are ascribed to a special operation of the Spirit of God. I may be able to send you a printed account of them soon from an impartial hand. I have much to say about our religious establishment or no-establishment. The subject can hardly be understood in your country—and here a wise man will speak cautiously. One thing we have found, that the absence of an Establishment is not synonymous with freedom, and that everywhere men must contend for their rights, if they would keep them.

Your sincere friend,
W. E. CHANNING.

What is the authority of Lingard's England?

To Miss Aikin.

Boston, December 13, 1827.

Will you permit me, my dear Miss Aikin, to introduce to you a friend of mine, Mr. Sparks, a gentleman who holds a conspicuous place in our literature, and who has many claims on the enlightened and good of all countries.

He is the editor of the "North American Review," a work which we think must have made our intellectual resources better known to England. He visits your country to get materials for an important historical work. I hope you will see him long enough to get at his mind, for he has some reserve. You have much curiosity about our country. I know no man who can give you equal information. He will give you his opinion on the question which you have asked me more than once, how we succeed without a Church Establishment. On this point I have deferred writing you, because a great deal is to be said. The danger which was apprehended from our experiment, that we should have no religious instruction, proves so far wholly imaginary. We have as much teaching as other countries, and all who make the comparison think we have better. But the great question, which is, how far intellectual liberty is promoted by it, is not so easily settled. Everywhere the *sovereign* is worshipped, and in countries where the people is the sovereign, this worship is not wanting. The love of place, office, consideration, is at work, and seeks gratification by flattering or not resisting popular notions. Independence of thought is a rare attribute anywhere. Here, as elsewhere, men of like views herd together, and love to rule by the authority of numbers; and not a few, mistaking the joint cry of a multitude for the strong, confiding tone of truth, give up their judgments to the majority. Sects, too, do not cease to be intolerant because formed in republics. I merely throw out these remarks in the hope of extending them. It is the ordinance of God that man is to be free in the true sense of that word—not through his outward condition, but through his own moral energy; he must fight for it, and win the blessing for himself. When is your work on Charles I. to appear? I look forward to it with anticipation of much pleasure and instruction. Your former works of this nature have given me a better insight into the times of which you treat than I had gained before from the historians. You know undoubtedly the delicacy of your task. L can hardly lay aside my professional tone, and refrain from *exhorting* you to be *impartial*. Liberty is not responsible for the faults and crimes of her adherents in former times, nor are we serving her by throwing their gross errors into the shade, or by the least injustice to her foes.

Very respectfully, your friend,
W. E. CHANNING.

To Miss Aikin.

Boston, April 27, 1823.

I beg to introduce to you, dear Miss Aikin, a friend of mine, who desires to know you, and whom I am equally desirous that you should know. It is Mr. Norton, of Cambridge, one of the professors of theology at that institution. He is one of our most distinguished scholars and writers, a man of taste and general knowledge, and a strong thinker. His lady, who accompanies him, is one of our most valued women. Her intelligence and virtues make her the delight of her friends. I am truly happy when I can bring the good and wise of our two countries to know one another. In a late letter by Mr. Sparks, I asked your opinion of Lingard's History of England. I am reading his account of the Reformation in that country. Is it not as impartial as the Protestant accounts? Nothing surprises me in that business so much as the case with which Henry accomplished his purpose. I think it not very creditable to the English character. I would ask if history furnishes an example of a people receiving fundamental changes in their religion with so little resistance? I know not how Lingard could have passed a severer rebuke on the Catholic Church in England than by recording, as he does, the almost unresisting submission of all orders, clergy and laity, to the subversion of the old system. The scarcity of illustrious martyrs under Henry shows a very rotten state of the Church. More and Fisher were victims to the suspicious cruelty of the King, and not to their own courageous assertion of what they thought truth. They would willingly have held their peace. The French clergy in the late revolution, whom we thought so corrupt, did far better. One would have thought that rather than substitute a temporal for a spiritual head, and submit to excision from the only true and apostolic Church, the English Church, not to say people, would have taken any hazard of a struggle with the Crown. I want some explanation of this part of your history. It would seem as if the Catholic religion had taken a feebler hold of the English than of other nations, and yet your previous history does not indicate this. Is Lingard's view of Cranmer to be trusted? Have you ever thought of giving us the memoirs of that period? I am looking with much hope for the memoirs of Charles I. I have received much instruction and pleasure from your previous labours in this department, and am somewhat impatient to know more of the secrets of the stormy time of Charles.

I hope soon to hear from you.

With respect, your sincere friend,

WM. E. CHANNING.

TO DR. CHANNING.

Hampstead, May 28, 1828.

Dear Sir,—A few days since I had the pleasure of receiving your valued and interesting letter by Mr. Sparks. I had long been your debtor for that which accompanied your admirable remarks on Napoleon, and I am now impatient to avail myself of the recovered power of writing, to assure you that I am not ungrateful. I say the recovered power, because I have been struggling for many months with a state of weak and precarious health, which by compelling me to remain in a recumbent posture, made the act of writing exceedingly troublesome and fatiguing. Though still much of an invalid, I am now considerably better, and my medical brother gives me at length assurance that I am proceeding, though slowly, towards complete recovery. This I had so little expected, that I have found some difficulty in returning to the interests of a life which I was fully prepared to quit: its cares and duties, clogged with a long arrear of neglected business, seemed to summon me almost rudely back from a state of languor which was not without its charms. In such a state, I have often repeated the line, "Resigned to die, or resolute to live," and thought the former much the easier part of the alternative; it must now be my endeavour to brace my mind for the latter. I have a great task before me to fulfil, and I pray God I may so fulfil it as to prove my gratitude to Him for life and all its blessings.

You will not wonder after this to hear that King Charles has been at a complete stand; yet I am not without doubts that the future work may have been gaining by an interval in which I have found opportunity for some general reading in history, and much meditation. Everything imprints more and more deeply on my mind the importance of the great historic virtue which I thank you for exhorting me to—that of impartiality. Certainly, instead of doing a service to the great cause of liberty by veiling the errors of its champions, we do it in fact the greatest injury, especially where we have failures to relate; for if the fault was not in the men, it seems a just conclusion that it must have been in the cause. On the other hand, by representing its opponents as worse men than they really were, we lighten arbitrary power itself of the reproaches justly its due, to discharge them on the vices accidentally adhering to its supporters. But certain principles have a tendency to produce certain effects, good or bad, on the minds and manners of their advocates; and the chief utility of introducing biographical details largely into works of history is, that these tendencies may be impressed and illustrated by examples; that both the rule and the exceptions to it may be fully understood, and thence just inferences may be drawn regarding principles themselves—and how can these *just* inferences, so important to virtue and happiness, be drawn from any but *true* premises?

You have done the world, I think, a great service, by your view of the character of Bonaparte, which appears to me a model of just and wise appreciation, and which has attracted with us much attention and applause. I lately recommended it to the perusal of an old lord, whose manly and rational mind seemed to me likely now to approve it, though in his youth he had visited your land in the capacity of aide-de-camp to Clinton; clearly he entertained no prejudice against the nation of the writer. I believe—I fear, that as long as there is man, so long there will be war upon the earth; and in war, as in all human things, good is mingled with evil, and sometimes we seem to see that Providence has effected great and beneficial changes by its means, which no other means within our knowledge could have produced; but this is no reason why a conqueror should not be shown as what he truly is—a scourge of the earth. Your view of the character of this surprising man delighted me the more, because I found in it a very remarkable correspondence with the sentiments which my dear father was accustomed to express; he, like you, regarded him as in most respects a man of vulgar mind, a mere soldier of fortune, and he expressed the same indignation against those who, calling themselves friends of freedom, yet ranked among his partizans. With respect to the style of your piece, I am almost afraid to express to you the extent of my admiration—but with what pleasure did I hear a literary friend, a few days since, decidedly pronouncing Dr. Channing the most eloquent living writer of the English language!

I am very much *enlightened* by what you say of religious sentiment amongst you. Certainly the sovereign will be everywhere flattered and worshipped; and in these matters the sovereign people is not likely to be wiser than other sovereigns. My father used to say of the popular systems that they *bid high* for mankind, and I believe mankind must become a good deal wiser before Unitarianism will be able to outbid them in the minds of the multitude; but certainly there is a progress in both countries: here it has lately been marked by the abolition of our Test laws, and you go on founding Unitarian churches. The celebrated political economist

Malthus, a clergyman, but a liberal—for he was brought up under my liberal grandfather at Warrington, and has always acted with our Whigs—slid into his pocket the other day my copy of your dedication sermon, saying, " It is a system which every good mind must wish to be true, but I think there are considerable difficulties from some of the texts." I have not yet had the opportunity of inquiring whether you have removed his difficulties.

I thank you much for your introduction of Mr. Sparks. I have yet seen him only for half an hour, and that was chiefly occupied by my questions and his answers respecting his objects of pursuit here. He has been illtreated at our State Paper Office, through the illiberality or exclusive caution of Mr. Peel, and was hopeless of being allowed to take copies of papers which were at first promised him; but I think means may yet be found, and I have set a friend to work, but without the knowledge of Mr. Sparks. Next week I hope he will meet at my tea-table the professor of modern history from Cambridge, Mr. Smyth, a very liberal and enlightened person, who will be happy, I know, in the opportunity of giving and receiving information; and two other literary friends, who will probably be able to assist his objects both here and at Paris.

I feel that I have written you an enormous letter, yet I think you will hear of me again before long. During my illness I have just been able to amuse myself with preparing a little lesson-book for children, most of which I had by me in pieces, written for my brother's young ones. Learning from Mr. Sparks that you have a little son, I shall venture to send you a copy, and with it a book for young people, which we have lately printed from a MS. of my father's.

Believe me, dear Sir, yours, with true esteem,
L. AIKIN.

To Dr. Channing.

Hampstead, June 12, 1828.

Dear Sir,—I have now the pleasure of requesting your acceptance of my father's little book and my own, which I hope may be not unwelcome to the younger members of your family. How deeply do I feel myself indebted to you for your introduction of Mr. Sparks! He is indeed a mine of information respecting everything which it is most interesting to learn of your great country; and I am proud to tell you that he did us the favour to communicate his knowledge and his sentiments with great freedom. His very looks bespeak goodness, and the more I conversed with him the more I was struck with the candour of his mind, as well as the strength of his judgment. I had the pleasure of introducing him to several literary friends, and all speak of him in terms of esteem and admiration.

He promises to visit us again on his return from the continent, and I hope by that time he will find all the obstacles surmounted which have been opposed to his consulting our State papers. It is plain that historians of the War of Independence are much more likely to arise on your side of the water than on ours; and those who are anxious that more than just blame should not be called on the measures of our Government, can do nothing so effectual as to promote the throwing open of all our documents to an American inclined to relate the facts with candour, and an endeavour at least at impartiality. Mr. Sparks assured me that the effect of all that he had been permitted to inspect at the Home Office had been to soften his feelings towards the British Government; and certainly this modification of judgment is the natural result of hearing both sides. I think you would rejoice to hear of the abolition of our sacramental test. It is the more satisfactory because the measure was carried in direct contradiction to the wishes of the King, by the sole force of public opinion declaring itself through the House of Commons with an energy which ministers found it vain to oppose. Alas! that the Catholic question should not also have been gained! All thinking people must dread the effects of renewed disappointment on the minds of so formidable a body as the Irish Catholics. In granting to them the civil rights of other subjects, I confess I see neither difficulty nor danger, neither probably do most of the opponents of the measure; but they say, Concede that, and they will next demand the establishment of their own hierarchy on the ruins of the Protestant Church of Ireland, on the plea that the Established Church ought to be that of the majority—a plea not easy to be refuted. In your country you have at least no dilemma like this to apprehend. I think I have never answered a question in one of your letters respecting the credit of Lingard's History. I have examined carefully the narrative of those reigns which I have studied, and I do not hesitate to affirm that, with all its apparent candour, it abounds in artful misrepresentations; but can or dare a Catholic priest be an honest historian of events involving the interests or the reputation of his Church? I greatly doubt it.

Believe me, dear Sir, yours with much esteem,

LUCY AIKIN.

To DR. CHANNING.

Hampstead, Aug. 12, 1828.

Dear Sir,—I hope you will have received before this reaches you my long-delayed little book and a letter accompanying it; Mr. Sparks put me in the way of sending it through his London bookseller, addressed to his care, by which direction you may hear of it, should it not have reached you, a poor return at best it is for the two admirable pieces with which you have last favoured me. Of the sermon I may truly say, that it was by far the noblest view of the Christian religion ever offered to my mind, and the most persuasive; it derives a novelty and originality from its sublimity, its purity and its simplicity; it is worthy of the most philosophic minds, the most enlightened ages, and I regard it as the best illustration of the idea of a *progressive Christianity* thrown out, as I remember, but not sufficiently unfolded, by that virtuous and accomplished, though not always judicious man and writer, Gilbert Wakefield. It is fitted to do incalculable good, and I am certain that in this country it will now find "audience fit," and by no means "few." The friends to whom I have communicated it are all ardent in their expressions of delight, and the forthcoming English edition is impatiently expected. Your further remarks on Napoleon are worthy of the same mind and pen; I subscribe to them with all my mind and heart, and regard them as no less enlightening on political than your other piece on religious topics. This, too, has been greatly admired with us, and read by those for whom ethical writings in general have no attraction. I have sincerely to thank you for the acquaintance of Mr. and Mrs. Norton; their society afforded me great pleasure, and I only regretted that their stay in London was not further prolonged. Mr. Norton was so kind as to send me his "Remarks on True and False Religion," which convinced me how well founded was your commendation of him as a deep and powerful thinker; his sensibility and amiable enthusiasm it was easy to discover from his manners and conversation; nor could the intelligence and animation of Mrs. Norton fail of attracting regard and interest. You put me on a great topic when you ask my sentiments of our religious reformation. A much better answer to your question than I am able to suggest you will find in Hallam's "Constitutional History of England," published last year, which I entreat you to read, as the most informing work on this and many other important passages of our national story which has yet appeared. The author is probably known to you already as the able historian of the Middle Ages, of the English part of which work his new one may be regarded in some measure as a continuation. This writer, it may interest you to know, was educated in the bosom of Toryism and High-churchism, being the son of a very courtly canon of Windsor, and brought up at Oxford. By the efforts of his own vigorous and independent mind, he has liberalized his politics and come to a judgment of our Anglican Church and Churchmen which galls them sorely, as you may see by Southey's furious abuse of him in the "Quarterly Review." He *knows* the dignified clergy *thoroughly*, and out of that knowledge contemns them as servile beyond any other class of Englishmen. From him they cannot pardon it. Et tu Brute! You will find that he ascribes the ready acquiescence of the nation in Henry's reform in great part to the wide though secret diffusion of the doctrines of Wickliffe, respecting which you may see some curious facts in Turner's "English History," which I think confirm Hallam. But I confess I think that great weight must also be given to the consideration that the memory of the civil wars was still so recent and so bitter, that Englishmen were then willing to yield to almost anything for a quiet life. It is also true that the personal character of Henry, by all its qualities, good and bad, was formed to assert a strong ascendency over the minds of his people, by whom he was at once more admired, esteemed and dreaded, than any other English king. It must further be considered that he innovated nothing in rites and doctrines; he hated and persecuted the Protestants; and so long as he did so, it is probable that the Catholics continued to flatter themselves that sooner or later he would return within the allegiance of the Holy Father. The ground of quarrel also was favourable to him; it was thought hard that he should be refused his divorce; it was visible that the Pope only refused it for fear of offending the Emperor, and the great body of English nobles had signed a threatening letter to Clement respecting it. Lastly, Henry was supported by Parliament in all his measures, and I have quoted in my Elizabeth the argument urged by the Attorney-General to More, founded on the omnipotence of that body: "You allow that Parliament may make kings; why not a head of the Church?" Still there ought to have been more martyrs among the clergy for their own credit; but the Romish Church had been so long triumphant, that we cannot be surprised to find it unprovided of the virtues militant. It behaved better afterwards; all Mary's bishops, with one exception, refused to crown her successor, and submitted patiently to deprivation. The Protestants had taught them to prefer conscience to interest. But I believe that under Elizabeth all the laity would gradually have conformed to Protestantism, but for that master-stroke of Rome, the institution of the order of Jesuits. They were a militia levied purposely to fight the battles of the Pope, and were certainly, in their way, a band of heroes. It is curious to see the efforts to revive them to meet the present dangers of the Church in France and elsewhere. My poor King Charles scarcely goes on, so very much am I impeded by ill health; but my mind still clings to the subject, and I live in hopes of being yet enabled to complete it. Have you seen the very able and accurate French work of Guizot on the "English Revolution," in which he includes the reign of Charles I.? I think it is the best history of the reign we yet possess. I have detected no errors and no important omissions, except with respect to the religious sects, of which he evidently knows but little.

Believe me, dear Sir,
With sincere esteem and regard, very truly yours,
L. AIKIN.

To Miss Aikin.

Boston, November 29, 1828.

My dear Miss Aikin,—I am indebted to you for two letters, and did you know the pleasure with which I contract such debts, perhaps you would be tempted to multiply my obligations. I have not received as yet the books by your father and yourself, but expect them by the next packet. Children's books, I think, should be written by those who are able to write for men, and I am glad to find such labourers in this field as yourself and your father. Your explanation of the causes of the faint resistance made to the reformation, or rather religious revolution, under Henry VIII., was very satisfactory to me. I rejoice with you in the repeal of the Test Acts, and still more in the cause of that repeal; I mean the power of public opinion. All your positive institutions seem to me fitted to build up and enrich the aristocracy. The hopes of the people seem to rest mainly, if not wholly, on the singular facilities enjoyed in your country for forming and expressing public opinion. I think there is no country in the world where they who think alike on great subjects may so easily understand each other, and join their efforts and ascertain and manifest the strength and extent of their views. The condensed state of your population, the intimate, vital connection of London with every part of the kingdom, and the electric speed with which the press brings a subject before the whole people at the same moment,—these things strike me as singular means of embodying and uttering general opinions with a force which cannot always be withstood. I feel, however, that the cause of the people has a very, very hard warfare to wage with the aristocratic principles of your government. By the cause of the people I mean nothing revolutionary, but a system of liberal or impartial measures, having the *common* good for their only aim. I hope indeed much from the culture of the intellect in the mass of the people; in truth, without this their case is desperate. But moral power is even more necessary than intellectual to the security of the just rights of the many, to the practical establishment of the great truth that the general weal is the only legitimate end of government, and I grieve to say that I do not see as decided marks of moral progress as I could desire. Excuse this long discussion which has filled my paper. The truth is, I have so deep an interest in your country, and such a conviction that it must exert an immense influence, whether for good or for evil, in the human race, that when I begin on the subject I know not where to end. I send you a discourse which I have just published. You have hitherto only commended what I have sent you. Believe me, if you would write to me with perfect freedom, and tell me where you differ and disapprove, you would confer a still greater favour.

Very sincerely your friend,
WM. E. CHANNING.

To Miss Aikin.

Boston, August 29, 1828.

My dear Miss Aikin,—It was with great pleasure that I received another letter in your handwriting. I had heard from some of my friends who maintain an active correspondence with the family of Mr. Kinder, that you were ill; and although I was not led to consider your situation as dangerous, I feared that you might suffer long. It is a dictate of nature to rejoice when our friends are restored, and I have never suffered any dark or philosophical views of life to check this spontaneous movement. I know that our Creator has better gifts and higher spheres of action than the present state. Yet when I see life so usefully and honourably filled as by yourself, it seems to me a great good; nor do I feel as if in detaining my friends here I were abridging the happiness of their whole being. May you be long continued, then, to enrich your own and others' minds! You speak as if you had thought death nigh. I recollect, when I was placed in that situation, I felt myself privileged, for I had before felt doubts as to the impressions which so solemn a moment might make. I delight to think of the support I found in religious principles and hopes. I was not, however, reluctant to return to life, as you seem to have been. I had much to live for, and I had found life a constantly increasing good. I trust that you will find that you have come back to an improving existence, nor will it be strange if the future shall be made happier and brighter by the sufferings from which you have risen. I hope you have resumed your more serious literary labours. The period of history on which you are to give us your lights is singularly interesting, and, like all periods of public distraction and convulsion, is very much obscured by the misrepresentations of party spirit. The men of that age were too much heated to judge calmly, and the world has not grown cool since their time on the great subjects which stirred them. I wish to know the Puritans better than I do. We here who have Puritan blood in our veins are never tired of celebrating their virtues. The first book which shook my faith in the common notions about them was Mrs. Hutchinson's Memoirs of her husband—a book which let me into some of their springs of action and more silent movements. A just, impartial estimate of the Puritans would be an important service to history and to the cause of religion and liberty. I saw a laboured and high-wrought description of them in the "Edinburgh Review" not long since, in which the writer seemed to me to be thinking more of himself than his subject. You will understand that I am speaking of their character. I have not a moment's doubt as to the good they did. Whether fanatics or hypocrites, or both, or men of sound and enlarged minds—whether governed by high or low motives, they served posterity almost beyond expression by their struggles for freedom or their resistance of absolute power. Can we judge whether they were most corrupted by the possession of power or by their religious extravagance? I know the first is considered the most active cause; but the moral sense is more injured than we suppose by fanaticism. I mean, however, to give no judgment. After reading the common books on history, I feel myself very ignorant and want to begin anew my studies. You promise me another letter. Do write often, for you give great pleasure.

Very respectfully, your sincere friend,
W. E. CHANNING.

To Dr. Channing.

Hampstead, December 26, 1828.

Dear Sir,—My paper bespeaks your patience for a long epistle; but I have two kind letters to acknowledge, and I perceive that the more we write to each other, the more we may write; for new topics of inquiry and discussion are constantly springing up between us, which is delightful. I have to talk to you of our old Puritans, of the present state of opinion and of morals amongst us, and of your own works; all which requires a large sheet. Your remark that fanaticism injures the moral character more than is usually supposed, has my full concurrence; and all I have learned of our old Puritans and their descendants confirms it. With fanatics, religion is rather a substitute for morality than a support to it; and I have seldom studied the character of a thorough-paced enthusiast without finding reason to believe that it contained a dash of knavery. Our old Puritans made their religion more directly instrumental to the purposes of worldly ambition than almost any other fanatics; the prediction that the saints should "inherit the earth," was constantly in their mouths; they declared that its accomplishment was close at hand, and they never hesitated to claim the character of saintship for themselves. I have been so fortunate as to procure a large collection of thanksgiving sermons preached before the Long Parliament, which will enable me to convict many of these holy men out of their own mouths. One example of the spirit they were of, I will give you. After a string of furious invectives and denunciations against the royalists and prelatists, the preacher turns round with a—" but it will be said that

Christians are commanded to forgive and love their enemies; certainly their own enemies, but not the enemies of God, as those ungracious persons are"! As for their descendants, the Calvinistic Dissenters, they had the misfortune of living in one of those middle states between direct persecution and perfect religious liberty, which sours the temper by continual petty vexations, without affording scope for great efforts or great sacrifices—which drives men to find a perverse pleasure in hating and being hated, and to seek indemnification for the contempt of the world in a double portion of spiritual pride and self-importance. "We can prove ourselves saints," "being Christ's little flock everywhere spoken against," is the plea put into the mouth of this set by Green, a poet, who was born and bred among them.

I have as much Presbyterian blood in my veins as any of your New-Englanders, and from the elders of our family I have picked up volumes of traditionary lore concerning the old Dissenters of Bedford, who built a meeting-house for John Bunyan, and their brethren of Northampton and Leicester—still strongholds of Calvinism. From the whole, I conclude that they were usually lordly husbands, harsh parents, merciless censors of their neighbours, systematically hostile to all the amenities of life, but not less fond of money, or more scrupulous in the means of acquiring it, than the worldlings whom they reprobated. Long before my time, however, my kindred—the Jennings', the Belshams, my excellent grandfather Aikin, and his friend and tutor Doddridge—had begun to break forth out of the chains and darkness of Calvinism, and their manners softened with their system. My youth was spent among the disciples or fellow-labourers of Price and Priestley, the descendants of Dr. John Taylor, the Arian, or in the society of that most amiable of men, Dr. Enfield. Amongst these there was no rigorism. Dancing, cards, the theatre, were all held lawful in moderation: in *manners*, the Free Dissenters, as they were called, came much nearer the Church than to their own stricter brethren, yet in *doctrine* no sect departed so far from the Establishment. At the period of the French Revolution, and especially after the Birmingham Riots, this sect distinguished itself by the vehemence of its democratical spirit, and becoming in a manner a faction as well as a sect, political as well as religious animosity became arrayed against it, and I now remember with disgust, not without compunction, the violent contempt and hatred in which, in common with almost all the young, and not a few of the more mature of that set, I conceived it meritorious to indulge towards the Church and the aristocrats.

The doctrines called Evangelical make all the noise now, both within the Church and without. Yet I fancy that their success is at its furthest, and I should not wonder to hear of a party professedly latitudinarian, and really Unitarian, beginning to show itself within the Church. Oxford partakes very little in the Evangelism of Cambridge. Of these Evangelicals, too, one encouraging symptom is to be observed—they have gradually and almost imperceptibly quitted Calvinism for Arminianism; therefore they feel less confident of being amongst the elect, and take more pains to work out their own salvation, not only by religious observances, but by deeds of beneficence and mercy. With much of the Puritanical rigour, in such points as the observance of the sabbath and the avoidance of public amusements, they are certainly a better set—indefatigable superintendents of schools, munificent patrons of Bible societies and missions, and incessant visitants of the sick and poor. Of course there must be many self-interested hypocrites among them, and not a few sour and censorious fanatics; and to a system so exclusive as theirs, some bigotry must adhere: but I think that many of them are so exemplarily good, and so sincerely pious, and act from so profound a sense of duty, that they must at length win from God the grace to think more worthily of His intentions towards the human race than they seem to do at present. I think, however, that their moral influence on the whole, and particularly amongst the lower class, is in many points unfavourable. They make religion exceedingly repulsive to the young, and the cheerful, by setting themselves against all the sports and diversions of the common people, and surfeiting them with preaching, praying and tutoring; they bewilder, and sometimes entirely overthrow, weak and timid minds by their mysterious and terrific doctrines; and they do much towards confounding moral right and wrong by the language which they hold on the efficacy of sudden conversions and death-bed repentance. The assurances of eternal bliss which they hold out to the most atrocious malefactors are often a just subject of scandal. On the whole, their system has much of the debasing, and, as it were, vulgarizing effect which you justly ascribe to such views of religion—and is perhaps one of the great causes of that apparent want of moral progress which you remark amongst us. Other causes are cheap poison in the shape of gin; over-population, which makes it hard to thousands to gain a livelihood by honest labour, and the improvident habits produced by our Poor Laws, and by the excess, or, in many cases, the injudicious application, of public and private charity. Our long wars, and the crushing weight of taxation which they have drawn upon us, are perhaps the remote source of most of these great evils.

Our state is a very strange one—unexampled activity in every kind of pursuit—excessive activity, I should be inclined to say—unexampled diffusion of knowledge, but bad institutions of many kinds, tending to crush the many, to exalt the few; abuse and corruption in every department; vast luxury and corresponding rapacity, and a great fund of stupid and illiberal prejudice diffused through all classes. We are, in the main, a Tory people; and, what you may well think strange, the greatest Whigs and reformers amongst us actually hail a Tory ministry like the present, because no other kind of ministry has ever strength or permanence to effect anything, being unwelcome both to the King and the people; and at a time when so much light and knowledge prevails, even Tories are influenced by public opinion, and often indeed by the necessity of the case, to favour *some* reforms (like Mr. Peel's of the Criminal Law) which in their hands become effective. If the Catholic claims be granted, it will be a concession which only a Tory minister could extort from our King, or carry against the clergy. The agitation of these claims, by the way, produces some of the strangest anomalies of our situation. Here are our highest Churchmen abusing without mercy the Catholics, whom Horsley formerly, with greater reason, declared to be "nearer and dearer" to them than any Protestant sectaries; and here are we *Liberals* almost driven into a league, offensive and defensive, with old Popery, whom we have been bred to scorn and hate from our cradle.

And now to my last topic. Nothing can be more sincere than the admiration I have expressed of your works, and none have I more admired than your last. Your views of the relation in which the Deity stands to man, and of the light in which He is to be regarded by rational beings, seem to me developments of my own thoughts, and the spirit of the whole discourse elevates, consoles, and delights me.

God bless you, my dear and valued friend!

L. AIKIN.

To Miss Aikin.

Boston, March 30, 1829.

My dear Miss Aikin,—This letter will be handed you by two of my most valued friends, Mr. and Mrs. Ware, of this city, the former one of our most eminent and enlightened ministers, and the latter a lady well known to your friends of the Kinder family, and esteemed among us as one of our most excellent women. I am truly glad to send to your country such specimens of our own. I think the time has come for breaking down the old spirit of nationality which had its rise in darker times, when men were hardly capable of any nobler bond, when it was a great thing to carry individuals beyond themselves as far as the borders of their country; but are we not now able to leap these borders? to feel that the natural tie of man to man is the most sacred of all? to sympathize with intellect and virtue everywhere? and to help in forming a great community of friends of virtue, piety and freedom, who, speaking in all lands, will put to silence the narrow prejudices in which tyranny, war and superstition find their chief strength? It is in the hope that this holy union is growing in the world, that I take pleasure in sending the intelligent and virtuous from this country to yours. I would ask if in your country the friends of old abuses are not most anxious to keep alive national feeling? There is an instinct by which such men know where their strength lies. I have no desire to extinguish patriotism; but unless it can be purified, this principle must be a bar to the progress of the mind. It certainly corrupts moral sentiment and narrows the heart.

Your last letter was very interesting to me. In much which you have said of the Puritans I accord with you. But have you made allowance enough for the power of self-deception? I suppose the best part of the sect came to this country, and they undoubtedly possessed much stern devotion to what they thought right. They had the stronger virtues in no common degree; but a false and narrow theology and the narrow maxims of their age turned their very strength of principle into harshness, intolerance, unkindness. The Puritans here were a more honest race than you suppose, but I am afraid not more amiable. Their fellow-sectaries at home were, I doubt not, terribly corrupted by struggles for power and by political success. I look for your book with much hope. Let me only repeat that you must labour to be the very personification of impartiality in treating of a period which as yet none of us view dispassionately.

Did you examine the authorities for Hess's Life of Zwinglius when you translated it? The book seemed to me not altogether trustworthy. At least I missed the philosophical spirit in it. I feared it was a panegyric. Still I have a great interest in Zwinglius, and want to know how far I may confide in his biographer.

Very affectionately your friend,
WM. E. CHANNING.

To Dr. CHANNING.

Hampstead, June 12, 1829.

Dear Sir,—Your friends Mr. and Mrs. Ware visited us last night, and I hasten to thank you most cordially for the acquaintance of these excellent people. If my letter, which is lost with the little books, had reached you safely, it would have told you how welcome were your other friends, the Nortons and Mr. Sparks; but they have returned to you, and have brought, I trust, no ill report of their reception. I know not exactly why it is, but your people always feel to me more like kindred than strangers; we are acquainted as soon as we meet. Simplicity of manners, with elevation of mind and a cultivated intellect, form a union admirable anywhere, but less rare, I apprehend, in your state of society than in ours; amid the bustling crowd of luxurious London it is a refreshment to the spirit to meet with it. Continue by all means to send us these noble specimens—it must tend to break down prejudices, and to strengthen the bands which ought to unite together the true friends of man in every clime. It is indeed time to throw aside the fetters of nationality already amongst us; the best men have the lead of it; and the blessed influence of peace which now renders an Englishman or an American free of the whole civilized world, emancipates the mind with the person and teaches it to scorn all littleness.

I have but a shabby account to give of Zwingle. I certainly verified nothing, and do at present regard that biography as a very rhetorical prize essay, and worthy of little confidence. My translation was made in early days, long before I became a searcher into history, and, truth to say, I undertook the task merely that I might have the satisfaction of earning a journey to Scotland by my own labour, instead of going at my father's expense. Zwingle however was an excellent man, and I was pleased to find that the best of English reformers and martyrs, Latimer, Ridley, &c., were followers of his pure and simple doctrine. Many thanks for your Fenelon. I thought there was a little inconsistency between the

agreement with some of his leading tenets which you begin with professing, and the very important disagreements which you go on to explain; but your sketch of the Catholic bishop is beautiful, and calculated to do much good; and, in a very different way, I regard your remarks on self-immolation as highly valuable. I remember making several reflections on the mischievous absurdity of that notion after reading a French selection from eminent Catholic divines for the use of young persons. The doctrine of original sin is the root of that and various other highly noxious errors in the popular systems of ethics; and though the *selfish system* has never satisfied either my reason or my heart, I think we owe great obligation to Paley and others who have set it up against its opposite. The Calvinists, by the way, stated the opposition between God and what they called Self as strongly as the Catholics. I found in some contemporary writers the cant term of *self-seeking* mentioned as a new coinage of the Scotch Covenanters; and looking then into the matter, I was inclined to think that the word *selfish* was scarcely of earlier origin, at least in its present acceptation. What a dreadful idea, that our Creator has planted within our bosoms a domestic foe, from whom we can never fly, and whose malice never sleeps a moment, an evil principle solely occupied in working our perdition! When will the most enlightened nations of the world take courage to banish from the midst of them superstitions far more baneful than the wildest dreams of savage ignorance? Did you ever read a Life of Fenelon by Charles Butler, the Catholic? It is a curious work, and I had some curious conversation with him respecting it. He plainly regards Fenelon's submission to the condemnation of his work, which Papists and courtiers united to call sublime, as something like a politic manœuvre. The whole story is an example, equally melancholy and instructive, of the sullying influence of temporal and spiritual despotism upon characters made for sincerity and magnanimity. But this further moral it perhaps did not suit the purposes of your tract to deduce from the history of one of the best men of his class.

Believe me, with the highest regard,

Most sincerely yours,

LUCY AIKIN.

To MISS AIKIN.

Boston, August 2, 1829.

My dear Miss Aikin,—I find so much in your letters to interest me, that to gain a new one I have more than once conquered my besetting infirmity of procrastination. Your last was particularly gratifying.

You seem to consider a lively religious faith as connected with constitution. I believe the vividness of ideas which have their foundation in the reason depends very much on the moral will. The faith of the imagination we cannot command, but that of the reason and conscience is in our power. The first I value not at all. The last seems to me the one thing needful, the pearl of great price. To *realize* our connection with the Supreme Being seems to me the great secret and spring of moral energy, moral victory, and unlimited progress in whatever ennobles our nature. It is for these influences that I value religion. The joys which the fanatic boasts of finding in piety, which have little or no connection with moral improvement, I hold cheap indeed But religion such as I learn it in the word and works of God is a very different influence. I know nothing to give unfailing moral energy to the mind but a living faith in a Being of infinite perfection, and who is always with us to aid, strengthen, reward, reprove, chasten and guide to immortality. I can set no bounds to the force of hope, resolution, love and effort, which such a principle can communicate; nor would I for the world lose the aid which the Christian religion gives in sustaining and strengthening this principle.

Since writing to you, I have read the work you recommended, "Hallam's Constitutional History," with great pleasure. It has carried me much farther into your history than I had gone before. It did not, however, remove all my perplexities. I was somewhat surprised to find Toryism so predominantly *High-church* as he represents it. I had supposed that this was essentially and chiefly a political heresy, and that it was characterized chiefly by devotion to legitimacy, arbitrary power and the crown, and that it supported the altar chiefly as a pillar of the throne. But I find that it clung to the Church more obstinately than to the Throne, and that its fanaticism outstripped its loyalty. How happened this? I can understand how the Tories after the Restoration came to hate Puritan and Dissenter with their whole heart, and made the Church an idol in opposition to these; but not how episcopacy became dearer than legitimacy. I am surprised too at finding the High-church Tory so perseveringly bitter against the Catholics, for the Romish Church had antiquity on its side, and was even the channel of priestly power from the apostles to the English bishop; and, besides all this, it had the Tory reverence for kings. I have long wondered how the High-churchman can be kept from breaking through the narrow barrier between himself and the Catholic. All his principles carry him to Rome. What force has driven him so fiercely in the opposite direction? I have been exceedingly struck with the hard fight which liberal principles had to maintain, and with the fact that they triumphed so much by the aid of religious fanaticism, now Puritan, now High-church. But my paper admonishes me to stop. When you write, I wish you to inform me of the progress of your work on Charles. I look for it with much desire and hope.

Very truly your friend,
W. E. CHANNING.

To Dr. Channing.

Hampstead, October 8, 1829.

Dear Sir,—I too, either from temper or habit, am a great procrastinator, and therefore I sit down to reply to your most welcome letter immediately, whilst the impression is quite fresh: I shall not be "gravelled for lack of matter." Hallam, I was certain, would both interest and inform you, and I wish you could put your historic difficulties to the author himself, as I did some of mine a few months ago, at a party where we were glad to discuss instead of dining. Such a torrent of knowledge he poured upon me! He talks faster than any other mortal who talks wisely and who has lost his teeth, and hard task it is to follow him. But as to some of your difficulties respecting our Tories and No-popery High-churchmen, I almost think I can give you some solutions myself. Toryism and High-churchism are so closely and naturally connected, that it is scarcely possible, in general, to estimate the separate influence of each; and in all our troubled times from the Long Parliament to the Revolution, it is plain that religious and political principles were both busy in the fray; but the shares belonging to each have been very differently stated by writers: thus Fox maintains that James II. was deposed chiefly for his tyranny, and Hallam holds that it was chiefly for his Popery, and I know not which is likely to be nearest the truth. However, it is certain that the smoke of Smithfield fires and the fume of Fawkes's gunpowder have to this day an unsavoury odour in the nostrils of the people. The clergy, as a portion of the people, partake of the same sense of things; moreover, the penal laws were a formidable obstacle to apostasy from the State religion. Laud himself, though in ritual and in some points of doctrine he wished to return as near as possible to Rome, felt that he could not conform entirely "till Rome were other than she is," and said "No," as you remember, to the Cardinal's hat. His master also seems to have been well aware at least that it could never stand safe upon the head of an Archbishop of Canterbury; moreover, he himself hated Popery, like his father, on account of its assuming power to depose kings, and he would not have resigned his supremacy. Now it has been a constant maxim of Rome to concede nothing to schismatics; all schemes of compromise between it and the English Church have constantly failed, and differences are sure to gain importance in the eyes of those who by experience have found them to be irreconcilable. Hence the determined alienation of some of our highest Churchmen from a Church which they would have met, perhaps, more than half-way. James II. strove to establish one exclusive Church on the ruins of another. In this extreme case the bishops must give up one of three things—honour and conscience, their mitres, or their favourite principle of passive obedience—and it is not wonderful if they judged the last the smallest sacrifice. In Dryden's "Hind and Panther," you may see, too, that Catholics, especially those who were converts or conformists to the King's religion, used at this crisis language sufficiently provoking and contemptuous to the Anglicans. With what intolerable point, and justice too, he tells them,

> But, half to take on trust, and half to try,
> It is not faith, but bungling bigotry.

After the Revolution, and down to George III., with the exception of High-church Anne, things were in a different position. The Court was by necessity Whig. The bishops, or those who desired to be so, were therefore, by like necessity, Whigs also; and the fight against Popery and arbitrary power, which always went together, was carried on by Low-churchmen and Latitudinarians, with Stillingfleet and Tillotson at their head; the country squires and country parsons meanwhile remaining in the enjoyment of their High-churchism, Toryism and Jacobitism. During the last reign, Jacobitism becoming extinct, *high* principles resumed their place at Court, and did their utmost to resist the spread of all freedom at home and abroad. Dissenters and democrats underwent much abuse and some persecution, and Horsley then spoke of the French emigrant priests as much "nearer and dearer" than the sectaries at home. Since that, however, the scene has changed again. Popery in Ireland is the religion of the mob; it has acquired a deep taint of radicalism; and its claims, being patronized by our Liberals, were opposed by the Tories of both islands till all statesmen saw that concession was unavoidable. The clergy, as a body, had interests of their own at stake, and stood out longer. "Give the Catholics this," they cried, "and you give them strength both in Parliament and without. They will resist the payment of tithes, they will overthrow the Protestant Church in Ireland, and then Heaven knows what they, with the Dissenters to help them, may attempt against tithes and Church in England." They struggled hard, and certainly scrupled no means to work upon the prejudices of the vulgar, high and low. But the spirit of the times, joined to the necessity of the case, proved too strong for the spirit of the Church; it has sustained a signal defeat and humiliation, and I hope good will come of it.

My health is still very indifferent; in particular I am much troubled with severe headaches, which so continually interrupt my studies, that I have the mortification to see my King Charles making very little and often no progress. With occupation it is comparatively easy to keep up the spirits under almost any circumstances, but compulsory idleness I sometimes find it a hard task to bear with cheerfulness. However, I do my best, and with time and patience I still hope that my health will be restored and my work finished. One advantage this delay brings me; it gives time for friends to take means for procuring for me family papers and other valuable documents, which one chance or other is continually bringing forth to daylight. In consequence of a base attack by Disraeli* on that patriot martyr, Sir John Eliot, his descendant Lord Eliot has rummaged out a correspondence between him and Hampden, and promises to put it into my hands. Pray procure, if you can, another interesting family relic lately published, Lady Fanshaw's Memoirs. She was a royalist, and I feel proud of the women on both sides when I place her account on the same shelf as Mrs. Hutchinson's. There is much less of literary skill on the part of Lady Fanshaw, but her artless tale is full of interest and amusement.

Passing from old times to new times, I have two pieces of intelligence for you, that German metaphysics (in the train of which German theology may follow) have got into Cambridge, where youths are puzzling their brains with Kantianism; and that it is whispered—monstrum horrendum!—that Unitarianism is infecting some of the

* The elder Disraeli.

most enlightened of the clergy of Oxford. What will the world come to? Some of these clergy, and those of Cambridge, also addict themselves to the modern science of geology and other branches of natural history—this connects them with the Geological, Linnæan, and other similar societies in London; at their meetings they come in contact with the men of enlightened and independent minds, and thus they rub off professional stiffness and prejudice, and learn to assert something of the birthright freedom of the mind.

I had a glimpse, and no more, of the Wares on their return from their northern tour. Mr. Ware was looking better in the face, and there was less of languor in his air, but there seems to be still great room for amendment in his state. He ought to recover with such a wife to nurse him. They did well to hasten to a more genial climate; ours has this season been unusually trying to all invalids. I am afraid that Canada keeps up in your country a somewhat bitter feeling against England which *here* is not reciprocated; for when we want to hate our neighbours, the French are far more handy than you.

You may wonder that I should talk of my inability to write a volume; but a letter may be written lounging, and requires no apparatus of folios and quartos.

Pray believe me, very cordially yours,
LUCY AIKIN.

To Miss Aikin.

Boston, December 31, 1829.

My dear Miss Aikin,—A packet sails to-morrow for Liverpool, and though pressed for time, I cannot let it go without an acknowledgment of your last very acceptable letter. Your solution of my historical difficulties about High-churchmen and Popery was very gratifying. By the way, Popery seems destined to call forth the zeal of all parties among the Protestants. New and great efforts are made here to subdue our Puritan aversion to Rome, and we are threatened with what I earnestly wish to avert, a Catholic controversy. Are you quite aware that one of the most powerful arguments on the continent in favour of Catholicism is what is called the *historical argument*, or that which is drawn from the subsistence of the Church through so many ages and perils? They who are open to this kind of proof must be very much confirmed by the present state of Popery, and probably see a miracle in its sudden rise from what seemed ruin.

Your news from Oxford needs confirmation. I am slow to believe that liberal principles in theology have scaled that fortress of orthodoxy. It is astonishing how far men's minds may be enlarged on other subjects and yet be stationary on this. I read last summer Dr. Whately's books on Rhetoric and Logic (he is of Oxford), and was much gratified with the sound judgment and manly reasoning with which they abound, and was then led to seek a volume of his on St. Paul's writings, hoping to find the same clear and vigorous intellect; but I was grieved to meet, not seldom, the same narrow, confused, superficial mode of thinking on several topics which mark the writers of his Church. I ought to say, however, that sometimes he shows his clear and strong mind. This more than anything has led me to question your news. As to Kantism, I shall be glad to hear of an irruption of it into any university or any part of your country. I want to see the English mind waked up on the great subject of intellectual philosophy. I know you look rather frowningly on metaphysics. But you have not perhaps separated the true object of this science from the idle topics which have been associated with it. The mechanical, necessarian philosophy of the human mind which has so long been the orthodoxy of England, I have no sympathy with. This leads me to ask who is the author of two books, "Essays on the Formation of Opinion," and on "The Pursuit of Truth," which have lately fallen into my hands, and which, though in many respects opposed to my views, I must own to show great power.

Will you forgive an almost illegible letter? I could write no other at present, and was unwilling to wait till I could find time for slower movement of the hand.

With earnest wishes for the restoration of your health and the progress and completion of your literary labours,

I am, very truly, your friend,

WM. E. CHANNING.

[It is clear from what follows that two letters of the correspondence are missing.]

To Dr. Channing.

Hampstead, June 1, 1830.

Dear Sir,—Many thanks for your welcome letter, which I was well able to decipher: I was the more glad to receive it, as I wanted such an excuse for writing to you, having, as you will find, abundant topics. My first shall be one concerning yourself—that article in the "Edinburgh Review." I am charged to convey to you the regrets and indignation of a large group of your unknown friends and admirers, who are hurt at it much less from any fear that it should either disturb your mind or injure your literary reputation, than from an apprehension that your country should regard it as a mark of national enmity, the more startling as appearing in a journal usually the organ of liberal principles. It is, in fact, the ebullition of one malignant temper, and it is easy to show you the sources of his hostility. The writer is William Hazlitt, a vehement admirer of Napoleon, of whom he has written a Life in a very different spirit from your remarks. He has also written on the English poets with an acute sense of their blemishes, and a very blunt perception of their beauties, another sin of *yours;* further, he is at enmity with your commender Southey; lastly, he was brought up at the feet of Priestley and Belsham, and probably retains of their system Materialism and Necessity, and little more. The matter was discussed amongst us at a literary dinner, and there wanted not those well disposed to make you *amende honorable;* but no one could suggest a fitting vehicle—if the attack had but come from the "Quarterly," the "Edinburgh" would have gladly received an appeal; but as it is, I believe it must be overlooked. I must tell you, however, that Mr. Hallam was one of the most indignant, and that he charged me to convey to you his wish to be regarded amongst your warm admirers, and his pleasure at learning that you had given some approbation to his labours. You would scarcely understand the reviewer's accusation against you as a trimmer; but seemingly he supposes that those who rank with the Priestleyans in theology ought to maintain the same doctrines in metaphysics, though it would be hard to show any necessary or natural connection between them. But what an obstacle is it to the progress of truth that a man must take or leave *all* the opinions of some party or leader, on pain of being accounted a time-server! It is one of the privileges of a mere spectator, like myself, to be free to accept or reject as conviction prompts, and accordingly I find myself often discarding old prepossessions, and striking out to myself new lights.

Now the time may have been that I did frown on metaphysics, and "as at present advised," I am a Lockist and Necessarian, and yet I am beginning to wish well to the progress of intellectual philosophy, and I will tell you why. This age and the men of it are "of the earth, earthy," and I wish to see some upward movement. There is a pseudo science called political economy which dries up the hearts and imaginations of most who meddle with it—there is Bentham's system, called the Utilitarian, which has a similar effect—there is Paley's system of morals, long the text-book at Cambridge, and just introduced as such, I am told, in the Scotch universities, which is another grovelling thing; and to all these, a lofty philosophy would act, I believe, as a counterpoise of great value. Metaphysical inquiries may, on many points, show only "how little can be known;" but when conducted in a proper spirit, I have seen them work much good on the mind and character; yet, as you say, they do not always make men the better reasoners on religion, or set them above vulgar cries or vulgar prejudices. Benson, now Master of the Temple, one of the most distinguished preachers and theologians in London—a Cambridge man—once favoured me with a luminous and beautiful lecture or harangue on Kantism; yet that man has renounced acquaintance, after a very long and dear friendship, with venerable Mr. Turner, of Newcastle, one of the best of human beings, on account of his Unitarianism, and has publicly preached that this faith was contrary to morals! Yet my Oxford news is true; not of any of their logical or metaphysical writers, that I know of, but of some of their geologists and other natural philosophers, who, turning the force of their minds to those branches of science in which they may speculate unshackled, whisper in corners to other men engaged in similar pursuits their contempt for the Articles they have signed. My brother Arthur hears such talk from Oxonian members of the Geological Society when they attend its meetings.

I have heard the two works you mention spoken of with high praise by a few good judges, but I have not yet seen them; the author, I am told, is a Mr. Bailey, of Sheffield, but this is all I can learn. You cannot conceive how much the lettered aristocracy of London society disdains to know anything of provincial genius or merit, at least in any but the most popular branches of literature. Montgomery, a Sheffield poet, being also an Evangelical, is tolerably well known in London, and may, in some companies, be slightly mentioned without committing the speaker. But a Sheffield metaphysician! bold were the London diner-out who would dare not to be ignorant of him! You once observed to me that everywhere the *sovereign* is worshipped; with us, that sovereign is an idol called Gentility, and costly are the offerings laid upon the altar. Dare to make conversation in the most accomplished society something of an exercise of the mind, and not a mere dissipation, and you instantly become that thing of horror, a *Bore.**

To Dr. Channing.

Hampstead, June 7, 1830.

Dear Sir,—By the kindness of Mr. Ware, I have it at length in my power to send copies of the two little books so long since destined for your daughter; and though I have written to you at large so lately, I cannot resist the

* The rest of the letter is missing.

temptation of adding a letter. I hope it cannot be very troublesome to you to read what it is so agreeable to me to write.

Your friend Mr. Goodhue spent an hour with me one morning, and I was much pleased with his mild and amiable manners, and the information which he gave me respecting many of your institutions and societies. I wished for more of his company, and invited him for the next evening, when I expected Mrs. Joanna Baillie, Professor Smyth, and another valued friend, Mr. Whishaw, a gentleman who has written little, but whose literary opinions are heard in the most enlightened circles with a deference approaching that formerly paid to Dr. Johnson. Mr. Goodhue was unfortunately engaged, but he sent me Mr. Richmond, and the result was, one of the most animated and amusing *conversaziones*, chiefly between him and the two gentlemen I have named—for we ladies were well content to be listeners—at which it has ever been my good fortune to be present.

A more fluent talker than Mr. Richmond I think I never heard, and I doubted at first how he might suit my two old gentlemen—both of them great eulogists of good listeners; but he is very clever, and there was something so *piquant* in his remarks on what he had seen here, such a simplicity in his questions, and, when he spoke of his own country, such abundant knowledge, so ably and clearly expressed, that they were content for once to take such a share of talk as they could get by hard struggling. I think the Professor of Modern History got matter for a new lecture on American law and politics; and he and Mr. Richmond took pains to contrive another meeting. But to me the most curious part was Mr. Richmond's wonder at having got into such high company as two or three baronets, a Scotch countess and some lord; and his difficulty to imagine, and ours to explain to him, how our difference of ranks *works* in society. He evidently supposed a much wider separation of classes than actually takes place. I believe the structure of society with us may best be expressed by what an eminent naturalist has said of organized nature—it is not a chain of being, it more resembles a net; each mesh holds to several others on different sides. Our complicated state of society, in recompence of great evils, has at least this advantage, that it brings the rich man or the noble into relation with a multitude of individuals, with whom he finds it necessary to his objects to associate on terms of social equality, notwithstanding great disparity of birth or fortune. Those very societies of which we agree in condemning the epidemic prevalence, are useful in our country by their levelling effect. In a Bible society or a missionary meeting, the zealous labourers, and still more the effective speakers, find themselves enabled to give the law to wealth and title. Scientific and literary institutions concur to the same results, and so does the cultivation in the higher ranks of letters and of arts. There is no fact, no talent, no acquirement, either useful or ornamental, no celebrity of any kind, but what serves its possessor as a ticket of admission to the company of some of his superiors. I imagine that in no country there can be less of undiscovered or unrewarded merit than in ours. Do you begin to suspect the insidious aim of these remarks? Your "Means and Ends of a National Literature" lies before me, and I am pleading for some exception as respects England to the general truth of your observation, that in Europe "it is for his blood, his rank, or some artificial distinction, and not for the attributes of humanity, that man holds himself in respect." Perhaps, however, my position, that men in this country value themselves, and are valued by others, very much according to their talents, tastes, acquirements, and their power and will to serve a sect or party, may not be irreconcilable with your position that they do not respect themselves sufficiently for the attributes—the common attributes—of humanity. Here in the lower, that is the more numerous class, it is too near the truth that "man's life is cheap as beast's." Your estimate of our literature I think very just. I am not, however, without hope that in labouring, as you say, for ourselves, which the difficulties of our present situation render imperative upon us, some general truths may be elicited which may be capable of extended application, at least in the other old countries of Europe, which continue to look to us for examples of many kinds; to you they will be less available.

The oldest minister of the Scotch Church, Mr. Somerville, author of a valuable History of the Reign of Queen Anne, died very lately at above ninety, but possessed of all his faculties. The venerable man uttered his "Nunc dimittis" on having witnessed Catholic emancipation; but one more triumph was in store for him in the perusal of your works; he said he rejoiced in them exceedingly; they formed an era in the progress of religion. This trait I have from his accomplished daughter-in-law, also a great admirer of yours. She is an eminent proficient in mathematical science, and now engaged in translating the works of La Place, and her countrywoman Joanna Baillie is no more modest, gentle and full of all goodness. Rogers the poet, having seen some of your pieces, told me he was going to the booksellers in search of all the rest. Merely as "means of moral influence" you may prize these testimonies.

It was with great concern I heard from the Wares that you had sustained a severe attack of illness, though I learned at the same time of your recovery. Pray take care of yourself for many sakes besides your own; you have yet much to do for the world; and pray take it into consideration whether you ought not to winter in a milder climate, such as ours. How very much we would make of you if we had you here!

Believe me, ever yours, with the truest regard,

L. AIKIN.

To Miss Aikin.

Boston, October 21st, 1830.

My dear Miss Aikin,—I owe you two letters, or two of yours are unanswered, and they furnish me topics for many sheets. But may I postpone all these for a moment? I have not written you since the *new Revolution* on the continent, and what else can I write about? It has filled my heart with gratitude and joy; not that I have yielded to any dreams of an approaching millennium. I have given up the character of prophet, and I neither expect nor desire any moral miracles. It is enough for me to see that great principles, on which the happiness and progress of society depend, have struck root in Europe too deeply to be plucked up by policy or force. I consider the late Revolution as putting to rest the great question, whether the liberal or aristocratic spirit is to triumph, whether human affairs are to go forward, or the old system be indefinitely perpetuated. If legitimacy would only open its eyes to read the signs of the times, to understand the strength of the principle of freedom and progress, and would be wise enough to make a compromise with it, so that it might make its way without convulsions, I should still more rejoice, and of this I do not despair.

Another thing which gives me great pleasure is the proof afforded by the French people of having *improved* by sufferings and experience. We hear much of *national education.* What nation ever learned so fast as France? When we compare this people with what it was a century ago, can we sufficiently wonder at the change? With the exception of one fatal idea, that of *military glory,* the national mind seems wholly turned on new objects, and noble ones too. The ideas of human rights, of the *true relation* of man to man, of the end of political and social institutions, are beginning to unfold themselves. How purified is the idea of Liberty since the Revolution of 1789!

To heighten my gratification, this Revolution has all the air of being a *popular* one. The *people* were more than mere instruments; they supplied the heart as well as the hands. A few leaders cannot claim all the credit for the energy and moderation of the movement. It puts one in mind of that fine passage of Paul: "Not many wise men, not many noble, &c., are called; out of the weak things, and things which are despised, are chosen to bring to nought things that are." Nothing delights me so much as good springing from the people itself.

The way in which England has received this great event does her much honour. You seem to be glad that your old rival promises or threatens to get the start of you. In good earnest, she does so threaten you, and I shall not be sorry to see you provoked to a right kind of jealousy. The friends of humanity are beginning to look to France as their chief hope. Not only her popular, but her philosophical mind seems leaving you behind. Still I do not give up my "venerable mother." In one thing you surpass or used to surpass France. That country thinks and acts too much in masses. The social spirit is too predominant. England *used* to have more solitary and independent thought. I say *used,* for I begin to be alarmed about you. Your rage for associations for everything seems to show that nobody can work alone or act from his own impulse. I rejoice to think that France has come forward so fast without that endless machinery of societies which absorbs so much of the intellect and capital of England.

My page admonishes me to stop, though I have a great deal to say. Let me only add, I never looked on any events more calmly than on what we have recently witnessed; nor will many sad consequences at all affect my views. I see great truths making their way and becoming principles of action. This satisfies me.

You amused me by the delicate manner in which you approached my article on National Literature. Did you know how I view what I give to the world, you would have fewer fears. I was probably right in the particulars in which you differ from me, for you who were born under aristocracies have no suspicion how much your judgment of human nature is perverted. We are darkened enough, but have a little more light. As to the article in question, I wrote it when sinking into disease, as I wrote my Election sermon whilst rising from disease. The body was indeed a reluctant instrument to the mind; and if the articles have any merit, it is to be ascribed only to my deep conviction of what I wrote, so deep as to break forth under great physical infirmity. I wish you would always speak most freely of what I write. Some here charge me with caring nothing for opinion. I say this to show you that I am not very vulnerable. I think they mistake me. What they charge on me as indifference is partly a natural reserve of manner, and I hope arises in part from my supreme interest in the *truth* which I labour to communicate. This makes me always dissatisfied with my mode of communication, and diminishes my concern for mere reputation. It was one of the beautiful attributes of Jesus that he preferred his truth to himself, and in this, as in all things, I would follow him. By all this I do not mean that I wish you to speak at all of my writings; but *when you do*, to come to the point without any fear. I find that I have not left space enough on this page to allow me to use it as a cover. I will add, then, that I am rejoiced to hear of the progress of your History. Do not keep it back too long.

I have recently been and am still amusing myself with Walpole's Letters. He shows what his power is by amusing me, for he offends my moral sentiments perpetually. I read him to learn something of a style of character and state of society of which I can know little by observation. I almost wonder that such an "upper class" as he describes was not overwhelmed and swept away by the impatient indignation of the other classes. I suppose the explanation to be, that the other classes were not much better. I will now release you.

With sincere affection, your friend,

Wm. E. Channing.

P.S. I forgot to ask you a question of some interest. I lately received a letter signed "William Burns," accompanying a large prospectus or exposition of moral and religious principles, headed by these words, "The New Era of Christianity." The writer lives in Scotland, I suppose the southern part, and I think his letter was dated Saltcoat, or something like it; but as it is in the hands of a friend out of the city, I cannot recur to it. He says that he has corresponded with distinguished men in France, and expresses the views of many in your island. I read several years ago two pamphlets by William Burns, which were full of mind and pleased me much. One was called the "Spirit of Christianity," the other exposed the Evangelical party. Is my correspondent the same with the author? What can you tell me about him? Such movements are very encouraging to me. The "New Era" is to be characterized by a new development of the *moral spirit* of Christianity. It seems that there are those in Scotland who want some higher form of religion than they yet find. This is a good sign. But I want to know more of them before I write to Mr. Burns.

To Dr. Channing.

Hampstead, December 14, 1830.

I had been quite impatient, my dear Sir, to hear from you, and I am almost equally impatient to answer your letter, which had a long passage, and is but two days arrived. I have volumes to say to you; but first of the last, for fear I should forget it. I was afraid W. Burns would prove a second Sheffield metaphysician, having never heard of him; but at length my friend, the Rev. George Kenrick, supplies full and satisfactory information. Twenty years since, when a Glasgow student, he often saw Mr. Burns at Professor Woodrow's. He was a very plain man, who had received the Scotch share of education, and no more, and whose style in writing was much more refined than in conversation. He had been a carpenter, but then lived without profession on a small fortune, devoted to reading and speculation. At that time he stopped short of Unitarianism, but adhered to the liberal party in the Scotch Church, and shared the odium attached to it in those evil days. He displayed a powerful and original mind, and was of high moral worth. Mr. K. thinks him to be not far short of sixty, and knows him for the author of the pieces you mention.

Several corroborating circumstances persuade Mr. K. and myself that liberal principles are now rapidly advancing in Scotland. Mrs. Joanna Baillie says the reason there are so few Unitarians there *out* of the Church is, that there are so many *in* it. Their ministers sign a confession at ordination, but having no liturgy, they are afterwards free to avoid all utterance of doctrine, if they please, or to teach their own. What an age have we fallen upon! Since the French Revolution we have had the Belgian, the Polish insurrection, and here we are in an English revolution! I can scarcely give you an idea of our state—we do not half understand it ourselves, but I am sure you will be anxious to hear as much as I can tell you. The panic occasioned by the postponement of the Royal visit to the city was at first indescribable; everybody said, "What must this danger be which frightens Wellington?" This soon subsided; it was admitted by all but a few of the highest Tories, that no case had been made out—that the Duke had either given in to a false alarm, or had wilfully raised one for political purposes. This, and his foolish declaration against Reform, turned him out. We have now a ministry pledged to reform and retrenchment—to non-interference with foreign states. It comprises so much virtue and talent, that if sufficiently strong and sufficiently lasting, it would seem likely to secure to us important blessings. But in the meantime we seem on the brink of that complication of all horrors, a servile war. You have heard, no doubt, of our burnings, machine breakings, and mobs attacking houses, stage-coaches, and passengers, for plunder. This, you may think, is no more than we have suffered before from the proceedings of Luddites and other collections of discontented workmen. But here is the difference—those were risings of the manufacturers of some one branch alone, confined to certain districts or towns, and comparatively easy to suppress. But this is a movement of the peasantry—the whole agricultural class almost throughout the country, and the means of quelling it are not obvious. The last thing in English history like it was the Norfolk insurrection, under Kett, in the reign of Edward VI., occasioned by the general inclosure of commons. Happily, our mobs have not collected by thousands, nor have they yet found a leader. The Tories, with their heads full of the French Revolution, have spread the idea that the conflagrations were the work of political agitators of a rank much above the peasants, whom they moved. But this appears an ungrounded notion. All the persons yet apprehended as ringleaders are loose and reckless characters from the dregs of the people; and herein, I conceive, lies the safety of the upper classes. Overpopulation is said, and I believe truly, to be the main cause of the distress which has produced these risings; but others have concurred, such as the laying small farms into large ones, rack-renting, the absenteeism of landlords, and various abuses in the administration of the Poor-laws. There is a strong feeling also amongst the people against tithes and against clerical magistrates. In general, the gentlemen have acted in these matters with a mixture of courage and humanity which does them honour. Very able judges have been sent down to try the delinquents in custody; the wages have been raised in most places; and I trust that at the price of some pecuniary sacrifices, and some correction of abuses, we may see tranquillity restored. In the meantime, both London and these villages swarm with beggars; some of them so sturdy and importunate, that there is but a shade between them and banditti. The ministry are in a situation of extreme difficulty and awful responsibility. They are pledged to some measure of Parliamentary Reform, for which this is certainly a very awkward season.

I am reading Jefferson's "Correspondence" with deep interest. I wept bitter tears at the recital of British cruelties during the war. I had no idea how horribly we treated you—pray forgive and forget; Jefferson did neither, but I dare not blame him. He speaks of "the half-reformation in religion and government," with which England has sat down contented, without thinking it necessary to cure her remaining prejudices.

Say not that France is outstripping us in philosophy, unless you have read the "History of Moral Philosophy in Britain," lately written by Sir James Mackintosh. It is a work of immense erudition, full of acute and original remark, and showing a prodigious comprehension of the subject; yet it is said to have been hastily written, and the style is not highly excellent. I am impatient for you to see it. Being written in a supplement to a new edition of the "Encyclopædia Britannica," it could not be bought in a separate form; the author only having a few copies for his friends, one of which was lent me. I tried to get possession of one for you, but failed. He was happily called by Mr. Whishaw, "an artist of conversation."

Brougham is our new Lord Chancellor—the Edinburgh reviewer—the radical-whig—the apostle of universal education and popular literature, whom we are astonished and delighted to behold in that highest dignity of a subject! This is the man, the only man, whose powers I contemplate with *wonder*. In society he has the artless gaiety of a good-humoured child. Never leading the conversation, never canvassing for audience (in truth he has no need), he catches the ball as it flies with a careless and unrivalled skill. His little narratives are inimitable; the touch-and-go of his remarks leaves a trail of light behind it. On the tritest subjects he is new without paradox and without effort, simply, as it seems, because nature has interdicted him from commonplace. With that tremendous power of sarcasm which he has so often put forth in public, he is the sweetest-tempered man in private life, the kindliest in its relations, the most attracting to his friends—in short, as amiable as he is great. His first great speech in the House of Peers on his plan for distributing cheap justice to the people, afforded a curious exhibition of the manners of that House. I have the account from Mr. Whishaw, who accompanied the Chancellor. "None of the cheers, none of the applauses of the House of Commons—no interest in so great and useful a subject. On the impassive ice the lightnings played." And when he had concluded, no one rising, no one thanking him—"they sat in their curule chairs mute and motionless (however wide of them in other respects) as the Roman senate in the presence of Brennus." No matter; England hears him. It is the news of to-day that the Prussians are rising, and Austria dreading disturbances in Italy. We shall be free—all Europe will. I cast away alarms and apprehensions as unworthy things, and surrender myself to the spirit of the age. Religious changes in this country become probable. It cannot, I think, be questioned that the Evangelical clergy have become odious to the common people by their meddling spirit, their hostility to all amusements, and the gloom with which they invest the offices of religion. To recover influence, the clergy must relax a good deal; if they do not, a season of Puritanism may again be followed by an age of utter profligacy. A well-informed friend just returned from Paris tells me, what others confirm, that with respect to religion the French mind is a "tabula rasa." "They do not write against Christianity," I remarked to one who knew Paris.

"No, they think that settled; they do not write against Jupiter." The churches are quite deserted, even in the south of France.—I am delighted at your amusing yourself with Walpole. All classes were very coarse then; they had not yet thrown off the pollution of the Court of Charles II. Lady M. W. Montague's letters tell the same tale—the Whig Horace Walpole-was aristocracy personified.

I hope you will again gratify me with a letter before it is very long—your letters give me much to think upon. Ever most truly yours,

L. AIKIN.

To Miss Aikin.

St. Croix (West Indies), March 4, 1831.

My dear Miss Aikin,—Thanks for your letter of Dec. 14th. I have just received it; for, as the date will show, I am far from home. My wife's health induced me to place her within the Tropics this winter; and I was willing to come myself, not only that I might see a "new nature," for such you find here, but that I might escape the severe trial of the cold season at home—a trial under which I nearly sank last year. Perhaps you have heard all this from Miss Taylor, to whom I wrote a few weeks ago. By the way, do you know that you are likely to have a rival in your friend Miss T.? She writes me letters *almost* as interesting as yours. Do not, however, be jealous. It is not true in the moral, as in the physical world, that one light puts out another. I find that new excellence gives me new sensibility to that which I have known and loved before. Certain it is that you and your letters are as interesting as ever, and I wish you knew how much so, for then you would find time to write to me oftener.

Your last gave me your views on a subject which presses on my mind with great weight,—I mean the condition of your country; and it was more eagerly read because here, in this little island—cut off by its position, and still more by the despotism which rules it, from the Old and New World—not a man can be found who has any comprehension or feelings of what is passing in the world. The great events abroad are of course known, but as for the sympathy which a human being ought to feel with the struggles, misfortunes and successes of his race, it seems to me wholly wanting. I think you ascribe your present convulsions too much to temporary causes. No doubt your superabundant population, Poor-laws, &c. &c., have their influence. But the great cause seems to me deeper. You are suffering from the hostility which subsists between your present state of society and the intelligence, the moral sentiments and general improvement, of the people. New and great ideas are stirring among you, which find little congenial with themselves in your institutions. That the general weal is the end of social institutions, is an old doctrine; but that the general weal is one and the same thing with the improvement and happiness of the *mass* of the people, has been very imperfectly understood. That the multitude, *because* the multitude, are the most important part of the community, is quite a new doctrine, and far from being comprehended in all its bearings. In England, the worship of the great has been the national religion, so that the new light, the juster estimate of human beings which is spreading among you, is an element of irreconcilable hostility thrown among your institutions, and will allow you no peace till it shall have brought things into some degree of harmony with itself. You say, "Here we are in an English revolution." You are only in the beginning of one. The reform which must take place in Parliament, and which will take the House of Commons out of the hands of the aristocracy and make it the organ of public opinion, will be as truly a revolution as if you were to make your government a republic or despotism. That you are in danger, I believe; and your danger seems to me to rise from the two extreme parties, the aristocracy and the radicals. The first will hold fast what they ought to concede, and the latter will insist on what ought not to be conceded. Could the aristocracy know their true position and catch a little magnanimity, it seems to me they might not only save the country, but raise it to new grandeur. I recollect that when in England I had some conversation with Mr. Southey on the perils which hung over your constitution, and among other things I observed to him that the time had come in which the aristocracy could only sustain itself by public spirit and by sacrifices to the public good; that its members ought to wake from their self-indulgence; that to secure their hereditary distinctions and wealth they must regard and sacredly use them as high *trusts* committed to them for the well-being of the State, so as to conciliate to them public confidence and favour. Your account of the manner in which the House of Lords received Mr. Brougham's speech on Legal Reform is a bad omen. They do not discern the signs of the times. They ought to be the *first* to carry justice to the poor man's door; the first to lighten the public burdens, to improve the character and condition of the people, so as to be recognized as the most distinguished benefactors to the State. The old relation of the aristocracy to the State was that of leaders and protectors in war. This has passed away, as well as the state of society of which it was so important a part. Can an equivalent relation take its place? If not, the aristocracy must go down. In truth, the progress of society is characterized by nothing more than by the subversion of all distinctions but personal ones. Men will cease to pass for more than they are worth. Woe then to the privileged classes, for the direct tendency of hereditary rank is to make men worth very little. I have little expectation that the aristocracy will understand their true position. They will probably fight an insane war against improvement in which they ought to be leaders, and thus will give their adversaries the better side. It will not be the first instance of the highest classes playing into the hands of the lowest. This is one of your dangers. Another, I fear, is, that your public men do not understand the greatness of the times in which they are acting. In the last number of the "Edinburgh Review," which I suppose to be the chief organ of the ruling party, I thought I discovered much more the tone of partizans than of men alive to the grandeur of the interests which are now at stake.—In looking over my letter I see that I have written too dogmatically. I rather intended to give you my views, that I may obtain yours. I am too far from you to judge of the true state of your country, and perhaps my error always is that I overlook details, and judge too much by general principles. Help to correct me.

I have left some interesting parts of your letter unanswered, but will not inflict another sheet on you. Do write to me as soon as you can, and address to me in my own country.

Your sincere friend,
Wm. E. Channing.

To Dr. Channing.

Hampstead, May 1, 1831.

Very happy was I, my dear friend, to hear from you again. There was no getting any tidings about you. I could not even learn for certain where you were, and I was anxious to learn how the change of climate had answered to you and Mrs. Channing in point of health. Boston is quite an easy distance to think of in comparison of that little out-of-the-world island which I never heard of before, and could scarcely hunt out upon the map. And Emily Taylor had not written me a word about you, for which I will scold her; but I will not be jealous of her, because I love her dearly—a purer or more amiable mind I do not know; she loves a joke, too, and we are very merry whenever we meet.

I have not been travelling for health, but keeping the house for it, which is worse. It is nearly three months since I have seen London, and I have been almost entirely disabled from writing, but I am again recovering. Great public events have occurred since I wrote last; on the whole, I think our position improved. The peasant risings are completely quelled; the Reform Bill absorbs all political feeling. It is a noble measure, and one which, when carried, will deserve to be revered as a new Magna Charta. It will render Parliament indeed the organ of the people, and put, I believe, an effectual check upon the corrupt and oppressive influence of the aristocracy. You express a natural apprehension that our aristocracy should not discern the signs of the times sufficiently to lead the people the way that they must and will go. Certainly many are even now blindly striving to resist what is inevitable; but the terrible examples of France have not been lost on the privileged

orders in general, and many individuals have shown
themselves actuated by a sense of justice and of true
patriotism, which is of the best augury for the country.
But the conduct of the King is our grand piece of good
fortune, and a most unexpected one. A patriot King!
Once in a millennium such a phœnix is seen on earth.
Alfred was our last. A levity in the manners of his
Majesty had caused him to be suspected of an unsound
head, but he has under this a plain good sense, and, what
is better still, a real love of seeing his people happy,
which in this instance has led him admirably right. His
appeal to the people on this great question has utterly
disarmed radicalism. The mob are ever king-worshippers
in all monarchical countries, and ours may be led anywhere to the tune of our "National Anthem." Hunt
and O'Connell hide their diminished heads; against a
king, and a sailor-king too, they are less than nothing.
On the higher classes, also, his influence is very considerable, and I feel almost confident that the measure
will be triumphantly carried in the new Parliament. I
agree with you that the want of harmony between ancient
institutions and modern light is the general cause of
commotion both in this country and throughout Europe,
and that the only general remedy is to be sought in a
comprehensive reform of institutions; but the particular
or immediately exciting causes are various; and to these
the attention of eye-witnesses is most directed, as being
those over which events, or what are unphilosophically
called accidents, have power. Thus, I should say, the
general progress of society must bring us Parliamentary
Reform during this generation; but the accident of a
George or a William on the throne, a good or bad harvest,
a prosperous or depressed state of trade, Whig or Tory
ministry, may make all the difference of our obtaining
it safely and peaceably, or through revolution and civil

war. But it is, in the main, the cause of the many against that of the few. I have convinced myself of this, and am become in consequence an ardent reformer. I boast of this as a self-conquest. Women are natural aristocrats, depend upon it; and many a reproach have I sustained from my father for what he called my "odi profanum vulgus." The rude manners, trenchant tone and barbarous slang of the ordinary Radicals, as well as the selfish ends and gross knavery which many of them strive to conceal under professions of zeal for all the best interests of mankind, are so inexpressibly disgusting to me, that in some moods I have wished to be divided from them far as pole from pole. On the other hand, the captivating manners of the aristocracy, the splendour which surrounds them, the taste for heraldry and pedigree which I have picked up in the course of my studies, and the flattering attentions which my writings have sometimes procured me from them, are strong bribes on the side of ancient privilege; but, as I said before, I have fought and conquered; and I confess that "the greatest good of the greatest number" is what alone is entitled to consideration, however unpoetical the phrase and the pedantic sect of which it is the watchword.

Of the integrity of the Chancellor, all distrust should cease. He has resisted more temptations than any public man in the country. An intense love of glory he certainly has, but it is for glory of the true sort. He is magnanimous and philanthropic; and these two last words I cannot write without being reminded to beg you to read the Life of Dr. Currie by his son. I knew the man—he was my father's friend—and the impression of the benefit and delight I received at an early age from his society and under his roof, will be one of the very last I can ever lose. I think him to have been one of the best and noblest of mankind, and the wisest I ever conversed with. And with these great qualities there was an elegance and tenderness of mind, a spirit of poetry, and a shade of constitutional melancholy investing the whole, which rendered him interesting beyond expression. Many of his letters are given in this work, and they are the man himself. The memoir has the very rare merit, from a filial hand, of being perfectly free from exaggeration—the simple truth. There are many matters in the book which will interest you. Currie was a wide as well as a deep thinker—few subjects of human speculation escaped him.

And now let me tell you how I have been attempting to fill up one of those languid pauses of existence in which one has little to do but to wait for the return of health and strength in patience, deceiving the long, and in my case lonely, hours as best one may. I have been reading metaphysics. And this was your doing: the mention which you make, I forget in which piece of yours, of the theory of Berkeley, excited my curiosity, and I have been reading him with great admiration of his ingenuity and his beautiful style, and wonder that so much is to be said for what seems at first view so chimerical. I have since been reading Priestley's "Disquisitions on Matter and Spirit," and his correspondence with Price. And what is the result? Why, that I am perplexed and confounded—utterly unable to take a side or form an opinion on subjects which seem to me, indeed, placed beyond the scope of human knowledge—yet pleased and *proud* that the human mind should dare to entertain such thoughts, to soar to such heights and sound such depths. Oh! the mind of man *must* be formed for progress, eternal progress; else why these thoughts beyond the measure of his frame? If the strengthening of this conviction were the sole result of pursuits like these, they were well and amply recompensed; but I have found in them other uses. They give me a more intimate sense of the all-pervading presence and agency of the *one* Cause. I did not before, if I may so speak, feel how *very near* it is—how closely it encompasses us on all sides. Second causes extend no way at all: they can account for nothing, effect nothing. I always saw that there was something amiss with Hume's famous argument against miracles, but I did not well know what—now I do; and now I feel the full force of your sentence, that it is "essentially atheistical." That imposing term, the laws of nature, may easily lead to great misconception. The correspondence of Price and Priestley is further interesting as a very beautiful exhibition of two characters of great but different endowments. Both have great acuteness, both great extent and variety of knowledge to bring in illustration of their topic; but the caution of Price, fertile in objections, is remarkably contrasted with the precipitation of Priestley, with whom "once to doubt" was "once to be resolved." Priestley was the more original thinker, the greater genius; but he could not feel difficulties; neither, indeed, on his own favourite topics could Price, whose political theories warped even his calculations. I have a vivid memory of Priestley, the friend of my father, the dearer and more intimate friend of my aunt, Mrs. Barbauld. In his manners he had all the calmness and simplicity of a true philosopher; he was cheerful, even playful, and I still see the benignant smile with which he greeted us little ones. It pleased me to find you referring to him when you mention Berkeley. I know you have disapproved him on some points—you differ on many; but you are brothers in the assertion of intellectual freedom, and the earnest search after and unhesitating avowal of truth. Oh! the noble, the glorious beings whom it has been my privilege to see and know! What would life be without the commerce of superior minds? what earth without "the salt of the earth"? And let us rely upon it that times like these will bring forth men equal to them. France is decidedly taking a higher moral station; and those gallant Poles, they *will* redeem their country. Here, too, I see much to rejoice in. Great borough owners, the Duke of Norfolk at their head, coming forward with alacrity to make the sacrifice of them to their country. Lord Grey—whose canvassing of Northumberland in former days was called Coriolanus acted to the life—the author of the great Bill. Lord J. Russell doing honour to his patriot line and to the tuition of excellent Playfair, whom I once saw him, in an Edinburgh party, pulling along by the skirt of his coat to be introduced to a lady of quality. (A little puny man is this Lord John, with a very small voice; sound sense his leading characteristic, and his style of expression simple, energetic and rigidly concise.) In middle life there seems to be a good deal of real patriotism. Even members of close corporations have sided with the public; and what is more, so have some of the clergy. It is observable that there is now scarcely a whisper raised of the Church in danger—when its peril was less, the cry of Wolf! was ten times louder. The lawyers, for the most part, take the reforming side. I scan not their motives. Both universities patronize darkness—but I blush most for the poets. A good while ago I saw Wordsworth in anxious museful mood, talking rather to himself than the company, as is his manner, against general education, and then bursting out: "I don't see the use of all those prayers they make the children say after their *fugleman*. Either it will give them a profane aversion to the whole thing, or make them hypocrites,"—in which I mutually agreed. Now, I hear, he says that if the Bill passes he shall fly his country. But whither, alas? Revolution may pursue him to Spain or Russia. And so ends my voluminous budget.

Believe me ever, very truly yours,

L. AIKIN.

To Miss Aikin.

Boston, June 22, 1831.

My dear Miss Aikin,—Give me joy on my safe return home. I enjoyed much on that little "out-of-the-world island" which you could hardly find on the map. But the balmy airs, bright suns, clear skies, and new and beautiful vegetation of the Tropics, could not conquer the instinct of country; and I was never more grateful than now for the sight of my native shores. I gained nothing in health, and perhaps I am not to hope for this; but I escaped a tremendous winter, under which I might have sunk. I wonder that the English, with their fine island Jamaica, do not visit the Tropics for health, instead of Italy. In Italy you have a half-winter, which is very trying; but in the West Indies there is not a sign or hint of that season. I incline, however, to think that the sick English will do well to keep at home, to keep in the land of comforts. These are as important as climate, and your southern coast is so mild that the consumptive may take the air freely most of the year. I am more and more satisfied that a degree of humidity is not as injurious in consumption as was once thought. Though I have found many comforts abroad, I have learned that home is the place for the sick—I mean the really sick. In incipient disease, and especially in disease where the mind plays a large part, travelling, change of objects, is often the best medicine. I wish your travellers would go to the West Indies to learn better the true evils of slavery. I know not a subject on which half-knowledge is more dangerous to legislators. I wonder that philanthropy, which is one of your fashions, does not come in aid of your restlessness, another English characteristic, and of the desire to see a new nature, and divert a part of your travellers to the land of slaves and palm-trees, of the sugar-cane and the acacia. I forgot to say, in speaking of my health, that it was not my motive for visiting the West Indies. I went to protract a life dearer than my own. My wife had long been losing strength under rheumatic complaints, and I resolved to make for her sake one great effort, and am happy to tell you that she has found a good deal of relief.

I thank you for your last letter, addressed to me in this country. I sympathize with you heartily on "Reform." I have thought since I last wrote you that I had viewed the measure as more revolutionary than it really is. In other words, it is only the continuance of a great revolutionary movement which has long been going on, and is by no means so great a step as is thought. For a long time power has been changing hands in England, or silently passing over to the people. Since Mr. Canning's adoption of more liberal views, public opinion has been continually manifesting itself as the destined, if not actual, sovereign; and the reform is only providing an appropriate adequate organ for this vast and growing power. Some means of action it must have. Hitherto it has operated through the press, by petition, by clamour; and it has been more clamorous because it could act no other way. Give it a legal, constitutional, natural, fit organ, and such representation is, and will be, much less liable to excess.

I am not surprised at the opposition to this measure. The High-birth and High-church party are, and must be (in the language of theology), "judicially blinded." To know how and when to give up power is a wisdom above their reach. Indeed, it is one of the hardest lessons for human nature under our present false institutions. I do wonder, however, that men can welcome and multiply causes, and then fight against their effects. Among your Tories, I suppose, are not a few who really rejoice in the diffusion of wealth and intelligence through your country; and yet how can a people grow rich and intelligent without taking a new interest in their government—without subjecting it to a strict scrutiny, and gaining an influence over it which they must always desire to extend? In giving wealth and intelligence, you give power; and a power which will assume a political direction more certainly than any other. No law of nature is surer; and yet there are those who think themselves the wise, who, instead of aiming to make this power a beneficent one, and to bring it into harmony with existing institutions, are making war with it and irritating it by blind opposition. I want nothing more to satisfy me of the expediency of reform than the general consideration that it springs necessarily from the improvement of the community in wealth and knowledge. It is a want of a people who are rising in civilization. They who do not so view it, ought at least to see that, be it good or bad, come it will and must; and that wisdom and patriotism call them to make the best terms with it in their power. I expressed to you my regret at the blindness of your aristocracy, because I should deem anything like revolution among you a tremendous evil, and I think it may be averted by wisdom in the higher order. England, with all her defects, and though less in advance of other nations than formerly, is still the first country on earth (nothing but truth would wring this acknowledgment from a Republican), and I cannot bear the thought of her encountering the chances of a violent change. I ask no quicker growth of Republican principles among you than is now going on; nor am I such a bigot as to insist on the expression of these principles in forms and institutions like our own. To these forms they will come at last, for every principle seeks its most natural manifestation; but they may exist for an age or more under other forms, and this is better than the hazard of civil commotion. Let society go on as it has done, and your hereditary distinctions will die a natural death. They cannot stand against the moral power which is establishing itself by the aid of the press, education, and a more rational religion; and to this mild but sure innovator I am willing to leave them.

The debates on the Reform question seemed to me very indifferent. Are they tolerably reported? Amidst the debates and declamation I found it hard to pick out a general principle, or find any large views. The tone of confidence was on the side of the anti-reformers. I commend the Reformers for abstaining from all promise of great immediate relief to the suffering classes through this measure. Such relief it cannot bring. The evil is too deep, I fear, for legislative remedies. When I look at the distress of the labouring classes, I feel the need of some great change in our social system. It is not right that so many of our fellow-creatures should be abandoned to want bordering on famine, to ignorance and degrading vices, whilst so many of us are rioting in plenty. There is a great fault somewhere. Some deeper reform than that of Parliament is needed. But this subject is as vast as it is painful. I will not trust myself with it. I have a great deal more to say, especially about your aristocratic partialities, which you have found it hard to overcome. They are founded partially in

E

truth, and are better than some levelling systems. But I cannot give my views now.

I rejoice in your metaphysical studies. I feared you were to be found among the scorners of that noble branch of philosophy.

Tell me if my letter is illegible. Mrs. Channing, who generally dots my "i's" and finishes my half-formed letters, is absent.

Your sincere friend,
WM. E. CHANNING.

To Dr. Channing.

Hampstead, June 28, 1831.

It is so agreeable a thing to me, my dear distant friend, to communicate to you my impressions of passing events, with the assurance, too, that I am doing what is acceptable to you, that I have felt impatient to amass materials for a second letter. But from my parlour sofa, to which I have been very much confined, I could only send you what my neighbours brought to me; within the last two or three months alone I have been enabled to go a little into society myself, and I now offer you my gleanings.

Parliamentary Reform is secure—the Tories may give some trouble by their factious opposition, but that is all they can do. The *people* have shown themselves much more zealous and united in the cause than public men on either side of the question were prepared to find them. The question therefore now is—what next? According to your prediction, we seem destined to proceed in the career of reformation until *all* our institutions shall have undergone a transformation. The friends of the Church dread that its turn will come next, and there are many tokens of it. A *stinging* "Letter to the Archbishop of York" has appeared, and the demand for it has been such as the printer could not keep pace with. The author declaims somewhat idly on the contrast between modern and primitive bishops—then inveighs with greater force against the alliance of Church and State, and its corrupting effects on the clergy; exposes their views broadly, and indignantly exclaims that a moral and religious people can no longer away with such unfaithful shepherds; and in the end boldly announces the fall of the Irish Establishment within one year, and the English within ten years.

Mr. Beverley, the author, whom I know a little, is a very elegant classic, a good writer, and a gentleman, but wild and eccentric to the brink of insanity. After many vagaries, he has just turned Methodist preacher. His pamphlet contains nothing like a reasonable plan for the settlement of religious affairs, but it is deeply imbued with the spirit of the Evangelical sect. It is professedly, at least, in love and reverence to religion that he would divorce the Church from the State, and place it on the common level of sects; and the extraordinary popularity of his piece seems to show that the large and zealous party to which he belongs are beginning to perceive how much the forms and the discipline of a church constructed on the model of the Romish—that is, on the taste of the middle ages—are at variance with the spirit of the present day, and hostile to their plans of empire over the minds of the people at large. I conceive that enthusiasm will always strive to burst through the fetters of articles and liturgies. I hear just now that the unpopularity of tithes is the chief cause of the currency of this piece. Another new and startling feature begins to appear. Hitherto both the Methodists and the Church Evangelicals have been distinguished by their indifference to civil liberty, and their attachment to "the powers that be;" lately they seem to have entered into coalition with the Radicals—at least, the lower class of Methodists, consisting chiefly of journeymen mechanics and other labourers in towns, are engaged in the *strikes* for wages which have been so frequent and formidable, and which their masters regard as the worst sign of radicalism.

The Marquis of Londonderry, a great coal-owner in the North, went lately and demanded a conference with the leader of the Newcastle *turn-outs*. He was referred to a person who proved to be a Methodist preacher, and who absolutely insisted upon the Marquis joining him in prayer (an exercise to which his lordship is little addicted) before he would proceed to business.

I own I am not quite pleased with the prospect of a second reign of the saints, for their rigour and intolerance go beyond the High-church themselves; but there would be hope, I think, if the Establishment were overthrown or considerably shaken, that a liberal party in religion might rise in some strength. I believe it is already pretty numerous, but shy of showing itself.

In the intervals of politics we talk of the Christian Brahmin, Rammohun Roy. All accounts agree in representing him as a person of extraordinary merit. With very great intelligence and ability, he unites a modesty and simplicity which win all hearts. He has a very great command of the language, and seems perfectly well versed in the political state of Europe, and an ardent well-wisher to the cause of freedom and improvement everywhere. To his faith he has been more than a martyr. On his conversion to Christianity his mother cursed him, and his wife (or wives) and children all forsook him. He had grievous oppressions to endure from the Church party on turning Unitarian. This was at Calcutta; here it is determined to court him. Two bishops have noticed him, and the East-India Company show him all civilities. But his heart is with his brethren in opinion, with whom chiefly he spends his time. I hear of him this remarkable saying, that the three countries in Europe which appear even less prepared than Asia for a liberal system of religion, are Spain, Portugal, and England.

You will read, I think, with interest, and in part with great satisfaction, Godwin's new volume, entitled "Thoughts on Man." Probably it will prove the last fruit of his mind, for he is now rather nearer eighty than seventy, and I believe declining. With all his extravagances of opinion, some of which in the early part of his career did considerable mischief and threatened more, I have always entertained a respect for some parts of his character, as well as a high admiration of his powers; and felt sincere pity for the long misfortunes in which partly his own errors, but still more the proscription of society, have involved him. I believe he justly describes himself in his new work as "one who early said to truth, Go on; whithersoever thou leadest, I am prepared to follow." And is not this of itself a noble character of a man? It was remarkable in him that the reasoning powers seemed to have been developed long before the sensitive part of his nature. Thus his system was originally constructed with a total disregard of the passions, the affections, and almost the instincts, of mankind. But it was beautiful to observe him, in his own experience of the tenderest ties of life, gradually expanding his groundwork to give admission to private and partial affections, and at length doing, as it were, public penance for the slanders which he had uttered against them in his days of ignorance. Those noble and rare virtues amongst the founders and champions of systems—candour and ingenuousness, have always attended him. And they have produced to him good fruit. They have enabled him, after discarding one error after another, to work out for himself principles which, in the midst of degrading embarrassments, and even of domestic dishonour, have preserved to himself respect, philanthropy, and cheering views of the character and destination of man. This volume is a repository of thoughts on many subjects, often I think original, often just as well as striking, and frequently expressed with great eloquence. He everywhere shows himself "lenior et melior." Do not almost all men grow better as they grow older? I was pleased to find poet Crabbe maintaining that they do, which from the tone of his writings I did not expect. Have you ever met with any writings of Paul Louis Courier? If not, you will know all about him from the very able notice of him and his works which appeared some time ago in the "Edinburgh Review." I have just been reading a selection of his political pamphlets, and with extraordinary admiration. His style is like that of Pascal, but still more lively and striking. A sharp thorn he must have been in the sides of the restored Bourbons, with their priest and emigrant faction—and it was this, probably, which caused his assassination. I had no knowledge, till I read his pieces, how the system of the Restoration had worked; but the oppression was terrible, especially in the provinces remote from the control of the public opinion of Paris. The maires and préfets, themselves slaves of the court, the ministers, or the Jesuits, were so many despots over the peasantry and middle class, and carried on a frightful persecution against the means and the principles of the Revolution. I see here abundant explanation and vindication of the Revolution of last July, and I judge the men who planned and achieved it to have been true benefactors to their country. Courier strongly asserts, what you likewise hold, the vast improvement of the national character since 1789. Possessed of personal liberty and a share in the soil of his country, the peasant has become industrious almost to excess, frugal and, generally speaking, moral; he has the virtues of a labourer in exchange for the vices of a laquais or the abjectness of a serf. It is from intimate views of private life in various ages and countries that the *moral* of political history is alone to be derived—and without this, what is the value of long tales of wars and conquests, and one king deposing and succeeding another, and republics changed into monarchies, and monarchies into republics? This principle has been always in my view in writing my "King Charles," and will impart, I think, its chief merit to my book; that is, should health and vigour be lent me for its completion. I have hope of it now; but I have been sorely tried by repeated disappointments on this head, and sometimes I have reached the very verge of despondency, and I have wished for the termination of a suffering and useless existence—my spirit beat itself against the bars of its cage. Then again I have called to my aid all I could summon of philosophy and religion, and I have soothed my soul by prayer.

I should like to know what you take to be the origin of the almost universal belief amongst mankind of a future state—was there, think you, a revelation to our first progenitors, of which all nations preserved some tradition? Or did it result from the reasonings of man upon the moral differences between individuals of the human race, not always accompanied here by corresponding rewards and punishments? Or was the wish for re-union with departed friends father to that belief? Or is it (with Locke's pardon) an innate idea, an instinct? I think there is something mysterious—something, if I may so express myself, *sui generis*—in so strong and general a persuasion, contrary to all appearances and unsupported by any real analogies. I should like to believe it a revelation; but there are difficulties.

I must not conclude without telling you some news of yourself. A friend of mine, just returned from Geneva, met there M. Vincent, Protestant minister at Nismes, a liberal and worthy man, who deplored the ignorance and narrowness of his flock, still buried in the gloom of Calvinism. He had set up a journal, in which, by mingling theology with literary criticism and general topics, he was gently insinuating into them more enlightened notions. My friend asked if he knew your writings, and finding he did not, she gave him several of them. In the first number of his journal, after his return, appeared as the leading article a translation of your sermon on the Resemblance of Man to his Maker. Thus the good seed is sown—you may water it if you think proper. I hear from further evidence that in several parts of France a simple form of Protestant worship, with liberal doctrine, would be highly acceptable to the people.

Have you heard of our absurd sect of Millenarians? Some say the end of the world is to be in the year 1860, others only give us to 1836, and one gentleman has actually turned his property into an annuity for six years.

Pray let me hear particularly of your health.

Yours, with the truest esteem,

L. AIKIN.

To MISS AIKIN.

July 14, 1831.

My dear Miss Aikin,—I wrote you a few days ago, but having a strong inducement send you another letter, which I trust will be of more moderate dimensions than my last. This will be handed you by a very dear friend of mine, Mrs. Farrar, a lady who does not perhaps need an introduction, as you knew her several years ago when she bore the name of Miss Rotch. She now visits England in company with Mr. Farrar, who is the Professor of Natural Philosophy in Harvard University, the most distinguished institution in our country, and who holds a high rank among our scientific men. He is singularly happy in communicating knowledge, and as a lecturer perhaps has not his equal here. I am sorry to say that the indisposition under which he suffers seems to have taken from his energy of mind as well as body. We trust that entire rest from his labour will restore him.

In your last letter you wrote about Price and Priestley. I wish you would give me some light about the latter. I have always esteemed him a good man, but I have had many doubts of his moral greatness. It is not a good sign when a man carries out his speculations without the least fear or hesitation, when they seem to shock the highest moral principles. Now Priestley's system of materialism, of necessity, and of the derivation of all our moral sentiments from *sensations* variously modified by association, does seem to strike a blow at our most intimate and strongest moral convictions, whilst it robs our nature of all its grandeur. Yet Priestley not only vindicated it as true, but entered into it with his whole soul. I cannot easily reconcile this with clear moral perception or deep moral feeling. I think of him as a man of amiableness rather than sensibility. The terrible amount of physical and moral evil in the world never seems to have weighed upon or burdened his mind. He imagined that he had got to the bottom of this mystery; he met it with an optimism more favourable to Epicurean tranquillity than to Christian sympathy and self-sacrifice. I have sometimes thought him a self-complacent, self-satisfied man, whose speculations were tinged by this quality of his mind. I am not now expressing my *deliberate convictions*, so much as suggestions and suspicions which cross my mind when I hear of Priestley. I am most willing to have my prejudices, if such they are, removed. I am fully sensible to his intellectual claims, to the range, rapidity and fruitfulness of his mind, to the beautiful simplicity and transparency of his style, &c.; and I know the impression his character made on his friends. Still he is not to me morally great. Price I have always delighted in. His book on Morals, though little read, took a strong hold on me in my youth, and helped to fix my moral convictions at that critical age. Here is a subject for a letter. I have another subject for you. I lately received a letter from Dr. William King, of Brighton, accompanying a series of papers called the "Co-operator." Dr. K.'s letter breathes a spirit of such pure philanthropy that I shall answer him immediately, and in the language of confidence in which a good man should be addressed. Still I should like to know something more of him, and something of this scheme of co-operation. Its object is the true one, and *must* be accomplished in some way or other. But whether this means be a wise one may be questioned. I trust that health is returning to you, and that I shall soon hear it from yourself.

Your sincere friend,
Wm. E. Channing.

To Miss Aikin.

Boston, August 27, 1831.

My dear Miss Aikin,—I thank you for your letter of June 28. I trust that before this you have found that you are not writing two letters for one. You tell me *reform is sure.* Of this I have no doubt. Good or bad, it must be conceded. I am not enough acquainted with your state to judge how far its provisions will extend the elective franchise. My only doubt about the measure has been in relation to this point. In this country the right of suffrage is next to universal. It may be said, everybody votes. But our situation differs from yours. Our people are *used* to the right. Then an immense majority have *property*, and are directly and strongly interested in the support of order and the laws. The breaking up of estates on the death of the owner, which almost always takes place, and the means of gaining property which our people possess in their education, in their early habits of industry, in the abundance of unsettled lands, in the immense undeveloped resources of the country, and in the absence of all obstructions to the freest use of men's powers,—these causes produce an equal and general distribution of property nowhere else known. Then the vast majority of our citizens may be called *educated;* and this we owe partly to a very honourable cause, our public provisions for instruction of all classes, and partly to what is our greatest reproach, I mean *slavery.* In the slave states, the only voters are the masters, and these from their condition enjoy many advantages of education of which they generally avail themselves. We have another security in the very *extent* of our country, which prevents sudden universal excitements, and scatters, as it were, the sensibility and interest of the community over a variety of objects. In these respects you differ from us. You have much more wealth, and many more poor; much more learning, and many more ignorant; and then your population is so dense, and communication is so rapid, that a day is enough to set the kingdom on fire. I have much confidence, however, in your leading men, and in their ability to adapt this great measure to the state of the country. In glancing over what I have written, I see that I have been guilty of something like a contradiction, for I have spoken of our enjoying *universal* suffrage, and in the next breath have spoken of the right of suffrage as confined to masters. I forgot that the *slave* was a part of the community having the rights of a man—so easily do established abuses obscure our perceptions. I now perceive that we have less cause than I supposed of boasting of the extension of the elective franchise here; for if our slaves are men, what a vast number do we exclude!

On this subject of slavery, *you* are far in advance of us. I almost envy your country the pure glory it has won by its sympathy with the oppressed negro. In truth, when I think of the state of the public mind here in regard to slavery, my national pride dies within me. Never did a people deserve chains more than we, who are vaunting of our freedom and holding one or two millions in bondage. This is truly our foulest blot, and I fear nothing will rouse us up to wash it away but the deep, stern, irresistible indignation of the civilized world.

In regard to your *Church* reform, it will be superficial for the present. Much good may, indeed, be done by a more equal distribution of Church revenues; but then the religion of the Thirty-nine Articles, which hangs as a millstone on the intellect and character of the nation, will continue to be taught. The object should be (considering what your Church is) to turn as much of these revenues as possible to education. The schoolmaster should take the place of the *priest*. By the way, have you ever considered that the minister of Christianity is nowhere in the New Testament called *priest;* that this term, which is very seldom used, is applied to the *whole body* of Christians; that there is no more reason for the distinction between *clergy* and *laity* than between lawyers and laity, or physicians and laity, and that the whole separation made between the clergy and the rest of society is unauthorized by our religion. I mention this, for it seems to me no mean proof of the divine wisdom of the Founder of Christianity. The office of *religious teacher*, properly understood, and so used as to promote intellectual, moral, spiritual freedom, is the *very noblest* and most useful on earth; but priestly usurpation, which, by the way, is as rife out of the Establishment as in it, seems to me at the present moment a great obstruction to the progress of religion and society.

I have not seen Godwin's last book, but will seek for it. There are some errors which show such a strange obliquity of intellect as to destroy my confidence in the judgment of those who adopt them. Godwin does not believe in a God, and such a mind must be as unsound as one which should not believe in the existence of the sun.

You ask me what I think to be the origin of the common belief in a future life. I go back to a primitive revelation of the doctrine, for we know that the first man must have received *some direct* instruction from his Creator, and it is natural to believe that he would be taught the great *end* or *purpose* of his being. I conceive, however, that revelation would be of no avail towards securing permanent and universal reception to a doctrine, unless that doctrine were founded in and congenial with our nature. All the great principles of human nature seem to me to demand and promise a future life. The reason, the conscience, the affections, all alike cry aloud for it. It is revealed to us especially in the capacity for moral and intellectual progress without end, and in the thirst for a higher existence which always grows in proportion to the right use and enlargement of the faculties. All the attributes of God, His wisdom, justice and goodness, point to another existence, and seem to require it for their own bright and full manifestation. The present life bears all the marks of an incipient, incomplete state, and constantly leads us to something beyond itself as its explanation and end. I think, too, that there is something still deeper in support of immortality. The mind which is *just to itself*, in the course of its development attains to a consciousness of its destination, to a pre-conception and conviction of its future perfection, power, glory, which it cannot communicate except to those who experience it. I could add much more, but perhaps I have answered your question. Your letters give me so much to write about that I continually pass my bounds, but you are a patient reader.

Very affectionately yours,

WM. E. CHANNING.

The account you give me of the favourable reception of my writings in France is very cheering and encouraging to me. I am solicitous to get some accurate views of the state and prospects of religion in that country.

What do you know of Miss Mitford? I owe her much for the pleasure her "Village" has given me. When I ask you about individuals, you will always feel yourself at liberty to be silent.

TO DR. CHANNING.

Hampstead, September 6, 1831.

Dear Sir,—I cannot longer refrain from acknowledging your last welcome letter, although I suppose you must have received one of mine soon after you wrote. There is always topic enough, since the interests of all mankind are ours. Just now my feelings are more cosmopolite than usual; I take a personal concern in a *third* quarter of the globe, since I have seen the excellent Rammohun Roy. I rejoice in the hope that you will see him some time, as he speaks of visiting your country, and to know you would be one of his first objects. He is indeed a glorious being—a true sage, as it appears, with the genuine humility of the character, and with more fervour, more sensibility, a more engaging tenderness of heart, than any *class* of character can justly claim. He came to my house, at the suggestion of Dr. Boott, who accompanied him, partly for the purpose of meeting Mrs. Joanna Baillie, and discussing with her the Arian tenets of her book. He mentions the Sanscrit as the mother language of the Greek, and said that the expressions of the New Testament most perplexing to an European, were familiar to an Oriental acquainted with this language and its derivations, and that to such a person the texts which are thought to support the doctrine for the pre-existence bear quite another sense. She was a little alarmed at the erudition of her antagonist, and slipped out at last by telling him that his interpretations were too subtle for an unlearned person like herself. We then got him upon subjects more interesting to me—Hindoo laws, especially those affecting women. He spoke of polygamy as a crime, said it was punishable by their law, except for certain causes, by a great fine; but the Mussulmans did not enforce the fine, and their example had corrupted Hindoos; *they* were cruel to women, the Hindoos were forbidden all cruelty. Speaking of the abolition of widow-burning by Lord W. Bentinck, he fervently exclaimed, "May God *load* him with blessings!" His feeling for women in general, still more than the admiration he expressed of the mental accomplishments of English ladies, won our hearts. He mentioned his own mother, and in terms which convinced us of the falsehood of the shocking tale that she burned herself for his apostasy. It is his business here to ask two boons for his countrymen—trial by jury, and freedom for British capitalists to colonize amongst them. Should he fail in obtaining these, he speaks of ending his days in America. The dominion we hold over India is perhaps the most striking circumstance of greatness belonging to our little island. Your acknowledgment of England for the first country in the world very much delighted me. Yes, with all its evils, all its errors, it is a land to be proud of. I have always felt with you on the calamitousness of any violent change amongst us. As long as I can remember, and through the times when French example had most influence, all the best friends of liberty and their country, at least its wisest friends, have constantly held that our evils were not nearly great enough to risk a revolution for their removal; and now, when so many peaceable and gradual reforms are taking place, the point is so very clear, that none can wish for troubled waters but those who would fish in them. You think we shall escape this danger through the moderation of the higher classes. We have a farther and perhaps a stronger security in the curious manner in which all our different ranks, classes, sects and parties, are *dovetailed* into each other, or, if you please, matted together, which precludes the possibility of such a clear separation of one from another as took place between the privileged and the unprivileged orders in France. It is an inestimable advantage that we have nothing answering to *noblesse;* that with us the younger sons of the highest peers sink back into the ranks, undistinguished except by the vague boast of blood or family, which now stands for little or nothing; whilst, on the other hand, the lowest birth is no obstacle to the attainment of the full honours and privileges of the peerage. Voltaire somewhere remarks, "In England, if the king makes his banker a peer, everybody, even the highest noble, gives him his title. With us, though Bernard is a real Marquis, more than hundreds who are so named, who would not laugh to think of calling him Marquis?" Thus our aristocracy is in a perpetual state of flux, and no one can say in any struggle who would or would not join its standard. The Tory party, again, is far from coinciding with any possible description of the aristocracy; it excludes the Dukes of Sussex, Norfolk, Bedford, &c., and includes the greater part of the London aldermen and most provincial corporations. Even the clergy are not all *serviles*, for some of them depend on Whig patrons. Neither are all Tories boroughmongers, nor all boroughmongers Tories. The High-church indeed are nearly all Tories, and Unitarians almost unanimously Reformers; but the Church Evangelicals, and all other sects of Dissenters, are divided. Our debates are, I believe, ably reported, but I wonder not that they disappoint you. The House will not listen with patience to general principles; they are supposed to be taken for granted; and the ability of the debaters is often shown most in a kind of apropos of time and person, in hints and allusions, skilful thrusts and dexterous wards, which none but the initiated can appreciate. Of late, the anti-reformers talk merely to consume time, and now and then to damage the ministers in public opinion.

Yes, we have many evils which lie quite out of the reach of Parliamentary Reform, and the extreme inequality of conditions is the one which must weigh the most heavily of all upon the humane and thinking mind. Probably it is an inseparable concomitant of commerce, manufactures, and a high state of luxurious refinement. Bad institutions and some combinations of political circumstances, however, have extremely aggravated the evil, and no doubt opposite influences may mitigate it, as I trust we may in time experience. I can trace much of the progress of pauperism to two particular sources, one of which has been but little noticed, and the other scarcely at all in public. The first was the anxiety of Mr. Pitt to keep the lower classes in good humour during the war against French principles, which led him to give to the system of legal relief its present pernicious extent, and to lay the foundation of the fatal practice of ekeing out wages by parish alms, which the landholders improvidently concurred in, from the selfish and shortsighted notion that wages once raised could not be lowered again, but that alms might be withheld when temporary causes of distress should cease. The other cause is connected with the spread and the converting spirit of the Evangelicals. Ever since Hannah More published her "Cœlebs," it has been held by a large party the indispensable duty of ladies, girls even, to spend much of their time in visiting the dwellings of the poor, inquiring into and ministering to their spiritual and temporal wants. Apparently, great good would result from these charitable offices to all parties; but you well know our national propensity to run everything to a fashion—a rage—and the result has been a great and pernicious excess. A positive *demand* for misery was created by the incessant eagerness manifested to relieve it. In many places the poor, those amongst them especially who have known how to put on a little saintliness, have been actually pampered and rendered like the indoor menials of the wealthy, lazy, luxurious, discontented, lying and worthless. Men have been encouraged in squandering their wages in drink and dissipation, by the assurance that the good ladies would not suffer their families to want; women have slackened their efforts to provide decent clothing for their children

—improvidence has become characteristic of both. These evils, however, begin to be felt pretty widely, and I expect "the fashion of benevolence" is beginning to abate. You complain that our restlessness does not carry us to the West-Indian islands. Two things are against it, the length of voyage and the shrinking abhorrence we all feel from the sight of slavery; but that senator would deserve praise who should defy them both in the cause of humanity. I have known these isles resorted to by consumptive invalids, and in one case within my knowledge, with complete success. I sincerely congratulate you on the benefit which Mrs. Channing has derived from her residence in the Tropics, and grieve that it has not done more for yourself. Would that you would both exchange your inclement skies for our milder ones, before another fearful winter sets in! You should pass the colder months in our Montpelier—Bonchurch, in the Isle of Wight—where a friend of mine, given over in Lancashire, has been marvellously surmounting her disease; the better seasons we would enjoy your society here. Pray think of it; health is even more than country, and is not this, too, your country?

We have little or nothing doing in literature; politics absorb us wholly. The state of the continent is an object of just anxiety. I dread beyond everything the demon of military glory which in all ages has possessed the French nation, and, combined with their treachery and love of intrigue, has always rendered them bad and dangerous neighbours. I do my best not to regard them as *natural enemies*, but it is difficult. They hate us, and with some cause too. I want to hear that your pen is again at work; we cannot afford to be deprived of its labours. You may still do much more for us, much as you have done already. As for me, I proceed in my task very, very slowly; want of health and its concomitant want of energy, the cause. Just now, however, I am in spirits; I have medical permission to make a little quiet week's tour under the watchful care of a kind brother, and we are going to view our English vintage, the Kentish hop-picking; also to see pretty Tunbridge, and make a pilgrimage to Penshurst of the Sidneys, or perhaps to Hever Castle, the birthplace of Anne Boleyn. Do you not a little envy us the historic recollections of an old country? I was present at the splendid spectacle of the opening of New London Bridge. It was covered halfway over with a grand canopy, formed of the flags of all nations, under which dined his Majesty and about two thousand of his loving subjects. The river was thronged with gilded barges and boats covered with streamers and crowded with gaily-dressed people; the shores were all alive with the multitude. In the midst of the gay show I looked down the stream upon the old, deserted, half-demolished bridge, silent remembrancer of seven centuries. I thought of it fortified with a lofty gate at either end, and encumbered with a row of houses on each side. I beheld it the scene of tournaments; I saw its barrier closed against the rebel Wyatt, and wished myself a poet for its sake.

Pray believe me yours, with most sincere regard,

L. AIKIN.

To Dr. Channing.

Hampstead, October 23, 1831.

My dear Friend,—Your two welcome letters have reached me both on the same day; of their various contents and of the Farrars I shall speak by-and-by; but the urgent thing is to enter upon the discussion of Priestley to which you invite me. I have long wished to get you there. I have just been talking him over with my brother Arthur, who was his pupil at Hackney, and had both the opportunity of knowing and the mind for appreciating him. He says that certainly in one sense Priestley was *self-satisfied.* He had emancipated himself from the yoke of Calvinism, which was little made for his sunny temper; and with such immovable, such entire conviction he had settled it with himself that all things must at all times be working for the best, because ordained and guided by the wisest and best of beings, that neither any misfortunes of his own, nor any disappointments to those causes which he espoused, were able to make deep or lasting impressions on his spirits. He was an optimist both by disposition and system, but from *Epicurean* tranquillity no one could be further. He was the most active of men; he could not have lived inactive; and to the propagation of this, his great principle, there was nothing he was not ready to sacrifice. My aunt has said of him, with as much truth as brilliancy, that "he followed truth as a man who hawks follows his sport—at full speed, straightforward, looking only upward, and regardless into what difficulties the chase may lead him." This sanguine spirit prompted him to adopt the maxim, that no effort is lost; he firmly believed that all discussion must end in the advancement of truth; and hence he could never perceive any mischief or danger in the fullest exposure of any doctrine which he believed. He was constitutionally incapable of doubt; what he held, he held implicitly for the time; but Arthur says he was not tenacious upon anything which did not affect his great principle of optimism—that is, of necessity. It may be considered that his system of the origin of ideas was derived from Locke and enlarged upon by Hartley, who also maintained necessity—and both these were revered names to follow. His system of materialism was more original and more obnoxious; but his own faith in a future state, being fixed on gospel promises, was quite unshaken by it; and he expected, I say not how wisely, to enhance the value of Christianity, and compel, as it were, the Deist to accept of it, by proving that there was no hope of immortality without it. All these doctrines, too, were in a manner sanctified to him by the often ingenious, often powerful use which he made of them in his attacks upon what he regarded as the most mischievous corruptions of Christianity. If he had promulgated these opinions from vain-glory, no doubt it would have destroyed his moral greatness; but as by the concurring judgments, I believe, of all who had the best means of knowing, his motives were purely reverence to God and good-will to men, I cannot agree that anything but imprudence ought to be imputed to him by those who may most distrust their truth and tendency. His private life was radiant with goodness. He was excellent in every relation; exemplary as a pastor, particularly for the unwearied pains he took with the young, for whom he composed catechisms and delivered lectures. His Birmingham flock has never lost the character of devout zeal which he impressed upon it. His disinterested love of truth manifested itself in his scientific pursuits. The moment he made a discovery he threw it before the public; not waiting to form a perfect system which would have redounded to his own glory, but eager to set other minds on the track of investigation, and provided truth were discovered, careless by whom. In charity and forgiveness of injuries he was a perfect Christian. "So kind was his temper," said my father, "that he would not have hurt his bitterest enemy." Think, too, of his zeal for civil liberty, and the obloquy and danger which he braved for it, and make allowances for the situation of a reformer rendered more positive by often dishonest opposition. No; he had a sanguineness of temper incompatible with true judgment, and perhaps with deep feelings, but I cannot deny him moral greatness; he would certainly have laid down his life for his faith and for mankind.

The doctrine of necessity has, no doubt, its dangers for inactive and self-indulgent tempers; and though I know not how to resist by reasoning the arguments which very long since rendered me an earnest advocate for it, I begin to *feel* against it. In affliction I have found that it rather rebuked murmuring than afforded positive comfort. I know not how any one contrives to hold it and the Scriptures together; moral responsibility is surely implied in their promises and threatenings; but, in fact, some of the necessarian Christians dilute and explain them away till they come to very little. What I can least afford to part with is the idea of being approved or disapproved by a heavenly as by an earthly parent or superior; of living "as ever in a great taskmaster's eye." It has sometimes overwhelmed my heart with a sense of desolation unutterably oppressive, to think, that by no efforts, no sacrifices, no performance of arduous duties with cheerful patience, it would be possible, if necessity were true, to gain the *moral* approbation of the Deity, without which I could not think of God as of a *Father*. Creator, I could call him, and Benefactor, but not Father, that dearest and tenderest of names. Your views on these subjects are so much more congenial to my feelings, that they have, I believe, very nearly become my own without my being aware of it. I am very much pleased with your account of the origin of a belief in futurity; it accords with my previous ideas. We cannot well believe in God without expecting that He will sometimes come, as it were, to an explanation with us on all the things which so perplex us here. In appealing to an inward light thus far, I think we are justified—it is rather dangerous ground, however; enthusiasm and superstition are very apt to take advantage of that inlet, as in the interesting case of Mrs. F. Of the Quakers, whom it was formerly my lot to know many rather intimately, I have always observed that, owing, I believe, to their want of professional instructors in religion and morals, either as preachers or writers, they are much more ignorant of first principles on these subjects than the members of other communities. Whenever they begin to inquire for themselves, their unpractised understandings soon get bewildered, and if they quit their own society it is usually for Methodism, Moravianism, or some other system where reason has least to do. A vagueness of thought, with a turn for mystery, almost always adheres to them, and it is very well if, in the midst of so much confusion, they form or retain very clear notions of moral right or wrong.

The Dr. King you inquire about, Mrs. Joanna Baillie knows; she says he is very upright and very benevolent, but not a man of sense. His plan, I believe, has been given up, though at first it seemed to work well. Miss Mitford I never saw, but I think her "Village" a very pleasing picture, and quite true to nature. She lives in a cottage with an old father whom she dotes upon. I hear she is very happy in her seclusion, and her friends speak of her with much affection; in London circles she rarely appears.

I was disappointed of the little Kentish journey I mentioned in my last by the sudden illness of my brother; but when he recovered I found myself better too; and "King Charles" is proceeding, though not the better for our political crisis, which so fills my mind that I fear its giving some tinge or some vices to my representation of the events of a former period of revolution.

No public event ever oppressed me, like this rejection of the Bill, with grief and fear. Delay—for it is but delayed—must evidently increase all its dangers. It gives opportunity for the intrigues of violent and designing men on both sides. The Tories are frightened now at what they have done. Many of them would never have given that vote but with the expectation of overawing the King and making ministers resign; they looked upon it as little more than a trial of strength between Grey and Wellington; they now know how the people look upon it, and how stanch the King is. The bishops are regarded as insane. We feel ourselves standing on a volcano. With all this, I love my country far too well to despair of her. I believe that the moderate party is strong enough to hold in check the two extremes, provided it *exerts* itself strenuously and skilfully for that purpose.

You have touched upon what must be the most grievous of all topics to an American who loves his country—slavery. We who praise republics hang our heads when it is mentioned. There is nothing by which Americans are so apt to give an ill impression of themselves here, as by unguarded expressions on this subject. The only time I saw Bishop Hobart, he said to me, in defence of creating new slave states, that "a man must be allowed to make the best of his property." There was a general shudder. I turned away and addressed him no more, and the hospitable master of the house never gave him a second invitation. Another American sometimes gave us unpleasant feelings simply by speaking of planters as his friends or acquaintances; we regard them as persons not to be mentioned without a necessity. I conceive that the greatest political difficulties and dangers which menace you are from this source: the crime will bring its own punishment.

It delights me to hear that you are writing again. Never can you put pen to paper without doing much good and giving great delight. In a general survey of the state of the world, facts will be of use to you as the grounds of reasoning, and I will take care to store up for you any I think useful. Mr. Whishaw is just returned from France, and I will keep my letter open till after to-morrow, in hopes of something worth writing.—No, he has nothing to tell me except that he found Paris so unpleasant from tumults that he left it in three days. But I have been questioning another friend, who has passed there the last year and half, on the state of religion. He says that, generally speaking, there is *no* religion at Paris. The Romish religion is considered obsolete, and very few but women attend the churches. The priests are from a low class, with a very small stipend from the State, which he believes their hearers never add to. He knows of no spread of Protestantism; some old congregations of Reformed there are, with Genevan ministers, who are by much the most eloquent preachers he ever heard; one congregation of English Unitarians, chiefly supported by Americans. These you doubtless know of; also that they have engaged an additional minister to preach in French. I hear from others that at Dijon a Catholic congregation went over in a body to the Reformed; that similar conversions have taken place at Lyons. The provinces are less irreligious than Paris. You have probably heard that the Genevan Unitarians have been at length provoked to enter into controversy with the Calvinists, who were carrying all before them.

I have been dining with two clergymen, who to my astonishment began a discussion upon the exclusion of bishops from the House of Lords, which they both thought impending. One said it would be a good thing, which the other did not quite deny, but thought this was *not the time* to strip the Church of honours. One of these was a Reformer, the other certainly a Tory; but being both, I believe, sincerely religious and honest men, they were equally ashamed of the conduct of the bishops, and sensible that temptation ought to be removed from them by the prohibition of translations and other means. There is extreme bitterness all over the country against the clergy. A gentleman who had been canvassing Liverpool for your friend Thornely was repeatedly told by Methodists and Calvinistic Dissenters, "We are willing to vote for a Unitarian, because he will be reasonable about the Church." A fearful sign for the Establishment when foes league against her! In the midst of this ferment the lower classes exhibit a growing depravity which gives true patriots many a heartache. None would wish to live in an *age of transition* such as we have fallen upon—none at least but the young and ardent, or those whose faith in the high destinies of man is firm as yours. I brace my mind as I can. In the storm there is sublimity, high thoughts are stirred, and even a woman may be called upon for the exercise of high virtues.

Farewell, my dear and honoured friend.

LUCY AIKIN.

TO MISS AIKIN.

Boston, November 20, 1831.

My dear Miss Aikin,—I received your letter of September a few days ago, and I am the more disposed to send an early answer in consequence of the news received to-day from England, which turns all eyes towards your country. We have just heard of the rejection of the Reform Bill in the House of Lords, and of the strong excitement produced by it in the community. I am grieved, greatly grieved, and for all parties. My great desire for England is, what I have often expressed to you, that your institutions may silently and gradually adapt themselves to the state of society through which we are passing, without the convulsions of revolution. This is the great object which statesmen should keep in view. All others are insignificant in comparison. But the chance of this seems to me now much diminished. That institutions should remain unchanged when all things are changing around them, is impossible; and how strange is it that any should expect it! Yet your aristocracy do expect it; and here we see one of the evils of Rank, that it places men in a position in which they cannot understand their age or the wants of society. Your nobility ought to make up their minds to meet the irresistible tendencies and vicissitudes of human affairs. It is demonstrable that as the mass of a people are elevated, the aristocracy must sink. The space between the different classes must grow less and less. The power must pass more and more into the hands of the people. This is a law of nature as irresistible as gravity, and wise men will conform to it; and this does not portend instant ruin to the aristocracy. Generation after generation *may* pass away without any *great* change in this form of your government, unless the privileged orders hasten their destruction by withstanding the mighty stream of human affairs. The aristocracy of England, as you observe, has no resemblance to the French noblesse. It is still strong, perhaps I should say *very* strong, in the hearts of the people. No body of nobles in any age can be compared with it in moral and intellectual qualities, unless you choose to except the patricians of Rome. As the representative and guardian of *property*, it holds an important place in your government, and I should think would be an object of great interest to the men of property throughout the kingdom. I grieve that it should become an object of distrust and aversion by trying to arrest what it can only modify and regulate. I throw out these remarks because the views of a foreigner are interesting, and I am willing to say something to prevent wrong impressions from some of my former observations on *aristocracy*. Viewing this institution abstractedly, I see it hostile to true elevation of mind, to the relations which ought to subsist between man and man, to that spirit of humanity which sympathizes with and reverences our common nature, and looks on all outward distinctions as childish badges. Christianity is at war with it throughout. But I have no spirit of violent revolution. Aristocracy may and should subsist until the national mind has outgrown it. In England you are outgrowing it, and I shall grieve if you get rid of it by more summary processes. Such are my wishes. I see, however, that Providence heeds not human wishes—that it seldom suffers nations to move along a smooth path any more than individuals—that it uses the earthquake and tempests in the moral as in the natural world. I pretend not then to be a prophet. I hope everything for England, but even she may tremble and disappoint hope. I confess my faith is somewhat shaken when I see the aristocracy, the conservative power in the state, doing so much to invite and justify sudden and violent changes.

Since I last wrote you, I have read Sir James Mackintosh's History of England, and I am prepared to retract some doubts which I expressed to you about his intellectual superiority. I think the History a noble one.

Perhaps I never read one with equal gratification. He knows on what parts of history to throw the strongest light. He judges past ages with discrimination and candour, and enters into their spirit, and knows the significance of actions in different stages of society. A genuine sympathy with the human race and a high moral feeling breathes through the work. He is a thorough Englishman, yet interested in the cause of mankind, and a stanch friend of liberty without giving in to the extravagance of Liberalism. It does me good to see a man so conversant with the world and with history holding fast his confidence in the power and triumphs of truth, freedom and virtue. A man may know the world, it seems, without despairing of it. I wonder how, with his mastery of language, he could frame so many intricate and encumbered sentences. My defect of vision obliged me to employ some of my young friends in reading the work, and they often lost their way in the labyrinths of a sentence. The style is sometimes obscure from condensation of thought, and this I never complain of; but this excuse does not always apply. I do not mean by these remarks to find fault with the style, on the whole, for it is very often felicitous. I have tried in vain to get Sir James' "History of Moral Philosophy." Cannot a copy be procured in England?

I was particularly interested in one part of your letter —that in which you describe the Evangelical ladies as patronesses of *pauperism* rather than of the poor. Be it so. Still, we must not condemn a good thing for its abuse. I desire nothing more than to see a free communication spreading through different classes of society, than to see the improved communicating their *minds* as well as wealth to the ignorant and poor; and this they may do, if they go about it wisely. They must visit the poor, not to school them, but as *friends*, with sympathy, and still more with respect. Poverty depresses the mind, and turns it away from all the noble uses of life. The end of visiting the poor should be to encourage them, to help them to understand themselves, the true nobility of their nature, the infinite good within their reach, and the art of making their condition a means to it. This they *can* understand. I have an intimate and intelligent friend devoted to the poor, who carries to them the highest moral and religious truths which we delight to talk about, and he tells me that *his poor* understand me better than *my rich* congregation. I know a few ladies who go among the poor with much of an angel's wisdom and love, and who have spoken of the effect produced on them by conversing with them on the paternal love of God, which has no respect of persons, and on the greatness of the soul, which is equally great in all ranks. That the Calvinists should fail is not wonderful, for they want humility and just respect for their fellow-creatures. Their spiritual self-conceit is as a great gulf between themselves and the poor. My Divine Teacher, whose wisdom penetrates me more and more, has said, that to be "great in his kingdom," or to be effectual promoters of truth and virtue, nothing is so needful as humility, the very grace in which the Genevan school is most wanting. I beg, however, to be just to the Evangelicals. They are far better than their system. It often gratifies me to see how the infusion of the undisputed doctrines of Christianity can sweeten the bitter waters of Calvinism. By the way, Calvinism is undergoing great changes here. The modern Puritan has the family likeness, but the old features are wearing away.

I have much to say, but have said enough. I rejoice in your improved health. I am happily well enough to do something, but I am expecting to be overcome by our winter. As long as I can work two or three hours a day, I feel myself a privileged man. I am looking at Godwin's last book. Though not a thorough thinker, he gives one much to think about. The cause of Reform has been injured in this country by the want of some good article or periodical to meet the able articles in the "Quarterly." I have not read the last, but they have made an impression.

Your sincere friend,
WM. E. CHANNING.

To Dr. Channing.

Hampstead, December 8, 1831.

I feel as if I were in some danger of becoming importunate to you by the frequency of my letters; but to converse with my "guide, philosopher and friend," has now become with me not a mere indulgence, but a want, and I trust in your patience. It is advisedly that I have called you my guide. I daily discover more and more how much I have come under the influence of your mind, and what great things it has done, and I trust is still doing, for mine. Let me gratify the feelings of a thankful heart by entering into a few particulars on this subject. I was never duly sensible, till your writings made me so, of the transcendent beauty and sublimity of Christian morals; nor did I submit my heart and temper to their chastening and meliorating influences. In particular, the spirit of unbounded benevolence which they breathe was, I own it, a stranger to my bosom; far indeed was I from looking upon all men as my brethren. Many things prevented it. A life, for the most part, of domestic seclusion; studious pursuits, and something of the pride and fastidiousness they are apt to bring; and, more than all, the atmosphere of a sect and a party, which it was my fate to breathe from childhood, narrowed my affections within strait limits. Under the notion of a generous zeal for freedom, truth and virtue, I cherished a set of prejudices and antipathies which placed beyond the pale of my charity, not the few, but the many, the mass of my compatriots. I shudder now to think how *good* a *hater* I was in the days of my youth. Time and reflection, a wider range of acquaintance, and a calmer state of the public mind, mitigated by degrees my bigotry; but I really knew not what it was to open my heart to the human race until I had drunk deeply into the spirit of your writings.

Neither was my intercourse with my Creator such as to satisfy fully the wants of the soul. I had doubts and scruples, as I have before intimated, respecting prayer, which weighed heavily on my spirit. In times of the most racking anxiety, the bitterest grief, I offered, I dared to offer, nothing but the folded arms of resignation —submission rather. So often had I heard, and from the lips of some whom I greatly respected, the axiom, as it was represented, that no evil could exist in the creation of a perfectly benevolent Being, if he were also omnipotent, that my reliance on Providence was dreadfully shaken by a vague notion of a nature of things by which deity itself was limited. How you have dispossessed me of this wretched idea I do not well know— but it is gone; I feel, I feel that He can and will bless me, even by means of what seem at present evil and suffering. You have shown me clearly a Father in heaven, and for nothing earthly would I exchange the heavenly peace which this conviction brings. It is surely the highest reason to believe that our finite spirits can never think too well or hope too much of His infinity, provided only we fail not in our parts.

From the time that I first became your reader, I had

a kind of anticipation that you would work considerable effects upon me; but it has been by slow degrees, and laborious processes, and hard struggles with deep-rooted prepossessions, that I have fitted my mind to give reception to so many of your views; and, but for the deep interest in them which your letters assisted to maintain, my resolution would have failed me ere the task was thus far accomplished. You have wished to interest in religion minds by which it was apt to be coldly regarded. With respect to mine, you have all that you desire; for the present I am little interested in any other subject; or, at least, I view all others as connected with this and subordinate to it. May God reward you! You have given me a new being.

All the principles that can support or elevate the soul are greatly needed with us now, to meet the tempests gathering thick and dark around us. Pestilence* advances, revolution threatens. With respect to the first, I feel only the dread of surviving those I love. A medical brother, pledged to go wherever called, is a great anxiety; but I will not dwell on possible evils. The poor in some European countries through which this scourge has passed, were possessed with the notion that it was purposely diffused by the higher classes to thin the numbers of the lower. I doubt not there was *talk* which showed at least profound indifference in the rich and great to this result, and unless people set a strong guard on their tongues, the same suspicions may arise here. It is felt that we have many spare hands. I have heard a good man say, that a decimation of London, if the lots fell *well*, would be no bad thing. But luckily there can be no security that the lots would so fall, if once the infection gained ground; and *therefore* we are cleansing the dwellings of the poor, and wrapping their persons in

* The appearance of cholera in England.

flannel; but is there not something frightful in this worthlessness of the lives of one class to another? What wonder that kings have made no spare of the blood of their subjects? I perceive more and more clearly what you first pointed out to me—the darkening effects of the spirit of aristocracy on the mind, its hardening influence on the heart. Distinct classes can never feel for each other as members of one body; and in the want of this sympathy all anti-social vices, oppression, arrogance, cruelty in the rich, envy, fraud, rapacity, and brutal insolence in the poor, take root and flourish. I am convinced that the deep dread with which the working classes begin here to inspire their *betters* is extremely wholesome; even such disgraceful excesses as those of Bristol have their use as warnings. Yet it is curious, though sad, to see how men drive away unwelcome thoughts, and hug again their old delusions. One day a threatened radical meeting in the suburbs puts all the magistrates and gentry on the alert; the police are arrayed, special constables sworn in, the rabble dispersed, the popular orators disappointed of audience for that time; and the next day you shall hear the aristocracy round their dinner-table confessing that some reform must take place, but assuring themselves and each other that a little will satisfy all the well-disposed, and concluding that "if the people will not be satisfied with moderate Reform (that is, something less than the Bill), they must be bayoneted." I give you the very words used to me last week by a mild, amiable, indolent young man of fortune, and one who thinks great scorn to be called a Tory. I begin to fear that if, I mean *when*, a struggle comes, that *dovetailing* of the classes into one another, in which I once confided, will be apt to give way. Yet there are noble examples of rich men, and even lords, who feel for the multitude. The Catholic peers have almost all sided with the people—by virtue, I suppose, of their want of attachment to the Church. It would shock you to be initiated into the abominations springing out of Church patronage. "What will you do with your nephew?" said a friend of mine to a great coal-owner. "Oh, if he turns out clever we shall make him a collier; if otherwise, we must put him into the Church." When there is a family living, commonly the most stupid of the boys, very often the most profligate, is made to take orders. In other professions success depends in some degree on merit. For the sake of electioneering interests, there is really *no man* whom a patron will scruple to entrust with cure of souls—provided only a bishop can be induced to ordain him—and there is always some bishop of notorious facility. I think there must, ere long, be considerable concessions to public opinion with respect to patronage as well as tithes; and these being reformed, doctrine will next come in question, I imagine. The substitution of popular election for patronage, and the abolition of pluralities, would infallibly procure us a more diligent, more moral, more independent clergy, and one better instructed in theology, and consequently more scrupulous of teaching what they could not themselves believe. After all, these are animating times to live in; they offer hopes well worth all the fears they bring. A friend just arrived from Italy brings me some curious particulars of the state of things. The Pope has nearly lost all temporal authority out of Rome. Bologna has refused, in the most respectful manner, either to admit his troops or to pay him any tribute. What is strange, the Roman censorship, though extremely jealous of religious heresies, takes no cognizance of political ones. You might almost publish there Paine's "Rights of Man." In Tuscany, on the contrary, you may print what you please on religion, but in politics you are much restricted.

A tragedy on the subject of the Sicilian Vespers had been repeatedly performed at Florence with immense applause. The French ambassador applied to have it prohibited on account of the reflections it contained on the French nation. "You need not stir," said the Austrian ambassador to him; "the letter is indeed directed to you, but its contents are for me." The representation was not forbidden, but it was long before the author could obtain license to print it. At last he did, on condition that it should not be in a separate form, but stuck in a thick octavo of his other works. He contrived to take off a few separate copies, however, and gave my friend one, which I have just read. It certainly breathes a strong spirit of resistance to foreign domination, and also utters very intelligibly that earnest desire for the union of all Italy under one government which now possesses her best patriots. Many of them, my informant says, would not object, on certain terms, to see the whole country under the dominion of Austria, which has the sense to govern Lombardy with a good deal of mildness and liberality. They hate the French.

The more I see of Rammohun Roy, the more I admire and even venerate him. Dr. Wallich, of Calcutta, himself an admirable person, tells me that he stands quite alone amongst his countrymen, with neither equal nor second in talent, in integrity, and in enlargement of mind. He has provoked the bitterest enmity of the Hindoo priests by his attacks upon their gainful idolatries: but Dr. W. says that, should he return safe and well, supported by the distinguished favour of the Company, and successful in his patriotic objects, a shock would be given to the whole Hindoo system, which would go near to overthrow it. He gave us this trait of the good Rajah. In conversation at the house of a Scotch gentleman at Calcutta, the question happened to arise, If two persons were drowning of whom you could save only one, and one were your countryman, would you not save him in preference? "Certainly I should," said the Scotchman. The Rajah reprobated the idea of making a choice between the lives of any two fellow-creatures at such a moment—he would save the nearest. "No," he added, after a pause; "there is a case in which I should make a choice. If one were a woman, I should rescue her." And this from a man brought up amidst widow-burning and the exposure of female infants! I have seen a good deal of the Farrars; Mrs. F. and I are sworn friends, and I have made her tell me a vast deal about you and yours; I can now fancy your happy fireside. She says your boy and girl are perfect specimens in their kind. I shall be anxious to hear how the winter agrees with you and Mrs. Channing. With us the weather is now almost oppressively warm, to the alarm of those who are dreading cholera. Nobody knows yet what our ministers are going to do about Reform; but they have declared they *will* not fail again.

Ever yours, with the truest esteem,
L. AIKIN.

To Miss Aikin.

Boston, December 29, 1831.

My dear Miss Aikin,—I received your letter, beginning with the vindication of Dr. Priestley, a few days ago. May every good and great man find as generous and able an advocate! I have no difficulty about receiving your impressions, for I have no prejudices or dislikes to overcome. I know little of his works, and probably shall not read them, for I have little sympathy with his ethical and metaphysical doctrines, and seldom turn my thoughts to the religious controversies on which he spent so much of his zeal. Still, I wish to be just to intellectual greatness and distinguished virtue, wherever or however manifested. The world is not, as yet, so rich in superior minds that we can afford to part with one. I need all the instances I can find of moral elevation to sustain my faith in the high purposes and destinies of human nature. How often this faith is assailed, almost shaken, by examples of degradation, I need not tell you. I will add that some of my speculations give me a *personal* interest in seeing all that is good and great in my fellow-creatures; for the connections in the intellectual or spiritual world seem to me so extensive and beneficent, and all excellence is of so expansive a nature, that I expect to be aided in some period of my existence by every mind which rises above my own. I trust, however, that I have a more disinterested joy in the contemplation of noble characters. I think you misunderstood me when I spoke of Priestley's philosophy as Epicurean. I did not mean that it tended to *inactivity*, but that he sought refuge in his optimism from that deep feeling of men's present miseries, that thorough sympathy with human suffering, which, I think, marks those whom God selects as the great benefactors of their race.

I have to acknowledge the generosity of Dr. Priestley's English admirers in forgiving me some of my remarks rather disparaging to their patriarch. I now think that I wrote with something of the Doctor's rashness. I doubt not his mild spirit will forgive any wrong I may have done him. I was sorry to find you so disposed to look with fear on the present condition of England. Many here are alarmed, but I am more hopeful. I am referred to antiquity for proof of the *tendency of the people to excess;* and I am told that human nature is the same in all ages. But I differ in believing that human nature has made some progress; that England is not Greece or Rome; that much more of intellectual and moral power is at work among you; that the industrious and domestic spirit of modern times separates them widely from the Old World; that the present wide diffusion of property is another distinction; that Christianity is not a dead letter; and that the infinite motives to order and peace will not be wholly put to silence by the passions. Your present discontents grow out of *improvements;* and this is encouraging. My fears are founded chiefly on the misery and depravity of your *lower* classes. You have a savage horde in the very bosom of your civilization, and I fear the more when I think that the luxury, vices and unfeelingness of your rich and noble classes have suffered this horde to spread among you—perhaps I ought to say, have done much to multiply it. I know the question will be put to me, How can we help it? I answer, *What cannot men help* who are in earnest to do good, who love and respect their fellow-creatures, who are prepared to sacrifice themselves to a great and godlike work? No, no; you have all to answer more or less for the frightful amount of ignorance, guilt and misery in what you call your lower classes.

With what face can your aristocracy talk of the perfection of your government and state of society, when so many myriads of desperate men are scattered through your population? Your great ones have retrenched no luxury, felt no anguish of spirit, in the midst of this moral pestilence; and yet they are indignant at the menace of revolution. I speak this in no bitterness of spirit, nor ought I to reproach England as alone guilty. The debt of the prosperous and enlightened classes to the depressed and ignorant is nowhere understood. We want a new era, when the ties of brotherhood shall be seen and felt to subsist among all who have one nation, and when justice shall be done to our nature in all classes. Then, and not till then, will revolution cease. This subject reminds me of *slavery*, of which you have written with a just indignation. But do you know how slaveholders reconcile themselves to their guilt? The language of intelligent men in the West Indies, and of men well acquainted with Europe, is—" Our slaves subsist more comfortably than the populace and peasantry of Europe." And I ask, do they speak without proof? Do their slaves suffer more than the sixty or seventy thousand poor who are said to rise every morning in London not knowing where to find bread for the day? The slaveholder says, Let the English provide for the Irish peasant as comfortable a hut and as good food as we provide for our slaves, and then they may come to improve the state of things here.

I acknowledge the sophistry, but I mourn that it should have so much foundation. I shudder as much as any man at the terrible vengeance which the degraded classes, when once let loose, take on their superiors; but when I think of the unfaithfulness of these superiors to their high trust, of the cruelty with which they have severed themselves from their less favoured brethren, perhaps trodden them under foot, I am compelled to acknowledge the justice of God in this retribution. May it not be intended that the great and rich and educated should be roused to their duty by their fear? that the *formidableness* of the lower classes should secure them a consideration which humanity and justice could not obtain?

I dread civil convulsions on account of the crimes which follow in their train, and of their tendency to give ascendancy to force and reckless ambition, and to issue in remorseless tyranny. If, however, the storm is to burst on the nations, as many predict, I shall not despair. I am sure that society will never be forsaken by its Author. I am not sure but that its present deep diseases may demand violent remedies. I have hoped for gradual progress, and have thought, and still think, that our present social condition contains the elements and promise of a happier state. I may err, and Providence may see that subversion, not improvement, of existing establishments is the only hope of the human race. Such will be my interpretation of violent revolutions, if they come; and I shall see in them motives to the disinterested and generous, for more strenuous efforts and more unsparing sacrifice for the regeneration of the world. I repeat it, however, my hopes prevail greatly over my fears as to the result of the present struggle, and I shall wait for darker omens before I grow sad.

What a race my pen has run on this subject of reform and revolution! I trust, however, that you will understand me. My mind is so alive to the present condition of society, that when I begin to talk or write about it I know not well when to stop. I must leave the other topics of your letter untouched.

Very affectionately your friend,
WM. E. CHANNING.

To Dr. Channing.

Hampstead, February 22, 1832.

My dear Friend,—I have many, many thanks to return you for those two excellent letters I have had from you since I last wrote. Nothing so much interests and delights me as the spirit in which you write of us and our concerns. Call yourself "a foreigner," if you must—it is a cold name, and one which we never give to Americans; but yours is a filial heart to Old England still, and beats true to her in all her trials and adversities.

If you have received two letters which I have written to you since the date of your last, you will have seen that I am still far from despairing of my country. I see dangers, indeed, many and of opposite kinds, and many more there must be which are invisible to me; I see the interests of various parties, sects and classes in society, roused into fierce opposition; I see all, the high as well as the low, exposed to peril, suffering under real evils and privations, and too generally disposed, by a short-sighted selfishness, to advance unreasonable claims, and to shift as much as possible of the burden from themselves to others; I see prejudice, ignorance, obstinacy at work, and in all classes too, to perpetuate bad feelings, urge on unprofitable courses, and resist wise and salutary reforms; I see, and with deep sorrow, much depravity in the lower classes, much too in the highest, and in the middle ones a sordid, grovelling selfishness, less scandalous but scarcely less pernicious. But I see, on the other hand, much true patriotism, and in high places too; much philanthropy, much enlightenment, active zeal, and in some bosoms fortitude and devotedness equal to any trials we can anticipate. There is also amongst all who have anything to lose a calculating coolness, a deliberate appreciation of present good, which is likely to range them almost universally on the side of peace and order. The long discussion of Reform has certainly had its advantages. You may observe that the highest Tories are now brought to admit that *some* there ought to be and must be. I firmly believe that, with more or less of modification, the Bill will now be carried; and with a popular House of Commons, whatever partial changes of ministers shall occur, and several are talked of, it is certain that many other salutary measures, now in preparation, will be brought in, and carried too.

The political unions seem to me to have lost ground since the affair of Bristol, and I do not in the least apprehend that they will be enabled to dictate to ministers or to Parliament, or materially to disturb the public peace. We have certainly in London no class of people capable of such deeds as the barricades of Paris. Our middling orders are men of peace, never drafted off by conscriptions; and as for our mob, they are profligate indeed, but seldom atrocious. I suspect you have been horror-struck, like some persons here, by the statements and descriptions of Gibbon Wakefield; but it is not on the word of an atrocious malefactor, seeking to rise again into something like credit, and also to sell a book, that frightful stories ought to be implicitly believed. I think, in short, that the general apprehension of a revolution will save us from the reality, and that better, not worse, times are approaching.

But what must I say to the heavy charge you bring against all the rich, the powerful, the improved, for the mass of vice, ignorance and misery, which they have suffered to accumulate about the poor of this country? I have pondered the matter over and over, for I cannot lightly dismiss from my mind such an accusation from such a quarter; and this is the best answer my lights enable me to frame. In England—I dismiss for the present unhappy Ireland—apathy towards suffering fellow-creatures is not a common fault. You have truly said that benevolence is one of our fashions. Political causes, misgovernment and bad legislation, have had by far the greatest share in producing evils for which benevolence, often misdirected, has found no effectual remedies.

It would require a pamphlet to expose all the particulars in which the administration of Mr. Pitt and the statesmen of his school tended to the increase of the curse of pauperism. During the war the enhanced price of provisions ought to have been met by a corresponding advance in the wages of agricultural labour; but this the gentlemen, from mistaken views of their own interest, opposed. Mr. Pitt legalized the payment of wages in part out of the poor-rate. In the southern and some midland counties, where this practice was adopted, continually increasing misery and degradation have ensued, and of late a desperate spirit of revenge, which is likely however to compel the adoption of effective remedies for the evil, some of which are already coming into operation. The fluctuations of commerce and manufactures; the transition from war to peace; the weight of taxation; the invasion of England by swarms of miserable Irish, who underbid our own working men in the already glutted labour market; the great extension of machinery; the general inclosure of commons, and the system of large farms, are some of the many causes which have fatally conspired to the same end; and you perceive that such of these as admit of counteraction are rather in the province of politicians and statesmen than of private individuals. That our legislation has not been idle in the cause, a slight survey of the objects of the greater part of the Bills brought in every session would convince you. When the great reform is effected, you will see the result. Meantime I regard all that is and all that can be done for the poor as palliative merely, and sometimes not that. The pauper is robbed of half his virtues as surely as the slave. He loses self-respect, the most irreparable of all losses; and neither the alleviation of his physical wants, nor even the acquirement of knowledge when the means are not earned by his own honest labour, but conferred upon him as the alms of his superiors, have any tendency to raise him in the moral scale. Neither does religious or moral instruction, so conveyed, work its proper effect. It is received as a tax upon the dole which is expected to follow. The cant of religion has been widely diffused amongst our poor by these means, but of the spirit and power of godliness little indeed.

I am convinced that an effective missionary must begin with, "Silver and gold have I none." He should be a poor man among the poor to reach their hearts and consciences. They have an incurable distrust of those who are called their betters in these matters—having indeed often seen religion perverted into an engine of state or an auxiliary of the police. More good, I believe, is to be done in this country at present by striving to diffuse pure and elevated and liberal views on religion and virtue amongst the higher and middling classes, through whom they may gravitate to the lower, than by attempting at once to confront degradation in its deepest caverns; though I would by no means discourage the glorious few who feel in themselves a mission for these heroic efforts of philanthropy. But the greater part of our would-be teachers of the poor stand themselves in great need of becoming learners, especially of humility and meekness. There are of course many, very many, of a better stamp; and I do look with a good deal of hope on the efforts now making for the establishment of Temperance Societies. But, alas! how are we to cope with the evils of an already redundant and daily increasing population? And Ireland, Ireland!

I have laid out of my account another dire calamity with which we seem doomed to contend—the cholera. Reached us it has, beyond question, and a few days will decide whether it be an infection from some single source, capable of being by due care extinguished, or whether it comes as an epidemic menacing myriads. In the most favourable case, much distress will arise—nay, it has already arisen—from the interruption of trade, by which thousands more must be thrown out of bread. But should it assume the character of a real pestilence, who can even imagine the confusion, the misery? Methinks I see the "grim features" of Milton's own Death exulting that his "famine shall be filled," and of the million and half of human creatures congregated in and near our vast metropolis! A remedy it may indeed prove for our over-population—but what a remedy!

To contemplate such horrors with perfect composure is a height of philosophy I by no means aspire to reach; but I trust I shall not be numbered with the panic-stricken. Hitherto, I have ever found that strength is given according to the call for it, to those who are not wanting to themselves. In the lives of those dear to me I am most vulnerable, but I bow to the Divine decrees; and I have been quite enough familiarized with affliction to know what precious medicine it contains. For myself, I have never at any period within my memory viewed death as a subject of dread; on the contrary, I have usually beheld it as an object of aspiration, and with a kind of solemn joy. I believe that at any moment of my life I should have welcomed a call to die nobly. To expose myself to infection when duty or affection bade, I have never hesitated yet, and I trust I shall not now.

It rejoices me to have been able successfully to vindicate to you the character and motives of Priestley. Too true it is that we cannot spare even one from our list of worthies. I long for a fuller development of your delightful idea of our personal interest in the high qualities of others. It is quite a new thought to me, and opens to the most inspiring views. Even in this state of being, the effects of a high principle, a grand discovery, a sublime poem, a noble action, extend quite out of sight and calculation. In other states they may reach to the whole race of man—I see nothing against it. Oh! who would bear the sight and sense of human misery—that has indeed a soul to comprehend and feel it—without the cordial of high hopes and noble aspirations! My thoughts are ever returning thither, to the invisible world; and, thanks to you, they never return thence without bringing in their train deep peace.

At length I am able to send you Mackintosh's "Essay," and I must give you the long tale which hangs by it. I long since *begged* Mr. Whishaw to *beg* one for you of the author, which he promised; but accident prevented his doing so till Sir James had, as he believed, not one left; but he was not quite certain, for he had been moving, and his books were in confusion. To add to the chance of sending one by the Farrars, I then applied to Rees, my bookseller, who said with alacrity, "I will write to the Edinburgh publisher, and if there is one left, Dr. Channing shall have it." He was as good as his word, and has sent one, which I see he hopes will be received in the nature of a peace-offering, from "Self and Partners, Proprietors of the 'Edinburgh Review.'" For the man has grace, for a bookseller, and besides he wants to stop my mouth about the odious article.

But in the meantime, the report of your admiration of his History so exceedingly gratified Sir James Mackintosh, that he renewed his search, found a copy, and gave it to Mr. Whishaw to bring to me. It would have been most ungracious to refuse it; I have therefore accepted it for you; meaning very honestly to keep it myself; which will be great luck for me, since it is not to be bought separately. I should have been mortified beyond expression if I had failed to procure one for you; and I hope it will not disappoint you, but I expect it will *pose* your young readers more than once.

Have you seen the spirited sketch of the history of the Italian republics by Sismondi, in Lardner's Cyclopædia? I think it very good indeed; in a high republican strain, like all his works; and the English very good for a *foreigner* (not being an American). The author is now on a visit to Sir James Mackintosh, his brother-in-law, and I am to have the pleasure of meeting him at a neighbour's in a few days, should I be well enough; but that is a great doubt, for I am a very poor creature, and seldom able to indulge myself with going into parties. The winter, however, has been remarkably mild with us; I hope it may have been so with you likewise, and that you have been able to retain the precious power of occupying yourself for the public.

I have written you an enormous letter, and I fear a dull one; I doubt that you will think too that I look coldly upon plans for the benefit of the most numerous classes. But it is not so; I only think that the political ferment must subside a little before anything effectual can be done. Our ministers seem to be dealing vigorously with the ills of Ireland; peace and comfort there would remove many of our grievances. I will yet cling to the hoping side.

We are very loth to send you back the Farrars. They have pleased universally. Since Mr. Farrar has improved in health he has shown us that his talents are of no common order, and nothing can be more unassuming than his manners. Without any tincture of his favourite sciences, I always found that it was easy to engage him in conversation in which he appeared to take interest.

I will now at length release you.

Ever your sincere friend,
L. AIKIN.

To Miss Aikin.

Boston, February 23, 1832.

My dear Miss Aikin,—I received a few days ago your letter of December 8th, and owe you more thanks than I can express. Living, as I do, in perpetual conflict with debility, and oppressed with a consciousness of doing little for my fellow-creatures, I receive unspeakable satisfaction from any proof of having aided others towards perfection and happiness. To know that I have aided such a mind as yours is a reward for which I am truly grateful to God. Mrs. Farrar told you truly that my lot is a singularly happy one. But I cannot escape the painful feeling that whilst I receive so largely, I communicate little. I look round me on the ignorance, guilt and misery of the world, and cannot think that I have a right to so much enjoyment without contributing more to the cause of humanity. What I have done I am apt to disparage, and the knowledge that my writings are not wholly lost is a consolation which I need. I feel more and more deeply how unchristian and guilty the lives of the prosperous classes are; how little genuine sympathy and brotherly affection we have towards the mass of our fellow-creatures. I see more and more distinctly that society needs a revolution such as history nowhere records. To *rise above others* is the spirit and soul of society in its present constitution. To *help others rise*, to use our superiority as the means of elevating those below, is the spirit of Christianity and humanity; and were it to prevail, would make a revolution more striking than any conquest has made. With these views of my relations to the world, and of the deep moral degradation of society, you will not wonder that my incapacity for exertion sometimes preys on my spirits.

Had I the energy of body and mind, how I should rejoice to enter on a new mission, to proclaim with a new voice the spirit of Christianity, to show how our nature is wronged by the institutions, civil and religious, the manners, distractions and maxims of life which are thought to favour it! But I can do little. The work belongs to another. It is my prayer, however, that before I am taken I may bear a stronger testimony to the great truths which are needed to regenerate the world. When I began this letter, I little thought of giving you this private history, and I am strongly tempted to withhold it; but after your frank disclosures, I ought to let you know something of the mind in which you take so much interest.

I shall not wonder if you think that you see some marks of *morbid* feeling in these views, such as may naturally be expected from a confirmed invalid. But "I am not mad, most noble 'lady'! but speak the words of truth and soberness." Nothing but patient meditation on the degrading influences of the present relations between man and man can enable any one to escape the power of habit, and to see society as it is. In many things you have the advantage; on this point I claim some superiority.

We are all waiting solicitously to know what the House of Lords will do with the Bill. Their position seems to me very difficult; they cannot by any act take back the suicidal blow which they struck by their former rejection. They then placed themselves in hostility with the nation, and the nation, I see, will now receive concession as a reluctant boon, wrung from them by menace and fear. Regard to their order is the ruling principle of the majority, just as all superiors through the whole range of society are anxious to keep down their inferiors; and this instinct, though quite sure in common cases, is a perilous guide in such extraordinary seasons as the present.

Your communications respecting France interest me greatly, and I beg you to tell me whatever you can learn about her from intelligent men. *You* have not yet shaken off your English feelings about this nation; but you must let philanthropy triumph over the old-fashioned patriotism, and must hope, as we do here, that France is to surpass England. We hope so, because her position gives her a moral influence over the world which England cannot exert. She is the heart of Europe, and has in trust the cause of liberal institutions more than any other people. It is the fashion to deny her the capacity of self-government; but I do not despair. She has certainly improved much since her first revolution. The school has been a fearful one, but never was a nation educated so fast. You see more good sense and deliberation in her public councils; and I do hope that the preservation of peace under such difficult circumstances is to be ascribed in part to a decline of her insane and childish passion for military glory. We are cultivating French literature here. A friend of mine is translating B. Constant's work on Religion, and a translation of Cousin's Lectures has just appeared. Degerando's "Visitor of the Poor" is just ready for the press, by another friend. It is a little remarkable that, with all your charitable societies and operations, you have not produced so good a work as this. So says a most competent judge. That religion is to spring up again in France, I cannot doubt. I indulge the hope that one design of Providence in suffering the old order of things to perish is, that Christianity may spring up in a new and purer form. I do not believe that the human mind is to repeat itself for ever. There are advantages as well as perils in a Christian nation separating itself from the past, as France has done. Human nature may disclose new depths of power, and move forward with a new life.

How heavily the *past* weighs on old nations! France is a new nation, and I look to her for some new action of mind. Religion must revive, because it is a deep, essential want of the soul; and Christianity must revive, because it meets this want. But I have no desire that it should rise again in any of its old forms. If it should, the chief benefit of the struggles of the age will be lost. You see the kind of interest I take in France. I wish my hopes had better foundation, but I cannot let them go.

Yesterday our whole country was engaged in one work —the celebration of the *centennial* anniversary of Washington's birth. What a singular event! Millions of freemen joining without a dissentient voice to pay grateful homage to the memory of their political father, and he a statesman and hero without *one blot* on his pure fame. Washington is the most remarkable man of modern times; not that he surpassed all in ability, for it is a question among us yet whether he can be called *great* in regard to intellect. But in a long life, passed among the most trying scenes, not a suspicion ever fell on his motives; and he inspired a whole people with a *moral trust* and *veneration* which contributed incomparably more than transcendent genius could have done to our freedom and union. But I must stop.

Very affectionately yours,
W. E. CHANNING.

To Dr. CHANNING.

Hampstead, April 7, 1832.

My excellent Friend,—Yours of Feb. 23 has just reached me. To find that the expression of my feelings respecting the effects of your writings had so gratified you, was delightful to me. But how is it that you can so underrate their power, that you can for a moment doubt the great, the inestimable good you are working on many minds in many lands? I must write to you a little more on this subject, and tell you what I think your greatest triumph, or at least that which most interests me, and it will lead me to a great topic hitherto untouched between us. The impression you have produced on the minds of *women* is one for which I bless God from the bottom of my heart. I need not tell you how precious your teaching is in the eyes of Joanna Baillie, and I have long since, I think, told you that admirable Mrs. Somerville was your zealous disciple (but make the Farrars tell you more of her). I have now to mention that you have another in Mrs. Marcet. This lady has published, but anonymously, so that her fame has been less than her merit and success—Conversations on Chemistry, on Political Economy, on Natural History, and on Botany—all elementary works of great solidity as well as elegance. She was the daughter of a wealthy Swiss merchant settled in London: her life has been almost equally divided between England and the continent; and her excellent qualities and rare powers of conversation give her great influence both here and in Geneva, which she now calls her home. She has a charming daughter married to Edward Romilly, "Of virtuous father, virtuous son," and from her I lately learnt that her sister, Madame Eugène De la Rive, of Geneva, was engaged in translating some pieces of yours for the "Bibliothèque Universelle," a meritorious periodical published there. The best and most sensible women of my acquaintance are, with very few exceptions, converts to your views. Now, considering that proneness of women to the religious affections, which is so capable of being either exaggerated into fanaticism or depraved into bigotry, I regard it as a circumstance of immense public importance that such ennobling, touching, and at the same time *sober-minded* views should be so respectably patronized amongst us. Whilst you take thought for the human race, I concern myself chiefly with my own sex, and oh! that I could raise a prevailing voice against the manners, the maxims, the habits, by which I see it fettered and debased! If I could engage you to plead in this great cause, I should esteem it half won. But I am ignorant how far the same evils and defects are common to us and our Transatlantic sisters, and I want much to discuss this subject with you.

We modestly esteem ourselves the first of womankind for knowledge, for accomplishments, for purity of manners, and for all the domestic virtues. I am not sure that we are mistaken in supposing that the *union* of these recommendations is more frequent in England than elsewhere; but even granting us the whole, there is much, much to be added and to be corrected. Amid all that is put into the head, the soul, and very often the *reason*, starves.

Women are seldom taught to *think*. A prodigious majority never acquire the power of reasoning themselves or comprehending the force of arguments advanced by others. Hence their prejudices are quite invincible, their narrowness and bigotry almost inconceivable, and amidst a crowd of elegant acquirements, their thoughts are frivolous and their sentiments grovelling. Exceedingly few have any patriotism, any sympathy with public virtue. Private feelings, private interests engross them. They are even more insensible than you charge our public men with being of "the greatness of the times in which we live." Rammohun Roy has been justly scandalized at the want of zeal for the Reform Bill amongst the ladies, and I sometimes pensively ask myself whether the country could now supply many noble Lady Crokes to exhort a husband to follow his conscience in public matters, regardless of the worldly interests of herself and their children. Luxury makes great havoc with the lofty virtues, even in manly minds, and woman it quite unnerves, for the most part. You look with some jealousy on the principle of patriotism as hostile to universal philanthropy; but I am sure you will agree with me that it is better to love our country even partially and exclusively than to love nothing beyond our own firesides, and, when public good and private interest interfere, to feel no generous impulse to sacrifice the less to the greater. I wish that more women were nurtured in, at least, the Latin classics, because from them they might imbibe *this* elevating sentiment, without which they can never deserve the *friendship*, whatever they may obtain of the *love*, of noble-minded men. If you will turn to one of Mrs. Barbauld's "Characters," beginning, "Such were the dames of old heroic days" (it was written, by the way, for the mother of Mr. Benjamin Vaughan, a grand-looking old lady, whose figure I still can recal), you will fully understand what kind of spirit I long to inspire into my sex. Almost all my life this desire has been one of my strongest feelings. When a little girl, I used to battle with boys about the Rights of Woman. Many years ago, I published "Epistles on Women," all to the same effect; and though I now think, I dare say, as ill as anybody of the *poetry* of that work, it contains many sentiments which I still cherish, and would give much to be enabled to disseminate. You may understand by this more distinctly what I meant by saying that the higher and middle classes required to be better taught themselves before they took in hand the instruction of the poor; and a great reason why I doubt of the good which women do in their visitations of cottages is, that I regard them for the most part as themselves the slaves of so many stupid and debasing prejudices. The theology of most of them is that of the Thirty-nine Articles, which you estimate as it deserves; and original sin and the atonement are the favourite themes of their lectures to the poor, even to children. Nay, our orthodox curate told me himself the other day that he had interfered to prevent the lady-managers of the infant school from giving the babies interpretations of prophecies concerning the twelve tribes of Israel, to learn by heart! So undiscriminating is their reverence for all that refers to the contents of any part of the Bible! You know well, too, how the precepts of Christianity have been pressed into the service of a base submission to all established power.

I am interested in your anticipations concerning France. It is much to require me to wish her to *surpass* my own country; but I may truly say that in any real, that is moral improvement of hers, I shall ever most cordially rejoice. This I hope I should do from a pure love of excellence, wherever it may manifest itself; but merely as a *patriot* I must wish that our next neighbours, with whom so many amongst us are inclined to cultivate the closest intimacy—from whom we derive many fashions, practices and opinions—from whom we receive (with horror I speak it) instructresses for so many of our innocent girls—should become more respectable and less a source of moral mischief to us. I own I still think extremely ill of their national character in every possible sense: they are regardless of the true, the sincere, the genuine, the natural; their vanity is odious to me, and their want of all decency, disgusting.

I am far more interested in the Italians. Debased and corrupt as they are, there are noble features in their national character; if free and united, I believe that they would again rise to glory of every kind; and their literature far more delights me than that of France— *they* have poetry, and a very noble spirit breathes in the works of Alfieri and some of their living writers. There are men of great merit amongst their exiles; if they have left many equals or successors behind them, the country must and will emancipate itself before very long. But, my dear friend, is it our duty to be always fixing our eyes on the destinies of nations, on the state and character of mankind at large? May we not often permit ourselves to dismiss from our care evils beyond our cure? Or may we not lull the pain which these general views are apt to inflict with some considerations like the following? This world with all its ills, man with all his crimes and miseries, are yet such as their wise and beneficent Maker designed that they should be, foresaw that they would be. That good preponderates we cannot doubt. All rational creatures, it is probable, find their life a boon even here—if not, how easily can futurity compensate transitory sufferings! Without falling into the Epicurean sentiment which you declare against, there surely is a sense in which we may say, "Whatever is, is right." We ought not surely to refuse ourselves to the advances of that sweet peace "which virtue bosoms ever," because of sin and suffering of which we are not the cause.

Believe it, we shall some time know how and why all these things are. In the meanwhile let the sensitive and ingenuous mind combat this anxiety as its "last infirmity," remembering that His eyes and His love are upon all, the evil as well as the good, the destitute and wretched as well as the happy. Pardon me, pardon me!

have I dared to exhort you? But no; I believe that it is the unworthy body which is in fault when you are overpowered by human ills, or unsatisfied with the amount of good which Providence has enabled you to perform. I know well how mighty that amount has been.

May you still be strengthened to go on adding to it many years! Our cholera turns out comparatively a trifle—what our Reform will turn out is still in dread suspense. I feel entirely with you respecting the position of the Lords. Should we, like France, be compelled, as you say, to separate ourselves from the old, there may be compensations for the inevitable evil of the parting, for posterity, scarcely for *us;* and yet the intense excitement would be worth having.

Ever most cordially yours,
L. AIKIN.

To Miss Aikin.

Boston, June 9, 1832.

My dear Miss Aikin,—I date from Boston, but I write from an inn in the interior of the country, where I am resting for an hour or two on a journey undertaken in the hope of regaining some strength. For above three months I have been useless; not sick enough for the physicians, but too sick for exertion. Our long-delayed summer seems at length opening on us, and I seek health where I have most frequently found it, at a distance from the city. I am more and more fearful that I cannot endure the rigours of our winter, and if a voyage were not so exhausting to me, I should be tempted to try for a season one of your southern counties, which Mrs. Baillie has recommended to me. But it is hard to leave my home. I have a mother about eighty years of age, who is capable of enjoying so much happiness from her children, and whose last days are so bright and peaceful, that I should grieve to place myself at a great distance from her. In truth, I form no plan. Like the birds, I welcome this joyous season, and leave the future to Him that "careth for us." I fear that one of my late letters gave you hardly a just idea of my ordinary state of mind. I recollect that after putting my morbid feelings on paper, I hesitated about sending them to you; but it seemed to me that I owed to your great ingenuousness some exposition of the occasional waywardness of my mind, if such it were. My general frame is anything but despondence. I am much indebted to you for two late letters; the first by the Farrars. These good friends reached us safely, and Mr. F. improved in health. They have communicated to me much about friends whom I love in England.

The principal topic in your first letter was our *debt to the poor*. I thank you for opposing me so frankly, but I think you in error. You hope little from the direct exertions of the rich on the poor. Shall I tell you the cause of your scepticism? You have not met with the rich who understand their relations to the poor, who have a true sympathy with them, and who have risen above all the distractions of life to a true reverence for our common nature. Nothing but sympathy and respect towards the poor, joined with a sound judgment, can do them much good, and these can do them great good. It is not the distance of the condition of the rich from that of the indigent which makes the difficulty, but *distance in spirit*. You would have the missionary to the poor a poor man, that he might come near them and may excite no mercenary hopes. I believe the rich *may* come still nearer. No one is so prepared to sympathize with poverty as he who has known a better lot, if he can only escape the blinding and hardening influences of his condition; if he can see in human nature something nobler than in property, and can carry with him a faith in the redemption or recoverableness of the fallen. As to the mercenary hopes which the poor must place in their benefactors, these would be inspired by a poor missionary; for if he had not a heart of stone, he will and must become a beggar for the sufferers whom he visits; and as soon as he shows a capacity of doing good, he will certainly be made an almoner of the rich. This is exemplified at this moment in Boston. No; the rich and instructed may do immeasurable good among the poor; and I say this from knowledge. I have now, as my companion, a friend whom I have taken from Boston, broken down by his labours among the poor. He goes among them in the true spirit of Christianity. He sincerely respects them, probably more than the rich; not from a prejudiced enthusiasm, but from close connection with them, and witnessing among them great virtues and rapid progress in virtue, that is, when measured by their condition. He has had very much your opinion about the greater good he might do if a poor man; and, though peculiarly blessed in domestic life, has almost wished, in seasons of great excitement, that he had not found these relations, in order that he might live among the poor, eat at their tables, and sleep under their roofs. I believe I have satisfied him of his error, and reconciled him to a lovely wife, fine children, and the comforts of life. Was ever minister before called to preach this form of self-denial? He proposes it as one of his great objects, to prevent the poor from leaning on him, to reveal to them the elements of power and happiness in their own nature, to show them that their great relief is to come from themselves, and that there is no limit to what they can do for themselves. He thinks nothing gained till he has touched the springs of mental energy and self-respect within them, and he has met with success.

This generous experiment on human nature has cheered me greatly, and strengthened me in my hopes for low as well as high. My good friend, do not talk of palliatives for the condition of the poor; that word is a dangerous one except in desperate cases. There is but one effectual way of improving human condition, and that is to act deeply and generously on human nature, to regenerate it in the true sense of the word. Forgive me this trespass on your patience, and be assured, though I am so confident, I am open to conviction if I err. I have spoken of one companion; I have another equally interesting, an inveterate hypochondriac, and who, with a great fortune, accomplishes less good than he should do in consequence of this terrible malady. Still, he is the truest friend of his race, and has more respect for human nature and a deeper feeling of the essential quality of human beings than almost any one whom I know. He is, too, a vigorous and original thinker. You can easily conceive on what subjects we almost talk ourselves hoarse. The condition, perils and prospects of our race —the passions and principles now at work in the bosom of society—the true character of Christianity, and the way to bring it to bear on men, and in general the means of human improvement—these topics never weary us. There are few greater blessings in life than this free intercourse with those who love God and their race with unaffected and enlightened fervour. There is, indeed, one greater good, and that is to convert our *speculation* into *reality*. Too many of us have glorious dreams, and keep on sleeping.

I can but touch on some interesting points in your

letter. I thank you for getting me Sir James Mackintosh's Dissertations. I have a short work in the press, which I hope soon to send to Sir James, and I will then acknowledge his politeness and kindness. I have read his work with great pleasure. It is a noble effort. He is the very man to criticise the labours of other great men. But I differ from him in theory. His attempt to unite Butler and Hartley reminds me of Nebuchadnezzar's image, with its head of gold and feet of iron and clay. Not that I undervalue Hartley. He was a great and good man. He made a precious contribution to intellectual philosophy, and his writings gave me a high idea of his character. Did you ever read his Prayers and Meditations? I know nothing of the kind which breathes so simple and sincere a piety. Still, his exposition of our moral nature is to me very unworthy, imperfect and degrading. It makes moral sentiments an illusion, and I am sorry to say that Sir James upholds it.

We have heard of the second reading of the Reform Bill in the House of Lords. It will probably receive some modifications there, which I rather wish, if they will leave the Bill acceptable to the nation. Compromise is the spirit of free governments, and your policy is to purify your institutions without civil convulsion. For want of a spirit of compromise, our own institutions are seriously threatened.

I cannot write about France. I grieve that you see no more signs of improvement in that country. Did you read in the last "Foreign Quarterly Review" an article on Louis Fourteenth's times? What a change in the French character since that day! and have not good principles made some progress?

I shall rejoice to hear of your better health.

Very sincerely your friend,
WM. E. CHANNING.

To Dr. Channing.

Hampstead, July 15, 1832.

My dear Friend,—I yesterday received yours of June 7, which gave me variety of pleasure and pain: the hope of seeing you—the fear that continued ill health might be the cause—sympathy in your sentiments towards a venerable parent, for such sentiments were my own whilst their dear object remained—all contended together; but being somewhat of an optimist, I settled it at length that *either* I should have the great delight of seeing you, *or else* the satisfaction of hoping that you were in better health at home. Ah! that health—what a blessing to those who recover it after long wanting it! I speak here experimentally. . For the last few weeks I have regained a state of ease and vigour which makes my whole waking time one song of thankfulness. And opportunely has this great change come! I had been so despairing of ability to complete my work, that I had fixed to print it a fragment, stopping at the beginning of the war—a bitter disappointment in many ways; when almost suddenly I rallied, found myself able to work, and now hope to bring out my Charles *complete* next winter. This makes me very busy, and I borrow from my sleep time to write to you. By the way, I have a long *unsent* letter to you in my paper-case. I wrote it on the passing of our *great Bill*, when we had just recovered from imminent dread of a civil war; but at that crisis we were so whirled about by the feelings of the moment, that I felt I might give you impressions to-day which I should find all erroneous to-morrow, and therefore I kept silence. I will now say that we feel the more happy and triumphant in the victory, because the people gained it for themselves, and by means so peaceable and orderly as showed them fit and worthy to obtain it; and because there is great reason to expect that excellent men will be elected to the coming Parliament. Nothing has ever given me such good hopes for my country as the conduct of the people at large on this occasion; good judges think they already perceive that the labouring classes are raised in their own esteem, and are becoming more estimable in consequence. The taste for other kinds of reading, besides political, seems rapidly to increase. The " Penny Magazine," set up by the Useful Knowledge Society, sells 120,000 copies; and this is only one of a multitude of cheap and wholesome productions which are eagerly bought up. To look back now upon the political state of the country, the state of knowledge, and the state of opinions within our own memory, and then to look forward, is absolutely dizzying. Happy they who have been spared to behold so bright a *dawn;* the *day* I think is yet to come. It will next be seen what we can make of a Church reform. The Irish resistance to tithes must lead, I believe, to vast consequences, here as much as there. A conscientious scruple of paying one's money is pretty certain to prove both obstinate and infectious.

I feel quite *enlightened* by what you say respecting the mode of acting beneficially on the poor. My own opinions, I must own, were not the result of any personal knowledge of the subject, and perhaps I was secretly swayed by a wish to believe exertions useless to which I was myself indisposed. It now strikes me that a person visiting the poor with such knowledge of their situation and such sympathy for them as the poems of Wordsworth display, could not but work much good; but, alas! to acquire such acquaintance with them is a business, a calling, and we cannot all devote ourselves like your admirable but enthusiastic friend. I will think more, however, on the subject; I have long felt an uncomfortable consciousness of deficiency in this great branch of duty.

Poor Mackintosh! You will, ere this, have learned that he is beyond the reach of your acknowledgments. He lies in the churchyard which I see from my windows. I thought there was a kind of appropriateness in the long train of *empty* coroneted carriages, with hat-band-wearing menials, which followed him to his long home, and then drove back at speed, without even waiting for the performance of the funeral rites.

I am not sufficiently acquainted with Hartley to give an opinion on his system, but it appeared to me in general that Mackintosh was fond of attempting to reconcile theories really incompatible with each other. And is it not rather too much of a subtilty to say that, although general utility is the *test* of right actions, it can never be an impelling *motive?* It is true that we cannot stop on all occasions to calculate the greatest good of the greatest number before we act, even if we possessed the necessary data; but surely we proceed upon a general idea of tendency to good in our actions; and is not the dignity of man more consulted by allowing reason that share in our determinations than by supposing them to be governed by a kind of moral instinct or appetite? But the more I think upon it, the more I am struck with the complexity of human nature, and the multifariousness of the influences to which every individual is exposed, and the consequent extreme difficulty, if not impracticability, of finding out what is primitive in him. In one sense we may regard his utmost refinement as a part of his nature. We can none of us remember ourselves *unsophisticated*, if the influences and suggestions of other minds be sophistications. We have never been left to the developments of our own powers, which is the reason that we know not by intuition whether or not we have any instincts unless those of suction and deglutition. I am disposed to question the soundness of all very simple theories of man, and that of association particularly, to which I also feel a repugnance in my heart. Oh! if you do but come to England, what prodigiously long conversations we shall have!—our topics will be quite inexhaustible. In writing to you I am always overwhelmed by the abundance of matter. I want you to know multitudes of English people who would be interesting to you in various ways, and yet I feel that extreme caution would be necessary to preserve you from being overwhelmed by crowds, which is the mischief and the misery to which *a name* subjects all here.

I find my historic task increase in interest as I proceed. The times are very favourable; they will allow me all the liberty of speaking I desire; and I have been fortunate in procuring unpublished documents. A volume of the Correspondence of Sir J. Eliot, the patriot-martyr, lies on my table. Hampden was his chief friend, and Eliot was worthy of all his affection. You can imagine nothing more firm, more philosophical, more truly pious, than his letters from prison. When, at Christmas, he was removed to a cell without fire, he writes to his friend: "I hope you will believe that change of place makes none in my mind." The cold was his death. A confession of guilt and a *humble* petition to the King would at any time have purchased his release; but this price he would not pay. Let me love the land which bore such heroes! Another family history lies before me, a folio manuscript. It is little or nothing to my purpose, but the writer was delighted to take a pretext for bringing it to me. He is such a personage as, I suppose, your country does not produce—a man who lives upon his pedigree. My friend is poor, for the entail was cut off, and the title came to him without an acre: his father killed himself, his wife has eloped—though still young, sickness has made his once fine person a miserable wreck; he has no career, and not even an heir male, but he knows that for seven hundred years a certain castle descended from father to son in his family; he can trace his ancestry to Saxon times; he has compiled their history with infinite labour; he knows that one committed a murder, that another was tried for treason; all this is a kind of *conscious worth* to him, and he is happy. Let me, however, give him his due. The polish of his manners has a kind of fascination, and it is impossible not to confess that pride of birth has made him at least *a perfect gentleman.* What is your opinion of this principle or sentiment? Some regard it as useful to balance the pride of purse; others look upon it merely as an arrogant assumption the more in society. I am inclined to look on it with some complacency as favourable to the graces, which certainly purse-pride is not; but I see that it often tends to political servility. A poor man of birth becomes almost unavoidably a hanger-on of the court or the minister, and in one way or other subsists at the cost of the people. A rich man of birth sometimes places his dignity in defying present power and protecting the weak. In our late struggle, the Howards, the Stanleys, the Russells and the Spencers, have deserved very well of their country. But here you will say that I confound the political effects of nobility with pride of blood, which is a different thing. Certainly reason cannot respect a man the more because his ancestors possessed certain manors for a succession of ages, and were sheriffs and county members in their turns. It is seldom that anything moral is connected with this kind of boast. Jesus set himself against the claims of those who said, " We have Abraham for our father." And yet temporal goods at least are represented to have been promised to the Jews on that very score. This strikes me as an eminent instance of what I should call his philosophical spirit, his sense of divine justice, or his enlarged philanthropy. It is somewhat in the same spirit with what you remarked of his instituting no priesthood.

I wish you would tell me whether there is any channel by which one could now and then send you a book which was likely to interest you, and which you might otherwise miss. I longed to convey to you a "Life of Wiclif," by Le Bas. You would find in it much curious and interesting matter. There is the very noble and striking character of the Reformer himself, with many instructive traits of his times—full confirmation of what I once assigned to you as the cause of the small resistance made to our Reformation, namely, the wide diffusion of Wiclif's principles; and there is curious proof how much an exceeding High-churchman of the present day, such as is Le Bas, falls short of the old reformer in simplifying religion. After great struggles he brings out the frightful fact that Wiclif would fain have abolished bishops and established a kind of Presbyterian discipline. This volume makes the first of a set to be called the "Theological Library," in which the ablest pens of the High-church party are engaged. Le Bas is noted as a bitter reviewer of polemics; he is certainly an able writer and affluent in knowledge.

My paper reminds me to release you. How eager I shall be for the next notice of your determination! Pray make health your first object.

Ever most truly yours,
L. AIKIN.

To Miss Aikin.

Boston, August 26, 1832.

My dear Miss Aikin,—I received yesterday your letter of July 15, and I hasten to answer it, to show you what a grateful reception it met with—and for another reason, which will not give you equal pleasure. I am suffering from a bad cold, the consequence of the unusual severity of the weather at this season (the thermometer this morning having been below 50, probably nearer 40), and after a night rendered *sleepless* by laudanum, I find myself equal to no task more severe than letter-writing. Among the many interesting and agreeable communications of your letter, the most agreeable was the good news of your restoration to health. It is very plain from what you say that the vital energy is far from being exhausted yet. Do not use it too freely. Watch over it for others as well as for yourself. I forgot what I wrote you about visiting England, but you interpreted me more strictly than I intended. I expressed wishes, I presume, rather than expectations. At present I am bound to my own country. The cholera is here, and every place expects it. I have no great solicitude about my immediate friends, for the temperate and prudent are generally passed by; but there are exceptions, and until a city has been visited by it, there is no certainty as to the classes on whom it will seize. In Montreal, the most virtuous and respectable were swept away as truly as the dissolute. I have great hope for Boston, for I believe no place on the globe has used more thorough and judicious means for averting or mitigating the calamity. One plan, I believe, is peculiar to our city. A Relief Association has been formed, the members of which are pledged to secure attendance to the sick whenever the aid of domestic friends shall be wanting. This Society embraces some of our most opulent and valuable citizens. No one therefore has any fear of desertion; and, what is still more important, moral courage and strength will descend from the higher to the less favoured classes, so that one great cause of the disease, terror, will cease, and the claims of humanity be respected everywhere. Have I not some right to be proud of my city?

You made me smile when you spoke as if my arrival among you would produce a *sensation*. Should I draw a crowd of admirers, the greatest wonderer would be the person wondered at, and he would be among the first to retreat. With all my efforts, I cannot connect anything extraordinary with the idea of myself. I am not insensible, I think, to my just claims. I believe that I have thought with some power and to some effect. But what I have done is so little compared with what I have hoped and proposed, and I see myself outdone by so many in various particulars, that my demands on the world's notice are very moderate. I do not mean by this language to represent myself as superior to the passion for distinction. But my love of domestic retirement, my great susceptibility of tranquil pleasure, particularly the pleasures of intellectual exertion and of communion with nature, and a conviction which very early sprung up in me of the worthlessness of most worldly applause, have prevented ambition from becoming my besetting sin. Were I to visit your country, after indulging myself liberally in your society and that of a few friends, I should incline to plunge into some beautiful retreat in Devonshire, or wherever you fix your *finest climate*. A fine climate! What a good these words contain to me! It is worth more than all renown, considering renown as a personal good, and not a moral power which may help to change the face of society. The delight which I find in a beautiful country, breathing and feeling a balmy atmosphere and walking under a magnificent sky, is so pure and deep, that it seems to me worthy of the future world. Not that I am in danger of any excess in this particular; for I never forget how very, very inferior this tranquil pleasure is to disinterested action; and I trust that I should joyfully forego these gratifications of an invalid to toil and suffer for my race. You see, then, the motives which would draw me to England. Notice, attention, celebrity, would not enter my thoughts. The hope of forming or continuing acquaintance, and still more friendship, with the distinguished in intellect and virtue, would be a strong attraction; but the strongest attraction would be a milder and more equal climate, where I might enjoy more of the tranquil pleasures which are so dear to me; and, above all, might be able to do something more than I can here for the cause of truth, freedom and humanity. Pardon this egotism. I will not trouble you again with so large a portion of it.

I earnestly pray that your anticipation from the Reform Bill may be realized. I doubt not that it will prove a great good, though mixed with evil, and slower in its operation than some imagine. My only fear about it, which I believe I expressed to you, has been that it might extend the elective franchise too far *at present*. This ought, indeed, to be universal; that is, a community should so instruct and improve all classes that all may be prepared to exercise it; but as long as an ignorant and degraded class exist, who would use it only for their own injury and that of the State, benevolence and justice require that they should be denied it. From the composition of your towns, I have feared that the qualification in those places was too low; but I cannot at this distance form a decided opinion. The conduct of the aristocracy through this whole affair has given me apprehension. It shows how hard it is for a privileged body to act with common judgment when their own privileges are touched. Your nobility would not and could not understand that Reform was not the cry of the mob—the populace—but of the nation; and they deliberately set themselves in hostility to the nation, and the King too, on a point which roused the whole sensibility of the people, and which was thought to involve their most sacred rights. How they could have contrived to make themselves more odious I do not know. Nor was this all. They invited contempt as well as hatred. They pledged themselves to resist this measure even unto blood. They affirmed that to concede it was to concede everything, so that the time had come to conquer or die for the constitution; but, when the voice of the people grew sterner, they shrunk from the position. What I fear is, that the relation between the aristocracy and the nation has become a hostile one, and this bodes ill for your domestic peace. I cannot regret that the bishops were struck with the same judicial blindness which fell on the nobles. The sooner they are dismissed from the Parliament, the better. Their proper influence, which is more spiritual, will be increased by putting off their temporal dignities. When thus confined to their proper sphere, I hope they will be liberally supported, and not exposed to anything like abuse from sectaries and ultra-liberalists. I know, indeed, that the present form of the institution is very childish. That an office which has but one aim, to teach men love to God and to one another, to teach God's equal parental interest in all mankind, should be tricked out in pompous titles, gorgeous robes, mitres, and civil dignities, is an incongruity at which one might smile, could we forget the influence of these puerilities on the fortunes of the race. Still, the bishops should be gently treated. I think not a little deference is due to the great multitude among you who still worship lawn sleeves; and then the bishops, generally speaking, are men of so much excellence as to deserve respect. At least I hear good accounts of them, always bating their political servilities. In proportion as the true, pure, simple idea of religion is brought out, the bishop and the priest must go down, and the process is sure enough to satisfy the rational friends of improvement.

You ask me what I think of pride of birth as forming the *perfect gentleman.* I have no room to reply. I will only say that I should reluctantly part with aristocracy, if I thought the perfect gentleman was to vanish with it. But I am sure that the grace, refinement and charm of the gentlemanly character may be much more effectually promoted by another principle, and I am more and more confident that through this they are to be diffused gradually through all classes of society. But more of this hereafter. I rejoice that King Charles is in progress; I look forward to it as one of my great pleasures.

Your sincere friend,
W. E. CHANNING.

To Dr. Channing.

Hampstead, October 15, 1832.

I will follow your example by answering your letter immediately—always the time when one is most disposed to answer. I liked everything in it but the report of your susceptibility to cold so early in the season. Here we have one of the finest autumns ever known. I wish I could bag up for you the west wind which is waving his balmy wings at my open window.

I still live in hopes that we shall some time or other lure you hither, and then you will know whether I was right or not in promising or threatening that you should be a *lion*. That you would soon be weary of performing that part I can readily believe, but I am sure that we *have* minds over which you must rejoice to feel the benignant influence which you have exerted. You desire me not to use my recovered energies too freely. There is no danger. Eager as I am for the completion of my long task, I am not permitted to sit too closely at it, for I am now surrounded by a close circle of friends and neighbours who tempt me daily into delicious idleness—if I may call that social intercourse idleness in which neither head nor heart is unoccupied. It will be three or four months yet before I shall have made an end of King Charles; but I begin to ask myself, what next? With my habits of literary labour, vacation will soon become tedious, and I must look out for another task. Pray assist me. I am resolved against proceeding further with English sovereigns—Charles II. is no theme for me; it would make me contemn my species. If I could discover how my pen could do most good, to that object it should without hesitation be devoted. Profit I have no need of, and of reputation I have all I want. My mind is often burdened with the consciousness of doing little good, and an ignorance in what way to attempt doing more. If I am capable of benefiting any class, it must be one considerably removed from the lowest, of whom, whatever you may think of the confession, I have never seen enough to know at all how to address them. One *comfort* is, that there is still plenty of ignorance and noxious error to be pointed out in all classes. But the office of *censor morum* is not one which I covet; for who and what am I? I can imagine, but I know not whether I could execute, something in the way of essays, or letters—moral, literary and miscellaneous—which might be made to serve good ends. But this is quite in the air.

Know that a great new light has arisen among English women. In the words of Lord Brougham, "There is a deaf girl at Norwich doing more good than any man in the country." You may have seen the name and some of the productions of Harriet Martineau in the "Monthly Repository," but what she is gaining glory by are "Illustrations of Political Economy," in a series of tales published periodically, of which nine or ten have appeared. It is impossible not to wonder at the skill with which, in the happiest of these pieces, for they are unequal, she has exemplified some of the deepest principles of her science, so as to make them plain to very ordinary capacities, and demonstrated their practical influence on the well-being, moral and physical, of the working classes first, and ultimately on the whole community. And with all this, she has given to her narratives a grace, an animation, and often a powerful pathos, rare even in works of pure amusement. Last year she called on me several times, and I was struck with marks of such an energy and resolution in her as, I thought, must command success in some line or other, though it did not then appear in what. She has a vast store of knowledge on many deep and difficult subjects; a wonderful store for a person scarcely thirty, and her observation of common things must have been extraordinarily correct as well as rapid.—I believe you may dismiss your fears of too wide an extension of suffrage under the Reform Bill. The total number of ten-pound householders turns out less than almost any one expected, and the "degraded class" are almost all lodgers, and the condition of a previous paying up of rates annexed to the privilege of voting has so much further reduced them, that in

many places the constituencies are manifestly still too
small to be out of reach of bribery. It is impossible
quite to suppress anxiety for the general result of the
coming elections, but all the friends of rational liberty I
talk with are full of happy auguries. It is quite true, as
you say, that the Tories have made, and are still making,
themselves both odious and contemptible; but I do not
think the public peace is threatened, because it seems
pretty certain that they will be left in a decided minority
in both Houses, so that the people can afford to forgive
them. John Bull is not of a vindictive temper, especially
when a plentiful harvest has put him in good heart and
good humour. You think quite as well of our bishops
as they deserve. The venerable Bishop of Norwich, of
whom Sydney Smith happily said, "he should *touch* for
bigotry and absurdity," stands very much alone amongst
them; however, I do not wish them hurt in the least,
nor frightened further than is necessary to urge them to
quit their political station. The separation of Church
and State is, in my opinion, by much the most important
victory which the people have still to achieve. When
our bishops shall be in the state of your bishops, certainly my animosity against them will extend "not a
frown further;" but till that happens, all fair means of
lessening them in the eyes of the people must be allowed. It is even marvellous to see how much the
Church is daily losing ground. It has no longer the
reverence of the lower classes in general, and by the
middling classes it begins to be regarded with the same
feelings as the lay Tories so generally excite. Its best
friends come forward with plans of moderate reform. So
long as Dissenters are compelled to pay towards the
support of a Church which they regard as corrupt in
discipline and doctrine, and the preachers of which still
thunder against the sin of schism and labour to bring

sectaries into the hatred and contempt of their hearers —so long the State religion must, and will, and ought to be the object of hostility and attack to all lovers of equal justice and of the best interests of man. Such, at least, is my sense of things. I think you can scarcely imagine the tone taken by High-church people of the upper classes on these matters. A lady who belongs to the first circles, taking for granted that one must be orthodox, expressed to me lately her horror at worthy and learned old Baron Mazeres, who " towards the end of his life not only became an Unitarian, but endeavoured to propagate those doctrines." As if a man ought to think his own opinions dangerous or pernicious to others !

Your cholera precautions are indeed admirable, and I trust they will prove effectual. Here the disease continues making considerable ravages, but we begin to grow used to it. It does sometimes, however, attack very sober and respectable people. I have personally known some victims of this class. Soon after it appeared in London, great alarm was excited by the death of a lady of quality, till it was charitably whispered that the *temperate* need not be the more apprehensive on account of this event. It is suspected that the Irish in St. Giles's and such places have perished in considerable numbers, but they disguise the cases from their violent prejudice against early burials without the accompaniment of a drunken wake. How are we to civilize these wretched people ? Not by dragooning them, say you, and I agree ; but this negative is more clear than anything positive respecting them. I wonder whether you have seen a small book published by Rammohun Roy containing translations of several of the Hindoo Veds ? I have found a good deal of interest in this view of theology and metaphysics of a nation so remote in every respect from us and our ways of thinking. The great point which the true friend of his country and his race has had in view in his various controversies with his own countrymen, has been to show that, although some idolatrous rites are sanctioned by their sacred books, yet it has always been the doctrine of the most authentic of these, that the highest future happiness was only attainable by a pure and austere life and the worship of the invisible, universal Spirit—that idolatry was for the gross and ignorant, rites and observances for them only. Thus he shows that eternal felicity—that is, absorption into the supreme Spirit—is promised to women who after the death of their husbands lead devout and holy lives; and only a poor lease of thirty-five millions of years of happiness with their husbands to such as burn with them, after the expiration of which their souls are to transmigrate into different animals. This you will say is mighty puerile, but it is at least meeting his antagonists on their own ground. Afterwards he details the many cruelties and oppressions to which females in his country are subjected by the injustice and barbarity of the stronger sex, and pleads for pity towards them with such powerful, heartfelt eloquence, as no woman, I think, can peruse without tears and fervent invocations of blessings on his head. The Rajah is now at Paris, where I doubt if he will find much gratification, as he is not well versed in the French language; he will return to us, however, soon after the meeting of Parliament. I dread the effects of another English winter on his constitution; and yet it almost seems as if a life like his must be under the peculiar guardianship of Providence.

What a charming poet is your Bryant! I am just reading Mr. Irving's collection of his poems. Do you know the author? I am curious about him.

I am not acquainted with anybody in your country who would take charge of a book for me; but anything that should reach either Robert Kinder, or Dr. Boott, or Mr. P. Vaughan, would be forwarded to me.

A brimful sheet, as usual! In writing to you, my excellent friend, I never want matter. May health and every good attend you!

Yours ever truly,
L. AIKIN.

To Dr. Channing.

Hampstead, November 19, 1832.

Oh, my dear friend! I was told yesterday that you had been very, very ill, and though it was added that you were now better, I have been able to think of little else since. What would I give to know how you are at this now that I am writing! This distance which separates us has something truly fearful in such circumstances. Would you had postponed all other considerations, however urgent, however affecting, to the one great object, your own health! Would you had sought our milder skies early in the autumn! I fear that, unless you should have embarked ere this, it must not be thought of till spring; but surely you will then transport yourself hither, and thus escape one of the trying seasons of your climate, which I take the early months to be. I have lately seen two or three very striking instances of the wonderfully restorative effects of our southern coasts in pulmonary cases. At this time I have a friend at Hastings reported quite well both by himself and others, who was absolutely given over last spring in London, and whom for some time in the summer, which he spent at Hampstead, I never saw within my doors without fearing it was for the last time. Another friend has been so fortified by two winters spent in the south, after the case seemed desperate, as now to be enabled to return to her native cold and wet Lancashire, where she has medical permission to winter. Well! I would not tease you with more of this; no doubt you have around you both the skilful and the kindest of the kind. My great inducement for writing was the hope that a little of this mute kind of chit-chat, which calls for no exercise of the voice in answer, might somewhat cheer your sick-room; at least you will accept it with kindness, as the only thing in which I can show my deep interest in the benefactor to whom I owe what is above all price—the sentiments which do most towards rendering us worthy of the future. Never, my friend, are you forgotten when my soul seeks communion with our common Father; and when I strive most earnestly to overcome some evil propensity, or to make some generous sacrifice, the thought of you gives me strength not my own.

I have written to you so lately and so largely, that some of my usual topics are nearly exhausted; still we have a little of novelty. In the beginning of November Term begins, and all the lawyers come to town. With their arrival commence my London dinner visits; for my most intimate friendships happen to be amongst this set, and I have already made one excursion to town, from which I gleaned a good deal. You know, of course, by reputation, our new Lord Chief Justice, Denman—the zealous defender of poor Queen Caroline, who in his excitation called our last king Nero, and our present one "a base calumniator." He wants caution, and is not the deepest of our lawyers; but his promotion is hailed by all congenial spirits as a triumphant example of the highest professional dignities attained by a man who never showed any other fear than that of being thought capable of sacrificing the most minute portion of truth, the nicest punctilio of honour, to any worldly interest.

Glorious days in which such conduct finds such acceptance! On his taking leave of Lincoln's Inn in consequence of his promotion, a speech was made to him by his old friend the Vice-Chancellor, complimenting him on the love of liberty he had ever manifested, in a strain which drew tears down the furrowed cheeks of the old benchers—practised worldlings as they must be. This glorious man—by the way, his person is made for dignity—was Mrs. Barbauld's pupil at four years old. I think it must have been chiefly for him that her "Hymns in Prose" were written; and he cherishes her memory most religiously. In a great public entertainment where I met him last year, he came up to me and said with a look of delight, "I dreamed of Mrs. Barbauld only last night!" He has a love and a taste for poetry and elegant literature worthy of her scholar, and I doubt not that she sowed the seed. In the move which Denman's appointment has made, another stanch friend of the people has become Solicitor-General. It is of great importance thus to recommend the laws to the many by the character of those who administer them.

I think I told you Hallam had become a Conservative and alarmist; but he seems to me to have recovered his spirits since last spring, and to be relapsing into a Liberal. He confesses to me that he is reading hard for a purpose, but will not yet say what. We again *croaked* together over the decline of literature, and modestly concluded that it was *our* duty to write as much and as well as we could. We canvassed much the good and evil of the new Penny Magazines and Cyclopædias, which are selling by hundreds of thousands; and all we could decide was, that condemning the superficial and desultory spirit which these and other periodicals and abridgments were fitted to diffuse, it was still impossible not to rejoice that food so innocent was found for the popular mind, and was welcome to it. An indirect benefit we also acknowledged from this new literature; its having to a great extent superseded the religious tracts of the Evangelicals, which their busy zeal threatened to render the exclusive study of the working classes. Perhaps it is in this last respect that the Useful Knowledge Society has proved most beneficial; and no doubt it was a leading, though unavowed, object of the founders thus to put fanaticism's nose out of joint (if you will allow such a grotesque expression).

Are we, or are we not, at war with our old friends the Dutch? This seems to be a question which nobody knows very well how to answer. For my part, I have such an opinion of the natural pugnacity of the human species, that I dread exceedingly these beginnings of strife; but poverty, the peace-preserver, still keeps watch over every European potentate, and I trust will withhold the means of mischief. There can be no doubt of the pacific dispositions of our present ministry; but they are unhappily committed in some degree by the acts of their predecessors, and there is also some danger that the obstinate King of Holland, by presuming too much on our forbearance, may render it a point of what is called national honour to forbear no longer. These are anxious considerations. No one can pretend to calculate the confusion and mischief which the expense of one campaign might cause to us in our present situation. But let us not be "over-curious to shape the fashion of uncertain evil."

These November fogs have brought me down a little from my high boast of health, and interrupted somewhat my historic diligence. I suspect that the weakness in my chest will oblige me to keep the house in all ungenial winds this winter. But no matter, my fireside is cheery. My dear new neighbours, the Le Bretons, are an inestimable acquisition. Here I paused to welcome Harriet Martineau, with all her blushing honours thick upon her. The Chancellor has sent for her expressly to write tales illustrative of pauperism, and has supplied her for the purpose with an immense mass of documents accessible only to official persons. I believe she will do much good; her motives and principles are pure and high, and success, as I predicted, has improved, not spoiled her. Indeed, she has very extraordinary talent and merit, and a noble independence of mind. I will stop here; may this little pledge of friendship find you in a state at least of tolerable ease. I shall inquire of you from every probable source of intelligence.

May Heaven preserve my precious friend!

L. AIKIN.

To Miss Aikin.

Boston, January 3, 1833.

My dear Miss Aikin,—Your letter of October has just reached me. It seems that in the letter to which you replied, I spoke of myself as threatened with disease. I proved too true a prophet. About the end of August I was driven to my chamber by a pulmonary complaint which wasted my strength and flesh so fast, that my friends became justly apprehensive as to the result. My mind sympathized more than ordinarily with the body. I retained clear and joyful convictions of the great truths with which I had been familiar, but was not equal to the least intellectual labour. Our autumn was singularly delightful; and when I was able to creep to the window, the most inviting prospects were spread around me; but the effort of looking at a flower or tree was too much for me, and I was compelled to turn away from the beauty after which I had sighed. I smile now when I remember how I felt the disappointment, and how I reconciled myself to it. I considered with Plato that this outward beauty was but a type or emblem of that spiritual beauty to which I had perpetual access, and that whilst surrounding nature would fade before I should gain strength to enjoy it, still the fountain of all its glories and loveliness was inexhaustible, and would never fail me. What strange beings we are! At the very moment when I was almost weak enough to shed tears at being cut off from the beautiful universe, I was able to find consolation and peace in reflections such as these. My recovery was rapid beyond expectation, after my disease was subdued, and I am not without hope that I may be better than I have been for some time. The last year has been an unfavourable one. For the last ten months I have preached but once, and my literary labours have advanced very little. But I do not despair of accomplishing some of my plans. At least it is a great happiness to have some worthy plans, towards the execution of which a step may now and then have been taken. During my recovery, a friend began to read to me Le Bas' Wiclif, which you had named to me. You little thought what a task you were imposing on me. The High-church notions of the writer troubled me not at all, any farther than it is sad to meet puerilities and absurdities in men who set up for oracles. But his High-church *style* was a real grievance. Very often my weak head was exhausted by the task of extracting the essential fact from the swelling, self-complacent rhetoric in which it was enveloped. Still there was much in the book to gratify me. Bating some extravagances of this radical reformer, he is more to my taste than his successor on the continent. I was sorry not to see the passages of Wiclif on which Melancthon founded the charge of *heresy*. I suspect the liberal and spiritual view of Wiclif would put to shame the Thirty-nine Articles. I ought to say that I found much relief to the weary hours of sickness in listening to some of Scott's novels. He was anything but a philosopher. But in *extent* of observation, in the quick perception of the endless varieties of human character, in the discovery of their signs and manifestations, and in the inventive and graphic power by which he embodies them and places them before us with the freshness and vividness of reality, where will you find his equal? I do not know the author who has given the same amount of innocent pleasure. Millions in both worlds are debtors to him. Others have done far greater good in *kind* or quality, but none in extent or amount. I forgive him his Toryism, and can even pardon his consummate weakness in attaching greater importance to outward distinctions than to his genius. This was Toryism with a vengeance; but I owe him too much to reprove him severely. I do not say that he ever touches the highest springs within me, but he has bound me by new sympathies to my race; and, what in such a world or, I would say, in such a body is of no small account, he has beguiled and delighted not a few hours which hardly any other books could have enlivened. Let me here say a word about Sir James Mackintosh. One of our reviewers has published an account of a conversation with him, in which Sir J. is thought sometimes to speak as a *Calvinist*. I have smiled at seeing him ranged under that standard. Can you tell me to what theological opinions he inclined? It is amusing to see how parties seize on great men as their property. We have lately had here Dr. Spurzheim, the phrenologist, who was eminently liberal in his views, but after his death some expressions in his lectures were made use of to press him into the ranks of Calvinism. Did you know anything of this good man? for such he seemed to have been. He made a greater impression in our city than any foreigner, and his death called forth a general sorrow. His lectures interested all ranks. He made few converts to craniology; but he was thought to possess a singular insight into human nature, and his hearers thought they gained from him that inestimable treasure, self-comprehension. I was too sick to hear him. Did he make any impression as favourable in your country? All who knew him here were struck with his unaffected philanthropy, and this was the great charm of his lectures. As far as I have seen phrenological writings, they breathe this spirit, and give some excellent views on the subject of the improvement of the race. I have this moment a phrenological head and brain on my table, and a young lady by the side of it, of a fine intellect and character, who has studied the science. She has been polite enough to find all the nobler organs in my head, so that I have no personal objections to the truth of the doctrine.

I will read Miss Martineau. I delight in every instance of the successful pursuit of great subjects by your sex. I almost wish at this moment that we had women at the head of our government. Do you know that we are threatened with civil war? I trust only threatened. But with women for our rulers we should have no bloodshed; and when I see how affairs are managed, I do not see how the ladies could do worse. It is consoling to see what progress the human race have made under bad governments. They have contrived to stagger forward under many a crushing load. How will they advance when set free? I do not mean by this that *we* are greatly oppressed; but excess of legislation has produced serious discontents. I shall rejoice to tell you in my next that they are removed.

If I can think of any work for you to engage in after

Charles is ended, I will name it. Generally, however, we are the best judges of what we can do. I wait impatiently for your book, not only because it is yours, but because I wish to understand that period better. May you preserve health, and may every blessing be yours !

Your sincere friend,
WM. E. CHANNING.

I have taken the liberty to publish in a religious paper your accounts of Miss Martineau and of Rammohun Roy's books. I wish to bring these persons before the public. Have you any objection to my using your letters occasionally in this way ?

TO MISS AIKIN.

Boston, January 12, 1833.

My dear Miss Aikin,—I received two or three days ago your letter of November 19th, and, though I wrote you last week, I cannot refrain from replying to it immediately. I thank you for the affectionate solicitude and the fervent wishes for my recovery which it expresses. The language of such friendship from one so distant, and who thinks herself indebted to me for some of her best blessings, is truly cheering and strengthening. My last letter will set you very much at ease about my health. I am living, indeed, very much in my chamber, but my lungs seem to be restored to their usual state. When the weather favours, I walk abroad and take the open air, which is one of my great luxuries. It seems to me that I enjoy the free air as few do. Perhaps I confirmed my late disease by sitting abroad after I had taken a cold. A balmy or bracing atmosphere is a constant delight to me. I think my sensations help me to explain one of the fancies of your noble Platonist, Henry More, who used to think, when a refreshing breeze was blowing on him, that the Holy Spirit was breathing on his soul. I am, however, most of my time a prisoner, and should rejoice to transport myself for a while to your southern coasts. I feel as if that climate might suit me better than any other. I have tried Italy and the West Indies, with little benefit. England seems to be the one retreat left. But at present I form no plans. I should not know what to do with my children in your country. My boy, now thirteen, is not prepared for the severe, perhaps I might say, barbarous discipline of your schools. He was never struck by a teacher, and an *English whipping* might ruin him. My daughter is the most social of human beings, and very susceptible of impression from companions, and in a foreign land the difficulty of choosing the best associates is great. You see how many mountains lie between us. I am willing, however, to make many sacrifices for health—not that I suffer greatly from the want of it, except in my capacity of labour; and this, indeed, is a melancholy exception. I feel as if I had done very little as yet of what I might do for my fellow-beings or for myself, but any considerable effort prostrates me. I have as yet done justice to none of my views, and showed their practical application very imperfectly; but enough of myself. You will excuse me when you consider that your interest in my present situation is my only motive for writing.

I forgot to answer in my last your inquiries about Bryant. He is a man in middle life, a native of this State, and brought up to the profession of the law in the interior. But literature seduced him from law, and he went to New York, hoping to live chiefly by his pen.

He commenced a review, which failed, and was obliged to become joint editor of a newspaper, to which he is now devoted. Mr. Bryant, though a partizan, has never been charged with unworthy motives. His poetry, I daresay, has led you to place him amidst woods and streams; but, instead of this, he lives amidst political storms, and is breathing the impure air of a city notoriously devoted to gaiety. This situation has almost necessarily turned him away from poetry. He writes seldom and makes no sustained efforts, but now and then his first love—Nature—haunts him amidst his labours, and wakes up his fine powers. He is generally placed at the head of our poets.

I wanted to write you about our political situation, which at this moment absorbs us, so that we think little of Europe. One of our States, South Carolina, has declared the recent tariffs imposed by the general government for the protection of manufactures, to be null and void, and threatens to resist by force the collection of duties within her borders. The President, on the other hand, threatens to reduce her to obedience by arms. You in England understand probably very little of the merits of the case, nor can you without understanding the relations between the General and State Governments, and the strange vacillations of our parties, which have wheeled and wheeled till they now occupy each the original ground of its adversary. I cannot now carry you over this field, and have only space to assure you that I remain

Your sincere friend,
WM. E. CHANNING.

To Dr. Channing.

Hampstead, February 10, 1833.

Many, many thanks to you, my dear friend, for your two welcome letters, and the excellent news they contain! It is indeed delightful to find you speaking so cheerily, both of the past, the present, and the future, and the most delightful of all is, that you still think of England. To level some at least of the mountains which, as you say, still rise between us, will be no hard task. First, the barbarous and odious practice of whipping is obsolete in nearly all our schools, except the public ones of ancient foundation, such as Eton, Westminster, &c., to which many other considerations would restrain you from sending your son. In that attached to the London University, to which my nephew goes, 230 boys are kept in order without any corporal punishment; in short, we would ensure your lad a whole skin. Then, as to your sweet girl, there would really be no more danger than everywhere arises from the little acquaintance which parents in general can have with the *individual* characters of the younger generation who are their children's contemporaries. You might easily be directed to families the most likely to afford fit associates for her. I cannot persuade myself that the very small difference of temperature between a *snug* situation in the immediate neighbourhood of London, and the southern coast, would be of moment to you; compared to the difference between the last and New England, it is nothing. Even in this village, placed as it is on a hill, very sheltered nooks may be found, and the air is eminently salubrious; and oh! if we could get you all here, how much we could do—I am confident we could —towards placing you in the midst of a small select circle where you would be appreciated, and your children would form connections such as you could not but approve! Several circumstances render society here peculiarly easy and pleasant; in many respects the place unites the advantages and escapes the evils both of London and the provincial towns. It is near enough to allow its inhabitants to partake in the society, the amusements, and the accommodations of the capital as freely as even the dissipated could desire; whilst it affords pure air, lovely scenery, and retired and beautiful walks; and because every one is supposed to have a London set of friends, neighbours do not think it necessary, as in the provinces, to force their acquaintance upon you; of local society you may have much, little, or none, as you please; and with a little, which is very good, you may associate on the easiest terms; then the summer brings an influx of Londoners who are often genteel and agreeable people, and pleasingly vary the scene. Such is Hampstead: ask Mrs. Farrar if I exaggerate. The subject threatens to run away with me; but here I leave it, for I have much to answer.

I like and can subscribe to your praise of Scott *as a writer*. Sir James Mackintosh was no doubt brought up a Calvinist; but I have seen a letter of his written from India to his old friend Robert Hall, then lately recovered from an attack of insanity, in which he warns him against dwelling on gloomy systems of religion as no one could have done who was a Calvinist, or, I should think, who believed salvation dependent on any *particular* creed. Read in the last number of the "Edinburgh Review," the article on Lord Mahon's History. I believe you will think the writer of it much improved since he reviewed Milton, and gave so dashing a sketch of the Puritans. This writer is Macaulay, confessedly the first *young* speaker in the House of Commons. As reviewer, as orator, as politician, he, if any one, promises to be the successor or rival of Brougham. I have never seen him, but I hear of him as presumptuous—at least this *was* his character at the outset. He grapples boldly and ably with O'Connell in the House.

On the brink of civil war yourselves, you might well be excused for thinking little of Europe and her concerns; but we here give you credit for too much wisdom by far to proceed to that dread extremity, and I trust that by this time you are coming to some amicable compromise; if so, you may be willing to hear something of the progress of our revolution. Yes, revolution; it is no less; of this it is impossible not to be more and more sensible every day. The Reform Bill now shows itself fully in the character of means to an end—and what end? Of this different parties would give different accounts; that is, some require more, some would be content with fewer, concessions of the few to the many; but all agree that numerous and important ones must and will be made. Ireland, miserable Ireland! a prey to so many evils, stained with so many crimes, and almost reduced to anarchy, what shall we do for her? To return into the right way after wide deviations, is as arduous a task in the government of nations as in the conduct of individuals; in fact, almost all the puzzling questions in public, as in private morals, arise from having set out wrong. The Protestant Church of Ireland is probably the most monstrous anomaly, the most barefaced wrong, in all ecclesiastical history; but it cannot be overthrown without some consideration for the *vested rights* enjoyed under it, and the same may be said respecting other interests there. Then, although the people are enduring many evils and oppressions, they must not be suffered to fill the land with robbery and murder; and the political *agitators*, though their views may be **patriotic, and** though by their efforts some wrongs have been and others will be redressed, must not be suffered to go on goading a ferocious people to fury, and an absurd people to folly and ruin. The Union must be preserved for Ireland's own sake. It is impossible to dwell upon these considerations without alternately blaming, pitying and dreading all parties. But how wonderful and admirable is the complication of good with evil in the whole system of things! How unexpectedly do the results of things come out! To the *Irish Papists*, the objects of their bitterest, their most inveterate hatred, have the descendants of the English Puritans been indebted for the establishment of their civil rights. To the crying iniquity of the Church of Ireland, English Dissenters are likely eventually to owe emancipation from the exclusive claims of the Church of England. I view with intense interest the progress of the Church reform in which we are engaged. Take my word for it, it will go far, and end in the acknowledgment of broad principles. *Protestant* exclusiveness, when cited to the bar of Reason, has nothing, absolutely nothing, to say; and this is a reasoning age. Thousands are coming to a clear perception how completely the interests of the Church and the interests of Religion are different, nay, opposite things. Nor do I fear that, according to the distinction of Hume, *fanaticism* should here gain what *superstition* is likely to lose. The schoolmaster is fast emancipating the people from both, and without producing irreligion.

Eternal honour to Brougham for his "Useful and Entertaining Knowledge," and his "Penny Magazine"! They have done very much towards beating Evangelical tracts and the *good-boy* books of the High-church Tories out of the field. The whole tendency of these publications, as far as I know them, is to instil that sober morality, that pure and simple piety, with which, as you would say, narrow and debasing views of God and of religion cannot co-exist. And do you think *you* have done nothing towards this great work? You should see a little work published by Mr. Tagart, a London Unitarian minister, the " Life of Captain Heywood," to learn in what esteem your writings were held by a nobleminded, beneficent, upright naval officer. There is a chord in all such hearts which responds to your teaching. I hear of your writings, see your name mentioned on all sides; even our clergy mention it with deep respect. Oh! come to us; breathe our air, which may preserve you in vigour, not alone for your own sake, or that of your family, but for England's and mankind's!

Mr. Vaughan's ship, with your precious volume, for which I return you my best thanks by anticipation, is not yet arrived; but he says he expects it daily. I have had a glimpse, however, of the English reprint of the book; a glimpse only, for it was lent to Mr. Le Breton* and to me, and in our mingled politeness and impatience we have been sending it to each other, and then snatching it back, so that neither of us has yet had much good of it. He has been an active circulator of your works, and no one more delights in them. You must know each other some time.—I lament over the unpoetical destiny of the poet Bryant; his admirers should have endeavoured to have procured for him some humble independence; but it will be long, I suspect, before you pension men of letters. We do little in this way. As to poor Spurzheim, I hear, for I never saw him, that he was much liked in society, and our anatomists much admired his mode of dissecting, or rather unravelling, the texture of the brain; but his system made few disciples amongst men of real science; and though I believe he individually was thought tolerably ingenious in it, a

---

* The late Rev. Philip Le Breton.

shade of empiricism was cast over him, which prevented his ever *taking rank* here; and his pecuniary encouragement was small. I think the spirit of philanthropy is almost a national characteristic of the frank and honest Germans; their writings, as far as I can judge of them from translations and critiques, very generally breathe it; and in the midst of their credulity and mysticism there is a deep and original vein of thinking which I should delight to explore if I possessed their language.

There is no hurry for a new scheme to succeed "King Charles" with me. Never was I so tasked; matter grows upon my hands; to condense it sufficiently is an immense difficulty. The book will certainly disappoint you when finished, in this respect if in no other. I have been obliged, in order to keep within compass and preserve the character of court memoirs, to say little or nothing of the Puritans after the beginning of the war. When the King quits his capital, so do I, and thenceforth he and his courtiers make my sole theme. I have still full three months' work to do; but I am pretty well, and work with pleasure.

What I wrote you of Miss Martineau and of the Rajah's book, I cannot now remember; but I have full confidence in your discretion, and shall be but too happy if anything I write you is capable of being made useful. Miss Martineau has been engaged by the Chancellor to write, from materials in the possession of government, a series of tales illustrative of the working of the poor-laws. She says the documents are rich in pathetic interest. I believe she is doing much good. Joanna Baillie has written some very affectionate lines on Scott, which she will send you. I know not why she should have taken this opportunity to strike at Byron. No need of crying down one poet in order to cry up another; nor will all the just censures of Byron's morality sink him in his poetical capacity, in which he will still be judged to soar far above the height of Scott, whom my father used to call the chief only of ballad poets. His stories in verse are now almost forgotten in his prose narratives, but I think undeservedly. It is true, indeed, that it is only in his novels that he displays that power of humorous delineation of character which was one of his greatest gifts.

Farewell, my valued friend! May health attend you, but may you seek it here!

L. AIKIN.

To Miss Aikin.

New York, May 30, 1833.

My dear Miss Aikin,—I received your letter of February at Philadelphia, where I have spent a good part of the spring. As soon as the cold relented so that I could travel, I left Boston, to escape what is more pernicious to invalids than the winter's cold—I mean the east wind which prevails during the spring, and brings with it, I suppose, from the banks of Newfoundland, a piercing quality peculiar to itself. Something like it, I have been told, is felt in Scotland; but you never feel it in England. You would think, were you exposed to it, that the particles of the atmosphere were specially sharpened for the season. What particularly strikes one is, that whilst the wind seems to pierce beneath the skin, and makes one shrink into the narrowest compass, nature is often singularly beautiful, the atmosphere never more brilliant, the clouds never more dazzling. I was once describing our east wind to a gentleman, who replied that according to my account it resembled "a beautiful shrew." I dreaded the shrewish disposition more than

I loved the beauty, and took refuge in Philadelphia, one of our most agreeable cities, which was founded, as you know, by Penn, and still retains something of a quakerish quiet amidst great opulence. The spring was uncommonly mild, and I gradually regained strength, so that I now consider myself in usual health. I have not, however, made trial of my strength, and am forbidden by my physicians to labour, and, on the whole, I am inclined to give myself the chance of longer rest. I thank you for your very, very kind invitation to England; you have learned the tone to draw me there. I can resist anything more easily than the urgency of sincere friendship. If I could satisfy myself that by crossing the ocean I should enjoy more advantages for regaining health, I should not hesitate a moment. But I have little to encourage me. I have tried all means with no permanent effect, and must wait for a new frame, a higher life, to give me the joyous consciousness of unfettered vigour. My burden I expect to bear, and yet the word *burden* is not the true one. When I make no exertion, I am able to enjoy much, perhaps more than most; and could I get rid of the feeling that a great work is to be done towards which I might contribute something, my lot would seem to be among the happiest. Excuse my egotism. Your interest in my health draws me into the weakness of an invalid. We will let the subject drop. I rejoice to hear that the rod is less used in your schools. It encourages one to hope that "other venerable remains of the olden time" are to yield to the "rash spirit of Reform." It seems from your letter that you are beginning to learn that reform means revolution. I hope it will not be the less welcome for its new name. I must rejoice in it, for I am sure that it is part of a noble movement, though I confess, I rejoice with trembling. The tendency of things is to a thorough, substantial improvement, a real elevation of the mass of the people, and this supposes that the old distinctions are to give way. To raise the low is to bring down the high. All other revolutions are idle, nominal, compared with this, and this must go on, peacefully I hope, but at any rate surely, inevitably. You write about Ireland. Public opinion here is against your coercive measures. We say, be just before you are severe; at least, let justice keep pace with severity. Redress the wrongs as fast as you punish the crimes of that miserable country. I give you the general feeling; but here, as in other cases, it is easier to blame than to point out a better course. Some good works I covet, but I envy no man the task of tranquillizing Ireland. *Our* civil war is blown over, and we had little reason perhaps to apprehend such an evil. I wish I could say the danger of disunion had ceased. But we have one cause of separation, which you can easily understand. Free states and slave-holding ones differ too much in social condition, feelings, modes of industry, and perhaps interests, to hold together strongly. The South and North (and these are our great distinctions now) do not love each other. Our Southern brethren, far from feeling the dishonourableness of their vocation as taskmasters to slaves, hold us at the North in a degree of contempt. They set up for chivalry, &c., and regard *us*, who are descendants of the Puritans, as heirs to the vices of the Roundheads. That they are altogether false in their judgment I dare not say. Your keen eye might detect among us some traces of the old Puritan. Oh that we could get rid of slavery! Of all our miseries and curses and reproaches, this is the worst. Some favourable changes of opinion seem to be taking place. Perhaps you are to give us emancipation. Set up an African empire in the West Indies, and you will break the chain here. Our people are reading, with all the zest of spite, the Travels of the German Prince in England. They think he balances our account with Hall, Trollope, and that band of worthies. I suspect our country is not the only one willing to put you down. England has made herself not a little odious by her haughtiness. She has been the Pharisee of Europe, given to "justify herself and despise others," and must pay the penalty of this vice. One good will grow out of the contemptuous manner in which England has treated this country. It will give us a real, substantial independence of the mother country. Resentment is doing what a virtuous self-respect ought to have done. One of our great faults is that, with all our vanity and loud boasting, we have been, and still are, prone to a servile imitation of Europe, especially England; and few things, I believe, have obstructed more the elevating tendency of our free institutions. Now the rude and abusive style in which your travellers have treated us is curing this folly. Captain Hall, especially, has done us good. The people here were weak enough to treat him as a great man, and his book, I think, will keep them from repeating the error. I grieve indeed that we are to learn independence through our bad passions, and for this, as well as other reasons, I am not very proud of my country; but in the present low condition of the race, we must be willing that nations and individuals should make progress, even by methods we disapprove. I think that in my last letter I spoke of Bryant as more immersed in politics than he really is. I learn that he is true to his first love, literature. I can add but a line about Miss Martineau. I have no great faith in some of her doctrines, but I delight in her stories. The Garveloch Tales are particularly good. What a noble creature Ella is! To give us in a fishing-woman an example of magnanimity and the most touching affection, and still keep her in her sphere; to make all the manifestations of this glorious virtue appropriate to her condition and consistent with our nature,—this seems to me to indicate a very high order of mind, and to place Miss Martineau among the first moral teachers as well as first writers of our time. Perhaps I may be partial. I feel so grateful to her for doing such justice to the poor and to human nature, that I am strongly tempted to raise her to the highest rank. I shall return in a few days to my home, where I hope soon to hear from you.

Very sincerely and affectionately, your friend,

WM. E. CHANNING.

To Dr. Channing.

Adelphi, June 13, 1833.

My dear Friend,—Congratulate me! Yesterday I corrected the last sheet of "King Charles." My long and arduous task is ended; my time is now my own, and the first use I make of it is, as it ought to be, to return you my thanks for your excellent volume, so long unacknowledged, and to resume the thread of our correspondence. You would take for granted that some of your discourses would be less to my mind than others, and so it is; but how can I sufficiently thank you for the profit and delight of those which give an echo to my deepest convictions, my loftiest feelings,—those which work out for me problems of the highest interest, on which my mind has often tasked itself in vain! The two sermons on Self-denial, and that on the Immortality of Man, are to me inestimable; nor is there one in the volume in which I do not find much to admire, to agree with, and to profit by. I think I perceive in this volume, as compared with your former writings, traces of recent and profound study in the science of metaphysics. I have been exceedingly struck by the newness as well as the cogency of some of your reasonings, particularly those in page 238. As usual, I feel how long it must be before I can make myself entire mistress of the bearings of writings which contain so much food for thought, which seem to me new at every fresh perusal; and one of the pleasures of my leisure will be to go through them again, pencil in hand, marking my favourite passages. You are full of *maxims;* I have often wished to collect them by themselves as hints for meditation.

As soon as my book is out, which will be, I suppose, in a week, I shall consign to Mr. Vaughan's care a copy for you. It is of no use telling you all my fears and misgivings about it; you will judge for yourself, and freely communicate to me your remarks. The times are undoubtedly favourable for uttering the facts which I have been most anxious to put in a clear light; and it is not nearly so much the fear of any criticism, as the sense of having after all done very imperfect justice to my subject —partly from the necessity of omitting a great number of matters which would have swelled the book inconveniently—that now troubles me. I am going to dissipate for a week in London, and that holiday I expect to enjoy; but domestic solitude and the habit of labour will soon be impelling me to seek a fresh pursuit, and my great care at present is to choose well and choose speedily. I certainly shall not go on to give the world a nearer view of the abominable court of Charles II., and this is all that I am certain of as yet. In other respects, "the world is all before me." I suppose that by the time this reaches you, Mr. Roscoe's Life will be on your table. I am just beginning to devour it; to you it cannot have all the same sources of interest it has to me; but I shall be much disappointed if you do not find it one of the most delightful of biographies and collections of letters. Per-

haps you will find in it a proof of what I have failed to
persuade you of, that in this country the spirit of aristocracy opposes no obstacle to the progress of real talent.
Mr. Roscoe was a splendid example of *rising from the
ranks.* I think I have never mentioned to you James
Montgomery, the poet; but you probably know some at
least of his poems, which would interest you from the
fancy and the feeling which animate them, and from
their deeply devotional spirit. He is a great master too,
as I think, in the art of versification. I wish I could
detail to you the particulars of his early life as he beautifully related them in letters to my father, whom he had
not then seen. It is enough, however, to tell you here,
that he was the son of a Moravian missionary, brought
up in one of their seminaries, and that he had never seen
an English verse, excepting their hymns, till he was
about fourteen; when one of the masters walking in the
fields with a few of his pupils, made them seat themselves on the grass, and drew from his pocket Blair's
" Grave," which he read them. " I seemed," said Montgomery, " to have found a language for sentiments born
with me, but born dumb." And from this time he became a writer of poetry. He quitted the Moravians for
the Wesleyan Methodists; has suffered at times from
religious melancholy, only less, I believe, than Cowper;
but of late years his mind seems to be tranquillized, in
part perhaps by the active exertions in which he has
engaged in behalf of missions, Bible societies, and other
religious objects. He retired from his business of a
printer some years ago, on a competence, and, what
seems to me very remarkable, has erected himself into a
critic. He has given lectures on Poetry at the Royal Institution, which were much admired, and lately he sent
me a copy of a publication of which they form the larger
and better part. I wish you could see it; there are

portions, especially some remarks on the themes of poetry and on its uses, which I know you would be pleased with. I am far from saying that I do not feel in the work the defective education of the writer in classical learning, and the prejudices rooted in his mind by the systematic fanaticism of the sect which brought him up; but still it is the work of an original and very interesting character, and the purity and tenderness of his mind and heart everywhere shine through. This fragment of a letter has travelled with me to London, and I can now tell you of some of my amusements. I dined yesterday in the company of Mr. Malthus and Miss Martineau, who are great friends and allies. Perhaps you may, and perhaps you may not, have taken the trouble to read the *pro* and *con* articles respecting Miss M. in the "Quarterly" and "Edinburgh" Reviews, of which the first is full of malice, and the second, I think, very empty of sound critical matter. She pursues her course steadily, and I hear much praise of her new tale on the Poor Laws, which I have not yet read; I fear, however, that it is the character of her mind to adopt extreme opinions on most subjects, and without much examination. She has now had a full season of London *lionizing*, and it is no small praise to say that, as far as we can judge, it has done her nothing but good. She loves her neighbours the better for their good opinion of her, and I believe thinks the more humbly of herself for what she has seen of other persons of talent and merit.

My bookseller tells me that the editor of the "Edinburgh Review" proposes now to give an article on my six volumes of Memoirs together. This annoys me not a little, and I will beg it off if I can. I have prospered pretty well under the silence of the critics, and it pleased me to have no thanks to give them. Also, I suspect I should fall into the hands of the same dull and tasteless critic, or rather gossip, who reviewed Miss Martineau; in whose prolix articles I have often stuck fast, and from whose remarks I should expect little benefit. It is likewise to be considered, that if praised in the "Edinburgh," I should certainly be abused in the "Quarterly."

Do you mark the course which our absurd Conservatives are taking? Nothing could be more fortunate for ministers or more dangerous to themselves than the vote which they carried in the House of Lords. I hear the Duke of Wellington is so violent that he would gladly push the difference between the two Houses even to civil war. What madness! Does he not perceive it would be the peers on one side and the nation on the other? And as for the bishops—No; words cannot do justice to their infatuation. Have you made this reflection on our triple legislature—that the King can free himself from an intractable House of Commons by a dissolution, that a House of Commons can compel a King to change his counsels by refusing the supplies, but that neither King nor Commons, nor both united, possess any regular or obvious means of controlling the Lords; consequently, that if they oppose the general will with obstinacy, they expose themselves to imminent danger of seeing their privileges curtailed or perhaps abolished. The bishops' votes especially hang by a thread.

How I long to know whether you are proposing to cross the sea to us! I cannot help thinking it would answer to you in every way. It is really a new world since you saw England. The progress in many ways has been of unexampled rapidity. You would find London embellished beyond expression. I ramble amongst the new buildings with unceasing admiration, striving in vain to rec .l the old state of some of the best known streets. We may now boast in the British

Museum of a collection to which the world has nothing comparable, and the suite of rooms lately added is worthy of its destination. What adds a moral interest to this assemblage of the treasures of nature and art is the splendid testimony it affords to the public spirit of Englishmen. The gifts of individuals to their country preserved here are almost of inestimable value, even in a commercial view. In France, on the contrary, their museums have been entirely furnished by the purchases or the plunder of the government. Not even ostentation there moves private persons to make presents to the public. There is another pleasing circumstance. A few years since, access to the Museum was so difficult that it was scarcely visited by twenty persons in a day; now, in compliance with the spirit of the age, it is thrown open to all, and Brougham's "Penny Magazine" has so familiarized all readers with the collection, that you see the rooms thronged by thousands, many from the humblest walks of life. I observed common soldiers and "smirched artizans," all quiet, orderly, attentive, and apparently surveying the objects with intelligent curiosity. Depend upon it, there never was a time in which true civilization was making such strides amongst us. You said very justly some time ago, that we were only in the beginning of a revolution; the spirit of Reform has gone forth, conquering and to conquer; every day it extends its way into new provinces; but it is, it will continue to be, a peaceful sway, a bloodless conquest. The strongholds of abuse yield, one after another, upon summons. Wellington himself will not be able to bring his "order" into conflict with the majesty of the people. I never looked with so much complacency on the state of my country. I believe her destined to a progress in all that constitutes true glory, which we of this age can but dimly figure to ourselves in the blue distance. The bulk of our people are at length well cured of the long and obstinate delusion respecting the wisdom of our ancestors, which so powerfully served the purposes of the interested opposers of improvement. Novelties are now tried upon their merits; perhaps even there is some partiality in their favour. Pray, pray come and judge of us with your own eyes!

Believe me, ever yours most truly,

L. AIKIN.

To Miss Aikin.

Boston, August 30, 1833.

My dear Miss Aikin,—I was truly gratified by receiving your letter of June, in which you ask me to congratulate you on the completion of your Charles. I do rejoice with you, for I believe you have finished one good work to begin another with new interest and new power of usefulness. My expectations from your History are not at all diminished by your dissatisfaction with it. When an author is satisfied with his book, nobody else will be. We have an artist among us who is said to find nothing in his paintings to correct, and the public find as little to admire. I can comprehend the jealousy of authors, but not their vanity. You see I expect the more from you for your humility. I have perhaps some interest in making this a test of merit, for it seems to me that the more I write, the less I am disposed to boast of my labours. I thank you for the kind things you have said of my late volume. When I began to print it, I expected to be able to make it more worthy of public attention; but I was obliged to give the discourses very much as they were preached, and not one of them had been written with care. I had thought much of the subjects; but the thoughts were generally thrown on the paper very rapidly. For the last year and a half I have done nothing to be named, and, though I am gradually rising in strength, I dare not hope that I can very soon return to labour. I have on my table two masses of materials which I have been accumulating for some time, but the intervals between writing are so long, that when I return to my task I forget where I stopped. Still my heart does not fail me. I live in hope of doing something before I die; and if this happiness be denied me, I shall find comfort in seeing what others do for mankind, and shall rejoice that this brief life is not the whole period of useful exertion.

I am reading Mr. Roscoe's Life with great pleasure. I am sorry that it was not more condensed, because I wish it extensively read, and I fear some may be discouraged by the size. Mr. R.'s admirable character interests me not only for its own sake, but as one of " the signs of our times." Do you think in any former age such a character could have been developed, that such a philanthropy, so comprehensive, so hopeful, espousing so many human interests, pursuing at once the advancement of civil and religious liberty, the diffusion of knowledge, the emancipation of the slave, the reformation of criminal law, the suppression of every abuse and form of tyranny, could have found excitement and a sphere of action? He belongs to a new era. In reading his life, I feel that the old want of faith in human nature is giving way, that the bounds of the old and narrow patriotism are broken down, that more is felt and more to be done for mankind than was dreamed of even a few years ago. I take pleasure in Mr. R.'s celebrity, for he did not command, compel it by singular intellectual superiority. His fidelity to the principles of justice and Christian love availed him more than genius. I almost envy him the happiness of his last years, when he witnessed the triumph of the great principles for which he had toiled, over obstacles which at first seemed insuperable. He did not live long enough to witness one triumph, which makes me envy your country as much as it puts me to shame for my own: I refer to the late Parliamentary resolution for the abolition of Slavery. England is winning another immortal crown, whilst America, free America, is sinking under the infinite disgrace of holding millions of human beings in bondage. I almost wish I were one of you when I bring this contrast to my mind. Glorious England! Yes, glorious in spite of the degradation of her lower classes, and of the corruption of the higher! I care nothing for your commerce and military greatness. That I do not envy you; and I smile with something like derision when I hear your writers pitying our new country for wanting the historical associations which haunt every spot of your land. What I mourn is, that we are suffering you to outstrip us in the spirit of humanity, and in efforts for human freedom and happiness. We have, it is true, a Colonization Society, which I hope is to do good in Africa; but if it does not make the condition of the black population which remain with us more sad and hopeless, I shall rejoice. I have my fears that the first effects of emancipation in your colonies may discredit the cause here. With the present feelings of the masters, I fear that relations of hostility will take place between them and their former slaves, which may spread much misery. Still, emancipation is right. The chains would never have been broken had you waited for masters to give freedom with a good grace. Emancipation so near us must do good, sooner or later, to this country. I hope, then, though I wish my hopes rested more on the moral principles of my country.

I have read no very important book from your country

of late. Sismondi sent me an interesting one—"The Prisons of Silvio Pellico." Have you read it? It is a beautiful manifestation of the power of high principles and of the benevolent affections. He relates his sufferings and wrongs with a mild, forgiving spirit, which calls forth, perhaps, deeper indignation against arbitrary governments than a vehement eloquence would have done. How I burned to pluck from the oppressor his abused power!

I have been much interested, too, in Mrs. Jameson's "Characteristics of Women," a work full of beauty, grace and feeling. I have not dared to recommend it, for the moral lies too deep for most readers. Most readers would gather from it that woman has no higher vocation than *to love;* that absorption in this passion, at the expense and sacrifice of every other sentiment and every duty, is innocent; and that she whose hope is blasted in this has nothing to live for, perhaps nothing to do but to die, like Juliet, by her own hand. I do not mean that these lessons are taught, but that such impression would be received by not a few readers from several parts. Mrs. J. discovers in her introduction so just an appreciation of woman, that I wonder a loftier, healthier tone does not decidedly characterize her book. Perhaps I am hypercritical, for in some of her characters she pays just homage to virtue and to the high destiny of her sex; and I feel almost ungrateful in finding fault with a lady who has delighted me so much by her fine perception of character, her richness of illustration, and felicities of style. I rejoice in your good hopes of your country.

Have you received a letter I sent you about the end of spring or the beginning of summer?

I remain, your sincere friend,
WM. E. CHANNING.

To Dr. Channing.

Hampstead, October 23, 1833.

My dear Friend,—Just as I had embarked in one of my pamphlet-letters to you, comes yours of August 30th; and it makes me begin afresh, that I may first notice its contents. I am glad you have been reading the Life of Roscoe, and feeling so much with me respecting it;— *how* much, you may learn if you please from the forthcoming number of the "Edinburgh Review," where I obtained leave to be the critic. But this pray keep quite to yourself; I never before wrote an article for any review but the "Annual," and should be very sorry to be known in this, as it might cause me to be suspected of what I never wrote.

You ask if I received a letter from you last spring or summer. I not only received one of May 30th, but wrote an answer, which I think you ought to have received before the one to which your last is a reply; I sent it as usual through Dr. Boott, and fear it may have been lost, perhaps delayed only. No, on recollection, I believe that letter of mine accompanied my book, which I hope you have by this time. Since that I have had your line by Dr. Tuckerman. I was in Kent when he called here, and therefore only saw him last week; but I am exceedingly struck and delighted with him, and impatient to hear him speak more of his noble exertions and designs. On Thursday next I hope he and Mr. Phillips will meet over my breakfast-table my friend Mr. Le Breton and dear Joanna Baillie. You will be with us in spirit, for many associations will bring you to the minds of all of us. When I have the privilege to be present at a meeting like this, of the gifted and the excellent from the far ends of the earth, it seems to me a foretaste of the happiness reserved for the world of spirits. Alas for one who gave me this feeling beyond all others—the admirable Rammohun Roy! He has been frustrated of one of his cherished hopes, that of seeing you face to face, either in this or the other hemisphere—but you were no strangers to each other. Scarcely any description can do justice to his admirable qualities, and the charms of his society, his extended knowledge, his comprehension of mind, his universal philanthropy, his tender humanity, his genuine dignity mixed with perfect courtesy, and the most touching humility. His memory I shall cherish with affectionate reverence on many accounts; but the character in which I best love to contemplate him is that of the friend and champion of woman. It is impossible to forget his righteous zeal against polygamy, his warm approval of the freedom allowed to women in Europe, his joy and pious gratitude for the abolition of *suttee*. Considering the prejudices of birth and education with which he had to contend, his constant advocacy of the rights and interests of the weaker sex seems to me the very strongest proof of his moral and intellectual greatness.

You are very kind in what you say of your expectations from my late work and my future exertions in literature, and this encourages me to talk to you a little of myself and my affairs. I am very well satisfied with what is said of my "Charles." All whose opinions I have heard seem to think I have been diligent and impartial, and they praise my style for its clearness and simplicity, my remarks for justness, and particularly for their moral tone. This is the kind of commendation which I most desired, and if I could find out in what walk of literature I should be most likely to earn more of it, that walk would be my choice. But I am still quite undetermined on this head. In fact, I have had as yet little leisure for reflecting upon it, as I can show. Early in August, having printed my second edition and seen my niece married, I set out for Sandgate, a very agreeable watering-place near Dover, where I should have enjoyed my leisure much had I found my strength equal to the fatigue of the little journey, and of the walking and riding necessary to explore the country. But I came back ill, and had scarcely done nursing myself when I was called upon to assist my poor niece in nursing her young bridegroom, who was three weeks confined in my house with a fever. I had the satisfaction, however, of sending him home well recovered, and next week I am myself proceeding for London, to take up my abode for three months with my brother Charles and his family. I go prepared to see and hear all I can, and thence to judge how I may best and most acceptably employ my pen. I sometimes think that a volume of essays might be useful, addressed to my own sex, and chiefly intended to point out the particular vocation of women in these times of change and improvement. I am of opinion that few of them have yet raised their minds to the "height of this great argument," and that there is no small danger of their becoming despicable in the eyes of high-souled men by an anti-popular spirit, and a determined preference of trifles and triflers to everything truly great and elevated. I am far from wishing to play the censor, or to lay down the law; a few suggestions modestly thrown out and temperately discussed would suffice for what I mean. Bulwer Lytton, in his "England and the English," a book which is making some noise here, falls violently upon the Englishwomen for their spirit of aristocracy, which, indeed, he considers as the prevailing spirit of the whole people; and I know you have the same idea. I want to go to the bottom of this matter, to consider what is, strictly speaking, a spirit of aristocracy—its causes, effects, remedies. One thing is plain, that in any country where, as in the old monarchies of our continent, noble birth should be the only passport to power, distinction and command, the spirit of aristocracy could never be that of the nation, but only of the privileged class which profits by it. If, therefore, it pervades all classes in England, it must be because no one is excluded by birth from the hope of becoming in some mode or other a member of that large and loosely-defined upper class which is supposed to comprehend all the meritorious and all the fortunate. Aristocracy in old France, in Venice, and in England, at the present day, are three things so distinct, that they ought not to bear the same name. Bulwer reproaches us ladies at our horror at associating with tradesmen, a horror which causes all young men who can possibly find the means to crowd into the professions, which are greatly overstocked. To this, perhaps, the ladies might be content to answer, that tradesmen, shopkeepers that is, are equally excluded from fashionable clubs and other resorts of gentlemen, that in truth their education and manners seldom entitle them to admission into either refined or literary society, and that individuals who deserve to be made exceptions to the rule usually are so. If ladies were equally guiltless of his other charges against them—that of flattering the follies and vices of the high-born and wealthy young men—it would be well. But the disgraceful practice of fortune-hunting, much more prevalent now among women than it ever was amongst men, renders this kind of vicious assentation very frequent, especially in the highest circles, and it deserves to be severely rebuked. There is great encouragement at present for all attempts at raising the moral tone amongst us. It fills me with joy and gratitude to contemplate the many reforms now proceeding with a reference to this end. The abomination of slavery put away from our people; poor factory children taken under the protection of humane laws; Church abuses effectually checked, and tithe compounded for; the criminal law amended; the poor-laws revised; election bribery severely repressed, and the boundless corruption and jobbing of close corporations cut up by the roots. Carry all these great measures from their causes into their evident and unavoidable results, and say if ever there was in the history of mankind a revolution so morally great and glorious! But I need not boast—you generously rejoice and triumph with us, and I on my part sincerely hope that your country will not long suffer us to put her to shame with the word Slavery. All fears for the working of emancipation in the colonies seem to have died away. I value commercial greatness as little, on the whole, as you can do, but yet I do rejoice in the present prosperity of our manufactories, because the full employment of the poor in most parts of the country will signally facilitate the meditated retrenchments of the relief granted at present by parishes to those who ought to live on the wages of their labour. To *dispaŭperize* the working classes must be the first step towards raising them from their degradation. After that, there will be a fair field for the efforts of Dr. Tuckerman and his missionaries; at present they would have to struggle against a system of premiums for improvidence and self-indulgence, such as no other nation ever had the absurdity to institute. Miss Martineau is doing good service in crying it down.

It rejoices me to find you so full of cheering hopes respecting your own health and capacity for further usefulness. In these cases we *can* very often when or because we feel strongly the wish and the hope, and I reckon upon seeing the two heaps of materials converted within a reasonable time into so many volumes. You have great influence here, and I cannot help wishing that you would take some occasion to explain to us the advantages of the perfect equality in which all religious sects are placed amongst you. With us, people are just beginning to perceive the injustice of assessing Dissenters to the Church-rates; this once admitted, long consequences may be deduced. I think our universities cannot long continue to require from laymen subscription to the Church Articles, since the sacramental test is in all cases abolished, and even Jews are now admissible to every civil office. Mrs. Jameson's book I have not seen, and scarcely heard of. "Silvio Pellico" has been much read and praised, but I have not yet found time to read it. I think you would be interested in the Life of that great preacher Robert Hall. There is something affecting in the evident struggle which his powerful mind and benevolent heart maintained for many years against the horrors and absurdities of the Calvinistic faith in which he had been educated, and into which he finally almost relapsed. He was also an illustrious example of the mind rising superior to dreadful bodily sufferings.

An intelligent friend of mine, lately from Paris, said to me of the Parisians, "They are the most irreligious people of the world, but yet they have five or six new religions which they have invented." She also said, "Morals are so very bad there, that I think they can grow no worse, or rather, that they are beginning to mend." She mentioned as a particular source of corruption the manner in which young girls of the higher class are married. A father says to his daughter, "You are to be married to-morrow." He names the gentleman, and it is one whom she has never seen. Yet she always submits without resistance or repugnance, regarding matrimony, like presentation at court, simply as the customary and indispensable preliminary to coming out in the world and being somebody. Young girls are never seen in company except at balls. The conversation in mixed society is unfit for them to listen to. Single women have there *no existence.* A great proportion of the marriages are brought about by paid brokers. Can you picture to yourself any state of things so utterly degrading to woman? It is remarkable that the French have no writers of any note at present, except in the sciences.

I have kept my letter open till I could tell you of the visit of your two friends. It was to me a most agreeable one. I was much pleased with the intelligence of Mr. Phillips, and the excellent information which he gave us in answer to our many questions respecting your country. Much of our conversation related to the state of religion and the arrangements for the conduct of religious worship amongst you, and I told them both that Americans could do nothing so useful to us as to publish these particulars in refutation of the prevailing notion here that religion could not be supported without an Establishment. Dr. Tuckerman is immersed in the study of our poor-laws; very few of us, I suspect, know so much about them. I am struck with his eloquence, and should like much to witness its effects on his poor hearers. Such self-devotion must command admiration and reverence from the most depraved. I held up to him your letter in triumph. "Let me look at his hand," he cried, and he took it and kissed it repeatedly. What a perfect friendship is yours! Long may you live to enjoy it! Nay, death will not end it!

Ever yours with true regard,
L. AIKIN.

To Miss Aikin.

Boston, December 28, 1833.

My dear Miss Aikin,—I am sorry to begin a letter with self-reproach, but I do blame myself for having delayed so long to write to you, and in such cases I find some relief to my conscience in acknowledging frankly my deficiency. Your letter of October 23rd, which I received last evening, was most welcome, and I cannot rest until I express my obligations for it, and for your late work, for which I heartily thank you. It has given me great pleasure. It seems to me a decided improvement on your preceding works. The style is more various, vigorous, free, and the narrative seems to me more skilfully woven. As to its impartiality, about which I have been most solicitous, I wish I were a better judge, but my knowledge of your history is not profound enough to make my opinion of much worth. I think, however, that you have been just to Charles, and have brought out his character strongly, though I am inclined to show him more mercy, or to make more allowance for the untoward influences under which he was brought up. It was next to impossible that he should comprehend the new ideas of his age. Indeed, what can a king see in the spirit of liberty, especially on its first waking from long slumber, but a fearful lawless power threatening ruin to the most revered establishments? As to Charles's great vice—deceit—I suppose it was sanctified in his own view by one of the ends for which he thought he was using it; I mean the Church. When the conscience exaggerates one duty, it is very apt to let others slip, and Charles seems to have imagined that he could expiate all his wrong doings by his faithfulness to the hierarchy. He is not the first man who has hoped to balance his bad faith in human concerns by his sound faith in religious ones. It is an instructive fact, that his fraud was not a whit the less ruinous to him on account of its union with his conscientiousness. Your History has given me a stronger impression than I had before of his ability and force of mind. I feel, too, more than I did that his wife was his evil genius. She undoubtedly confirmed him in the dangerous maxim that no faith was to be kept with heretics, and made his propensity to intrigue a desperate disease. I was sorry you could not let us more into the character of the Puritans as a sect, and of their leaders. Let me ask if you have not gathered materials in your historical researches for a volume of interesting essays? You have taken, I doubt not, some new views of public character, and great events, and of the progress of society, and I hope they will not be lost. Do think of this suggestion. I could fill my letter with remarks on your book. I have expressed my pleasure on the style and execution. Now and then, however, I met a word not in sufficient use, perhaps not to be found in the dictionary. Did I not see the word "complicity"? The spirit of your work is a noble one. You have kept throughout your loyalty to the great principles of freedom and virtue. You disturbed a little my opinions and feelings about Falkland. I do not love that such an image should be dimmed; but let truth prevail. You have given me another subject to think and write about, Rammohun Roy. I feel his loss deeply. I cannot name a stranger whom I so wished to see. Do treasure up your recollections of him, and give them to me and the public. I lived in hope that he was to visit this country, and now I can only know him by following him into the common country of all pure and noble spirits. May we all meet there! It seems you wish to make *woman* more worthy of the homage which the Rajah paid her. I like your project much, and I should think such essays as you propose would excite attention. The work, however, is a delicate one. You must make women patriots without turning them into partizans, increase their force without taking from their loveliness, and cultivate the reason without encroaching on the affections. It is an important part of woman's vocation to give refinement, purity, gentleness and grace, to social intercourse; to wear off our rough edges; to rescue us from absorption in grosser interests by awakening in us some taste for beauty. It is a greater work to lay the foundation of the future patriot and Christian; to infuse into the child, whether boy or girl, the spirit of the philanthropist, hero, martyr; to give just and large views of life, and of the true means of promoting human happiness. There is no greater work on earth, and none requiring a more generous culture of all the powers. If you can turn your sex to the high purposes of their being and of their peculiar relations and endowments as women, what a benefactor you will be! You speak of Bulwer's remarks on Englishwomen and their aristocratic tendencies. I doubt not they are true in the main. I have read only the first volume of his work as yet—a remarkable book, especially considering the haste in which it seems to have been thrown off. I felt that a man who could write so good a book ought to have written a better. He is generally superficial, and yet looks so often beneath the surface, that one wishes he had been more just to himself and his subject. His notions of religion are very crude. With all his egotism, he writes like a true friend of the people, of the mass of men. Is he not worthy this highest praise? I delight in your good account of your own country. I am not, however, as sanguine as you are as to the safe working of the late scheme for emancipation in the West Indies. Would the master become the friend of the slaves and heartily co-operate with Government, he could make their transition to freedom easy, safe, and mutually beneficial; but he seems disposed to throw obstructions in the way, and the hostility which may consequently spring up between the two races may be ruinous to both. Perhaps you do not comprehend how hard it is for the master to meet as a freeman, and in some respects as an equal, the man whom he has commanded and treated as a brute. It is as great a revolution as would be the abolition of castes in India. I suspect the love of power is more wounded than the passion for gain. We here have the deepest interest in the success of the plan. Let emancipation succeed in the West Indies, and slavery must fall in our Southern States. Let it fail, and our prospects, which are dark enough, will be next to hopeless. My mind is painfully alive on this subject. I want to write, to act; but I must work alone, for I do not agree with our abolitionists, and I have not health, even if I had ability, for a single warfare. Our union and institutions are threatened by slavery, and we can look up to Heaven with no hope whilst this national guilt, the greatest a people can contract, is not only perpetrated, but more and more accumulated.—I have been lately looking at a biography of Bentham, and his general principles of legislation, by Dumont. The book is from Neale, one of our countrymen, who was secretary to Bentham. The effect of the whole is not to raise Bentham in my estimation as a philosopher, however great may have been his sagacity in detecting abuses in the present system. I mean to look at his larger work on morals and legislation, though, if I may judge from this specimen, he knows little of man's moral nature. Neale pronounces him an atheist. I am glad you have seen my friends, Messrs. Phillips and Tuckerman. The latter gave you a somewhat characteristic proof of his friendship for me. I want to advise him to be more on his good behaviour, for sometimes strangers, seeing his ardour, distrust his judgment, which is sound. He has a noble spirit. I miss him and Mr. P. much, but I hope to enjoy them more for absence.

Your sincere friend,
W. E. CHANNING.

To Dr. Channing.

Hampstead, February 2, 1834.

My dear Friend,—On my return yesterday to my own house, after a sojourn of three months at my brother Charles's in London, I found your kind letter just arrived to welcome me, and I will not resist the impulse to make an immediate return to it. You gratify me much by what you say of my book; I perceive, however, that you think I a little want indulgence to Charles. This makes me regret that I forbore to sum up his character. I shrunk from the task as a difficult, and in some sense a dangerous one; for I should have made for him such allowances on account of education and the influences generally to which his situation exposed him, that the almost unavoidable inference would have been, that all kings must be, more or less, the enemies of liberty, of public virtue, of the happiness and progress of mankind. I have come as near this inference as I well could, by showing that Charles was absolutely suckled in falsehood and dissimulation, and that *as prince* he thought himself as much above the laws of social morality as those of the land; but I believe I ought somewhere to have distinctly stated, that in his most unprincipled acts he was probably never self-condemned, except in the case of Strafford. I plead guilty to *complicity*. I knew that this French word was scarcely naturalized, but it had been used; I had a vague idea that my father thought well of it; and knowing no English word of the same meaning, I ventured. May one not *now and then* do these things with good effect? I am not conscious of any other offences in this way, but it is likely enough that I may unconsciously have picked up odd words from my old authorities. Certainly, in the course of my labours, collateral subjects of remark did now and then occur to me; but I fear I have let them slip away. I do, however, feel some temptation to venture into the essay line, when, perhaps, thoughts might recur on the morals of history. At present, however, I am absolutely, like poor Burns, "unfitted with an aim." One friend suggests to me Memoirs of Caroline, queen of George II.; another would have me go on to Cromwell; another would send me back to Edward III., as a subject out of harm's way, involving neither theology nor politics. "The literary class," said the very sensible advocate of the last scheme, "are almost all for Church and State, and your last subject is one which they do not like. They would not have much inquiry into King Charles." This remark might lead me wide into a dissertation upon our present state of political and religious feeling; but before I enter such a field, I think it prudent to answer some passages of your letter.

I wonder not at your deep feelings on the subject of Slavery. It is worthy of you so to feel, and to devote your powerful pen and all the energies you can command to that great theme. I am quite incompetent to pronounce any opinion of my own on the state of our islands, but that excellent old abolitionist, William Smith, seems to me highly satisfied with the working of the new system hitherto, and Dr. Lushington also. It has been said that the planters begin to judge it conducive to their own interests—a grand security for their exertions to make it answer. It seems that the protection of the black population will be secured, so far as law can secure it, by depending on a reformed magistracy, which, in other respects, is likely to be welcome to the planters. But I know not the particulars.

Excellent Rammohun Roy! I wish I could obtain more particulars of him to offer to you; but, like all remarkable foreigners in this, and I suppose in other countries, he was beset by the enthusiastic, the ignorant, the impertinent, and often the malignant; in his case political and theological passions conspired, and he was misrepresented on all hands. That good man Dr. Carpenter has published an account of him, and I know of no better. It is now known that the title of Rajah, which some suspected him of unwarrantably assuming, was conferred on him regularly by the Great Mogul, or King of Delhi, as he is now called, in the character of his ambassador. He was able in negotiation, and obtained for his master the large sums which he claimed of our Government. In his demeanour there was all the dignity and gracefulness of *high caste*, tempered with not only courtesy and benignity, but with a kind of humility only to be accounted for, as Dr. Boott acutely observed, by recollecting that he belonged to a conquered people, and had been compelled in India to submit to social inferiority. It was impossible, however, to charge him with servility. He sometimes evaded indiscreet questions, but the information which he gave voluntarily was so precise and satisfactory that it was impossible to question its perfect truth. His knowledge of languages was prodigious, and when he spoke of the light cast by an acquaintance with Oriental literature and manners on the sense of Scripture, or when he explained the laws and customs of his country, with the modifications which they had sustained from its Mussulman conquerors, you perceived that he was able to draw from all that he had learned and seen the inferences of a clear, sagacious mind. But perhaps his greatest charm was the atmosphere of moral purity in which he seemed to breathe. To women this was peculiarly striking; he paid them a homage reverential as that of chivalry, without its exaggeration. Absolutely new to their society, as he must have been, an innate sense of propriety revealed to him always the right thing to say and do. Persecution, calumny, injustice, public and private, only strengthened him to endure in a good cause, without either saddening or embittering his spirit. Benignity was the leading characteristic of his countenance and his expressions, his love of liberty was fervent, and nothing which concerned the welfare of his brethren of mankind was indifferent to him. May we indeed meet that pure and noble spirit where only such are admitted!

Bentham I did not know, and I have never heard anything respecting his religious opinions. There is no hint of atheism in his theological works, nearly all of which I have read; these are full of logical and critical acuteness. His dissection of the "Church Catechism" in his "Church-of-Englandism" would amuse you, as well as his sarcasms on "My Lord the Bishops," whose "very footmen are clothed in purple." Mr. Whishaw, I think, characterized him very happily when he called him "a schoolman born some ages too late." He lived latterly in a narrow circle of worshippers, reading nothing and writing incessantly; and probably did not sympathize extensively enough with other men to understand human nature profoundly. Consequently he was rather fitted to supply legislators with principles and suggestions, than to legislate himself. Brougham has very handsomely acknowledged his obligations to him for the idea of many of his reforms, particularly, I think, his legal ones. Romilly, a man of great piety, lived in strict friendship with him. Neale seems to be a slight and rather paltry person, very little qualified to measure the mind of Bentham, and probably only knew him in extreme old age. On such authority it would be unwarrantable to impute to an innocent and certainly a benevolent and public-spirited man, one of the ablest thinkers and the most skilful logician of his age, the brutish absurdity of atheism—a word, as you well know, used by ignorant or prejudiced people often without any definite meaning. The masterly lectures on Jurisprudence published by my friend Mr. Austin, a very zealous promulgator of the utilitarian system founded by Bentham, are firmly based on theism, though they make no reference to Christianity, with which, however, their subject had no concern. I have just been assured, on what I think pretty good authority, that neither is Godwin an atheist.

During my stay in London, it was my great object to learn what *our* world is doing and thinking—and this is what I make out. Literature is low indeed—*swamped*, as our phrase is, by the *tract-makers*, with the Useful Knowledge Society at their head. Bulwer has protested with good reason against the prevalent practice of anonymous writing. We shall at this rate soon have no such character as an author amongst us; the public will account it as idle to inquire who wrote an essay, or even a book, as who set up the types—and one artificer will become as much a mere labourer for wages as the other. But that this state of things cannot well become permanent in a civilized country, it would almost break one's heart. In the meantime, the nullity of literature leaves all the thinkers and all the talkers at leisure for a few great practical subjects which must become the business of Parliament in the coming session. These are Church reform, Poor-law reform and general Education. On the first, some things are decided, as far as ministers are concerned. They will bring forward a commutation of tithe, and probably some new regulations against pluralities and non-residence. They will propose to grant the Dissenters redress of their grievances in respect of marriages, burials and birth-registries, and may perhaps be willing to exempt them from Church-rates. But here is the danger: The orthodox, that is, the Calvinistic Dissenters, or Independents and Baptists, emboldened by their great and growing numbers, and by what they view as the spirit of the times, have plainly declared that they regard the whole connection of a favoured sect with the State as an abuse and an injustice, and that they will never be satisfied till it is totally dissolved. This decision, made in defiance of the prudential remonstrances of the calmer and better-informed Unitarians, is beginning, as it seems, to produce a strong reaction in favour of the Church; to which, with a small exception for Catholics, and another for Unitarians, the whole of the two Houses of Parliament and of the nation, down almost to the shopkeepers and mechanics, is at least nominally attached; and which carries with it also most of the agricultural class, and a good portion of every class. There is danger, therefore, to the most moderate claims of the Dissenters, should the ministers desert their cause; to the ministers themselves, should they remain steady to it; and I dread from the whole affair a fierce renewal of religious dissensions, and of a persecuting spirit directed against all sectaries and free inquirers. It would be most unfortunate should a measure of general education be proposed and carried into effect during such an access of High-churchism, as its character would of course be narrow and exclusive, and the effect would be to fix on the children of Dissenters a universal stigma. It is also certain that nothing would strengthen so much the hands of the Tories as a rally for the Church. Nor would the Poor-law question be uninfluenced by such a crisis. To promote a spirit of independence amongst the labouring classes would not be the aim of triumphant squires and parsons. I am obliged to state all this very crudely, but *verbum sapienti*. You will see, on the whole, that our state is an anxious one. I could wish that the Irish Church question were first to be dealt with. It was Catholic emancipation which repealed the English Test and Corporation Acts. You will not wonder that, with my *historic experience*, I dread beyond everything the mingling of ecclesiastical disputes with questions of civil government, especially as our people are much less advanced in religion than in politics.

Fear nothing for Dr. Tuckerman. He interests us the more for his bursts of sensibility. "He has enthusiasm," said Mr. Le Breton* happily, "but no fanaticism." We all love him, and his suggestions are heard with respect by persons who have both the will and the power to carry them into effect to some extent. He could not have visited us at a better time: the state of the poor has become such, that all agree *something* must be done to amend it, and every one who can speak from experience on the subject is heard with deep attention. There is much benevolent activity amongst us, which only wants and asks to be well guided. We are all struck with his eloquence. "He took me by the button," said Mr. Le Breton, "last time I saw him, and certainly preached a short sermon; but I did not wish it ended." In fact, the oftener he is heard, the less one wishes him to end. Since I finished the last sentence, I have taken

* The Rev. Philip Le Breton.

two ladies to call on him; I never heard him so interesting and eloquent in the illustration of his principles and plans. The ladies were all attention; and one of them, who lives with her brother, a country clergyman, and devotes herself with him and his daughters to the welfare of a village, found much correspondence between their modes of proceeding and his—except that they talk to the people of original sin. I admired the dexterity with which he slid over this difference. He has more tact and sagacity than I ever saw united with such ardour.—You trace a beautiful outline of what essays for women ought to teach. I fear I could not fill it up; but I feel that in these days knowledge of points of debate is necessary, to prevent our quick feelings from making us fierce upon them. Ignorant partizans are always the most violent. Candour, the virtue of the wise, is that in which women are most deficient.

I fear I must at length have quite wearied you; in writing to you I know not where to stop.

I rejoice in the good account you give Dr. Tuckerman of your health.

Believe me ever most sincerely yours,
L. AIKIN.

To MISS AIKIN.

Boston, April, 1834.

My dear Miss Aikin,—It is a long time since I have heard from you, though I hear of you through my friends in England. You are well and cheered by success, and I trust have found a new subject worthy of your powers. Have you never thought of memoirs of the Commonwealth? or are you so much of a royalist that you can only write memoirs of a court? Speaking of history, I am reminded of a fine review of Guizot's Gibbon in the last "Quarterly." With the exception of a thrust at Priestley, its tone was singularly liberal and generous for that periodical. Is it not remarkable that France should furnish the first Christian annotator on Gibbon? It is a good sign. I must hope more from that country than you do. Is Milman equal to the work of furnishing additional notes to Gibbon? I wish the same office could be done for Hume which Guizot has done for Gibbon. What a flood of light has been thrown on your history since Hume's time! and yet the work will always be read. Can no impartial friend of freedom supply an antidote to his errors?

I think when I last wrote you I was reading Bulwer's England. I rose from it with admiration of the various powers and respect for the philanthropy of the author.

One of your gifted countrywomen here lately recommended to me Godolphin (a novel by I know not whom) as giving the best views of your highest classes. Have you read it? is it an authority? It is certainly written with power, and interested me a good deal, which is what I can say of very few fictions, excepting Sir Walter's. The writer makes the stream of aristocratic life shallow and turbulent enough, and so it must be. It is impossible that they whose whole existence is founded on superficial distinction should understand true greatness or happiness. Nothing is more natural than that they should resort to vulgar, i.e. outward, means of cherishing and manifesting that consciousness of superiority which is the very breath of their life. When is this spirit of hollow pretension and exclusiveness to cease? Not till it is met by a just self-respect in other classes of society. The true self-respect would put the spurious to flight at once. Let true dignity be understood, and the false could not hold up its head.

All pretension thrives through some intellectual or moral deficiency in the community. The book says something, though not as much as I expected, of that exclusive spirit which, as I learn, has penetrated the ranks of aristocracy itself, which sets up *fashion* against birth and titles, and which pronounces some of the highest nobility, and even Majesty itself, "en mauvais ton"—that, I believe, is the phrase. When I hear of the delicate tact of these fashionables, which detects the minutest particles of vulgarity, and the almost imperceptible lines of high-breeding, I wish that a kindred power might be brought to bear on morals. How little we understand yet the refinements of virtue! The assailants of aristocracy, such as our author, little understand that their principles, fairly carried out, would bring on a revolution in society far deeper than changes of constitution or dynasties, and such as they would not relish much. No matter. They are ministering unconsciously to the purposes of a higher Wisdom and Benevolence than their own. I wish you could name to me some good novel or light work. Sometimes I want easy reading, but find it hard to satisfy myself. Books which do not set me to thinking are generally dull.

We hear good accounts of England, though I do not see much prospect of relief and improvement to your uneducated and depressed millions. I cannot forget these, and they darken your country, and make me almost shudder at your luxury and prosperity. What a tremendous price you pay for what is called your civilization! Were your higher ranks virtuous, I could be more reconciled to the ignorance, vice and misery of the lower; but the eye finds little relief in passing from the squalidness of the pauper class to the pomp and glitter of the rich and noble. Of my own country I have not much to boast. The warfare of our headstrong, arbitrary

President with our National Bank has turned our prosperity into commercial distress. Selfish partizans are at work on both sides, and new combinations of parties are formed, bringing together those who a year ago could say nothing too hard of one another. All this would do well in an old corrupt monarchy, but does not suit the paradise of a young republic. Could I see any moral elevation growing out of our pecuniary losses, I should welcome them; but not a knee the less bows to gold. I am not disheartened, however. It is hoped that the usurpation of the President will be put down, and that he will be the means or occasion of introducing important improvements into our Banking system, which, without a check, might have produced wide mischief.

I hope to hear from you soon.

Very sincerely your friend,
Wm. E. Channing.

To Miss Aikin.

Boston, May 5, 1834.

My dear Miss Aikin,—Thanks for your letter of February 2nd. You need not fear wearying me. Your long full sheets are most welcome. You amuse me with the advice given you as to the next subject you are to write on. I protest against your going back to Edward III. Write what will bear on the present. Always keep in sight the highest principles at which your mind has arrived, and on which the best interests and progress of your race seem to depend, and choose topics which will give you means of confirming and diffusing them. If I understand you, a noble aim will do more than anything to bring out the whole force of your intellect. You must not think that I would confine you to the didactic.

There are a thousand forms of manifesting great principles, and I have no disposition to prescribe a form to another mind. Your letter gave me a more discouraging view of the state of opinion and feeling than your former ones. You plainly think that Church reform is not making much way. I fear so, and I will assign some causes which, coming from a distance, may interest you, and about which I wish your opinion. First, I fear too many of your advocates of Church reform are mere politicians, worldly reformers, who cast a wistful eye on the revenues of the Establishment, and are willing to disturb old titles; and in this way the cause of the Church has become identified with the cause of Property, the chief idol of a commercial people. Next, the Church is really reformed to a degree. Its ministry was never so respectable, faithful, useful, and it is willing to part with many abuses which are not necessary to its strength. Again, Dissent, by growing milder in its doctrines, by parting with the old Calvinistic, Puritanical rigour, has approached the Church, so that none need become schismatic for the sake of a "purer faith," especially since the Evangelical party has grown up in the Establishment. Again, I suppose that your late political changes have brought many of the natural friends of the Church into Parliament on the side of your Whig ministry. But the great cause remains to be named. You have not the *spirit* of religious reform, of better religious institutions, among you. Here is the root of the evil. Your people have no passion for truth, no enthusiasm about high principles. There is no brighter light breaking in among you, producing restlessness, discontent, and a desire of something better than you have. Perhaps England was never more destitute than at this moment of a thirst for the higher order of truths. You have a low, earthly, material, utilitarian philosophy. You have no intellectual and moral philosophy. Your religious system is a relic of former times, retained from the absence of sufficient spiritual activity to change it, and held with little intimate conviction, so that it secretly favours the scepticism which it talks against loudly. Your moral system is—I know not what. It would be comforting to see any great principle fought for to the death. Even German mysticism is to be preferred to this absence of spiritual life. There is much intellectual action among you, but spent on the surface and tangible realities of life. Such a country is the very spot for an Establishment remarkable for decorum, order, show without gaudiness, and a grave magnificence, which neither tasks the intellect nor tortures the conscience, which knows how to make a compromise with the pomp and vanities of the higher classes, and yet inculcates, in word at least, the precepts of Christianity. This is strong language, and I have thrown it off very much as earnest people talk, who venture on hyperbole to make a truth palpable, and neglect to modify, in their zeal to make an impression. You must not take me to the letter. I wish to give you my general view of the English mind. What you say of the strength of Toryism goes to prove that I am right in the main, for Toryism is essentially blindness to spiritual truth. It never penetrates beneath the exterior of human nature, birth, rank, wealth and manners, to the divine principles in the soul. Now you have the character of being all Tories at heart, and how can you expect a real religious reform, or any great improvement in religious institutions? I began with telling you that my reasons for the strong tendencies to Church-of-Englandism which you speak of, might interest you as coming from a *distance*. On this account I distrust them. It is hard for a stranger to know the true state of another country. Do set me right. After talking so freely of your country, I incline to take some liberties with my own, and this I do because we are told that Miss Martineau intends us the honour of a visit. I am truly glad, and shall give her a hearty welcome; but I do fear she will be disappointed here, and will receive less pleasure than she will give. Almost all your travellers have carried away from us unfavourable impressions. *We* ascribe it to national prejudice; but there must be a broader cause; and this is to be found in our state of society, which has features not very inviting to a foreigner. We have one unlucky trait for our visitors. We are a *reserved* people, rather cold in manner, and wanting in expressions of sympathy. I ascribe this in part to our Puritan descent. Our fathers came over, you know, to establish *their church*, and they lived together in the character of church members, who were to keep what they called "a godly watch" over each other. Accordingly, every man was under surveillance, and one consequence was the suppression of all feelings which did not suit the sanctity of the age. Society was frozen by a jealous caution; and, notwithstanding great changes, this sin of the fathers, I fear, is visited in a measure even on the present generation. Another cause of our reserve may be found in our political institutions. This will surprise you; but you know everything is worshipped, and here *the people* is king. A man, to rise, must get the favour of the people—thence a great deference to popular opinion when once pronounced, and much wariness against giving offence. Another cause is the early period of life in which the young are thrown on themselves, cast on the world. A young man begins to support himself, becomes a man of business, sooner here than elsewhere, a circumstance very favourable to morals; but one consequence is, that the tide of youthful feeling is sooner checked, and habits of caution and calculation sooner begin their war on the enthusiastic principle of our nature. Once more, the necessity under which we are all laid of labour, prevents much cultivation of the art of social communication. *Society* is less an object; graceful and easy conversation less studied; awkwardness and diffidence less resisted. That a stranger should find us more shut up, should think that we want heart, you will not wonder after this detail. Another thing which I find strikes the English when they visit us is the apparent want of *filial* deference. Our children are subjected to fewer outward restraints than yours. We profess to rely more on inward restraints, on the affections, reason and conscience of the child; but in many cases these higher principles are neglected, and the stranger is shocked by domestic insubordination. Another unpleasant feature in our society is the want of good domestics, one result of easier or more honourable means of subsistence. No one in this country thinks of being a servant *for life*, and the demand for labour in other departments of industry is often so great, that in many places a favour is conferred by going into a family in this capacity. Now, to a traveller the annoyance arising from this deficiency in our domestic establishments is often great, and especially to the English, who are so well served at home. You will easily see that a country such as I have described, however distinguished by private virtue, general intelligence, and strong domestic affection, will not show well to a foreigner, unless to one who can get admission into the interior of our social system, which is seldom the case. Miss Martineau will bring with her the repulsion of celebrity as an authoress, an additional difficulty in the way of free communion, which, however, may be done away by genuine affability and self-forgetfulness. But let her come; and let her tell the truth, too, of us. I want that we should know our faults, and, if nothing else will do, be scourged out of them; but there is no need of this severity; there is a spirit of improvement at work among us, and a wise, philanthropic traveller may do us good. To use your own language, I fear I have wearied you.

Your sincere friend,
W. E. CHANNING.

I have had no time to speak of Rammohun Roy. Why cannot Englishwomen combine their efforts to elevate *their sex* in Hindostan? There is a noble and fit object for women. I should rejoice to have an association for this end bearing Rammohun Roy's name. Could a better monument be raised to him? I hope sectarianism would not deny him this honour. If so, the object might still be accomplished. The Hindoos, I believe, are willing to have their women taught by Europeans. Is not this as great an object for philanthropy as abolition of slavery? Perhaps greater. Have you no disposition to labour in the field?

To Dr. Channing.

Hampstead, May 29, 1834.

My dear Friend,—In your welcome letter received about ten days since, you said it was long since you had heard from me; but I think you must very soon after have received a long one from me; at least, I wrote one, and consigned it as usual to Dr. Boott. This is to go by Dr. Tuckerman, whom we are very loth to part with, for we all revere and love him; but there is some satisfaction in his assurances that he also loves us, and will do his utmost to send you to visit us. Mr. Phillips we hope to keep a little longer. He is a general favourite, and perhaps even better liked in society than his friend, whose mind is almost engrossed by one subject. It mortified me to catch only a glimpse of Mr. Dewey; his stay was so short that he was gone before I could find an opportunity to invite him. I heard great praise of his pulpit eloquence from very good judges. Send us more such visitors; they will do much to overcome prejudices on both sides. And now to reply to the questions in your letter.

"Godolphin" I have not read. I understand it was written by a Mr. Sunderland, who is genteelly connected, and was educated at Oxford; but as his extreme youth cannot have allowed him extensive opportunities of observation in any society, it would be unreasonable to put much faith in his view of manners. All novelists run into exaggeration of one kind or other, for the sake of effect. Formerly, they were chiefly reproached with painting "faultless monsters," whose charms and graces threw all living merit into shade, and disgusted young people with the sober realities of life. But this was a splendid sin compared with that of the present fashionable school, who exaggerate nothing but vices and follies, and delight in representing as odious or contemptible those classes who will nevertheless continue to be objects of envy to most of their inferiors. In high, as in low and in middle life, there will always be many who yield to the peculiar temptations of their situation, but many also who resist, and I know no reason whatever for believing that our aristocracy are worse in any respect than in past ages; on the contrary, I know some strong reasons for thinking that in several respects they are better. No one denies that they are much less addicted to drinking, less also to gaming; for men play less, in general society at least, and women scarcely at all. I cannot say whether there is less licentiousness; but you who have read Walpole will not dispute that there is much more decorum, much more of at least outward respect for religion and virtue, and I think it is plain that even hypocrisy must put some restraint on vice. Then it is certain that the circumstances of the times keep the higher classes in a state of extraordinary mental activity; that they feel it necessary to cultivate all their talents, to inform themselves on every question of practical importance, and at the same time to preserve the graceful accomplishments which may serve to conciliate public approbation.

With respect to what you have heard of a class of fashionables who set their own pretensions above those of rank and title, there is something in it; the most fashionable persons in London are so rather by *merit*, if one may so apply the term, than by birth. A certain talent, or tact, is necessary to become an "arbiter elegantiarum;" and although there may be not a little of presumption and conceit amongst the *exclusives*, they have at least the recommendation of daring to show great lords and great ladies that they may be looked down upon in society if they rely too much upon mere rank and pedigree. You cannot without seeing it imagine the charm which waits upon a patroness of Almack's. Perfect good-breeding is a beautiful thing to behold, and no *fine art* deserves to be more studied.

I leave it to Dr. Tuckerman to describe to you the society in which he has lived, which consists chiefly of the higher part of the middle class, and is the same with which I mostly associate. I know he will give you a good account of it, and that he will especially attest the zeal prevalent in this set for the improvement of the character and condition of the poor. *Much* is doing for the ignorant and degraded, and I trust that they will not long be numbered by millions, even in Ireland. Immense things are in agitation regarding the poor and regarding the Church, and both subjects are approached by many, especially the first, in a pretty good spirit. I do not yet wish to see the Establishment overthrown, because at present the fanatics would be able to seize the chief power and oppress all free inquirers; but it will do Mother Church no manner of hurt to be put in mind of her end, and the Dissenters are willing enough to jog her memory on this subject. The worst is, that we must expect an increase of bitterness and animosity as these Dissenters proceed, for when was ever an ecclesiastical question settled in a Christian spirit? And in the meantime, I grieve to see literature *swamped* as it is between politics and theology. You may inquire in vain for light reading. Poetry we have none; and though we have novels not a few, I really know of none which are much praised by people of taste. We can scarcely find new works sufficient to keep our Book Society alive. The dearth is something quite strange, and hardly credible at a time when everybody affirms that there is more reading than ever in the country. I suppose people will be tired of twopenny tracts ere long, and then there will again be a demand for *books*. In France there is an equal stagnation; in Germany alone literature really flourishes, although, or perhaps *because*, literary labour scarcely brings there any pecuniary reward, on account of the impossibility of securing copyright beyond the limits of a single state. The most laborious works, I hear, are composed by professors of universities, as in some measure a part of their duty, or a means of distinction. I wish I could tell you that I am again settled into some substantial work, but I cannot yet fit myself with a subject. Two in English history have engaged my attention; that which you suggest, the Commonwealth, and the two first Georges. But I rather dread the quantity of dry reading, especially of the polemical kind, which the first would require, and in general the *ruggedness* of the theme, on which it would scarcely be practicable to strew flowers. The second also somewhat affrights me by its magnitude, for the materials would be redundant, and it also repels me by the want of great and interesting events; in short, I am not enough pleased with either of these periods to be willing to *live* in it for years. Sometimes I meditate another kind of writing—essays, moral and literary. I seem to myself to have some thoughts which it might be useful or agreeable to put on paper; but here fears and scruples of many kinds assail me. If I were to give the rein freely to my speculations, I know not whither they would lead me—most likely into a kind of Pyrrhonism which would give great offence to this dogmatizing age. I am not here referring to religious topics, on which I should never think of addressing the public; besides that, on these my mind is pretty well settled, though not in opinions which would be approved; but I have in view many points relating to morals and the conduct of life, on which I am much more convinced that error generally prevails, than prepared to pronounce what is truth or reason. I am a little disposed to envy those who can adopt a sect or party, and stick by it with unfaltering allegiance. Such people know at least what to wish for, what to aim at, what to praise or blame, what and whom to love and to hate. With me it is quite the contrary. I remain suspended and neutral amid the unceasing clash of parties and principles which rages around me. I listen to both or to all sides till I can take part with none, and I fold my arms in indolence for want of knowing anything to be done which might not just as well, or better, be let alone. Can you prescribe any remedy for a state like this, which I am disposed to regard as a morbid one, because one sees that if it were to become epidemic, the whole world would go to sleep?

Events press fast upon us. Since I began this letter, a few days only ago, a split of the Cabinet has been announced on the important question of the appropriation of the temporalities of the Irish Church. Mr. Stanley and two more, who insisted on preserving the whole to the Protestant Establishment, go out; and we may consequently expect to see the cause of Church Reform espoused by the government. In this I do unfeignedly rejoice. It gives some reason to hope that a compromise may be effected with the *English* Dissenters also, which will divert them, for a time at least, from seeking the utter overthrow of the Establishment. But much will depend on what cannot well be reckoned on, the prudence and moderation of our Upper House, especially the lords spiritual. There are sinister reports concerning the sanity of our poor well-meaning King. A regency, with a Tory Queen at its head, might prove under present circumstances a dangerous incident. Political unions are said to be spreading over the country, or rather trades' unions, which, on the slightest cause of jealousy given by the government, would immediately become political ones. I should exceedingly dread to see more power fall into the hands of the low and ignorant, the selfish, and, on the whole, not moral classes, of whom these associations are composed; and nothing can preserve us from this peril but a wise, just and liberal, but moderate administration. After all, though I have been murmuring at the *swamping* of literature between religion and politics, I feel that I cannot myself resist the influence of circumstances. We are in a state of revolution, it cannot be denied, and however one may wish to divert one's mind from the present and the directly practical, it will not be; and those who do not pretend to be able to instruct the public on the great questions of Church and State (and I am sure I do not), must be content, as matters stand, to hear, see, and say nothing. I am reading a long and a great work, Sismondi's "History of the Italian Republics." It errs somewhat on the side of minute detail, as might well be expected, considering that the author had occasion to take for his authorities the native historians—those masters of prolixity. But with this abatement, the work is surely a very noble one, full of interesting circumstances and lively, graphic descriptions, both of places from personal knowledge and of characters and incidents. The moral tone is admirable. The author seems to me unerringly faithful to the best interests of mankind, except that he perhaps prizes a little too highly the turbulent liberty of Florence; fertile, however, it must be owned, in great men in every line. I am told that Sismondi's "History of France" is, however, his best work; and if I do not set myself to writing, I think my next task may be to read it. History never tires me.

Pray make Dr. Tuckerman tell you a great deal about all *us*, especially ask him about my friend Mrs. Coltman,* in whom he delights, and then figure to yourself how you will enjoy finding yourself surrounded by such disciples (for all this set are your disciples, and have received your friends in your name).

An unpleasant suspicion comes over me that I have been inditing a vastly dull epistle: pray excuse it, if so it be. There will be better and worse in letters, as in other things: there is a happiness in topics and expressions not to be commanded; and if my letter be good for

* Afterwards Lady Coltman, wife of the late Judge.

nothing else, let it at least serve to assure you of my continued esteem and friendship, and my anxiety to keep up my privilege of communication with you.

Ever most truly yours,
L. AIKIN.

To Dr. Channing.

Hampstead, June 19, 1834.

Mr. Phillips offers me conveyance for a letter to you, and though rather pressed for time, I will begin: at least I may be able to thank you for your last admirable letter, and to convey my sense of its contents. I am very much enlightened as well as pleased by your remarks on your own country. What very curiously corroborates their justness is, that the characteristics which you note as of Presbyterian origin are, or were, almost equally observable here in the Scotch and the old English Dissenters. The same coldness and reserve of manner—the same repression of enthusiasm—the same caution and mutual superintendence, I have been struck with in them ever since I have been able largely to compare them with our Episcopalians. Miss Martineau, being herself of Dissenting parentage and connection, will be fully prepared to find warm hearts under cold manners, but even our sauciest travellers bear ample testimony to the hospitality they find amongst you. Do you know I am half inclined to quarrel with you for calling us *foreigners* with respect to you? I think we never call you so. Our common origin, common language, and common history down to a period not yet beyond the memory of man, forbid the use of that chilling word. Pray leave it off.

I think you quite right in the main respecting our religious state. There is, however, a great deal of earnest belief amongst our Evangelicals in and out of the Church, and a good deal of unobtrusive piety amongst individuals of all communions; and I would say that the warm reception your works have found from persons in as well as out of the Establishment is a strong proof that spiritual religion is congenial with many minds. In the meantime, the present struggle between the Church and the Dissenters must be regarded as partaking more of the nature of a civil than a religious contest. The question is, Shall the Church monopoly be suffered longer to exist in all its rigour, or shall it be made to yield more or less to the spirit of the age and the demands of justice? You will see that the Bill for abolishing subscription at the universities as a condition of graduation has been carried by a great majority in the Commons, being supported by most of the Scotch and Irish members. It is probable that the Lords will throw it out; but it will, nevertheless, be a great triumph to the Dissenters to find the representatives of the people so decidedly in their favour. The question of the appropriation of Tithes in Ireland particularly will next come to be discussed; and should the two Houses form opposite decisions on this question likewise, very long and very important political consequences may, *must* be the result. The Establishment is by no means so willing as you have been led to believe to correct its own abuses. It is highly probable that Brougham's Church Bill will also be lost among the lords spiritual and temporal. It will, unless a salutary fear of provoking one knows not what, should seize upon these noble and right reverend personages. I am surprised at daily proofs of an alienation of the minds of men from the Church, for which, as you know, I was not in the least prepared. In no one county, town or city, have the friends of the Establishment ventured to call a public meeting for the purpose of raising the cry of "The Church in danger!" The blustering of Oxford, with its military chancellor,* has failed to excite emulation. I believe that if the Church is to stand, great concessions must be made, not only on the points of pluralities, sinecures and non-residence, but in the matter of Church patronage. The Scotch General Assembly has found it expedient to allow the parishioners at large a negative on the appointment of the patron, and I look daily for some similar claim here. Now all these may be regarded as tendencies towards what is called the "voluntary" Church system, which I have no doubt you will allow to be much more favourable to *spirituality* than an Establishment dependent chiefly on the Crown and the hereditary aristocracy of the country.

You will gather from all this that I conceive the popular interest to be fast gaining ground, and that I believe it must finally carry every point in contest, whether civil or ecclesiastical. I believe also that important reforms will thus be effected, and the well-being of the people at large promoted. Nevertheless, I cannot exult in the tone of national feeling. I fear we do indeed deserve to be reproached as a nation of shopkeepers: all our quarrels are money-quarrels—every question in high debate may be resolved into one of £. *s. d.* Ask the trade unions what they require? Higher wages. The shopkeepers? The repeal of the assessed taxes. The manufacturers? Free trade, especially in corn. The landed interest? The continuance of the corn-laws, and of all others favourable to the maintenance of their rents. Now this universal worship of Mammon makes me sigh and blush for my country. In the first political struggles I can remember, great and noble principles were at stake; now it is a vulgar dispute who shall pay most, or least rather, towards a long reckoning. Fox was the type of

* The Duke of Wellington.

the former period, Joseph Hume of the present. But looking at the causes of this extraordinary activity of the mercenary principle amongst us, I am willing to believe that they are in great measure of a temporary nature. The taxes have pressed with crushing weight on every class and interest by turns. It was the hope of relief from pecuniary distress principally which has brought the people into collision, first with the borough-owners, now with the tithe-owners. Some burdens have been already lightened by our reformed legislature, but the Court and the Tories still resist retrenchment, and it is necessary that even a clamour for it should still be kept up. But let reforms in expenditure once have been carried fairly through all departments, and this extraordinary pressure removed, and the active spirits of our people will demand higher and better occupation. Then shall we find the great results of the illumination of the popular mind, which has been all this time proceeding with a constantly accelerating pace; then expect from us moralists, poets, philosophers. I will tell you a little anecdote which has made me hope highly of the effects of the diffusion of literature amongst the lower classes. Dear Jane Roscoe, whose head is all benevolence, having accidentally discovered that various cruel practices prevailed amongst the market people at Liverpool, caused a committee of ladies to be sanctioned by the mayor for the prevention of these offences. It then occurred to her that, to go to the root of the evil, the market people themselves should be humanized by knowledge, and she got a society instituted by ladies for supplying them with a circulation of books. Soon after, the wife of a small butcher requested of her, on the part of her husband, a second view of one of the volumes. "He says, madam, that they say the tracts the gentlefolks give us poor people to read are books for children, but that he is sure this is a book for a man, and such a book as he never saw the like of; and never anything did delight him so much; he can talk of nothing else." It was "Paradise Lost."

The Archbishop of Dublin (Whately) is doing much good by reconciling the Catholics to the national schools, from the system of which he has banished everything offensive to their religion. "To be sure," said an old Oxford colleague of his to me, "he is the very opposite of the sort of person I should have chosen for the situation; I would have had a man remarkable for mildness, patience, willing to hear and to answer all objections; but God knows better how to appoint His own instruments. I know many people who, if the Archbishop were to be roasted, would go to get a bit of him, because he has yielded to the Catholics respecting giving children the whole Bible. But he goes on, and he could not care less for abuse if he were made of wood. He says of the Sabbath, 'Spend if you please, or if you can, the whole day in religious exercises, but put things on the true footing; do not tell your children it was instituted by God's command to Moses to commemorate the creation, but tell them it was fixed by the Apostles to commemorate the resurrection. Give it all the sanctity you please, but not on a wrong ground.' This has given great offence. So has a very learned and philosophical work in which, by tracing the origin of many Romish superstitions to the principles or the weaknesses of our common nature, he has been charged by some with extenuating them." He added, that the Archbishop had a great fondness for parables in conversation, which were often rather homely ones, and for experiments. One day, at a great set dinner at the Lord-lieutenant's, a question arose, how long a man could live with his head under water. The Archbishop quitted the room, and presently returned with a great basin full of water, which he set on the table and plunged his head in before the whole company. Having held it there an enormous length of time, he drew it out, crying, "There! none of you could have kept your heads in so long, but I know the method of it." Another time, also at a formal party at the Castle, he spoke of the great weight a man could support on the calf of his leg, bending it outwards. "If your Grace of Cashel," said he, "will stand upon mine, as I stretch it out, I can bear your weight without the slightest difficulty." But his Grace of Cashel would not have done so odd a thing in that company for millions. I take a fancy to a metropolitan who dares to be odd, to conciliate the Irish Catholics, and to provoke the saints, alias bigots.—No, I shall not go back to Edward III., never fear. No black-letter documents for me! But I am not yet the nearer to finding work for my pen. I do want a *noble* subject, and I cannot find one in our history after exhausting Charles I. I am in a thoroughly unfixed state of mind, which begins to feel irksome to me. This whole London season I have been much in society, and I have seen so many and such various people, and have put myself in the way of hearing such various opinions, that I feel as if I had been on an excursion with the Diable Boiteux; that is, I seem a spectator of all things, inclined to be satisfied with that indolent amusement, and to take part in nothing. I suppose there is a limit to the benefit of hearing all sides. La Fontaine came at last to the two maxims, that Everything may be true, and that Everybody has reason on his side. With such notions I do not see how any one could write eloquently, or indeed give himself the trouble to write anything at all but tales and fables to divert idle people. If my letter is to go to-day, as it ought, I must not fill up my corners as usual, but despatch this hasty scrawl, in which you will find, I believe, some things contradictory of my former views of things,—an inconvenience not to be avoided when every day develops popular feelings more and more.

Believe me ever, with true esteem,
Your attached friend,
Lucy Aikin.

To Miss Aikin.

Boston, August, 1834.

My dear Miss Aikin,—I received your letter by Dr. Tuckerman a few days ago, and I am the more disposed to answer it soon on account of one of the topics in which I feel much interest. You tell me you are not yet suited with a subject for your pen, and that you are wavering between *history* and *essays* on society, &c. I am not very forward to be a counsellor on such a subject, because I feel that one's own consciousness and preference are generally the surest guides as to what one can do best; but as you seem to invite my opinion, I cannot but express my hope that you will fix on the essays. I think that you have looked on society with a searching eye, and can help it to comprehend itself. I would have your essays turn on the past as well as the present. In your historical researches you must have taken many general views of society not given in your Memoirs, and must have materials for many striking comparisons between the past and the present. Portraits of distinguished individuals, the character and influences of sects and parties, the connection between the great social revolution of our own day, the civil and religious revolutions on which your attention has been turned; in a word, the philosophy of history as far as you have explored it,—all these topics might find a place in your volume. I have no fear for your severity, if you will only watch over your motives, and will reprove in the spirit of philanthropy, and with a sincere desire to remove obstructions to the progress of your fellow-beings. This I have wanted to say to you; but let me add, be guided by your own mind. You are, after all, the best judge of the subjects into which you can throw your whole strength. I shall be glad to know that you agree with me, but shall be very tolerant if you differ. I have forgotten to state one reason for my choice, which seems to me of weight. I think you will benefit your own mind by giving it a *new action*, by exercising it on a new field.

My remarks on your aristocracy have led you to say a good word in its favour, which I am glad to hear and not at all disposed to gainsay. I can easily believe that among those who occupy a false position there may be not a few who overcome its disadvantages, especially at times which demand great effort. I believe that the tendencies of aristocracy are hostile to those of Christianity and civilization; that it is a principle of *division*, whilst these bring together and harmonize mankind; that it generates a spurious self-respect and an ungrounded and unsocial consciousness of superiority; that it confers on outward accidents the honour, distinction, influence due to merit alone; and that it is out of place and must be a perpetual spring of jealousy and disunion in times like the present, when we have learnt that the general weal is the only object of social institutions, and that every human being has a right to the means of improving his nature. I will not deny that it was in place in former times, when the community was hardly capable of any stronger or more generous bond than loyalty or devotion to chiefs. But those times are past; not that *loyalty* is superseded, for it never will be; but as men make progress, loyalty becomes more and more a sentiment of moral reverence, exalting alike to him who yields and him who receives it. There will always be an aristocracy; but the *natural* aristocracy, that of intellectual and moral endowment, is to take place of the conventional. Happy it will be for you if the latter shall pass into the former, at least so far as to prevent violent changes. These I dread. Though born in a revolution, I am anything but a revolutionist. My hope is in the regeneration of the world by the peaceful influences of Christianity and increasing knowledge. Sometimes, indeed, society must be convulsed to give these principles any chance of action, but you are not in this case. May you be quiet for ages!

You are alarmed by the trades' unions. I have perhaps less fear, but think of them with as little favour as yourself. You must bear them, however, for they are necessary. They belong to the times. Everywhere you see men running into masses, and abandoning solitary for joint and public notice, and there are reasons why this tendency should manifest itself peculiarly in the *people*. The people are individually insignificant, and can accomplish nothing but by overwhelming numbers. The lighter the particles, the more must be accumulated to produce any considerable weight. Then it is only by banding themselves that the people can get a share of political power, the passion for which is the keener for having been repressed so long; and I see not how the aristocracy, who are devoured by this passion, can with any show of reason find fault with it in others. It is also true that the people have been taught by experience, that they can only secure their rights by an alarming manifestation of force; right must thunder to be heard; and surely the aristocracy cannot blame them for using an instrument which they have themselves made necessary. In another way the old order of things has given rise to these unions. It has produced a strong feeling of opposition of interests between the high and low, a feeling very much exaggerated by the ignorance in which the masses have been kept. Is it strange that the people, conscious of individual weakness, as fond of power as their betters, stung with the idea of wrongs, loving excitement, bent only on physical advantages, and as impatient as children for immediate, visible effects, should partake in the general propensity to run into masses, and to carry their points by imposing co-operation? You know I am no friend to this rage for association. It seems to me a bad sign when the individual loses the consciousness of power, when nobody can do anything alone, when even books, once the products of independent and solitary agency, must be made by literary co-partnership, and even genius becomes a drudge for a "Library." I know the explanation is found in utility. I should look for it in the want of spiritual development. But to save you a metaphysical disquisition, I will only add that my interest in the people (who have my chief sympathy) makes me regret this kind of action among them beyond a narrow limit. I want the people to learn their work and dignity as individuals, much more than their *force* as a *mass*. The latter discovery is full of peril, unless checked by the former. The people, organized and banded in seasons of excitement for their particular interests, lose the little wisdom they have, see everything by their passions, are maddened by jealousies, and fall a prey to their selfish leaders. Sometimes they do infinite mischief; but I do not fear this among you; for, unless I mistake, your lower classes are too broken down to do anything unless in questions like the Reform, where the great weight of the middle class is on the same side. The beginning and end of my preaching is, Let it be the first object of a community to elevate the great mass of its members. There I find myself on the brink of another discussion, but I will spare you. I had a word to say about your Church reform, which will be no reform at all, for you are incapable of one. Your Church is probably better than any of the popular sects, especially if its old insolence has been put down by recent events; but it is utterly unequal to the religious wants of the present state of the world.

You wrote me a little while ago about our poet Bryant. He has now gone to Europe. I spoke of him as more immersed in politics than he is. I have lately heard of him as given to objects more accordant with his fine genius. I hope he will find a good reception.

Our Republic is in quite an amusing condition as far as names are concerned. Our Conservative party has taken the name of *Whigs*, and is trying to fasten the name of *Tory* on the Democratic mass. But your Tories may comfort themselves; their name cannot be made to stick to the mob.

Do write me some other letters as "dull" as your last. I ask nothing better. Were it not for fear of plagiarism, I should be tempted to apply the epithet to this epistle. Perhaps it is only *grave*, the next fault to dulness, or rather one with it, in the judgment of multitudes.

What is the best History of England for my daughter? Have you read Mignet's French Revolution?

Your sincere friend,
WM. E. CHANNING.

To Dr. Channing.

Hampstead, October 19, 1834.

My dear Friend,—Your welcome letter arrived as I was actually putting pen to paper to inquire after you and petition to be written to. Thank you very much for the interest you take in the employment of my pen, and your suggestions on this subject. My own inclination is likewise to essay-writing; but I feel diffident, well knowing it to be a difficult and an exhausting kind of composition. Sometimes I have thought the form of dialogue a convenient one for exhibiting the different sides and bearings of a subject, and I have lately made one or two attempts in this kind, and shall perhaps proceed a little further. I think, at least, I have made up my mind not to search further for a historic subject. But I am again impeded in my pursuits by a failure in health, and am not able to apply much force of mind to any object. I read, however, much and variously, and seek to lay in ideas for more propitious seasons—should such be in store for me. It would be a great undertaking to "teach this age to understand itself;" one ought first to be very certain of its being understood by the teacher. That spirit of aristocracy of which you speak, is of itself one of the most perplexing and, at the same time, important subjects of meditation and inquiry that I know, especially with reference to these times and this country. I have not only thought and conversed, but even made several attempts at writing on it, without being able to come at all near to the end or the bottom of it. Is it true, I have asked, as some people say, that the English have more of this spirit than any people in Europe? Certainly not, if by the terms it is meant that the distinction of noble and plebeian families is broadest here.

We have, in effect, no *noblesse* in the sense of old France or present Germany. Only the head of any family is a nobleman; the younger branches are all commoners, and do not even retain a titular distinction beyond the first generation from a peer. Yet there is some reason to assert that haughtiness of demeanour towards inferiors acknowledged as such, and, still more, an extreme jealousy of rank and precedence, and an indignant rebutting of the pretensions of those a very little below themselves, are striking characteristics of our people. And why is this? I believe because there never was a country or a state of society in which men were so much the artificers, not only of their own fortunes, but of their own rank, as modern England. Every advantage, every distinction, is held forth to be struggled for. Each is striving to surpass his neighbour, and still more to be acknowledged by his neighbour himself to have surpassed him. It has been a frequent remark with our essay-writers and novelists, that persons of real rank and gentility were much less arrogant than pretenders or upstarts, which is likely enough to be true as a general rule. But in this land of merchants, manufacturers, men of science, men of letters, orators, preachers, politicians and dandies, you may easily imagine that there are hundreds of pretenders and upstarts, or at least of men who have raised themselves, for one person of established, acknowledged hereditary rank, fortune and consequence; and thus perhaps, in some degree, have arrogance and insolence become unfortunately almost national characteristics; at least this seems likely to be the solution of the fact, if fact it be. When you reflect upon the activity of all these various competitors for the respect or admiration of society, as well as its more tangible prizes, you will perhaps better understand the grounds of what little partiality I may feel towards the old aristocracy, the claims of which sometimes act as a useful counterbalance to other claims not better founded, and urged with more offensive self-sufficiency. But the tendency of our political state is to diminish all kinds of personal pre-eminence, a tendency of which, as you are aware, the associating spirit is both effect and cause. The diffusion of knowledge is in some respects to all the aristocracy of this age, what the discovery of gunpowder was to the military aristocracy of one age, and the Reformation to the ecclesiastical aristocracy of another. As for the trades' unions, I had absolutely forgotten that ever I had been afraid of them. It is now manifest that they cannot become *political* unions. They are not, as you seem to suppose, combinations generally of the poor against the rich, but of one particular class, the journeymen mechanics, against all the rest of society beneath and around, as much as above themselves. The unreasonable attempt of this class to enhance the price of *their* commodity, skilled labour, would, if successful, cause a general advance in the money value of all other commodities, which, by disabling our manufacturers from maintaining their ascendency in foreign markets, must bring poverty on the journeymen themselves in the first place, and then on the nation. This is so clearly perceived, that they have found no sympathy anywhere, and the delusion amongst themselves is subsiding, or will subside.

You may be right that we shall have no religious reform, but I think we must have various Church alterations before long. In Scotland, which has now first become a free country, and is likely enough to give the tone to England on several topics, the seceders have lately increased prodigiously; and it is not on doctrine that they depart from their Church, but on what they call the *voluntary* principle, that is, that the minister should be elected by those who are to attend upon him, and paid by them alone. The refusal of vestries to impose Church-rates, which is becoming general, proceeds on the same principle. In this trial of strength, or at least of numbers, between the Church and Dissenters, the Church, which is almost synonymous with the Tory party, has been on the whole signally defeated. Even Church congregations begin to kick at patronage. Just now, a populous and respectable London parish, on losing its rector, sent a deputation to the Bishop of London, the patron, which took the novel' liberty of requesting him to appoint a particular clergyman, unconnected with the parish, whom they named. The bishop replied that, in that case, they, not himself, would be the patrons, which he did not intend to permit, and so sent them off malcontent. Tithe must be abolished forthwith in Ireland, and must, I conceive, be much modified here. Now, though these be in themselves secular matters, they indicate in the middle classes an hostility to ecclesiastics and their authority and interests which cannot be without its influence on religion itself, at least on the public exercise of it. The Evangelicals have not made a conquest of the whole people—far from it—as the defeat of their Sabbath Bill by the representatives of the people abundantly proves. Those, too, whom they have not subjugated they have vehemently provoked by their sourness and their spirit of dictation and exclusion; and I see great reason to believe that a large proportion of those who now unite with the *serious* party against the Church, would equally oppose giving either additional wealth or power to them.

It strikes me also as unlikely in itself that ecclesiastics should escape being losers by that tendency to the leveling of all personal distinctions which I have already noted as belonging to this age. Their authority is more immediately dependent on public opinion than any other. It may seem an obvious remark, yet I know not that any one has made it and observed its bearings, that the necessity and value of oral instruction of every kind is, and must be, exceedingly diminished by the vast extension now given to the art of reading and the circulation of books. A well-read layman, even of a humble class, will be little inclined to bow to the mere authority of a pulpit. Unless, therefore, some man of genius should arise to promulgate some new system peculiarly adapted to the tastes, the feelings and the wants of this age and people, I prognosticate a period of religious indifference and wide-spread disbelief. Even from the higher literature of the day, one may infer the rising of a different spirit from that which, not five years ago, prompted all candidates for popular applause to mix up something of piety with every tour, every novel, every song, and every sonnet. I doubt if "*Sacred Annuals*" will long continue in vogue. "May religion," I once heard a devout man say, "be always in honour, and never in fashion." Whatever has been in fashion will soon be out of fashion. Now in this land religion has been for a good while in fashion. The mode is changing. How I run on, as if I wanted to practise essay-writing upon you!

As to a History of England for your daughter, there is none for anybody's daughter. Hume is still the only very agreeable one, and his deficiencies and partialities you well know. Lingard is biassed by his profession and religion; and Turner is warped by systems and crotchets. However, they all deserve to be read, and out of them the careful reader may pick a history. What Hallam has given us, both in his "Middle Ages" and his "Constitutional History," is of inestimable value to the student, but too deep and too technical for young ladies. There is a "History of Great Britain," by a Dr. Andrews, a Scotchman, which I read with great pleasure in my youth. It is written on the plan of giving in separate chapters the civil history of a reign, then the ecclesiastical, then the history of commerce, of literature, of manners, &c. There is no great merit in the style, which is flat and commonplace, and the first chapter on manners is rendered strangely absurd by his deriving those of the ancient Caledonians from Macpherson's fabulous Ossian; but in spite of these deductions, it is a valuable and agreeable work for the early periods. It stops at either the death of Henry VIII. or the accession of Elizabeth. I have not seen the work for years, and later ones, Turner's especially, may have gone deeper into the topics of manners and literature; but I suspect it first opened my mind to those uses of history which produced my own works in this kind, and I therefore owe it a good word.

You tell me nothing of your own plans or pursuits. I fear you are not coming over to England for the winter, as we had all been hoping—which is very shabby in you. We shall but just be able to forgive you should another report prove true, as I trust it is, that you are writing a book. That will be some compensation; but indeed you must not give up the dear project of coming hither and introducing your young people to English society. Recollect what you have sometimes written to me on the advantage of your best people coming and making themselves known here. I shall make diligent inquiry after Bryant, whom I long to see. Poets are rare with us. Coleridge we have lost, and where have we his poetic equal? Of which of his contemporaries can we say that he has written too little?

Will you think me outrageously sentimental if I confess to you that I have deplored even with tears the conflagration of our two Houses of Parliament, rich as they were in historic recollections? The name of Pym was still to be seen cut over the place which he occupied in the House of Commons, the Armada tapestry still lined the House of Lords. St. Stephen's Chapel was built by our third Edward. In the Painted Chamber James and Charles used to lecture their sturdy Houses of Commons —and all are now ashes and ruins! We must be thankful that Westminster Hall itself did not share the same fate. There was great manifestation of feeling amongst the spectators of every rank. With all our faults as a nation, few of us are without a touch of filial love for Old England, and pride in the memory of her glories. How absurd to call your mob *Tories!* I trust your Whigs will defeat them. There can be no fear of your lower classes not having power enough.

With every good wish for you and yours, and particularly that you would give us the opportunity of showing you hospitality,

Believe me yours with true regard,

L. AIKIN.

To MISS AIKIN.

Boston, January 5, 1835.

My dear Miss Aikin,—How shall I begin my letter? I owe you two letters, and it is a long, long time since I wrote you; and what is worse, I have no sufficient excuse for my negligence. I can only say that I have long been good for little or nothing. I have wanted the inward spring of exertion. You probably know what it is to be capable of passive enjoyment and nothing more. I have read a good deal, thought a little, relished nature keenly, longed to write, and written scarcely anything. Do not think that your letters are less welcome because they have failed to stir me up to answer. If you knew the pleasure they give, your benevolence would be motive enough for continuing them.

I am just rising from a sickness of a month, which has been rife here under the comprehensive name of Influenza. In some parts of the country it has been mortal. Without severe suffering, I lost all my strength. On rising, I was driven to books of amusement, and read Bulwer's last novel. Perhaps my wearied head was in fault, but I found little in the work to take hold of me, except as it gave some vivid pictures of antiquity. No justice was done to the primitive Christian, and in this, as in his other works, I felt the want of *life, reality*, in the higher characters. I have heard the word "washy" applied to the superficial style of painting, where the figures have no depth, massiness, substance, and the epithet seems to me to suit a good deal of the fashionable poetry and fiction. One admirable exception I lately met with in Philip Van Artevelde. Here I found myself amidst real beings, breathing the breath of life, and, in spite of some affectations of style, speaking and acting from their own souls, and not graceful or sentimental puppets, through whom the author shows you his skill and fine thoughts. Who is Mr. Taylor?

In your last you speak of your plans. As to *dialogues*, I think they may usefully be mixed with essays. A volume of them is somewhat hazardous. You are one of the few to whom I could recommend this mode of composition. Generally it is a failure, for it requires dramatic skill, spirit, life. The reader is disappointed when in a dialogue he finds a dissertation, the different sentences which are put into different mouths, but have nothing characteristic, nothing of the freedom and animation of conversation. I am sure you will do well. I recollect no late colloquial writing which has interested me, except Southey's Dialogues on Society (Sir T. More was chief speaker), and in these probably the singular beauties of the style and the greatness of the subject made me overlook defects. Speaking of style, I have been struck with the superiority of the three Lake-poets, as they were once called, in this particular. Who of their contemporaries can stand by their side, especially by Coleridge's? I might add to them one who seems to have been of their set, Lamb, in whose Elia are some passages exquisitely written. By the way, what do you think of Taylor's criticism on your admired Byron in Artevelde? Byron's want of comprehensiveness and depth of thought is beginning to be felt. I should not wonder if his letters, bad and repulsive as they are in point of morals, should be appealed to more than his poems as proofs of his scope of intellect.

I have not strength or time to write you about politics. So you have a Tory ministry, and under the worst circumstances; that is, the Whigs have fallen through very weakness. Perhaps a Tory ministry may be best for you. So much the worse. Louis Philippe's arbitrariness is said to be best for France. You can judge of a people's condition pretty surely by learning what is *best* for them. The amount seems to be, that your people have not enough of wisdom and principle, of clear-headedness and right-heartedness, to govern themselves, and the power has fallen to a class who are separated from them, want sympathy with them, and look down on them as inferiors, and have no sincere desire to serve them. The papers say that the new ministry will be liberal, &c.; but save me from *reform* in the hands of its foes! Nothing will be conceded but by *necessity*, and the concession will be robbed in every possible way of its significance and worth. The Tories have one advantage; they have *fixed principles*, as all Conservatives have. Reformers are necessarily unsettled in many points, and hence division, mistake and weakness. My principal solicitude is about the influence of this change on the cause of improvement and liberal institutions generally. I do not, however, despair at all. The eddy is not the current, and the current sets the right way. I ought to say that I have written the above with very little knowledge of the facts of the late changes.

You interested me much by your remarks on the state and prospects of religion in your country. If you will look at my last volume of Sermons, page 58, you will see in the last sentence but one a *hint* of what you have suggested as to the influence of the press on the demand for the Christian ministry. I have no belief, however, that any improvements will supersede this institution; and the present low state of all classes in regard both to the theory and practice of religion and morals reduces them to great dependence on the minister. That scepticism may spread more widely is to be feared. The singular worldliness of this money-getting, utilitarian, material age, is directly hostile to the nobler sentiments, especially to *faith*. Then the old bands of authority are loosened, many old supports of religion are weakened, and the true foundations are imperfectly explored or made known. Then there seems no religious class among you to answer the needs of the time. Unitarianism was palsied at its revival by the doctrines of materialism, necessity, &c., which Priestley associated with it, and its spirituality suffered from its political connections. The other sects have given perpetuity to the forms of darker times. Still I see no signs of such a terrible shock to religious faith in your country as France experienced. It cannot be said of your Establishment, as of the Catholic religion in that country, that the edifice was too far gone for repair, and needed leveling to make way for a better. It is my earnest hope and trust that England is to enjoy reform in all its departments without revolution.

I want now to say a word about my own concerns. Have you any friends in Dorsetshire who can make inquiry whether *my name* is known in that county? My ancestors came from Dorchester, or its neighbourhood, near the beginning of the last century. I have seen a letter written to them from Abraham Channing, a minister, who resided, I think, at Cranbourne, north of Dorchester. I have no expectation of finding an illustrious ancestry, and should not of myself have made this application; but I have a brother who wishes to mount or rather descend our genealogical tree, and his conversation has stirred up a little my curiosity. Our coat of arms is three Moors' or Negros' heads. I have understood Mr. Canning had the same. Perhaps among my family in England (and I am pretty sure it is not extinct) there may be some antiquary, and I should like to bring him and my brother into connection.

Do present my best respects to Mrs. Baillie. I am in debt to her as I have been to you; but not a bankrupt as I hope to prove soon. I shall rejoice to hear of your improved health.

Your sincere friend,
WM. E. CHANNING.

To Dr. Channing.

Hampstead, March 10, 1835.

Avaunt! carpenters, bricklayers, gardeners, painters, and upholsterers, and let me hold converse with my dear distant friend! These people whom I exorcise are employed, be it known to you, in preparing for my reception a house to which I hope to remove very shortly; but this being Sunday, they and I enjoy a respite. It is no long flight, only to the opposite side of the street; but it will give me, besides better rooms, a delicious prospect from my windows—thirty miles of varied and verdant country, sprinkled only with white houses, and bounded by the range of Surrey hills. This will be a new pleasure to me; I shall scarcely feel my solitude in the presence of so much of nature, and I *do* promise myself that, in the intervals of gazing through my window, my pen will exert itself to better purpose than heretofore.

All that you say on the subject of dialogue I think just. The chief advantage of that form is, not in conveying information, for which it has many inconveniences, but in representing discussion, and thus prompting the reader to exercise his own powers of reasoning and judging. It will serve to *hint* subjects of inquiry which it may not be convenient to treat more openly; and it may save a writer from hostile criticism, by enabling him to plead that he has represented both sides of a question without pronouncing for either. Call these paltry utilities if you please; but amongst a people where ancient prejudice is *hugged* by the million, the best friends of man's best interests may be thankful to take advantage of them. At present, however, I have scarcely made a beginning of my work; that is, I have got only one dialogue and a half, and some scraps which I think will hatch into essays. But of this enough. I have had by me for some time a message for you from a Prince (but, thought I, I shan't write purely for that; the republican doctor will laugh at me). This Prince, however, is a man of merit; it is the Duke of Sussex. At a dinner which he gave some time since to the Fellows of the Royal Society, of which he is Presidsnt, and a few others, he beckoned to him my brother Arthur, to talk aside on the topic that he loves—religion. He spoke with delight of your sermons—said he had read every one that was printed. He had heard (would it were true!) that you were coming to England in the spring. "I understand," he added, "that your sister corresponds often with him; tell her that when he comes I shall think it a great honour to be introduced to him." Will nothing tempt you to come to us? Surely, after the illness you have had, you would find travelling a restorative; and should you not like, "antiquam exquaerere matrem," to make your own researches in Dorsetshire? Meantime I shall not lose sight of the object.

The first time I can get sight of Joseph Hunter, of the Record Office, our first living topographer, one of our first genealogists, and withal a York student and Unitarian divine, I will mention the subject; and I dare say he can at least inform us how information can be gotten. It happens that I know absolutely not a person in that county. But you are Cannings, you say; and if so, I am afraid you must be content to take, along with the eminent statesman, a certain Bet Canning, who about the middle of last century contrived to make herself the talk of the whole kingdom by a well-invented tale of having been carried off and kept prisoner in a lone house near London, from which she made a marvellous escape. The particulars might be found in an old "Annual Register," if you are curious; but perhaps you are not. I believe she is mentioned (either in the "World" or "Connoisseur") as the rival of a certain Mrs. Tofts, who professed to have brought into the world—a litter of rabbits.

Talking of pedigrees, I think I never told you that I saw, too late for my book, one of Queen Elizabeth, kept at Hatfield House, and certainly drawn under the eye of Burleigh, in which she is traced up to a personage called "the second wife of Jupiter," and collaterally to no less a worthy than Cerberus himself; whence, no doubt, her habitual vigilance and occasional *doggedness*.

I quite agree with you as to the *prose* merits of our Lake poets. Southey is an excellent prose man. The first circumstance which tended to redeem style from the cold regularity of the French school and the pedantic Latinism of Johnson, was the appearance of Percy's Reliques; from that time, and by the help also of the *true* elucidators of Shakespeare, Steevens, Malone, &c., old true English has been understood and written by all our writers of genius. There is no better English than that of poor Charles Lamb—a true and original genius—the delight of all who knew, still more than of all who read him, and whom none who had once seen him—my own case—could ever forget. Your praise of Artevelde I cannot quite agree in. The energetic simplicity and purity of the style, indeed, I much admire, but I cannot say that his personages do strike or interest me greatly. But I may be biassed. The detestableness of everything relating to the depraved creature whom he has made the heroine of his second part—the unspeakable coarseness and vileness of the man who is represented as running a long parallel between her and the virtuous wife whom he has loved and lost—these things we women could not bear or pass over. We have made no outcry, however, but our silent indignation has been felt. I thought his criticisms on Byron able, and to a certain degree just, but invidious. Byron's deficiencies, however great, do not prevent his having in some kinds, and in some passages, exhibited merits and beauties of the first order. Mr. Taylor is, I think, somewhat of a heretic in poetical doctrine, inasmuch as he says in company, that he holds Wordsworth for a much greater poet than Milton.

Twelve years ago I saw at Dr. Holland's a man of three-and-twenty, tall, rather well-looking, with an air of talent, promptitude, and moderate self-confidence. He was the son of a clever gentleman-farmer, and just arrived from Northumberland to seek his fortune in London, bearing a letter of introduction from excellent Mr. Turner, of Newcastle, his father's friend. Within three days, Wilmot Horton, then colonial secretary, said to Dr. Holland, "These lords' sons do no good in our office; I wish you could recommend me a young man who would be willing to work." The doctor mentioned the young Northumbrian; he was examined, approved, and immediately installed in a lucrative situation, which he still retains—and this was Henry Taylor. He printed some years ago a tragedy, which had no circulation. He was often at Coleridge's evening parties, and long ago I heard of his provoking some of the company by an *invidious* eulogium on the Koran. They were the more angry because he possessed the slight advantage in argument of being the only person present who had read the book. I think, or hope, that he will yet write things worthy of ungrudging praise; and I much approve his manly style, as an antidote to the sentimental jargon of which we have so much; but he must cultivate moral refinement, to give pleasure where he must wish to please. Above all, he must never again make his hero exclaim, "How little flattering is a woman's love!"

Almost two great pages without a word of politics! Not that they are not *the* object of interest at present; but what to think! what to remark or to predict! In the first place, however, I am not surprised at anything that has happened. I always thought it likely that the Tories would make some effort to reinstate themselves in what they have so long regarded as their birthright—the government of the country, with all the advantages, privileges and emoluments thereunto belonging. Something like treachery on the part of the King was also highly probable, considering the natural antagonism between Royalty and Whiggism. But in all this *I* see nothing alarming. With such a House of Commons as the present proves itself to be, in spite of the utmost efforts of the Tories, who scrupled nothing of corruption, or intimidation either, to pack it to their minds—reforms we must and shall have, and effectual ones too. It is, I believe, not amiss that every step of amelioration should be won with some effort and struggle. Every reform is the more valued, as well as the better understood, for being the result and reward of long agitation. We might therefore afford to have patience with the reluctance of ministers to proceed in the road which, after all, they must travel, were delay the only evil of the case. But I confess I feel hurt at the restoration to power of a party which I regard as essentially that of injustice and abuse —a party which in its best measures must always be open to the reproach of acting inconsistently with its own principles. Surely its reign will not be long. It is hazardous, however, to predict in circumstances unprecedented. A ministry outvoted in the Lower House, and an opposition outvoted in the Upper, is a new dilemma in the history of our mixed constitution. It is the opinion of wise men and friends of religious as well as civil liberty, that great part of all the reaction that there has been against reform has arisen from the rash declarations of certain classes of Dissenters against an Established Church. They egregiously miscalculated their strength if they supposed that the Church could, yet at least, be outvoted, and the natural result of their vehemence has been that of rousing the clergy to tenfold fierceness against all sectaries and all liberals. There may be some chance, however, that ultimately the *sacred order* will find itself to have sustained irreparable injury, in my opinion, by the exhibitions of its temper, and its maxims which have thus been drawn forth. I stand by my belief, that no form of religion in this country is extending, if preserving its authority over the minds of men.

You may be interested to hear that Brougham, like Cicero in his banishment, flies for support under political disappointments to the study of philosophy. He wrote the other day to an old and respected friend of his and mine, to send him the works of Tucker, the answer printed, but not published, by Mill to Mackintosh's attack on Bentham, and several other books on ethical subjects. Will you charge yourself with my cordial thanks to Dr. Tuckerman for his ordination sermon and his pamphlet, from which I am glad to learn that his noble experiment proceeds and prospers? Your charge has very much delighted us all. One point, however, I want to discuss with you. It is the opinion given by both you and Dr. T., that, as well with you as in Europe, it is the tendency of modern improvements to increase the distance between the upper and lower classes. Now, with respect to your own country, it seems to stand to reason that it must be so; because you are beginning, and but beginning, to have a class *born* rich, and also because parts of your country are become densely peopled, and of course the wages of labour no longer there bear the same high proportion to the necessaries of life. But I doubt whether there is this tendency in *any* of the kingdoms of Europe, and here I discern more signs of an opposite one. I grant, indeed, that in some districts over-population, combined with neglect of the wholesome old law that no cottage should be built without a considerable garden attached, has depressed the condition of the agricultural labourer; but this effect is partial, and affects only the cultivators. In towns, wages were never, I believe, so high in proportion to the price of the articles of consumption; and never was education so widely diffused, never were the people so experimentally convinced of the great truth that knowledge is power. On the other hand, several circumstances have combined to bring down our aristocracy. The depressed state of agriculture has shorn down their incomes so low, that to pay the interest of their mortgages is more than most of them know how to compass. The Reform Bill has deprived them of the great resources in money and preferments, civil and ecclesiastical, which they used to derive from their borough interests, and places and sinecures are much diminished. In the mercantile class it is certain that much fewer great fortunes, and many more moderate ones, are made by trade now than some years ago. I throw out these hints hastily, but you will know how to put them together. I must now conclude.

Ever yours most truly,
L. AIKIN.

To Dr. Channing.

London, May 13, 1835.

My dear Friend,—Mr. Phillips shall not return to you without at least a few lines from me, and I take up the pen in London, and amid many distractions.

See if I was not right! The Tories are out again. The will of the King put them in, the will of the House of Commons has nevertheless turned them out. Still our state is not altogether satisfactory; it is evident that severe and perhaps dangerous party struggles await us. I wanted to tell you—but when I wrote last had little heart to mention politics at all—that I think you simplify too much in your views of our state. It seems that you think we have but two parties—that of reform and that of abuse; but we have twenty, besides infinite shades of opinion, and there are pure patriots and corrupt and selfish designers in all. You will perceive that this must be so, when you consider that now, as in the days of the Stuarts, religion, or at least theology, mingles in the fray, and sec's make factions. More to embroil the scene, we have persons who desire reform in the Church and not in the State—the case of numbers of the Evangelicals; others, ultra-radicals, who in new-modelling the State would destroy the Church. The champions of civil liberty are compelled to fraternize with rank Irish Papists, who have perhaps for their ultimate object the separation of their country from ours, and the establishment of their own Church. These are but a few of the perplexing combinations of elements naturally discordant which we see taking place around us. There is much in our moral world to remind one of the old theory of the formation of the physical world by a dance of atoms and their fortuitous concourse; but as yet we have not risen out of chaos—the order and beauty are all to come. I found the other day in that most original work, Tucker's "Light of Nature," the startling remark, that few people know what their own real opinions are; and I have since felt the truth of it, by reflecting on the *backward and forward talking* of almost all one's acquaintance—excepting those who have tangible interests involved in questions at issue. One day you find a man a decided Reformer, the next day he becomes Conservative, then he appears fixed in Whiggism—till the next turning of the vane. Now the love of novelty, now the force of old associations, becomes predominant. Hope, fear, and memory play their busy part, and fixed principles are found scarcely anywhere. I speak the more feelingly on this head because the case is very much my own. The ultras of all the parties inspire me with repugnance, and perhaps fear; but there is a wide middle space which with me is land debatable, and through which I pick out an uncertain course. In theory I find it impossible to controvert the principle, that the will of the majority ought to prevail; but when I reflect on the blindness, the ignorance, the gross selfishness of that majority—that headlong multitude—I cannot but wish that it would be content to submit to the guidance of a wise and disinterested few; but then how are these few to be discovered and invested with power, and how are they to be preserved from being corrupted by it?

After all, I believe our people are improving in knowledge and in virtue under the discipline of these struggles, and this ought to reconcile our minds to the inevitable evils attending them.

Read, pray read, Wordsworth's new volume of poems. You will there see how the dread of innovation has acted on a mind of no ordinary powers of reflection, not warped either by any immediate self-interest, but perhaps we may say, dominated by poetical associations with old castles, cathedral service, and village steeples. As a poet, I think he rather advances than declines; for though not a few of his new pieces appear to me failures, none of them have the puerility into which he used so often to fall, and there are some which I esteem of surpassing excellence. What a treasure of original thoughts, and sublime and touching imagery, and exquisite harmonies, is his ode "On the Power of Sound"!

Montgomery has likewise given us a new volume. It has some very striking narrative poems and many fine stanzas; but how is his strain marred by his devotedness to a monstrous system of religion! I cannot easily understand how a mind so benevolent as his should have found the peace he says he has under his tremendous belief; but is it not true that there are some secret contrivances by which the worthy mind escapes from the consequences of shocking theories which it believes itself to admit, and thus secures the serenity which is virtue's right? Thanks for your sermon on War. I am not sufficiently informed of the facts of the case in your dispute with the French to be able fully to appreciate the weight of your arguments; but I trust that, after all, your President will not find it necessary to carry his threats into execution. I believe the genius of civilized nations is becoming less and less warlike.

Last night I saw Mr. Hunter, and asked how we could get any answer to your inquiries respecting your family. He said that he thought it very likely Channings were Cannings, and that the only *gentle* Cannings whom the heralds had been able to discover were seated in Oxfordshire—that George Canning's Irish family was *perhaps* a branch of it. If the Dorsetshire Channings were people of a certain consequence, some notice of them *might* be extant in Hutchins's "History of Dorsetshire"—if not, the only course would be to make inquiries of some Cranbourne person, if the name was still known there. But I think yet I shall be able to find something out by other means.

I must here bring my epistle to a conclusion.

Ever most truly yours,
L. AIKIN.

To MISS AIKIN.

June 22, 1835.

My dear Miss Aikin,—So you are building a house! By what sympathy is it that we are carrying on the same work at once? I hope, however, your practical wisdom has kept you from my error. My house threatens to swell beyond my means, so that I cannot think of it with a perfectly quiet conscience. This is the only point on which I am in danger of extravagance. I spend nothing on luxuries, amusements, show. My food is the simplest. My clothes sometimes call for rebuke from an affectionate wife, not for want of neatness, but for their venerable age. But one indulgence I want, a good house, open to the sun and air, with apartments large enough for breathing freely, and commanding something of earth and sky. A friend of mine repeated to me the saying of a child, "Mother, the country has *more sky* than the town." Now I want "more sky" than other folks, and my house, though in a city, gives me a fine sweep of prospect, and an air almost as free as the country. I do not, however, suffer even a house to be an essential. When I think of Him who had not where to lay his head, and of the millions of fellow-creatures living in outward and inward destitution, I feel doubts and misgivings in enjoying the many accommodations which respectability is thought to require. Alas! to a Christian, to one who hungers and thirsts after moral excellence, what perplexities and obstructions are offered by the present condition of society! How hard to realize our conceptions of disinterested virtue! How the fetters of custom, forged by a self-indulgent world, weigh on us, and enthral the purer and more generous feelings! Were I entering on life, instead of approaching its end, with my present views and feelings and with no ties, I should strive for a condition which, without severing me from society, would leave me more free to act from my own spirit, to follow faithfully and uncompromisingly the highest manifestations of virtue made to my mind. I mean not, however, to repine. I have not been wholly a slave to outward and inferior influences, and there *is* a world of true, perfect freedom. You hope much aid to your intellect from the beautiful prospect your new house is to give you. Do not be too confident. The intellect, in the common sense of the word, may be aided less than the imagination and the heart. I am now spending the summer in the country, and I find myself lured perpetually from my books and papers, to saunter among the shrubbery, to listen to the wind among the branches, to enjoy flowers whose names I cannot remember, to let the affections rise or expand at will. I begin to think there is more wisdom in these affections than in much which passes for philosophy; but perhaps you have not lived long enough to learn this, and may blame your beautiful prospect for troubling the intellect. Let me intercede for the prospect. In the end you will write better books for it. Your house has filled so much of my letter, that I can answer little to its other topics. I am indeed grateful for the attention with which the Duke of Sussex has honoured me; and, were I thinking of a visit to England, I should anticipate an introduction to him among my pleasures and privileges. Let me say, however, that your testimony to his character gave me much more pleasure than his message. I had often heard before of the liberality of his sentiments; but the truth is, that the reputation of your Royal Family, as respects morals, is so low in this country, that we have never felt as if any class of Christians were aided by their sympathy or patronage. I rejoice to learn that the Duke of Sussex is so esteemed, as your letter implies. I love to think well of one who is pledged to principles which I hold sacred and dear. I cannot gainsay your criticism on Van Artevelde. The truth is, I read the second part in great haste and at odd moments, and spent no thought on it. I was offended by the scene you refer to, but am not sure that it is untrue. As far as my recollection goes, this part was intended to show the sad process of a mind, originally reserved, unbending and self-relying, yielding itself to the corrupting influences of the passion for power, of victory and empire; and the question is, whether, in such a case, tender recollections of a holy love may not mix with the encroachments of criminal passion ? The style of the book is often encumbered by an affectation of archaisms, &c.

As to politics, what shall I say ? Your letter was written during the reign of Toryism (how happened it to have so long a voyage ?), and I know not in what condition this letter will find you. I am almost discouraged from writing on this subject by an increasing conviction of the difficulty of understanding a foreign country. I receive different, opposite opinions, even from your own people who visit me; and the fact that my own country is so misapprehended by strangers makes me distrustful of myself. I have been struck of late with the disposition manifested throughout Europe to throw the blame of all that is evil in this country on our *free institutions*, as if freedom were the only element of our social condition. The truth is, that freedom, at this moment particularly, has less influence than other peculiarities in our State. Our most striking peculiarity is that we are a young people, bringing all the powers of an advanced civilization, and very singular energies of industry and enterprize, to bear on a new country of inexhaustible resources. Every day discloses to us a new mine of wealth. In addition to our capital, which has increased immensely, foreign capital is pouring in, and opportunities of profitable investment seem to increase in still greater proportion. The consequence you can easily conceive. The minds of the people are intoxicated with a stimulant which human nature has never yet been strong enough to resist. The spirit of speculation, the passion for unbounded accumulation, rages among us. We think very little about politics compared with "public improvements," as they are called, new applications of steam, railroads, new settlements in the "far West," &c., &c. In such a state of things no man has a fixed position. Hardly any man has the strong local feelings of older countries. A mighty stream of population, bearing away our adventurous youth, is setting westward. Journeys of five hundred or a thousand miles are amusements to us. The imagination is at work continually on the distant and vast. The consequence is, a very vigorous but very partial development of human nature. We understand positive material interests better than any other people. We already surpass *you* in manufacturing ingenuity, and a British vessel cannot easily get freight when an American one is the competitor. But the result of this infinite external activity is, that the inward, spiritual, higher interests of humanity are little comprehended, prized or sought. We surpass even England in worldly utilitarianism. The worth of the higher intellectual and moral culture, of arts and studies which refine and elevate, is not felt as it should be; but this has nothing to do with our freedom, or is not to be charged on our free institutions. It is a remarkable fact that, with all this worldly activity, there is a higher standard of morals among us than anywhere else. My personal observation is indeed confined very much to Boston. I have seen the population of that place quadrupled, and its wealth multiplied in vastly greater proportion, and I am confident that there has been a decided advance in religion, philanthropy, and general virtue, as well as in intelligence. I fear that the same praise cannot be given to the other large cities, for they have been overflowed by emigrants, particularly from Ireland, and have wanted our means of education. Still when I consider the tendency of our peculiar situation to unsettle and materialize the minds of men, I wonder that our moral condition is as sound as it is, and I see in it a much stronger argument for than against free institutions. To those who measure institutions by *prosperity*, ours must be the very best ever devised, for never were people so prosperous. For myself, I would we were less prosperous. Our freedom and glory are endangered by our rapid growth, especially by our growth from abroad. Our foreign population is becoming a great evil. Our fathers, never dreaming of what has taken place, and wishing to make our country "an asylum for oppressed humanity," began with granting the rights of citizenship on too easy terms, and we have gone on from bad to worse, until the elective franchise is lavished on ignorant hordes from Europe who cannot but abuse it. This profanation of so high a privilege moves my indignation. But I must stop. I determined when I began to confine myself to a sheet, but on some topics I do not know when to stop. You misunderstood me when you supposed me to say that our present civilization increases the distance between the higher and lower classes *generally*. I said that it creates a more degrading *pauperism*. Write me often and fully. Are not *complete editions* of Coleridge and Lamb expected?

Your sincere friend,
W. E. CHANNING.

P.S.—I intended to say that I do not despair on account of the material tendencies of my countrymen. Perhaps it is well that human nature should work itself out fairly in one direction. It is too noble and various to work always in one way. A higher activity is to take place here, though perhaps not in my day.

To Dr. Channing.

Hampstead, September 13, 1835.

My dear Friend,—Your welcome and long-expected letter arrived a few days since, just as I had begun one to inquire what had occasioned so long a suspension of our correspondence. I cannot account for the long delay of mine, unless by the supposition that it must have waited long at Dr. Boott's for an opportunity of sending it. I have certainly written you one since—by Mr. Phillips, surely—which I hope you have received. English and American will, I suppose, in process of time, become distinct languages, at least as to familiar idioms. When I told you that the workmen were preparing a *new* house for me, you understood that I was building one: an Englishman would have understood only that I was *changing* my house—which was the fact. My present dwelling would be regarded as a venerable relic of antiquity in your country. I dare say it has much more than a century on its head, though it is still strong and in good condition. Thanks to the remission of taxes since the Reform Bill, and of rates since the amendment of the poor-laws, I have now a much better house than formerly for about the same money. Pray do not grudge yourself your healthful, exhilarating, only luxury. I know how deeply you both understand and feel the claims of the poor on their more prosperous brethren; the beautiful sermon you last sent me is a striking proof of it; but depend upon it you are doing more for them, and for the world at large, by keeping *yourself* in spirits and vigour, than by any amount of money you could bestow in deeds of charity; not to mention that by giving employment to the industrious, we are often putting money to its most philanthropic use. You lament the fetters placed by custom upon the free energies of virtue, and most assuredly there *are* those whose own sense of the good and the beautiful would far excel any agency from without, both as motive and restraint. But are not those fitted, as well as " content to dwell in decencies for ever,"—that is, the mass of mankind—the better, do you think, for the habit of submitting to restraint?. If they had more free-agency, would they not rather stray into absurdity, or lose themselves in recklessness, than rise to any higher notions of excellence? But in how many different forms are the questions continually recurring—When to take off the leading-strings or *when* to remove the fetters? All the questions of internal policy which have been and are still shaking our State to its very foundations, may be resolved into these; and even where the restraint is one which has most manifestly originated in nothing but the prevalence of might over right, it is often held a point for grave consideration, how speedily or how entirely it is wise to take it off. With us there are many who hold that the " Voluntary Church system," though best in itself, would not *yet* be best for the English people. Our Tories were loth to allow that Dissenters, Papists, Irishmen, and negro slaves, ought *yet* to be free from their wholesome restrictions, and the other day our House of Lords decided that a few links of chain ought still to remain around town councils. At the bottom of my heart I have a persuasion that the generous and especially the disinterested are the advocates of the earliest and the most complete emancipation; and my sympathies go with them; but then the alarmists and the weighers of expediency come round one with so many plausibilities, that I often, on particular points, become staggered at least, and, if not convinced, I am silenced. With respect to our country, however, I am entirely of opinion that the *when* is the only question. The popular cause has already gained victories which must lead to further and full success; unless, indeed, the Reformers should offend the characteristic moderation and prudence of the nation by some strange ebullitions—hardly to be apprehended. The detection of this widely-spread conspiracy to overpower a reformed ministry and liberal House of Commons, on the part of the Orange Association, headed by that disgrace to human nature, the Duke of Cumberland—shared in by many principal Tory peers, and diffused widely through every rank in the army—is in every way a fortunate event. Its result must be, I think, to bring upon its knees to the people a faction which might have continued to be very formidable, had it not rendered itself detestable, and by its dark machinations brought itself within the danger of the laws. There can be no doubt that Cumberland's aim was to make himself the head of a party strong enough to place him on the throne, to the exclusion of his niece—a mad design indeed, unless he believed the whole people to be enamoured of the character of Caligula. He has been driven from the country, never, I trust, to pollute its soil again, and his principal abettors will not, I suppose, choose to abide the proceedings of the attorney-general. These are strange events, and of absorbing interest to those before whose eyes they pass.

You have well traced out to me the circumstances which are exerting the chief influence at present over your national character. No! with you politics cannot now be the ruling interest. Your fathers have won for you the unmolested enjoyment of the greatest inheritance upon earth; you have now to explore, improve, and enjoy it. You are destined to the good and the ill of a state of unexampled prosperity—unless the slave question be preparing a division of your federal union, with all the formidable results which would plainly be inevitable. To adjust the balance of moral good and evil in the causes which act largely on the character and manners of a nation, is probably a task beyond human power. All that the most enlightened philanthropy can perhaps wisely attempt, is to lean against the prevalent vices of the time, and cherish its virtues. At all times, in all countries advanced in the arts of life, there must be abundant scope for the preacher or the philosopher to cry aloud, "Be not conformed to the world;" be not immersed in matter; forget not the invisible, which alone is real and permanent! Long has your voice been heard, and much longer may it yet be heard, sounding these great warnings in the ears of men, and impressing on their hearts truths of the highest order! For myself, all my exertions are confined to the forming of projects destined very probably never to be executed. During several months I have found myself in a state of languor which reminded me of the knight, in I forget what tale of chivalry, who had drunk unwittingly of the unnerving fountain, and lay stretched upon the grass, lost to all deeds or even thoughts of "chivalrous emprize," and unable to lift the spear or sustain the burden of his crested helm. I ascribe this listlessness partly to a very weak state of health, aggravated by the unusual heat of the season, which is now happily abated, and partly to the deep impression made upon my spirits by very melancholy circumstances affecting those whom I dearly love. I think I must have mentioned before that Mr. —— was tried by severe sickness in his family. He has now two lovely daughters in confirmed declines, and one of them in the very last stage of this dreadful and hopeless disease. This last sweet creature, who has just attained the age of one-and-twenty, has one of the noblest yet softest minds I have known—one of the finest, purest and least earthly spirits. She long suffered her father and sisters to believe that she was ignorant of her state: at length she confessed that for months she had been fully aware of its hopelessness, and since that avowal she has at once wrung their hearts with grief, and warmed them with admiration by a bright manifestation of the treasures of her soul. "In observing the state of her mind," wrote her father to me, "I rejoice with trembling; the question constantly · recurring to me—Is it possible this can hold out to the end? Such firm composure—such a calm contemplation of her approaching departure—such confiding trust in the power and fatherly goodness of God—all this is more than could be anticipated even from her." In this situation, which has now endured about three months, your writings have been her constant solace and support. Everything I had of yours, which she was not before acquainted with, I have sent to her. Her father's last account, too, has this passage: "She said yesterday she should have liked to be under the observation of Dr. Channing, and speculated upon the nature of the advice he would have pressed upon her in her present state; whether he would not have considered her impatient under her trial —not sufficiently disposed to bear, as well as to do, the will of God." I had written to her, that you were full of cheerful views under a dangerous illness some time since, and she begged I would send her an extract from a letter of yours describing your feelings. This account I could not forbear giving you. Poor —— will be released, in all human probability, long before this letter can reach you, or I should have asked some little message for her; but perhaps you will give me a few words in your next for the heart-broken father and his other dear sufferer, also of a most angelic sweetness and goodness, and quite devoted to the service of the sister still more oppressed with illness than herself. But let me quit this melancholy subject.—You have read, or you must read, "Mackintosh's Memoirs" by his son (not the Life prefixed to his historic fragment). It will certainly interest you in many ways, though I think you will agree with me that the impression on the whole is rather a painful one. Mackintosh, with all the ambition of his countrymen, had neither the frugality nor the steady industry by means of which a Scotchman usually climbs to fortune or to power. I am inclined also to believe that his abilities were overrated, or at least wrongly rated, by himself and many of his friends, especially in the beginning of his career. Hence his life offers the history of little else than abortive attempts and half-executed designs. The wide range of his reading, the promptness as well as the accuracy of his memory, and his power of just and sententious remark, gave so much power to his conversation—rendering it, in fact, so like a clever book—that the hearer involuntarily gave him credit for more than he in fact possessed of the powers of a fine writer; as a *debater* in Parliament he had no talent, and even his set speeches were delivered to half-empty benches. His highest efforts, in whatever line, went just so far as to prove that he was *all but* a man of genius. He had attained self-knowledge when he said that his true vocation was that of a professor in a college; but to this his ambition and his passion for shining in London society made him disdain to confine himself. Coleridge's "Table-Talk" is full of strange and rash opinions. I believe it to be neither an impartial nor an intelligent report of his sentiments—and yet a man with his habits might often talk wildly enough: you will find the book worth looking through, however. The second volume improves upon the first, and some of the literary remarks seem to me both fine and just. If I find myself gaining strength and able to write without great fatigue, I will not neglect your kind request to write often and fully.

I have not yet seen the Ticknors, but am to do so on their return to London next month.

Ever believe me, with the greatest truth,
Your obliged and affectionate friend,
L. AIKIN.

TO DR. CHANNING.

Hampstead, January 17, 1836.

My dear Friend,—I will not wait for your acknowledgment of my last letter to write again, knowing by experience how long my letters, committed by Dr. Boott to private hands, have often been in reaching you, and more than suspecting by your silence respecting them, that two or three have never reached you. . . . .

In literature, by much the most considerable publication since I wrote last is Joanna Baillie's three volumes of dramas, which you will no doubt see. She tells me that her own favourite is "Witchcraft," and I think that it perhaps goes deeper into human nature than any of the rest. But I nevertheless prefer her tragedies in verse, and "Henriquez," and still more "Separation," charms me. All these new dramas being of the domestic kind, necessarily fall short of the majesty of "Ethelwald" and of "Constantine," but I think they have as much or more of pathos than her former ones, and not less of poetry; and in the arrangement of the plots and other points of dramatic skill, she has improved very considerably. To those who know her well, the value of all she writes is incalculably increased by its affording so perfect an image of her own pure, benignant and ingenuous spirit. Her character, more, I think, than any I have ever known, deserves to be called a heavenly one; and when I think of it in conjunction with her rare genius, I can scarcely help regarding her as a being of a higher order.

Never in my life has reading been so constantly, almost so incessantly, the business of my life. My state of health confines me very much to the house; of society I have but little; yet the time very seldom indeed hangs heavy, for I can always lose myself in a book. My pen is seldom in use; I am too much cut off from opportunities of informing myself by conversation, too unable to run about in search of documents, to pursue any kind of historical inquiries, and it is but now and then that a subject for a brief essay or dialogue occurs to me. Perhaps indolence grows upon me; it is the natural companion of a monotonous and solitary life, in temperaments not irritable and not enthusiastic; and unless improving health should hereafter enable me, as I am still in hopes it may, to apply the stimulus of change of scene and company, I believe I must be content to allow myself to be numbered with those that *were*, by all but a few dear friends and relations. You will find me but a dull correspondent, I fear—but a very grateful one ever for the pleasure and the benefit of your letters. I will trust mine no more to the precariousness of private hands, for I am quite sure that several proofs of my punctuality, if of nothing more valuable, have not reached you.

You have sometimes been inclined, I think, to reproach us with the miserable state of a large portion of our population, especially the congregated poor of our cities. I am happy to acquaint you that this great evil is rapidly diminishing. Never were manufactures, arts and commerce in such a state of activity amongst us. An extraordinary impulse seems to have been given to *everything;* whence derived in the first instance, I know not. Manchester daily puffs forth fresh volumes of black smoke from more and more huge steam-engines. She invites all agricultural labourers who want work to come to her, and sets them down instantly to spin and to weave. Norwich, which I have known from my childhood as the melancholy seat of decaying manufactures and redundant population, has not now one ablebodied man on the parish books, and twice within six months the doors of her empty jail have stood wide open, for forty-eight hours each time. Our new Poorlaws have happily co-operated with this state of things to raise the moral tone amongst the poor, by compelling them to rely more on their own exertions. With the outward prosperity of this class, there can be no doubt that their desire of giving school-learning to their children will go on increasing. The difficulties of establishing a national system of education I believe to be insurmountable in this country of religious divisions; but I think the object is likely to be on the whole better accomplished by the efforts of the labouring classes themselves, aided by the voluntary exertions of the benevolent and enlightened working on their own plans and within the limits of their respective religious societies. I apprehend that some kind of parish provision for the wretched poor of Ireland will be established in the coming session of Parliament; but there, also, religious divisions formidably obstruct almost every plan for the general benefit. There is, and must be in a Protestant Government, a reluctance to entrust large funds for the support of the poor to the management of the ignorant and bigoted and furious popish priests of Ireland; yet they are indisputably better acquainted with the necessities of the people than any other persons, and the want of a middle class, consisting of substantial farmers and decent tradesmen, in almost all the agricultural districts, seems to point them out as the only qualified dispensers of parish relief. I like to state to you such facts as these, that you may not underrate the difficulties or the efforts of our statesmen, amongst whom I believe that there is at present much wisdom and a very pure love of the public good. In a new country, or under a despotism, a general system may be laid down and carried into effect with little or no modification; but here, hampered by ancient usages and inveterate prejudices amongst the people, compelled on all sides to respect vested rights, and yield to powers of resistance in bodies and in individuals, an administration can do no more than apply partial remedies to inconveniences, and carry plans and principles into a modified and restricted execution. There is, however, this great compensating advantage, that no changes can be made by any other power than that of public opinion, deliberately formed and strongly pronounced; and that a habit of discussion is thus formed and preserved, by which one cannot but hope that much truth important to human happiness will continue to be elicited, especially as reasonings on practical questions of government and political economy are here continually made the subject of actual experiment.

We have all been sympathizing with the sufferers in the conflagration at New York, one of the greatest, I should think, within memory, and we have felt for them the more, on account of the spirit and energy with which they have set themselves to repair their losses by their own exertions, which have been surely admirable, and quite in accordance with your national character.

Winter is dealing rather severely with us, and I fear

with you likewise. I shall be happy to learn that you have not been a sufferer in health by it.

Pray believe me ever yours most truly,

L. AIKIN.

To Miss Aikin.

Boston, March 12, 1836.

My dear Miss Aikin,—I received to-day your letter of January 17, and I cannot let the day pass without answering it. You fear that your letters have not been received, but it is not so. They came in due time, and the blame of my silence lies wholly on myself. I hope you will not visit my offence severely. I told you long ago how prone I have always been to remissness as a correspondent. My faithfulness in this respect towards you has been remarkable. Let this plead for me. My late negligence is not to be ascribed to any want of strength, but to the reverse. I have been uncommonly well since the beginning of the last summer, and the consequence has been an *increased activity.* A European student would smile at what it amounts to. Still it has been enough to weary me and to lead me to postpone letter-writing. This is a poor excuse, and you deserve a better return for your letters. They always give me much to interest me, and I thank you for continuing them. Your last was particularly gratifying by the accounts it contained of your national prosperity. I wish I could look as favourably on our own. *Your* prosperity brings relief to suffering multitudes. *Ours* multiplies comforts and luxuries to those who were well off before, and who have always had the means of improvement. The present effect here is a kind of intoxication, a wildness of enterprize, a more intense worldliness; not that I incline to take dark views of the present. I rejoice to see that the infinite activity of our times is not all wasted in inferior interests. There are good powers at work, better views of the uses of wealth, generous hopes for the race, generous spirits willing to be spent for it. I do not respond to the croakers who see nothing but germs of revolution, convulsions, in the present restlessness of society. Property is everywhere a conservative principle; and when I see the multitude everywhere seeking this by industry, I have no great fears of general confusion. To be sure, this is not relying on a very generous sentiment; but, you know, the ballast which keeps the vessel steady is of little worth; and we must keep her steady some way or other, or the more spiritual forces which carry her forward would soon make a wreck of her. There is more of rhetoric than logic perhaps in this illustration, and I do not mean that I would admit base principle even to keep the State steady. The truth is, that with much excess there is also much well-considered self-interest in the present pursuit of property, and this is legitimate ballast.

Mrs. Baillie's plays have not reached me yet. I look forward to them as a great pleasure. I believe all you tell me of the beauty of her character. My friends whom I introduce to her return with delightful recollections. I felt she took some hazard to her peace in publishing a work so late in life, and your account of the work is very gratifying, as showing that she will not suffer from severity of criticism. I trust her last labour is to be reviewed with a respect and grateful approbation which will cheer her declining years.

Your friend Miss Martineau has spent some time in Boston, and found a hearty welcome. I am sorry that she is here at an evil time. The country is agitated by the question of Slavery, and I have never known our society present a worse aspect. Miss M. has mixed herself up a little with the controversy, that is, she has expressed very strongly her sympathy with the party called Abolitionists, who have contrived to arm against themselves not only the fury of the South, but the prejudices of the North. Still I hope she will not complain of us as inhospitable, though in some instances she has been treated rudely in the papers. Her sincerity and moral independence secure respect even where her opinions are not approved.

I am reading a French book on moral science which interests me much—"Cours de Droit Naturel," by Jouffroy. I am struck with his intimate acquaintance with the English schools of moral philosophy. The French have great merit as expositors of philosophical systems, and I hope through them at last to understand the philosophy of Germany. It is a striking fact that the disinterested character of morality is more insisted on in France and Germany than in England. I welcome every sign of a sound and elevated philosophy on the continent.

We thank England for her disposition to preserve peace between this country and France. Every year of peace seems to me a great gain to the cause of humanity; for peace is not now what it used to be, a mere truce, a time to sharpen the sword for new conflicts, but it is multiplying continually friendly relations, complicating the interests of nations, establishing new means of intercourse, increasing the necessity of peace. Let war be kept off somewhat longer, and a weight of opinion and interest against it, such as has never been known and cannot easily be withstood, will be the result. This good comes from the spirit of commerce.

I hope to hear a better account of your health. Give

yourself repose; I will ensure you against habits of indolence.

Your sincere friend,
WM. E. CHANNING.

Miss Martineau sends her kind regards.

To Miss Aikin.

Boston, May 10th, 1836.

My dear Miss Aikin,—I have had no answer to my last letter, but wish to expiate my long silence by writing without such a motive. I think I told you in my last that we had enjoyed Miss Martineau's society. She makes firm friends wherever she goes. No stranger was ever domesticated in so many families among us, and she has inspired confidence and attachment wherever she has been, and it is creditable to both parties that this kindly intercourse has in no case been interrupted, as far as I can learn, by the great frankness with which she gives out her whole mind. She has made some enemies by taking an open part in the Slavery question which is now agitated here, but alienated no friends. We feel that her deafness is a great obstacle to a just estimate of persons and things here; but should she write about us and give false views, we shall know that she has not erred from want of kindness or of reverence for the truth. I am more and more satisfied that one people cannot be made known to another by travellers. The traveller gets half-truths at best. He is struck most, not by what reveals most a nation's mind and heart, but by what contrasts most strongly with his own manners and habits of thought. A traveller helps the people of whom he writes to understand themselves better by showing how they differ from others, and by an analogous process he comes to understand his own country better; but he is a poor mediator between the two. A nation's history and literature are its best interpreters.

Speaking of travellers, I have amused myself with looking over Mrs. Trollope's Paris. She is certainly clever at observing the surface, but, like other superficial book-makers, leaves you about as wise as she found you. You see through the whole that she is plotting future visits to Paris, and means to be well received. The tone of fearless truth, which cares not for giving offence, is singularly wanting. I was quite amused with her Toryism. It aims to be authoritative and dignified, but cannot rise above scolding. I hope much more from the French than you do; but they need great changes, and such seem to be beginning. Madame Trollope is most angry with them for the worship of Reason in the days of their madness. Such freaks cannot last. To me, their worship of the agreeable, of pleasure, their idea of life as given for sport and bagatelle, their out-door, superficial, epicurean mode of living, the apparent absence of all consciousness of the serious and sublime purposes of human existence,—this is to me most discouraging. The great work of Paris is to solve the problem how the most continuous pleasurable sensation can be secured, and they have learned that the gentler and more moderate pleasures, the little "agrémens," the courtesies and graces of life, are vastly more effectual in exorcising the demon ennui, than more vehement and passionate enjoyments. They are the wisest and most practical epicureans; but, to my apprehension, Paris is one of the last spots on earth for comprehending or securing the true happiness of a human being. There is one striking proof of the folly of their philosophy. In the city, where people live most for the present moment, contempt of life is more frequent than anywhere else. Where but in Paris would you have had such an exhibition as the execution of Fieschi and the other conspirators? Mrs. Trollope even says that every week there are cases of suicide for no other object but to be talked of, and to awaken wonder for a day. I will not answer for the truth of this, but I cannot think that, where life is laid down with so much sang-froid, its true happiness has been found. Mrs. Trollope's book is an amusing comment on the national vanity, not by her description of it, but by the degree in which she has caught the contagion herself. She has given with much seriousness a ludicrous scene, the reading of Chateaubriand's Memoirs before a select circle, a most truly Parisian affair; and the complacent authoress, in her delight at finding her way into this precious coterie, has not the faintest suspicion of the smiles she is exciting in the reader at her own expense, and the expense of the other worshippers of that distinguished man. But is France always to be so superficial? The change in her intellectual philosophy is remarkable; but passing over this and other refined agents, a grosser instrument is working a revolution in France, and indeed in all Europe. I refer to the Spirit of Trade, the Spirit of Railroads, and other material improvements, the impulse given to all industry. The French may even rival *you* in wealth-worship and in the passion for accumulation; and when men begin to build up a fortune as the great interest of life, though they may not be morally better, they will certainly be more serious, earnest, thoughtful of the future; and here is a groundwork for something nobler. In proportion as the people grow industrious and rich, they will be less in the streets; and in proportion as they cease to live perpetually in one another's sight, they will learn to look into themselves; something *inward* will take place of the outward, the superficial, the frivolous.—I little thought of making out my letter on one topic. You will see that I have caught nothing of the French volatility of spirit; and you may wish that I had taken some lessons in the Parisian art of touching a subject lightly and gracefully, and glancing from one to another; but you will accept kindly what is done in kindness. I have not strength enough to write another letter, or make this more legible.

Very faithfully your friend,

WM. E. CHANNING.

To DR. CHANNING.

Hampstead, June 12, 1836.

This is indeed an awakener to my conscience! A second kind and delightful letter from you, whilst an answer to the first is still lying half-written in my desk, where it has remained untouched, I believe, a full month!

My only excuse is one which I rejoice that you had not to plead—an unusual severity and continuance of illness and debility, and perhaps an indolent disinclination to exert the little power which I still possess. But away with such impediments! I will make mind victorious for once over body! Your account of Harriet Martineau gives me great pleasure. I rejoice that her remarkable and fearless sincerity has been rightly appreciated among you; it sometimes made me fear for her in London; but there also what friends she made she kept. No doubt she will write a book about you; but I entirely agree with you that travellers always see imperfectly, and with a bias. Nevertheless, I should like you to look at Von Raumer's account of us. I believe him to be upright and sincere, and he gave me the idea of an industrious, and zealous, and rather able man of letters. The curious thing is, the coolness with which he takes for granted that Prussia is much further advanced than England in the science of legislation and government, as well as in the arts of music, painting and sculpture; and the patronizing tone with which he honours us on these matters, doing homage, however, to our surpassing wealth and luxury. It is true that Prussia may boast of a national system of education which imparts the rudiments of several kinds of knowledge, and of *singing and playing* to all; and that *they* have advanced so far as to put all religions on the same footing, not only with regard to civil rights, but to state endowments. Yet I believe we shall not be brought to look up to any despotism, however mildly or prudently administered.

Germany is a country which now interests me much more than France, though I am struck with your ideas respecting the means now at work for her improvement, and I shall rejoice to see them verified; but to us Germany is of more importance. It is a school in which numbers of our young men are learning lessons, the results of which are likely, unless I mistake, strongly to influence religious *feelings*, rather perhaps than religious opinions, amongst us. One of these gentlemen, now about thirty, poured out his whole heart to me on these subjects the other day, taking me, I believe, to be the only female relation he had who could understand or would bear with him. He had returned some years ago from a first visit to Germany, resolute not to fulfil his destination to the English Church. A second residence has only confirmed him in his abhorrence of creeds and articles, and admiration of the freedom of a German university, where all varieties of opinion are represented by one professor or another, and the students may attend whichever they please. He seemed to me devout as well as sincere. The cheap and simple life led by the inhabitants of Munich, where he has also found an agreeable circle of lettered and polished society, delighted him much. He will probably return to it, at least for a season; but in the meantime he is connected with a set of young Germanized Englishmen, who write in a new British and Foreign Review, and are labouring to instil their free opinions into our public.

Full time it is now that I should thank you for your introduction of your nephew and his family. My illness, indeed, has prevented my seeing the mother and son more than once, when they paid me too short a visit, and your niece I have not seen, but I was very much struck and pleased with Mr. Channing. He instantly revived my recollection of you, which was in itself a great merit in him; but I can well perceive that he has much besides. His manners are such as no teaching could give; they are evidently the emanation of a noble and elegant mind. I was particularly struck with the candour he evinced in all his judgments, and the fine tact manifested in all he said and did. I congratulate you with my whole heart on possessing such a relation and such a friend and associate as I am sure he must prove to you. I hope for one more glimpse of them before they finally quit London. Ah! why will you not come yourself?

I am all but a prisoner to my house and little garden. I am a miserable walker, and unable to bear without injury the motion of a carriage even for a short drive. I accommodate myself, however, to my circumstances better than I could have anticipated. Whilst I have books always, and the sight of friends sometimes, I find life more than bearable. The only thought which sits heavy on my mind is that of my own inutility. Alas! what important end of existence do I fulfil? To whom is it of any real consequence whether or not I continue to fill a place in the world? I hope only that involuntary uselessness will not be imputed, and that we may say, "They also serve who only stand and wait." The thing I find chiefly to be guarded against is indolence, or the habit of filling up time with trifling occupations which unfit the mind for any strenuous effort. I own myself guilty this way; I promise to amend—but how difficult to *make* motives for exertions! A necessarian would say, impossible. The thought of necessarians brings me back to that system of Hartley which you dislike so much. Surely it must be wrong to trace human character or human actions to any single principle, whether that of association or any other, for we cannot well help observing in ourselves the operation of a great complication of causes. But yet I suppose you would admit that there is not one of our active principles which is not strongly influenced by the power of association. How then do you limit its sway? The more I reflect upon the formation of human character, the more impracticable I feel it to reduce the facts to any general rule. It seems as if the doctrine of association had been employed by the French *philosophers* to represent that chance to which they were willing to ascribe everything. But the pious Hartley no doubt believed, "All chance direction which we cannot see." Still, I never could understand how his system was really compatible with moral responsibility —with the sense of human actions which God himself has surely implanted in our souls. I do not wonder that Mackintosh struggled so hard to find a middle way between two systems which appear each of them false and each of them true, according to the side on which they are viewed. This is all very crude, I am sensible; but I want to strike a light out of you if I may.

Pray believe me ever most truly yours,

L. AIKIN.

To Miss Aikin.

Boston, November 21, 1836.

My dear Miss Aikin,—Your letter of June 12th deserved an earlier answer; but I have for some time shrunk from any effort, except in cases where I had a special object which required immediate attention. At the end of the summer I was attacked with a short illness which left me prostrated for weeks, from which I am not yet entirely restored. I find that we may learn to suffer, as we learn other things. I do not mean merely that we may make a wiser and more effectual use of religious principles and hopes, but that we may learn abstinence from ineffectual attempts to mitigate pain which only disappoint and make bad worse, and get the art of turning to better account the little intervals and alleviations of suffering which belong to sickness. I find it better to look the foe (that is too hard a word) in the face, and to make up my mind to pain, instead of inquiring for and multiplying remedies, and watching solicitously their operation. I have fancied, too, that by analyzing our sensations in moments of suffering, we might find some pleasurable ingredients which escape us without such attention, and which may be brought out and fill larger space by a wise care. Much may be done, where there is any command of thought (and this is seldom wholly lost), by choosing topics of thought of an interesting nature, such as our past lives, the modes in which certain principles or habits grew up, the influences of such and such friends, or the characters of friends revealed in all that we know of them. I suspect that the retirement of a sick chamber, so spent, will make us better acquainted, not only with ourselves, but with others, than a long intercourse in which we have never concentrated our observation. I am satisfied a good book might be written on the *art of suffering.* Our intellectual philosophy might furnish many hints. The expedients to which impatience recurs for relief almost always aggravate the evil. Why not make this the subject of one of your essays? It would be worth a few fits of illness to be able to teach others how to bear it.

In looking at your last letter, I see you recur to some of my opinions about the change going on in the French character. After sending that letter, I feared I might have written unguardedly. I meant only to give facts, not to express approbation of them. The spirit of trade, enterprize and accumulation, is working mighty changes, supplanting the spirit of war, the old aristocracy, &c., bringing forward the inferior classes; but there is much in it I detest. It is removing many abuses, undoing the past; but I do not see that it is to re-construct society so as to answer at all the hopes of a wise philanthropist. Our country this moment is suffering severely from the madness of what is called "speculation." The insane lust of gain has hurried multitudes into over-trading and wild schemes, and we all suffer; but the suffering is nothing compared with the infinite moral evils of this reckless, daring selfishness. I was exceedingly struck with the deep impression made on Lamartine (in his Pilgrimage) by the quiet, unaspiring, unsolicitous spirit of the East. Have you read that book? Its descriptions of scenery are wearisome, but the views of society are exceedingly interesting. He evidently thought that there was more virtue as well as happiness in the abandonment of the Oriental to the present moment, to the influences of nature, to spontaneous, unsought pleasures, to the natural affections, than in the restless, feverish, anxious pursuits of avarice and ambition which characterize Europe. I have no doubt that the true religion is the reconciliation of these two elements of repose and activity, so seldom harmonized now; nor do I believe in any other mediator.

Your account of the probable influence of Germany on your country was exceedingly interesting to me. I know nothing of the new British and Foreign Review. Anything to stir up the unphilosophical, stationary mind of England on moral, religious, spiritual subjects, must do good. The Church seems to you in danger. At this distance, it seems to be embraced with new zeal by a formidable party, and the public mind seems to be running into a religion most falsely called *evangelical*. The signs of a purer, nobler faith do not appear as yet. That there is an under-current of scepticism, I do not doubt: so much the worse. At this moment, religion seems to be doing nothing to elevate the national mind. I trust it lays restraint on vice, and this is a great good. Write me more on these points. Write me soon, and tell me you are better and able to labour. I must stop. What is taking place is chiefly of local importance, though very exciting. We have passed through an election of President in the most quiet way, though the parties are much inflamed. I took but little interest in it, for the chief points of difference are financial, or relate to banks, revenue, &c., affairs beyond my capacity, and understood very little by other people.

Your sincere friend,
WM. E. CHANNING.

I have not yet read Raumer. In truth, I have been a sad idler for three months. A friend read to me, whilst convalescing, a powerful, but strange, I fear unprofitable, book, called "Physical Theory of another Life." It is worth reading.

To Dr. Channing.

Hampstead, December 10, 1836.

My dear Friend,—Will you, or not, regard it as a palliation of my shameful deficiencies as a correspondent, that I have had in my paper-case for above two months a letter to you half-finished, which I have never found resolution to complete? The fact was, that I had there entered into some political speculations, the soundness of which I began to distrust as soon as I saw them on paper. I said to myself, "Let them wait till I see more of the course of events in Ireland." And thus they remained till a few days since, when I finally condemned them. Wiser people, and much more skilful politicians, than I, have been as much perplexed to know what to expect, or even what to wish, for that luckless country. It seems to me that all the really puzzling questions in public morals, as in private, arise from having previously gone wrong. The straight line is generally obvious enough to those who have never quitted it, but hard to be distinguished by such as, having deviated, are anxious to return to it by the nearest way. This is what one feels about the Protestant Establishment in Ireland. The wrong step was to set it up whilst the majority of the people were Papists; but to give to that abominable superstition the triumph of seeing it now at length pulled down again, goes very much against one's feelings and all one's better hopes for mankind. Still worse would it be to see the re-establishment of Popery, which seems to be aimed at by O'Connell and his red-hot followers. Meantime, there is unmingled satisfaction in observing the equal justice which is now administered there between men of the two religions, and the means taken to civilize their fierce manners, and to relieve their wants. Should this system be steadily pursued for some time longer, it may so mollify angry spirits as to render an equitable adjustment very feasible.

The warmest wish which my heart now forms for my country is the cessation of the vehement party struggles which have agitated us so long. To say nothing of the interruption of old friendships and of the comfort of general society which they occasion, they occupy many of the ablest heads and most accomplished characters, to the exclusion of objects of higher, because more extensive and permanent, importance. Literature, as you well know, is in an unsatisfactory state amongst us. By writers, it is too much regarded as a mere trade; by readers, as one only of the contrivances for filling up the vacant spaces of life; like dancing, singing, or sight-seeing. But we may live to see a change. I have lately been paying a good deal of attention to the literature of the time of William and Anne; and it is cheering to observe what an impulse was given to it by that revolution which, like the one in which we are now living, was peaceable, and carried in favour of freedom, by appeals to the reason, the best feelings and the true interests of Englishmen.

Pray read, as I am doing, the "Literary Remains" of Coleridge. In one passage he denounces with such indignant scorn those readers who presume to intimate that an author does not understand himself, when it is only that their stupid or ignorant minds are incapable of understanding him, that I certainly dare not intimate any such suspicion regarding him. I will only say that he has very many passages which pass my comprehension: some, indeed, which are quite too deep in scholarship for me; others which I do comprehend, but which seem to me exceedingly absurd; others, again, which have more of the philosopher, and more of the poet, than we can hope from any one of our living writers with whom I am acquainted. His native proneness to the mystical seems to have received added force from his study of the German philosophy; but from that deep I often perceive that pearls are drawn up. I have frequently wished myself a diver in it. I feel, as I know you do, the "flat, stale and unprofitable." of our utilitarianism in everything. It rejoices my spirit when Coleridge launches a thunderbolt at that clay idol of our universities—Paley. As to his assaults upon Unitarianism, I do not suppose they will much either irritate or alarm you. He is a perfect enthusiast for the Trinity, and especially for the doctrine of the fall of man. Of the last he says, that it is not only inconceivable to him *how* it should be true, but *that* it should be true; but that *it is*, his conscience tells him so. As if a man should say, I know I am a beggar, and that convinces me that my great grandfather must have had a fine estate and forfeited it for treason! Next to these grand mysteries, he seems to cherish the notion that the genius of Shakspeare was actually superhuman; and he approaches an *apparently* absurd or immoral passage in his writings with full as much awe as a text of scripture—the plenary inspiration of which, by the way, he strenuously denies. Yet his lecture on English Literature, and particularly his remarks on Shakspeare, are full of deep thought, exquisite discrimination, profound sensibility, and brilliant and truly poetical illustration. It is a great pity that, as he delivered them almost entirely without notes, we have them only in the imperfect memoranda taken down by his hearers. They were perfectly *dazzling* as he delivered them. I was so fortunate as to hear two of them, almost thirty years ago.

I have not yet seen Miss Martineau, though several notes have passed between us relative to the memorial of English authors to your legislature concerning copyright. Mr. Farrar says the business would have been more likely to succeed if our Government had interposed by its minister, and so I think too; doubting a little whether Harriet's interest at Washington will prove as powerful as she imagines—but the effort seems at least not likely to injure the cause, which is surely a just one. There will be, I hope, a good deal of curiosity to see our friend's book; but, unluckily, we have been inundated with books on America, and it will be difficult for her to find unpreoccupied ground. The Slavery question is a rock in her way which will require wariness. Our public may think that *we* have purchased a right not to have our feelings further tortured with details of negro suffering. She will regard herself as addressing, perhaps equally, both sides of the water—for she seems to have left at least half her heart behind her—and this, I conceive, will make a difficulty. Miss Tuckerman paid me a short visit the other day, and left me desirous of seeing more of her. There is the stamp of something noble upon her, as indeed might be expected of her father's daughter.

With me time passes—as I believe it never does with you—heavily, languidly. I read and read, but can fix my mind to no pursuit, and my pen is quite idle. It might seem strange to say I am idle because I am alone, and yet I verily believe this to be the case. Under the perpetual misfortune of domestic solitude, I find it impossible to raise my spirits to the tone necessary for composition; idleness re-acts on my spirits; and unless I can make to myself, or circumstances should make for me, some kind of stimulus, this unsatisfactory state may continue to the end. Change of scene would be a grand medicine to my mind, but unfortunately travelling disagrees exceedingly with my health. Why do I trouble you with all this? I believe in excuse for a dull letter, or else from the pardonable wish of gaining a little sympathy.

Again my letter has suffered an interruption of many days. The melancholy of the last paragraph was, I believe, the gathering of a fit of illness. It is now dispersed, and I am going to enjoy myself at a friend's house in London, where much good company is to be met. I shall have the opportunity of asking Mr. Hallam when he intends to give us his history of the literature of (I think) the fourteenth and fifteenth centuries, which I am impatient to see. Just now I am reading—what indeed I have often read before, but the changes in our own sentiments often make an old book seem new to us—the great epic of Tasso. I never admired this noble work so much, and I am now wishing to see a critique worthy of it by some modern hand. The division of the poetry of Europe, since the revival of letters, into the classical and the romantic, is, I think, a good one; but it would be hard to say which school may best lay claim to Tasso; their respective shares seem balanced to a grain, reckoning, that is, by the number of lines which seem to belong to each. As to the value of the respective parts, the case is very different. From the ancients, Virgil in particular, he has servilely translated many passages and transferred some whole incidents; what is in the romantic style is full of life and interest, and, so far as I know, of originality. In one part he appears only the elegant scholar and versifier; in the other, the great poet. Had he not, from melancholy and distrust of himself, submitted his work to the tyranny and pedantry of classical critics, I cannot but think he would have given us an epic all romantic, and all worthy of his genius, which was not less fertile than graceful. How unaccountable it is that he should everywhere call the Mahomedans *pagans*, so intimately as

Moors and Saracens were then known all over Italy! Did ever religious animosity so mistake the matter as when Italian Papists reproached Mussulmans with idolatry! Ariosto misstates this matter as much as Tasso. I live upon the old masterpieces; lately I treated myself with the re-perusal of "Don Quixote," which Coleridge, by the way, has very admirably and eloquently characterized. You are a great optimist; but will you give me any hopes that we shall ever see greater, or so great, works of genius again produced? The presiding power of this age is the steam-engine, and what has that to do with anything morally or spiritually great?

Pray believe me ever yours, with true regard,

L. AIKIN.

To Dr. Channing.

Hampstead, February 12, 1837.

My dear Friend,—Many thanks both for your kind letter and for your dedication sermon,* in which I found much to interest me, although the general strain of sentiment is, as indeed it could not but be, very similar to what you had before expressed. I was much pleased with your biographical notice at the end of it. Here I reckon myself upon my own ground, and I entirely agree with you that "no department of literature is so false." Give us more of these sketches of your old worthies; this must bear to the mind of every reader the stamp of truth and resemblance, and the manner in which its subject dealt with his horrible system was very original and remarkable, and much worth recording. I formerly heard, from the lips of a large and free thinker, this problem:—Suppose that it were necessary, in order to

* Discourse at Dedication of Unitarian Church, Newport, Rhode Island, July 27, 1836.

carrying into effect the system which should produce the greatest amount of good upon the whole to the human race, that a few individuals should endure unrequited misery, such as should make existence to them a preponderance of suffering: would you say that it was inconsistent with the justice of God to adopt that system? I could find no other answer than this:—That if it were believed that there was to be even one such victim, as no man could tell that the doomed one might not be himself, it would destroy reliance upon the justness or goodness of God in every mind, and I could not believe in an unjust Deity. But Dr. Hopkins would have said this was a selfish, wicked view of the subject. Somewhat a similar conclusion, though from very different premises, Mackintosh comes to in one of his speculations, where he seems to say that a man ought to be contented with believing that the *race* would go on indefinitely advancing in knowledge, virtue and happiness, and discard the weakness of wishing or hoping that his own existence should be continued to be a witness of that advancement. But this is too sublime a height of virtue for me. After all, the origin of evil is *the* difficulty; it lies at the bottom of every system, whether of religion or philosophy, and by whom has it ever been solved? You express curiosity respecting our *visible church*, and want to hear more fully the grounds of my opinion that it is in danger, notwithstanding the stout rally apparently making in its favour. No doubt the sense of danger has called up zealous defenders, and to a small extent a coalition may have taken place between the orthodox, that is the half-Romish, and the evangelical, that is the half-Puritan, parties within our Establishment. In fact, the ritual superstitions of one sect, and the doctrinal superstitions of the other, are not so absolutely incompatible but that interest may sometimes reconcile them; and it is from no advancement of human reason upon these points that I augur ill for the ecclesiastical fabric, but from more earthly considerations.

The spirit of our liturgy and of our clergy is basely, slavishly loyal. "Fear God, and honour the King," are injunctions which they have always coupled together as equally obligatory and sacred. Now the spirit of this age, as I need not tell you, is anything but this. Hence a wide and deep ill-will among the numerous classes towards the system, and still more towards the men. For proof of this, I cite the success which has attended all late attempts at abridging the exclusive privileges of the Establishment. The new Registration-law, just coming into action, takes from the clergy, and without pecuniary compensation, the monopoly of performing marriages. It likewise adds a universal register of births to the registry alone of baptisms performed by the parochial clergy, and this too without compensation for probable diminution of baptismal fees.

The imposition of Church-rates has been so vigorously opposed by the advocates of the *voluntary system*—comprehending many Churchmen, with the whole body of Dissenters—that the ministry *must* abolish them. Tithes in England have probably been saved for the present by a commutation; but High-churchmen, with some reason, regard this as placing the revenues of the Church on a less independent and less secure foundation, making them stipendiaries rather than freeholders. In Ireland the tithe is certainly at its last gasp. The only claim advanced by Dissenters in which they have been as yet unsuccessful is that of admission to Oxford and Cambridge without a declaration of belonging to the Establishment; but it has been found necessary to grant power of conferring degrees without that condition to an academic body in London, and probably the universities will find it their interest soon to yield.

Another awkward circumstance for the Church is this. The vast increase of our population was naturally judged to require an addition to the number of places of worship. Parliament under the Tories, and with many bitter speeches from the opposition, granted large sums for building churches, and by the activity of zealous persons, especially the Bishop of London, large subscriptions have since been raised for the same purpose. But how to endow the officiating ministers, and provide for current expenses, has become a greater difficulty than raising the edifices. Tithes and other Church funds being already appropriated, it was necessary to have recourse to pew-rents, and it appears as if the children of the Establishment, accustomed to get their religion gratis, so grudge this payment, that the new churches and chapels mostly turn out failures, and starve their ministers. A person above this sordidness, but more attached perhaps to the doctrines than the forms or rites of the Church, and caring more for the preaching than the Prayer-book, is tempted to say, however, "If I pay, let me at least pay to a chapel, where I may hear a minister chosen by myself and the rest of the congregation, and not forced upon us by the rector or the bishop." And thus it seems as if Dissent would gain by the very measures taken to counteract its increase. To call in the voluntary principle *in part* is hazardous for an endowed Church. There has also been a little civil war between a commission, chiefly bishops, appointed to attempt some gentle reforms in the Church, and the deans and chapters, whom the pious prelates have defrauded of some patronage, and converted to their own benefit. Sydney Smith, that bright wit and independent politician who founded the

"Edinburgh Review," is one of the aggrieved, and has stated their case in a keen pamphlet which unmasks that would-be Laud, the Bishop of London, and which—contrary, I believe, to the author's intentions—gives a handle to the enemies of the hierarchy altogether. These are the signs of the times on which I found my auguries; but very much of the fate of the Church, as well as State, will depend on the event of the renewal of that grand conflict between our two Houses of Legislature which is now imminently impending. For my own part, I see indeed many dangers, many evils, on both sides of the question; but I feel my heart beating stronger and stronger towards the cause of the people; regarding that cause, however, as what would be best promoted by the preservation of our triple form of government, with some modification of the authority of the peers, and especially with the great improvement of the exclusion of the bishops from their house.

I do not wonder that you regard the kind of religion now prevailing here as little fitted to elevate the mind, and useful only as a restraint. In fact, the *currency*, whether stamped with the effigies of prelate or heresiarch, is of base alloy; but our *cabinets* contain thousands of pure gold medals. The present concern should be to cry down the base coin; afterwards we may raise the standard. You will see my meaning if you will examine an article in the "Edinburgh Review" on Evangelical Preaching. I know not who is the author, but I think him on the right track. It would break my heart to believe that superstition and hypocrisy were to hold in perpetual bondage my dear and noble country. They must not—will not—shall not!

Since I began this letter I have had the pleasure of a visit from your friend Mr. Gannett. We seemed acquainted at once, and had a long and animated conversation, partly on the topics of this letter. I am much pleased with him. It is impossible to mistake his sincere devotion to the highest and best objects. I hope we shall return him to you well recruited for future exertions. In literature I have seen nothing lately of much interest, for I have not yet seen Mr. Hallam's new work. There is a Life of Goldsmith, prolix, and in every respect meanly written; the account of his early days, however, is worth reading, as a picture of Irish manners about a century ago. Nothing is more remarkable than the loose notions of property among persons of some education. Those who wanted, however much it was their own fault, asked as a matter of course, and what is more, received as a matter of course, relief from persons whom the same carelessness might reduce to beggary to-morrow. It seems that the description in the "Deserted Village" of the exemplary clergyman who so freely received all beggars and vagabonds for his guests and companions, was a true draught from Irish life, such as the poet saw it in his own father's house. According to our Irish poor commissioners, the same amalgamation seems still to subsist between the begging and the farming population, and I apprehend it had its root in the old Brehon law which gave the property of land to the whole *Sept* in common, and merely temporary occupation to individuals. One might say that the Irish have never owned anything but land, and in that, or its profits, all have regarded themselves as entitled to some share. In this there seems to be some natural justice; but how incompatible with civilized English notions! Poor Goldsmith, with his boundless sympathy and goodnature, and thus brought up, became in London a constant prey to rapacity and imposture, and when brought to distress he preyed on others by running in debt to them. His habits of life were far from right and correct; but still he had "a spirit finely touched;" he always served virtue with his pen, and his delightful works seem no nearer oblivion than when they first appeared. I am glad to see him brought again before the public.

I have heard no more since my last writing concerning our German students; in fact, we are too busy at present with practical matters concerning our Church and State to have much leisure for the speculations of philosophy, in which the Germans may freely indulge. I wish we also found ourselves too busy to dip into the infamous and corrupting novels now so prominent a part of the literature of France. You may see that our reviews, under colour of reprehending, are exciting curiosity respecting them, and I fear they are fast gliding into a half-secret circulation.

Our whole country has been saddened by a severe epidemic, under the name of influenza, of which many, chiefly of the aged and the weakly, have died. It is abating now. With me it dealt lightly, and I am now in usual health.

I rejoice to hear good accounts of your recovered strength.

Believe me ever truly yours,
LUCY AIKIN.

To Miss Aikin.

Boston, April 1, 1837.

My dear Miss Aikin,—I received two or three days ago your letter of February. It gave me great pleasure. Your previous letter had been written under disease and depression, and gave me some concern for you. I rejoice with you in your improved health and spirits. I cannot think of you as restored. Both of us, I suppose, are doomed to find the body more or less a burden to the end of our journey. But I repine not at the doom. What remains to me of strength becomes more precious for what is lost. I have lost one ear, but was never so alive to sweet sounds as now. My sight is so far impaired that the brightness in which nature was revealed to me in my youth is dimmed, but I never looked on nature with such pure joy as now. My limbs soon tire, but I never felt it such a privilege to move about in the open air, under the sky, in sight of the infinity of creation, as at this moment. I almost think that my simple food, eaten by rule, was never relished so well. I am grateful, then, for my "earthly tabernacle," though it does creak and shake not a little. It has stood this winter's blasts wonderfully. I do not know when I have passed through the cold wind so comfortably. Pardon my egotism. I should not have yielded to it, had I not felt that I had a good account to give of myself. Happiness, perhaps, makes us more egotistical than suffering. My sufferings I wish to shut up, but would it be grateful to give no tongue to my joy? The habit which I have of looking at what is interesting and great in human nature has no small influence in brightening my life. To be a spiritual being, to have the power of thought, of virtue, disinterestedness, progress without end—this does seem to me an infinite good. If this inward life can be strengthened, it seems to me of little importance what the outward life is. I have only had a gentle touch, a slight taste of poverty, not enough to let me know fully what this dreaded calamity is; but it seems to me I should not care much for it, if the consciousness of my *inward* spiritual being should remain to me. Again I must say, forgive my egotism. I am almost tempted to begin a new letter, lest what I have written should give you some false impression of my feelings; but your knowledge of human nature will tell you that misgivings and self-reproach must mix with these brighter views. My present mood is cheerful, and allowance must be made for it.

I have read very little of late, because I have been well enough to act. Books are my amusements rather than employment. Yesterday I was reading a story of Richter (Jean Paul), and was a little struck with finding there at full the thoughts which I had expressed in my last letter to you, on the power of a *great idea*. Perhaps one reason of my interest in German books is, that I meet so much of my own mind in them. I well remember when I read Madame De Stael's Germany, on its first appearance, how amazed and delighted I was to find it overflowing with thoughts which had been struggling and forming in my own breast, some half-formed, some matured. Mr. Hallam's new work has not reached me, nor Goldsmith's Life. I shall be glad to get some more favourable views of the latter than Boswell has given. I have sometimes been almost ready to pronounce Goldsmith the finest specimen of English style. He unites with Addison's wonderful ease and *nature*, a sweetness all his own. Such writers as Addison and Goldsmith make me feel my own great defects. The eloquent style, as it is called, I might make some approach to. But the spontaneous graces of these writers are beyond me. I do not enjoy them the less on that account.

I was much interested by your news of the Church question, and am looking with great concern to the struggle in the present Parliament. Success to the good cause!

Your sincere friend,
WM. E. CHANNING.

Mr. Norton, whom I introduced to you, has just published the first volume of an important work on "The Genuineness of the Gospels." I have read the text only, not the notes, which form the bulk of the volume. It has great merit. Do read it.

To Dr. Channing.

Hampstead, April 23, 1837.

My dear Friend,—The very great kindness of your last, which I received lately, impels me to answer it speedily, though I think you will ere now have had one of mine, written in much better spirits than that which so much excited your concern for me. Yes, body is to blame, I believe, whenever my spirits are depressed without any evident cause, for they are usually victorious over all minor miseries, and they, like my health, are now recruited. It appears that thousands have been attacked, during our long visitation of influenza, with this dejection of mind; that in many cases it has formed the leading symptom of the epidemic—so mysteriously do mind and body act and re-act upon each other. This extraordinarily prolonged winter has aggravated all our evils, and we are but just beginning to feel a milder air breathing upon us. The face of nature is still wintry and dark. Fortunate may those account themselves who, like myself, have not been called to mourn for any very near and dear; the mortality has been appalling. The weakly, and particularly the aged, have been mown down in heaps. Since the plague of London, so large a proportion of its population has never fallen in a single season.

Do you inquire what our public is now occupied with? We have forgotten our epidemic, we have waived politics for a space, and have been supping full with the horrors of a bloody murder. Not that we care so very much for the simple circumstance of a man's killing a woman whom he pretended to be on the point of marrying; but to have cut off her head and limbs afterwards, that is what has shocked us beyond measure. I believe, however, the general feeling is in this instance right, and that, even of the persons capable of a cold-blooded, mercenary murder, but few could bring themselves to attempt such a mode of disposing of the remains. I should be sorry to see our populace cured of all reverence for the shell which has once contained a human spirit. In this case, the police were obliged to fight hard with the mob to prevent them from tearing to pieces the murderer, and a woman, his accomplice.

Are you aware that the humanity of our rabble is one topic of our national boasting? Unlike the French, mobs with us never shed the blood of any whom they regard as their own political enemies. I am not aware that they have massacred since the days of Jack Cade. Then they always take the part of the weaker. A man could scarcely do anything so dangerous as to treat a child with cruelty in the streets of London. Formerly, they were unfeeling towards the brute creation; but owing, I think, to two circumstances—the diffusion of the taste for natural history by Penny Magazines and by the Zoological Gardens, and the enactment of penal laws against cruelty to animals—a great and admirable change has taken place, insomuch that it is now a protection to cattle to be driven to market through the great thoroughfares of the city. I am inclined to think that no evil propensity is so generally counteracted by the influence of education as that to cruelty—the vice, peculiarly, of the unthinking and the uncivilized. In this point, at least, the connection between knowledge and virtue is perfectly clear. Would it were equally so in many others!

A strange thing, good sir, that you should have been preaching here in Hampstead church, fifty yards from my door, without letting me know a word of the matter! It must have been you, no doubt, for I am credibly informed that a stranger delivered in that pulpit, a few Sundays ago, one of Dr. Channing's most admired discourses, changing nothing whatever but the text. Yours is a wide cure seemingly! This brings me to what you say of the value of a *great idea*, which gives " unity to our inward being." You have a great right to speak of what you know so well from happy personal experience. I will add that I regard it as the highest privilege of your profession, when embraced from pure motives and strong convictions, that it connects by so close a bond the inward and the outward life. It is the single care of the good pastor to put his most intimate thoughts into all his judgments upon the practice of others. From this concentration of his whole being, he derives that mighty power which enables him to wield the minds of men almost at his pleasure. No other class is thus privileged. A physician, for example, may overflow with devout feeling in his closet, but when he quits it he must take up studies and occupations quite unconnected with religion, which he cannot even introduce into his discourse but at the risk of giving offence, or of incurring suspicions. He must not take upon him to be weighing the actions and characters of other men in the scales of the sanctuary; if he makes them his own standard, he cannot very gracefully proclaim that he does so. Hence a kind of complexity in the scheme of life, and especially a separation between inward and outward, unfavourable to ardour and to strong moral effects. The same may be said of persons engaged in every other walk of active life; but the contemplative and the literary, if they are willing at least to live almost out of the world, may in good measure *enact their own ideal.* The ancient philosophers appear often to have done so, and they also were able to form schools of disciples, as were Godwin and Bentham in our own times. But for this, a spirit of dogmatism is requisite, with which many neither are nor would wish to be inspired. Certainly a *great idea* is like the faith which could remove mountains; but to think we have found a *great,* and at the same time a *new* idea, that is the difficulty. I own I have as much hope of finding the philosopher's stone. Continual reading, if desultory and without a definite object, favours indolence, unsettles opinions, and of course enfeebles the mental and moral energies. Writing, on the contrary, concentrates the thoughts and gives strength to convictions. I feel that since I have disused it my mind has become, if I may say so, of a thinner consistency. When by chance I turn to some passages of my James or Charles, I am apt to say to myself, Surely I was a *man* when I wrote that, who am now a mere old woman. This is lamentable enough. I wish I dare promise to find a remedy; perhaps I may, however; for since my health is amended, I feel an appetite for labour to which I had long been a stranger.

As to public affairs, we are all *at gaze.* Must the Whigs go out? Dare the Tories come in? Will the Commons pass this Bill? Will the Lords throw out that? These are the questions which everybody asks, and nobody can answer. The King will not let the Parliament be dissolved, that seems certain; and parties are so nearly balanced in the legislature at present, that neither seems able to do more than obstruct the measures of the other. It is like a great stoppage of carriages in the street; the people who sit fretting in their coaches think it will never be over; but sooner or later some broad-wheeled waggon or brewer's dray will move out of the way, and people will proceed on their various errands as usual. We are waiting for some accident or incident. Meantime all parties are much out of humour; in particular the *odium theologicum* is in high venom.

Poor Lord Melbourne is half distracted whenever a bishop dies, because there is such a difficulty to find Whig parsons out of whom to make a new one—that is, such as are old and seasoned; plenty may be had made up in haste, on the spur of the occasion, but those are liable to warp by change of seasons. The last who died, Bathurst of Norwich, still more venerable by his virtues than his ninety-three years, was a true patriot, a fine scholar, a finished gentleman, and what might be called the Christian of every church. *Because* he believed his own church the truest and the best, he was anxious to remove all such bulwarks from about her as tests and subscriptions; *because* he was a really pious and exemplary man, he disdained affected rigour and evangelical sourness. I once heard him deliver a charge to his clergy, which was the best adapted to inspire at once veneration and filial affection that could be conceived, and the gracefulness of composition and delivery was inimitable. On being introduced to him, I almost wished to beg his blessing. Norwich is one of the poorer sees; and, highly endowed and highly connected as Bathurst was, he might have insured a speedy translation on the usual terms; but having opposed a Tory ministry on an important question, he said, on returning from the House of Lords, "I have lost Winchester, but I have satisfied my conscience." If you look into Lockhart's "Life and Correspondence of Scott," of which one volume has appeared, and as many more will appear as the public will submit to pay for, you will find an amusing fragment of an autobiography, comprising enough of the early years of this extraordinary man to show distinctly the circumstances by which the turn was given to his tastes, sentiments and pursuits. Much of his sickly childhood was passed at a farm-house, where his chief companions were cattle and the peasants who tended them. His predominant inclination being to hear stories in order to tell them, he soon made himself master of all the epics of that border country, and hence his heroes are always of the moss-trooping order, and his machinery consists of brownies, kelpies and fairies. Hence, too, his unquenchable animosity against the *Southrons*. Observe how seldom he draws an Englishman but as a coward or a fool. His vivid fancy, his animal spirits, his good-humour and habitual kindliness, and his perfect freedom from affectation, must be liked, and might be envied; but the furniture of his mind was really made up of trumpery. Elevation of sentiment he had certainly none, and philosophy was far from him as the antipodes. Mr. Whishaw said once, of Bentham, that he was a schoolman born some ages too late: Scott was a stark moss-trooper in the same predicament, and a Jacobite.

Since I began this letter I have been making a *reviving* visit in London, in the midst of kind old friends, liberals and literati. One tone I find pervading all the men of deep and sound learning in whatever department, and it is what you will not like to hear of. It expresses a full conviction that the attempt to diffuse knowledge by means of society tracts and mechanics' institutes began in enthusiasm and proceeds in quackery; and they deprecate it, not in the spirit of aristocracy, but in the name of good letters, which they see to be sustaining severe injury by the attempt, on every subject, to write *down* to the dull or ignorant. It used to be said of learning in Scotland, "that all had a mouthful, and none a full meal," and it is to be feared that something like this will be the case here; at least so say the croakers. I hold out the consolation that the multitude will throw down their books when nobody is watching, and take up some pastime which suits them better; and then the old distinction of learned and unlearned will return. But there is a strange tendency to fly from one extreme to another. I perceive that young ladies, fatigued with lectures and languages, have fairly returned to the stupid cross-stitch works of their great-grandmothers; and who knows but they may resume the laudable practices of spelling at random and writing from corner to corner! My present occupation is reading history; that of the Romans occupies me at present. I have purposes in this course of study, but no formed plan as yet.

Believe me ever very truly yours,
L. AIKIN.

The Duke of Sussex desires I will lend him your last sermon. He has been ill, and loves religious reading.

To Miss Aikin.

September 8, 1837.

My dear Miss Aikin,—I ought perhaps to begin, as I have often done, with apologies for delaying to answer your last very acceptable letter of April, but my confidence in your candour encourages me to leave my defence to yourself. I thank you for recalling to me in your last the kindness of the Duke of Sussex, from whom you had formerly transmitted a message. When I understood that he had borrowed from you my last discourse in his illness, I remembered that I had been wanting in courtesy and gratitude, and resolved to clear my conscience by sending him a recent publication, with a few lines. In accomplishing my task, I found myself unable to adopt the usual mode of address; for so indifferent have I been to your aristocracy, that I have not even inquired into the titles by which the great are approached. I respected the Duke, however, too much to think that he would take offence at my republican plainness, and despatched my packet. You see my old want of respect for your hereditary distinctions is undergoing no change, though I honour many who bear them. It is a matter of amazement that a people generally so wise and proud as the English, should confide from *choice* a power almost irresistible to a body wanting sympathy with them and looking down upon them as an inferior mass. I believe I never told you that when in England I almost envied the aristocracy one possession. It was not their social rank, or their palaces in the city. These I should not have been willing to accept. But their ancestral country-seats, with the ancient forest, the garden, the lawn, the park, the riding—these did almost move me to envy. When I now think of revisiting England, next to the pleasure of seeing a few old friends, great men, perhaps nothing attracts me more than the prospect of visiting some of the Edens which England embosoms. I do not, however, murmur; I spend my summer on a delightful island, and live in the sight of a beauty which inspires constant gratitude.

I have had a letter from Miss Martineau. Her book, though so able and so often breathing a noble spirit, is in bad odour here, as bad as Mrs. Trollope's—perhaps worse. I hear with perfect composure the unsparing criticisms made on her mistakes and harsh judgments, but cannot hear with the same indifference the imputations cast on her character. I honoured her reverence for truth; but those who did not know her give her no credit for this. She certainly has given us much praise as well as blame, to neither of which, however, do I attach much importance. For instance, she insists, again and again, on the abundance of *good-temper* among us; from which I only infer, what I have heard, that as a people you are not remarkable for this quality, and that she judged us by contrast. Certain I am that we have no excess of this virtue, and I should never have thought of ascribing it as a distinction to my countrymen. I am quite indifferent to the opinion of foreigners about us, for they are little more than guesses. What troubles me is, that through them the honour of free institutions should be wounded. Speaking of good-temper, I think our feelings towards Miss Martineau show that we do not deserve to be sainted for it.

In your letter you speak again of Scott in a way which I feel to be unjust. I know he is no philosopher. He has no gift for analyzing our nature so as to search its elements, nor does he arrive by any high processes at its great laws; but its actual combinations, from the throne to the cottage, its free, varied play through a vast range, he has a wonderful power of seizing and portraying. His broad, keen views of life, and his exhaustless invention, give him a wide-spread empire, which belongs only to genius. I read his Life with great pleasure; it answers the first end of biography—that is, helps you to judge of the hero as if you knew him, a condition fulfilled by few Lives.

So the Conservatives are almost in the ascendant. Strange people! The French, whose king-worship a century ago was their religion and patriotism and principle of honour, are utterly weaned from kings and nobles; and John Bull, shrewd, proud, practical as he is, clings to these as if they were his life. His son Jonathan, with all his bad manners, is certainly more of a man in these respects than his father. I suppose the No-Popery panic has a good deal of influence on your politics. Is it true, what the papers say, that bribery was never so profusely or unblushingly used? If so, aristocracy is not to be envied its triumphs. I promise myself a great treat in Mr. Hallam's new work. I rejoice in your better health. Use the only true specifics for keeping it, exercise, temperance (in the large sense of the word) and cheerfulness.

Your sincere friend,
WM. E. CHANNING.

To Dr. Channing.

Hampstead, Oct. 14, 1837.

My dear Friend,—Your welcome letter, yesterday received, contains matters which will not suffer me to leave it a day longer unanswered. With regard to Miss Martineau's notions of the political rights of women, I certainly hold, and it appears to me self-evident, that, on the principle that there should never be taxation without representation, women who possess independent property *ought* to vote; but this is more the American than the English principle. Here it is, or was rather, the doctrine that the elective franchise is a trust given to some for the good of the whole, and on that ground I think the claim of women might be dubious. Yet the Reform Bill, by affixing the elective franchise only, and in all cases, to the possession of land, or occupancy of houses of a certain value, tends to suggest the idea that a single woman possessing such property as unrestrictedly as a man, subject to the same taxes, liable even to some burdensome, though eligible to no honourable or profitable, parish offices, ought in equity to have, and might have without harm or danger, a suffrage to give. I vote for guardians of the poor of this parish by merely signing a paper; why might I not vote thus for members of Parliament? As to the scheme of opening to women professions and trades now exercised only by men, I am totally against it for more reasons than I have time to give.

But there is more. In a very merry little female circle, at the time I mentioned, and I have never seen her since, we hailed Harriet Martineau as our champion, between joke and earnest, and she then told us of the scheme of a periodical devoted to the good of the sex, of which she was to be the editor. The chief points she then dwelt upon were, the sufferings of the *most unhappy* class of women, and the necessity of taking more pains to explain to poor girls at school the snares which encompassed them, and the utter ruin to which one false step exposed them. In this I zealously concurred. . . . So far, and only so far, do I agree in any opinions peculiarly hers . . . . I impute to her no designed misrepresentations; but indeed, indeed, it is somewhat hard that on her eulogy of American good-temper you should found a charge against us of ill-temper. Poor stupid John Bull has generally been reckoned good-natured at least. But what presumption in any individual to speak of the tempers of a whole nation! What false judgment do we often form of those of our familiar acquaintances!

I have no doubt your packet would be exceedingly welcome to his Royal Highness the Duke of Sussex, notwithstanding any republican plainness in the address —I conclude you do not direct to Mr. Augustus Guelph. You say you do not care enough for our aristocracy to learn their titles, and at this I do not wonder. The history of nobility in England is, however, a curious subject, on which an essay might be written, and I rather wonder such an one has not been written, capable of throwing much light on our history, and of explaining that attachment to the peerage which now perplexes you. It is because the nobility formed a *caste* in France, but has never done so in England, that the order is viewed with such opposite feelings in the two countries. In France, all the descendants of the noble were *noblesse*, and enjoyed immunities given to the detriment of the people at large, and which no *bourgeois* or his children could hope to share. Here the children of the highest peer are, all but the eldest, and that after his father's death, commoners in the eye of the law. They enjoy no immunities, and the humblest man in society is not always without a chance of seeing his son a peer, spiritual or temporal. The father of Lord Nelson was an obscure country clergyman; the father of Lord Lyndhurst, an American painter; of Bishop Blomfield, a parish-clerk. Lord Ashburton was himself a merchant. And these are the circumstances which attach the middle class to the lords: they are their own flesh and blood, and even in their haughtiness they take a natural kind of pride. To this you must add the respect which an Englishman can scarcely help feeling for the ancient families, sprung from those barons who wrung Magna Charta from a mean-souled tyrant, and who at many other trying periods of our history bought with their blood our laws, our liberties, and our glory. Think how many lords stood for the people against Charles! Almost all the Parliament's first generals were peers. And it was by a few Whig lords that the Revolution of 1688 was planned and brought to effect. Long live the principle and practice of religious dissent! As a mass, zealous Churchmen of every rank are Tories at heart. The principle of passive obedience, the worship of the powers that be, is almost inextricably interwoven with our Establishment—certainly the most systematically servile in

Christendom. Of the present reaction, as far as it exists, several causes may be assigned, of which I take the strenuous efforts of the clergy trembling for many things —their surplice fees among the rest—to be one of the chief. There has certainly been much bribery, and still more intimidation, on the part of the Tories, and a very unjust cry raised against ministers on account of the new Poor-law, in favour of which none of them were more warm or decided than Wellington and Peel. But several of these obstacles to the popular cause are temporary in their nature, none of them absolutely invincible; and if our young Queen should continue her confidence to Lord Melbourne, whom at present she delights to honour, and who has had the wit to surround her with Whig ladies of the household, I see not but that the small ministerial majority may suffice to keep the Whigs in office. At any rate, I strongly confide that all really useful reforms will sooner or later be carried, even without invading the constitution of the House of Lords. The fact is, that the sovereign, if sincerely bent upon it, has always means sufficient, by the application of certain court rewards and punishments, of commanding a majority in the upper House; and the Commons, by their command over the purse, can *compel* the sovereign to use this power in conformity with their will. Thus the result of all is, that a majority of the lower House can always make itself obeyed in the long run. The House, like the nation, is at present nearly equally divided; but with the spread of light and knowledge, I believe that the party of liberty is also diffusing itself—and think what victories it has already achieved! Rash or unjust measures on either side may temporarily depress, by disgracing, one or the other party, but I do not greatly fear the ultimate event. This great nation *will have* what appears to itself a good government. Indeed, to say the truth, we have not now a bad one, though, like all human institutions, it might be improved. I wish I could see the people better. But the crying sin equally of our nation, and of yours, and of all commercial nations, the "auri sacra fames," goes on augmenting with the growth of trade, of manufactures, of mechanical inventions, and even, I fear, with the diffusion of the elements of knowledge. To give men new wants is indeed the way to make them industrious, but it is also the way to make them rapacious, dishonest, gambling speculators, and in public life corrupt.

Reverting to what you say of the imputations cast on H. Martineau in your country, I think it due to her to state, that I have never heard of anything against her, and large allowances must be made for the hatred which she has meritoriously drawn upon herself from your slave-owners and their base abettors. . . . . . There are no new books much worth mentioning to you; indeed, this is not the publishing season. I hope Hallam's volume will soon appear. I hear he is now able to employ himself, though still very sorrowful for the loss of a lovely, lovely daughter, who was his worthy pupil and delightful companion.

Adieu, and believe me ever truly yours,

L. AIKIN.

To Miss Aikin.

Boston, February 7, 1838.

My dear Miss Aikin,—I thank you for your good long letter; but before answering it, let me ask you one or two questions, which I have more than once forgotten. What is the character of the "Philosophy of History, by George Miller"? I believe I have the title. What is the merit of Alison's "French Revolution"? By the way, have you read Carlyle's extraordinary History of that wonderful period? Does it offend your classical taste? It finds great favour with many intelligent people here. They seem to think that the muses of History and Poetry have struck up a truce, and are henceforth to go on lovingly together. I must confess myself much interested. Carlyle seems to be an example of the old proverb of "the prophet without honour in his own country." He has many ardent admirers here—so has German philosophy and German literature. You see we are not so hopelessly unenthusiastic as we are sometimes called. Your travellers look at the surface—but there is fire at the heart.

You seem to think that I bear too hard on John Bull, that he is a more good-natured person than I suppose; and in a former letter you spoke of your common people as free from cruelty. Different impressions prevail here. The *boxing* among that class seems not more humane than bull-baiting. We are told that the lower class are cruel to inferior animals; and, still worse, that they are severe to their wives. Not long ago, a clerk in a church here, an Englishman, was complained of to the rector for whipping his wife. He (the rector) had been a good deal in England, and dismissed the complaint with much nonchalance, saying, that "the English whipped their wives."

Your explanation of the influence of the aristocracy in England is satisfactory. It shows, however, the strength of the principle among you. Human nature has many hard battles to fight among you before its rights will be recognized, before the self-evident truth will be recognized that the inward is worth more than the outward, that humanity is worth more than its accidents. You will tell me that the aristocracy of commerce is worse than that of rank, and I shall not quarrel with you here. The aristocracy of wealth is good only as it is revolutionary, as it breaks down the old feudal one, as it stirs up the more depressed classes, and tends to mix all classes together. In itself it is low enough, and I can join with the old nobility in laughing at it. All these efforts of man to sever himself from his brother are my abhorrence; they must all yield to nobler sentiments. I have faith; I am sure of this; but when, I know not. You will think this is playing the prophet safely.

We have had a new History here, the History of Ferdinand and Isabella, said to be very good. Bancroft's History of America is much praised. We have a good deal of intellectual life; I think increasing. Let me ask you a question of orthoepy. Do you in England pronounce the words "holy" and "wholly" alike? If not, can you give me the difference?

Very truly your friend,
W. E. CHANNING.

To Dr. Channing.

Hampstead, April 18, 1838.

Ah, how kind! You write and thank me for a letter of I know not how old a date, when my conscience has been reproaching me, I know not how long, for leaving your last but one unanswered. But how could I write with any comfort so long as that sad Canada business remained unsettled?—whilst I could not tell whether violent spirits might not even make us *foes*—as far as national hostilities could render us so? Happily, most happily, these fears are all at an end. We have all possible reason to praise and thank your government for its conduct towards us, and it has taken away our common notion that your central force wanted strength to control the self-will of your borderers. Democracy has done itself great honour by you. For a while, I knew not what to say for it, to myself or to anybody else.

It is very difficult for our two nations to understand each other, yet I assure you I have long given your people credit for that "fire under snow" which some Frenchwoman ascribes to Englishmen. With regard to our *boxing*-matches,* I have only to say that they are not a *popular* amusement; being totally illegal, they are never held in cities, but only in by-places, and are frequented by few except those called, in *slang* phrase, "the Fancy"— that is, an assemblage of gamblers, sharpers, ruffians and profligates of every degree, from the duke to the chimney-sweeper. Respectable men, even of the lower classes, never need witness them, and seldom do. I think I mentioned mercy to animals as rather a *new* feature of our national character, brought out by laws and education. The same causes have produced a striking amendment in respect of profane swearing; I am told that no member of a mechanics' institute ever utters an oath, and even coachmen and cabmen shock the ears less than formerly. Your rector who said the English whipped their wives, I take to have been regardless of truth; at least, in my whole life, I never either read or heard of one single instance of that infliction; though of many, alas! of husbands injuring, or even killing, their wives by kicks and blows of the fist. In ninety-nine cases out of the hundred, intoxication—either of the man, the woman, or both—is the occasion of these brutalities. If, or let us say *when*, we grow more temperate, we shall mend in this point. Our law does what it can for beaten wives, by binding husbands over, on complaint, to keep the peace; and I am told that the merest clown feels

* Since this was written, the United States have sent us their Heenan to meet our Tom Sayers.

deeply the disgrace of this, and seldom offends again. *Paddy* is a much more frequent offender, by pugnacity of every kind, than cooler *John Bull* or *Sandy*.

No!—born champion of my sex, as I may almost call myself—I say deliberately, on good knowledge and careful consideration, that there are only two points in which it seems to me that our laws bear hard on women. The first is, in the want of a stricter hand against the inveiglers of girls for wicked purposes; the second, in the full power which the father is still allowed to retain over his children when *his* offences have compelled an innocent wife to obtain a divorce from him. It is surely most monstrous that a woman should be restrained from separating herself, under circumstances of the most aggravated offence, from a brutal and unfaithful husband, by his inhuman threats of never letting her see her children more—of placing her daughters under the very care of his mistress—a menace which I know to have been uttered!

On carefully comparing the Code Napoleon with ours, I am convinced that we have the advantage of French women. Yet, understand me not as admitting that we have nothing to complain of. Society wrongs us where the laws do not. The *life* of a woman is esteemed of less value than that of a man. Juries of men are very reluctant to punish the slayer of his wife as a murderer. Her *testimony* is undervalued; men-juries often discredit her evidence against a worse than murderer. She is wounded by the privileged insolence of masculine discourse. "Woman and fool," says spiteful Pope, and dunces echo him. Any feeble-minded man is an "old woman;" fathers cry out to their boys in petticoats not to care what their elder sisters say to them. These and the like insults, when my blood was hotter than now it is, have cost me many a *bitten lip*. One of our legal exemptions signally offends me. It is that which grants impunity even for felony committed by a wife in presence and under control of her husband. Has a married woman, then, no moral freedom? Must her vow of obedience include even crime? Surely this disgraceful exemption ought now, at least, to be withdrawn, when that immoral vow is no longer an essential of the marriage rite. On the whole, however, I think the present age is more favourable to our sex than any former one. Women are now, with us at least, free of the whole circle of arts and sciences; they have neither ridicule nor obloquy to encounter in devoting themselves to almost any department of knowledge. All men of merit are forward in cheering them on; they are more free than ever. Alas! I speak of women, but you may say I only mean gentlewomen. In truth, I *can* speak of none else with personal knowledge—the miserable drudges, the beaten and half-famished wives, and a class still more miserable, are never seen, never heard of by me in my tranquil home. I know not whether it ought to humble me—perhaps not, all things considered—but the fact is that I know scarcely more by actual survey of the dwellings, the manners, the characters of the most numerous class in England, or even in Hampstead, than of the inhabitants of Pekin. As to the attachment of women to priests, it is curious to observe how little there was of it in England a century ago. Recollect how bitterly Swift complains of their contempt for divines, and exclusive preference of *beaux* and the military. *Ladies* are, no doubt, much superior now in education, tastes, and manners, to that generation: then they played quadrille; now they read theology, and attend lectures, and gather pence for missions and Bible societies. In this country we are subject to *rages*, and these things are, or have been, the rage amongst us. But the influence of the clergy over women is so natural, that the wonder is to find that it was ever suspended. They seize the female soul both by its strong and its weak sides—its spirituality, its thirst after perfection, its docility, its hopes, its fears, its melancholy, its lively and often ill-regulated imagination, and its general averseness or incapacity for close reasoning. And this last defect, little is done by modern systems of culture to correct. I see numbers of men, and a still greater proportion of women, full of acquirement and accomplishment, but mere children in reason—absolutely destitute of the first elements of philosophy, and willing to give up their souls to the guidance of the first who will take the charge. Many times of late it has been a project with me to write something or other respecting us Englishwomen; but, alas! I have lost all energy, and my projects come to nothing. If you were to lay your commands upon me to write you some letters on this subject, perhaps —for think what I have just said of clerical influence over *us*—and I declare that if any reverend gentleman has power over me, it is you.

Carlyle *does* offend my classical taste; but the worst of it is that I have been absolutely riveted to his first volume, which I have this minute finished, and that I am hungering for the next. A very extraordinary writer certainly, and though somewhat, I must think, of a jargonist, and too wordy and full of repetition, yet sagacious, if not profound, and wonderfully candid. I think, too, that he shows an exactness and extent of knowledge of his subject which very advantageously distinguishes him from poetical historians in general. I assure you he is not without enthusiastic admirers here; his lectures on German literature last year were a good deal talked of; and I see he has announced a new course on general literature, which I must inquire about. I am ready to hail almost any striking phenomenon in literature; we have had little but mediocrity lately. Of your two books, "Miller" and "Alison," no notice whatever has come to my ears. I have just heard that "Alison" is praised in "Blackwood," therefore ultra-Tory. . If they be new works, as I suppose, the first cannot be written by Professor M. of Glasgow, nor the second by Alison (of Taste), who is now very old and quite infirm; I believe it is his son.

Pray read Guizot's "Histoire de la Civilisation en Europe," a small book which will give you much matter of thought.

No, our pattern speakers do not confound hōly and whŏlly; to the short vowel in the last word they give a sound between o and u, if you can imagine it. Trent-north, a grand boundary of dialect, the provincials say *woley* or *wooley*, and in Norfolk they say hully; but stick you to whŏlly if you would pass for a member of your much-respected the English aristocracy.

I really am totally unable to understand your faith in the coming of a time when all men will be regarded by all as equals. Such a time can plainly not come without community of goods, and to that I see no tendency; nor can it arrive whilst any division of labour exists. As long as one man works only with his hands and another with his head, there will be inequality between them of the least conventional kind; inequality in knowledge, in the objects of thought, in the estimate of existence, and of all that makes it desirable. Among the rudest savages there has always been inequality, produced by that nature itself which gives to one man more strength and more understanding than another; and all the refinements of social life open fresh sources of inequality. Even in a herd of wild cattle there is inequality produced by differences of age, and sex, and size; and what imaginable power or process can ever bring human creatures to a parity? As little can I see how such a state would be the practical assertion of the preference due to the "inward over the outward," to "humanity over its accidents." Are not many of these sources of inequality really inward? Are not these accidents inseparable from humanity? The things which elevate man above his fellows are all *powers* of one kind or other: wealth is a power, since it can purchase gratifications and services; birth is a power, where the laws have made it the condition of enjoying privileges or authority: where they have not done so, it speedily sinks into contempt. Genius is a power; weight of moral character is a power; beauty is a power; knowledge is a power. The possessor of any of these goes with his talent to the market of life, and obtains with it or for it what others think it worth their while to give—some more, some less. Can or ought this to be otherwise? The precious gifts of nature must be valued so long as humanity is what it is; the results of application, of exertion, mental, bodily, cannot cease to bear their price without deadening all the active principles in man. I see, indeed, a tendency in high civilization to break down in some degree the ancient barriers between class and class, by opening new roads to wealth, to fame, and to social distinction. Watt and Davy, Reynolds and Flaxman, could not safely be treated with disdain either by Howards and Mowbrays, or by the "millionaires" of commerce; but this does not assist those who have nothing to rest upon but mere human nature itself. These may be equal to their more privileged brethren before God; they may and ought to be equal in the eye of the law; but socially equal—I do not see the possibility. You approve the aristocracy of wealth so far as it tends to break in upon that of rank, and to mix all classes—but how far would you carry this mixture? Shall I begin tea-drinkings with my maudlin washerwoman? Will you invite to your table the bow-legged snip who made your coat? How soon, alas! at this rate, would the rivulet of refinement be swallowed up in the ocean of vulgarity! What models would remain of manners, of language, of taste in literature or the arts! What a mere worky-day world would this become! The coarse themselves would grow coarser, and in the end sensuality would rise victorious over all. The opinions in which all could agree must be absurd and extravagant ones; for, as Locke observes, "Truth and reason did never yet carry it by the majority anywhere." The talk in which all can join is seldom such as any one is much the better for hearing. If it be true that "there is no man of merit but hath a touch of singularity, and scorns something," surely merit must always be allowed to scorn ignorance or grossness incapable of estimating it; and this cannot but include a kind of disdain of the society of the lower classes. Pray answer me all this, for I think I must have misapprehended your idea.

Not yet have I thanked you for your two kind presents of your "Temperance" and your "Texas." I admire the first particularly for its discrimination, by speaking of the Temperance Societies as symptoms, rather than causes; you have explained what I before thought a puzzling phenomenon. I could, if my paper allowed, cavil at your opinions on public amusements; but another time. "Texas" seems to me your greatest effort yet. May success reward the patriotic virtue which inspired it!

Ever believe me, my respected friend,
Yours most truly,
L. AIKIN.

To Dr. Channing.

Hampstead, July 16, 1838.

My dear Friend,—There are two urgent reasons why I must make Mr. Gannet the bearer of a letter to you: first, because it is always a pleasure to me to send you a friendly greeting; and secondly, because I wish, whilst the impression is still fresh, to express the gratification I have felt in his society, and to thank you for the introduction. On his first arrival here, the lamentable state of his health and spirits obscured, though they could not quite conceal, his admirable talents and qualities; but they now shine forth, and we all find him an exceedingly interesting companion. Of his powers as a preacher I have not enabled myself to judge, but I can bear strong testimony to the perfect modesty and simplicity with which he receives tokens of a success which would be sufficient to turn most heads. Mrs. Joanna Baillie told him truly, that he had been talked of at a time when we had scarcely leisure to talk of any one—so full were all heads with our grand Coronation; and I never saw anything more beautiful than the unaffected, modest dignity with which he received the compliment—it would have delighted you to witness. He carries back with him the esteem and good wishes of all whose testimony is worth having, in spite of very industrious efforts to injure him—I believe you know from what quarter.

And what have you thought of the fever-fit of loyalty which has seized "universal England" on occasion of setting the crown on the head of our young Queen? Perchance you may have viewed it somewhat in the spirit of the laughing philosopher; but if you had been an eye-witness of what passed, I think you would have sympathized in our emotions more deeply than you now believe possible. This young creature has thus far conducted herself most admirably. Her behaviour at her first council was described to me by an excellent judge who was present, as combining the highest degrees both of self-possession and of sensibility compatible each with the other, and such has been the complexion of all her conduct since. Her steadfast adherence to a Reforming ministry has been of inestimable value to the cause of liberality and improvement; her perseverance in the same course is what we have most to wish, and to let her see the popular attachment which it has already gained for her seemed the most likely means of securing this great object. The people have to support her against the aristocracy, and I have heard it said, I believe with as much truth as point, that the ministry is kept in place by the Queen and the shopkeepers. In the meantime, it seems to me that we are going on well; reforms proceeding slow and sure, and decidedly the tone of at least a large portion of society becoming constantly more liberal, both in religion and politics—the natural effect of the continuance of a Whig and Low-church administration. I perceive signs also of a revival of literature, which now again is able to hold up its head in the presence of science, by which it was for some time in apparent danger of being totally overshadowed. In particular it pleases me to perceive that historical literature is cultivated with great activity, for which there are two obvious causes: a state of public feeling which allows history to be written freely without incurring persecution either from the government or the mob; and, with respect to our own country, a great accession of new information from the printing of the public records.

These favouring circumstances, I think, will enable even me to conquer my long desponding indolence, and attempt a new design. My plan is not yet matured, but it is only *entre nous* that I give any hint of it; but I am turning my thoughts towards something like a view of letters and social life in England during the first sixty years of the last century, i.e. the reigns of Anne and the two first Georges. This will differ from my former works in excluding civil history entirely, for which I could not now undertake the labour of collecting materials, and my chief doubt at present is, how far the work can be rendered sufficiently interesting without it. I must intersperse biography largely; and I propose entering deeply into the subject of female manners and acquirements. At present I am only collecting materials, but that is no disagreeable or uninteresting part of the business. You may infer from my entertaining so bold a design that my health is stronger than it was, and I expect to find it still further benefited by plunging into business, which will alleviate the constant weight upon the spirits of domestic solitude.

I wonder whether you have ever been a great student of the works of Addison, especially of his periodical papers. It seems to me that justice has not even yet been done, or at least is not done in this generation, to his unrivalled merits. To women he was the greatest of benefactors. By his arch ridicule and gentle reprehension of their follies, especially of their idleness and their ignorance, he worked a wide reformation. By teaching them to deserve the respect of the other sex, he enabled them to secure it. No systematic advocate of the rights of woman, especially none who is herself a woman, will ever, we may safely predict, do them half so much service. I have a good many remarks to make on this topic, which I believe will be new, and I hope may be useful.

Did I not say to you in my last letter, that a gay

young, play-going Queen would make a formidable counteraction to the progress of the Evangelicals? I will now add that they have been receiving a great injury from the hands of their own adherents—the sons and biographers of Mr. Wilberforce. The book is luckily so tiresome as well as so sour and so narrow, that it meets with general abuse, in spite of the efforts of the Edinburgh reviewer, a nephew of Mr. Wilberforce. Everybody sticks fast in the perusal, and it has damaged the subject of the book scarcely less than its authors. It is plain that whatever other merits Mr. Wilberforce might have, he was by no means a man of strong understanding; and the curious disclosure of his practice of wearing pebbles in his shoes by way of penance, is little likely to do him honour with the English of the nineteenth century. The Life of Hannah More was a much more readable book than this, because she both wrote and received many agreeable letters *before* her conversion; but even that made no great noise out of her own set, and I believe did no good to her cause. Our rigorists of the Establishment seem now to be swinging towards that kind of High-churchism which is but just to be distinguished from Popery; which will do less harm, because less likely to be taken up with enthusiasm by the common people, than the high Calvinism of the Evangelicals. The intolerance and the pharisaical arrogance of the two systems is much alike.

One trait of popular sentiment which I observed in watching the Coronation procession may interest you. There was vast applause of the Queen, great applause of her mother and of your friend the Duke of Sussex, and a kind recognition of the other members of the royal family; there was generous applause of Soult, because we had formerly beaten him, but not the slightest notice of any other foreigner. The ambassadors-extraordinary might display as much pomp as they would, and certainly such splendour of equipages had never before been exhibited in the streets of London; still honest John remained obstinately mute, or contented himself with whispering, "Depend upon it, those coaches are English built, and the horses bought here." Whence I infer, that national pride was the leading principle in the popular mind; such part of the show as each man might tell himself he had helped to pay for delighted him; the rest rather provoked his surliness, and he was little disposed to thank foreign kings for all their civilities.

I trust your pen is not idle; you must go on writing, if it were only for the sake of your public here, which becomes a wider one with every new piece you give us. Texas we most of us consider as your best effort.

Pray believe me ever
Yours, with the truest regard,
L. AIKIN.

To Miss Aikin.

August 24, 1838.

My dear Miss Aikin,—I thank you for your letter of July 16. I do not know that I had earned it by answering your preceding, and I therefore hasten to reply, though I have not time to say much. Your pages did not overflow as usual; I wish you to feel that you cannot write too much. I was amused by your notice of the Coronation. I should undoubtedly have smiled, as you suppose, at the vain show had I been present; but I am not sure that I should not have shed tears too. The enthusiasm of a multitude is the most contagious thing on earth. The last thing I could resist is a universal, deep feeling essentially generous. My reason, however, would have thrown a good deal of cold water on the fire. I have no great respect for what is called national sentiment, though I think it holds a useful place in carrying a man beyond lower workings of selfishness, and in many minds it has even some disinterested elements. I see in it signs of what man may be. It is no sign that he is such already. As to loyalty too, this has something generous in it, at least as called forth at a Coronation; for on such occasions, the imagination of the multitude invests the idol with the greatest attributes of which it has any comprehension, and the worship is addressed to something more than human. It is painful, however, to see the noblest sentiments of human nature wasted on what is of little worth. Misplaced veneration has ever been one of the chief pillars of priestcraft and despotism, so that man has been degraded by the very principle which was meant to connect him with greatness. But let me stop. I am beginning to be too grave. Your Coronation, I believe, was one of the most innocent. I like your young Queen much, from what I hear of her, and I have no great fear that she is to bring back chivalry and the dark ages. Men's positive interests, if not their principles, are too strong for this. I believe, as you say, the abstract love of monarchy is not growing strong among you, and yet I do not think your monarchy unsafe. It rests more and more on a rational foundation, and this in the long run is the strongest. You all feel that, in your present civilization, the highest office in the state is too great and dazzling a prize to be thrown open to competition. You see *reasons* for the Throne, and therefore it can stand without reproach. But the *reasons* for an aristocracy are beyond my comprehension. The relations of the aristocracy to the government seem to me reversed by the changes of society; and instead of making property more secure, it is perhaps more likely than anything else to cause a rising against property. It is every day taking an attitude which must prove fatal to it, that is, of hostility to public opinion — not to gusts of opinion, but to opinion as determined by the progress of society. I feel that these are views which need a good deal of explanation, but I feel more and more the error of applying our old notions about forms of government to the present state of the world.

I am glad you have found a subject, and I like it much. I enter fully into what you say about Addison. He is my delight, strange as you may think it. My style, indeed, is anything but Addisonian; but I do not enjoy him the less on that account. His nameless grace is quite out of my reach; and when I read him, I think of my style as badly as the Edinburgh Reviewers do. My position has hurt me as a writer. I have grown up amidst war, and this makes a man strain himself; but my taste for the truly simple has not been lost. You are not quite just to Mr. Wilberforce. I saw him in London, and could not but respect him, though I saw not a sign of intellectual superiority. He asked me about the Unitarians of Boston, not suspecting me of the heresy; and when I told him that I was one (though some of his family did not receive the communication with the kindness which hospitality required), the good old man went on to talk with undiminished complacency. On my leaving him, he took me into his study, gave me to understand that he thought more of a man's temper and *spirit* than opinions, and chose to write my name and his own on a pamphlet which he presented as a memorial of our interview. I doubt not he had force, though I did not see it, and he certainly had goodness.

Your sincere friend,
WM. E. CHANNING.

To Dr. Channing.

Hampstead, November 16, 1838.

My dear Friend,—You like overflowing letters, you say, and I have no great difficulty in finding materials for such in writing to you; the worst is, that I grow tired, throw aside the half-filled sheet, and leave it in my writing-desk till it is too stale to send. This is what has happened now. I have just condemned a fragment to the flames, and whether this present attempt will have better success remains to be seen. You inquired if I had read Prescott's "Ferdinand and Isabella;" and hearing much of the work, particularly that so excellent a judge as Lord Holland called it the best History written in English since Gibbon, I was unwilling to write till I had at least seen something of it. I have now finished the first volume and entered upon the second, with very great satisfaction. The spirit and sentiment of the work is admirable; there is enough of reflection, and not too much; the narrative is lively and flowing; and great judgment is shown in the proportions assigned to the various topics on which it treats. It is entertaining, with every mark of strict adherence to truth, and instructive, without deep philosophy indeed, or sententiousness of remark; but by means of a pervading spirit of candour, good sense and liberality, the interest of the subject hurries one on, at first reading, too fast, I believe, for the credit of the writer; and I have little doubt that a second perusal would disclose many fresh merits of detail. As for the style—the diction rather—*it is pretty good for an American.* " Civil !" cry you; but like our Members of Parliament, I disclaim "any personal application." In fact, it is not in a style like yours, which neither is nor ought to be a colloquial one, that any difference from that of an Englishman can be detected. Neither, indeed, is Mr. Prescott chargeable with using words or phrases peculiar to your country. If it were possible in these days of steamers and railroads to imagine an Englishman possessed of the knowledge and literary talent of this writer, who should never have mingled with the good society of London, he might be expected to compose in the same style—that is to say, provided he had never made a study of his own language. He, like Mr. Prescott, might employ the Scotch term "a border *foray;*" he might call artizans *operatives,* the slang word of Glasgow weavers; he might transplant from the newspapers, French, military, and other terms; he might, perhaps, want the tact to exclude from the style of history several mere colloquialisms, as well as corrupt uses of words which might be enumerated. Considering this work as one which will attain a permanent station in English literature, I cannot but regret these blemishes, and wish to see them removed in another edition. But there is a special reason why I mention them to you, which is this. You tell me you can see no use in our aristocracy. This is a use—to establish a standard of taste and refinement in language as in manners; to rebuke pedantry; to set a mark upon ignorance, provincialism and vulgarity; to preserve the native tongue in equal purity and vigour. No one, without having frequented those London circles where lettered men and women of rank associate with lettered men and women without rank, can form a just conception of the grace and beauty of which our language is susceptible in its colloquial forms. No one without this advantage can attain finished elegance in any style of composition, except the most grave and dignified—that of the pulpit and the schools; at least, such attainment is so rare, that when we meet with it, as in the works of that *low Irishman* Goldsmith, it fills us with surprise as much as admiration. No Scotchman has ever accomplished a perfect English style. Blair and Robertson escaped faults by rejecting all idiom from their composition; but at the expense of all originality and charm. Hume supplied his want of English idiom and disdain of Scotch by seizing upon French phrases. Burns, in prose, wrote no language at all; and Walter Scott is full of provincialisms and barbarisms, some of which, through his popularity, threaten to naturalize themselves amongst us. Charles Lamb, a Londoner, gained a pure and very racy English by study of our old writers, especially the dramatists, but he acquired at the same time a quaintness which only the best society could have taught him to discard. Dryden, Cowley and Addison, our three great masters in the middle style of composition, all lived first with scholars, as they were themselves, and afterwards with courtiers, nobles, statesmen, great lawyers and great ladies. A sound classical education, with assiduous study of our best writers, might indeed suffice to forming a pure and correct style, provided their effects were not counteracted by hearing vulgar speech and reading the bad writers of the day; but in general all people read the current trash more or less, and those who have no access to elegant speakers will scarcely escape the infection derived from coarse ones. An upper class, a metropolis, and a court, can alone preserve the language of an extensive empire. Therefore, woe unto you Americans! It amuses me to think that I, who have all my life belonged to the democratic party, and have earned the lasting enmity of the admirers of King Charles and his cavaliers, should, with you, take the part of a champion of monarchy and aristocracy. You may place it, if you will, to the account of that spirit which the lords of creation affirm to be so prevalent in our much-libelled sex. But when you profess that "the reasons for an aristocracy are beyond your comprehension," I own I wonder a little. Allowing that I may be too much inclined, as Bacon said of James I., "to take counsel of times past," I still must hold that a philosophical thinker ought not to shut his eyes to the large fact that, until the establishment of your States, the whole world, as far as it is known to us by history, had never seen a nation, barbarous or civilized, destitute of some kind of hereditary nobility or aristocracy, excepting those Eastern monarchies where all were equal, because all were nothing, beneath the rod of the despot. A counterbalance to the absolute power, whether of a king or a people, has the most obvious utility, and I offer it for your consideration, whether that very propensity to form associations which you have found it necessary to rebuke in your own country, is not the consequence of the want of one. In a land where "the right divine of *mobs* to govern wrong" is consecrated as a first principle, how can any sect or any party propose to itself another mode of carrying its points, than persuading or compelling the adherence of a numerical majority? Where the co-operation of king, nobles and people, is required to every public measure, all interests must be consulted; that even of the few must not be absolutely sacrificed to the many; reason, justice, fairness, must be allowed their plea; above all, full liberty of speech is secured. In a despotism, whether of one, of the few, or of the many, "sic volo, sic jubeo," is sufficient. With regard to our nobility, every impartial person who will study thoroughly the history of its political conduct, must own this: that it gained Magna Charta; that it opposed effectual resistance to the despotism of the Church and its head, and the introduction of the slavish maxims of the civil law; that it controlled in many important instances the encroachments of our kings; that in the great struggle of Charles and his Parliament it endeavoured, however vainly, to hold the balance; that it gave many confessors to the cause of liberty, several distinguished generals to the people, and that the abolition of its constitutional powers was one of the most guilty acts of the military usurper; that it gave us our glorious and bloodless Revolution, and by its resistance to a Tory House of Commons, Tory squires, and Tory clergy, saved us from the return of the tyrannical and bigoted Stuarts; that even at the present day a majority of the high and old aristocracy, which owes not its honours to the trade-pampering policy of Pitt, adheres to Whig principles, though it repudiates Radicalism, that is, the supremacy of the rude and selfish and ignorant many. With such past claims to our gratitude, and in my opinion so much of advantage to be hoped from it for the future, I say to the illustrious order, with all its faults, its errors, sometimes its provoking obstinacy—" Esto perpetua!" Were you more intimately acquainted with the feelings of our people, I believe you would soon renounce the opinion that the existence of the aristocracy endangers property. One proof of the contrary is, that those notable public meetings in which the working-men take care to show our optimists how very little their notions have advanced since the days of Jack Cade, all take place in manufacturing towns—the very places in which the aristocracy do not reside and exercise no influence. Even in London, where the influence of the aristocracy is rather that of the class than of individuals, the ultra-Radicals could make no hand of it; indeed, I believe they are everywhere pining away under the contempt of their superiors and the neglect of the Attorney-general. Ignorance is weakness. Ignorant I believe the bulk of our spinners and weavers must in the nature of things always remain. In your young and unexhausted country, with land cheap and labour dear, all is different. May you be able to realize the beautiful idea of a nation self-governed with wisdom and justice! With us, the old distinction of governors and governed must still subsist; but we may indulge the hope that public opinion, which in all classes above the very lowest has made, and is daily making, a real progress in light and liberality, will irresistibly urge upon rulers a constant attention to the interests of those who know not what is truly good for themselves. Thus only can we hope to see them preserve that "national feeling" which, cheap as you may hold it, Mr. Burke truly entitled "the cheap defence of nations." Since beginning this letter I have been proceeding with "Ferdinand and Isabella" with still increasing interest and approbation, and I beg that when you write you will give me any particulars you think proper of the author, as I cannot help feeling great desire to know something of his personal history. What think you of our new Oxford set of *Laudists* or semi-Romanists? They at least serve as counterbalance to our Evangelicals. I must now conclude, having an immediate opportunity of sending my letter to London.

Ever truly yours,
L. AIKIN.

TO MISS AIKIN.

Boston, Jan. 15, 1839.

My dear Miss Aikin,—I thank you for your aristocratical letter, and not the less for its opposition to my own opinions. How we should fight our battles in the same room may be questioned, but battles across the ocean are bloodless, and cannot harm, but rather strengthen, such an old friendship as ours. I have no disposition to fight out the historical argument for aristocracy. In barbarous times, barbarous institutions have their use. In the infancy of European society, a brute force was needed to hold men together, and the bloody barons performed this part to admiration. It was a lion rule, but better than no rule. Royalty and the priesthood, comparatively moral powers, fortunately sprung up to share the spoils; and through the conflicts of these different usurpations, a new power was gradually developed, that of the people, of the human race. Gradually the people learned, and their masters learned, that they were made for some other purpose than to be ruled, and they are now spelling out the lesson that the million are not only *something*, but even *more* important than the few. Aristocracy is no longer what it was. Its original relation to society is changed, and its great function now, which is to represent and protect property, is rendered unnecessary by the character of our civilization, which worships property, and secures it, not by concentration, but by diffusion. Aristocracy is a *caste*, has the spirit of a caste, legislates as a caste. Is not the world fast outgrowing it? Is it fitted to the great work of our times, which is that of raising the mass of the people to the rank of men? Must it not die, in proportion as a just respect for the human being, as reverence for what is truly, essentially and eternally venerable, spreads through a community? I was much gratified with your account of the highly polished and intellectual society produced by the meeting of men of rank and men of letters in London. I should enjoy it much as one of the phases of humanity. How far I should enjoy it as *society*, I am more in doubt. Reserved as I am thought to be, I delight in the *free*, the *spontaneous*, in social intercourse.

I love to see people *in earnest*, and this is hardly consistent with strict observance of all the rules of good breeding. A man speaking from the heart, will *insist*, too much for the comfort of all, on what he feels—will forget some conventional observance—will sometimes trouble us with his idiosyncracies; and yet, as we cannot have all good things, but must make our choice, I incline to the earnest man. The fundamental rule of polished society I take to be to spare your neighbour's self-love to the greatest possible degree,—a very good rule as the world goes; but, for myself, I would rather read a good book in my study than mix much with society which rests on such a basis. I must go into society, not *first* and chiefly to please or be pleased, but to be true to myself and my convictions, to speak and act from the highest in my own breast, and to require the true, genuine and pure in others. On this foundation build the graceful, the ornamental, the amusing, the winning, as much as you please; but leave me something *firm* to stand on. I have feared that intercourse with people of rank would receive a taint from their consciousness of superiority founded on mere outward distinctions. This I suppose is smothered a good deal in courtesy. But "what is *in* will *out*." I have seen great courtesy which said, "Keep your distance." Still, I doubt not there is a charm in the society you describe, and that the art of communication is better understood among you than here, where we go into society to rest after labour, more than to exert our powers.

I come now to what chiefly stirred me up to answer your letter so promptly. I want to know something about the Popish explosion at Oxford. I am more interested in it because it does not seem to me a mercenary cry of "Church and State," to answer the low purposes of the priest and Tory, but a genuine fanaticism or enthusiasm, which has generally something respectable in it. Does the infection spread? How is it regarded by men of influence in the Church? Is it a signal of the old leaven of Popery working extensively in the Church? I want next to know how I am to interpret the bigoted assaults on the bishops who subscribed for Dr. Carpenter's and Mr. Turner's books. Is such intolerance a safe game in the Church? Will public opinion allow it? I read an extract of the Bishop of Durham's letter, in which he seemed to cower before the fierce spirit of his adversaries, and to write as if it were worth a man's character to express common humanity towards the Dissenters. I would fain hope that this energy of intolerance is the energy of despair. Is it so? I think little at present about your politics, though always grateful for your views on the subject, but the state of religious liberty among you always interests me.

You ask about Mr. Prescott. He is a quiet student, a man of great modesty, highly esteemed by his friends as a man, and the more to be honoured because he has carried on his great work amidst outward prosperity, which has relieved him from all necessity of labour, and opened to him all the indulgences of life.

Very sincerely your friend,
W. E. CHANNING.

To Miss Aikin.*

Boston, February, 1837.

My dear Miss Aikin,—I have received your letter of Dec. 10, and am grieved by the account you give of yourself. Your mental state requires change of place, and it seems you cannot bear travelling. I trust that I

---

* This letter is misplaced: it should have followed Miss Aikin's letter of the 10th December, 1836.

have done you good by furnishing you with a motive to the effort of writing a letter. If so, go on writing, and do good to more than yourself. Your incapacity of exertion comes, I am sure, from a physical cause. Perhaps, however, it is aggravated by a moral one. Perhaps your inability "to fix your mind on any pursuit" would not be so painfully felt, had you concentrated your soul more on some great object. I have often been struck with seeing the power of a great idea, especially of a noble one, in neutralizing adverse influences, in overcoming painful sensations, in giving the soul something to cling to and sympathize with in all changes. Literature, by furnishing a succession of agreeable engagements, is undoubtedly a great protection against weariness; but it cannot satisfy us either in the most earnest and solemn or the most languid hours of life. Besides, by scattering the mind among a great variety of objects which have little connection, it may prevent that *unity* of our *inward being* which is the secret of strength to do and to suffer. The *great idea* of Christianity seems to me alone equal to the wants of our nature. It reveals an infinite end, an ultimate good, on which all things may be made to bear, and is, in this and other ways, a perpetual spring of interesting thoughts and efforts.

I am glad you turned your attention to Coleridge's Remains. I am now in your condition, shut up very much by indisposition and cut off from labour, though hoping for release very soon, and I am reading the same book. Coleridge's worship of Shakspeare seems to me to have been one of his most innocent excesses. Was it not a good? Where else could he have found an influence so fitted to counteract his morbid tendencies and errors? Coleridge, I believe, loved truth; but, I fear, he loved more that subtle, refined action of mind, by which he was authorized in his own judgment to look down with contempt on the common judgments of men. After wandering in his regions of mist and abstraction, what a benefit to him must it have been to enter the clear, mild, beautiful daylight of Shakspeare! The influence of Shakspeare on English (I include American) literature is invaluable. It is impossible, whilst he is made the great standard, is enthroned in the general mind, is more universally read and admired than any other author, that a false, perverted, unnatural taste should long prevail in any literary department.

It is so long since I read Don Quixote, that I cannot judge as well as you can of Coleridge's criticisms on it. I observed one inconsistency. In one place he exculpates the knight from vanity, and in another charges him with it in a very selfish form. He is right in the first instance. The knight had identified himself too entirely with his romantic ideas to be personally vain. It was not from self-love, but pure admiration, that he aimed to realize what he had read. I see that you enjoy Don Quixote more than I have done. To me, the book seems to have a great defect. I love and respect the hero too much to consent to the indignities with which he is treated. He carries my sympathies too much with him, and I am ready to fight his battles for him. I must confess, too, that I have little relish for the wit which lies in blows. I suspect there is something wrong in myself when I differ from the general sentiment, but I believe there is something right too in my feelings on this point. I fear that I have not expressed enough in these remarks my admiration of "Coleridge's Remains." Few writers give me such an impulse. His invectives against my religious peculiarities pass me as the idle wind. I hardly give them a thought. I find much to interest me in his criticisms on great authors, and in his distinctions and discriminations in psychology; but the peculiarities of his mind, and still more the infelicities of his character and life, unfitted him for the study of religion. I have been sorry to see great disingenuousness in his attacks on Unitarianism. Will you accept this as an answer to your last? I feel that I ought to write, and I wish to express my sympathy with you, but am incapable of writing more.

Your sincere friend,
W. E. CHANNING.

To Dr. Channing.

Hampstead, March 23, 1839.

Months ago did I say to myself, "My Boston friend will be making inquiries about these Puseyites before long, and I must take care to be provided for him." At the same time I do not think them of much consequence or likely to be so; and although the sect seems to have its fanatics, it is no new illumination, but mere Laudism— an extreme of High-churchism, which cannot prosper without much more countenance from the magistrate than it appears that it has any chance of receiving. Dr. Pusey was some time ago the ringleader in a plot for depriving Dr. Hampden of his Divinity professorship, on account, or on pretext, of an explanation given by him of the doctrine of the Trinity, which Pusey and his followers called heretical. But their zeal or malice having impelled them to go beyond the authority given by the statutes of the university, they were called to order by the government; and Dr. Hampden, after making a sort of recantation, obtained preferment, *although* he had openly pleaded for the admission of Dissenters to the universities, his worst heresy. As for the origin of the sect, some say Cambridge having had her Simeon, Oxford must have her Pusey. But the root lies a little deeper than this. Our Church, as you know, is a Janus, having one face towards Geneva, the other towards the city upon the Seven Hills. Of the sour Geneva face, as exhibited by the modern Evangelicals, our gentlemanly clergy began to grow very sick, and to fancy they should prefer the other, which at least becomes a mitre far better.

For the purpose of inclining the minds of the people in the same direction, this party have for several years past been publishing panegyrics in reviews and sermons, and panegyrical biographies of our elder divines, with cheap editions of their works; endeavouring quietly and gradually to bring into fashion again that edging on toward the Roman creed, that exceeding almost scriptural tenderness for the divines of the fourth, fifth and sixth centuries, which distinguishes the Church of England dignitaries from Elizabeth inclusively to our Revolution in 1688 from other Protestants; concerning which edging Coleridge in his *latter* mind says, "I scarcely know whether to be pleased or grieved with it." Yet in an earlier passage of his "Literary Remains" we find him confessing that there was a strange lingering of childish credulity in the divines of the episcopal church down to the time of James II., when the Popish controversy "made a great clearance." But this by the bye. Besides the increased reverence for priesthood by episcopal ordination derived from apostolical succession, and the notion of *authority* in the Church to make orders for externals, and decide questions of faith which the study of these writers was fitted to instil, an important advantage may have been calculated upon in a great controversy. It begins to be clear to all parties, that the doctrine of the Trinity cannot be defended by Scripture, so many of the texts formerly relied upon having yielded under the assaults of modern criticism; but *make Scripture* of the Fathers of the first four centuries, and you have all the authority for it that you can possibly desire. The atonement also might be much strengthened by making an apostle of Augustine; but this perhaps is rather the affair of another party. Now, although this scheme had something plausible, I doubt its solidity. Of all attempts, the least promising is that of restoring things gone by. *I*, indeed, believe folly to be immortal, but individual follies certainly live out their day and die. Much as it would redound to the glory and profit of the clergy "to lift again the crozier," it cannot be done without the concurrence of the State, without the restoration to the Church of coercive powers long since lost, without an authoritative quashing of controversy, without a commanded exterior reverence to things fallen into general contempt; such, for example, as the keeping of Lent, so scouted in the House of Commons the other day. Therefore, depend upon it, one Pusey will not make a Laudian church. I should not wonder to see a part of the real fanatics of this sect turn Papists ("go the whole hog," as *you* say): the others will cool down into proud, stiff, High-church people—nothing more. The best is, that they thwart the Evangelicals, and thus divide the house against itself, for which it will not stand the faster.

With respect to the bishops who subscribed to the sermons of my venerable friend, a little allowance must be made for them. Men who are governors in a Church with such creeds and such articles, cannot very consistently appear as patrons of Unitarian sermons; the Bishop of Durham,* accordingly, had stipulated to have his name suppressed, and might justly be a little vexed at the breach of this condition;—the more, as he was baptized and bred among the Unitarians, and has always

* Dr. Maltby.

been of a very suspected orthodoxy. The other bishop I take to be a timid Liberal. On the whole, I think what you would call rational religion is silently working its way in society. It is remarkable that the Unitarian sect, confessedly one of the very smallest in the country, has more members of Parliament in proportion belonging to it than any other denomination whatever,—a strong presumption, as it appears to me, that many more favour and secretly entertain these opinions than think proper as yet openly to avow them. The orthodox Dissenters, who have not a single member, are enraged at this circumstance, and I have no doubt it sets an edge on the polemical zeal of the clergy. An Unitarian has also been made a baronet, one of the best of men. The present ministry are constantly upbraided by their opponents as enemies to the Church, and not entirely without reason; yet they are supported by majorities, though small ones.

Pray observe that it was chiefly as a school of taste that I commended the society in which rank and talent meet. I am sensible that some who frequent it too much lose that earnestness on which you justly set a much higher moral value. But I see also those who, with manners rendered adroit by the intercourse and example of the great, know how, in more select and private circles, where they meet equals, to maintain excellent opinions on the highest subjects—to maintain them with the more effect for never losing command of themselves or a just deference to the claims of others. These indeed are the *élite;* as to either commonplace or merely worldly people, they certainly are rendered less displeasing by polished manners, and neither more insipid nor more hollow.

One word more as to aristocracy. In this country it cannot be said to have accomplished its vocation of keeping the peace so long as we have such frightful inequality of property—that is, so long as our population continues (and what should prevent its continuing?) so excessive in proportion to the means of support. Eight shillings a week is the present pay in many parts of the country of an agricultural labourer, and hope of ever mending his condition in the common course of things he has none. Dare you trust such a man with a vote? Political power in such hands would soon conduct us to universal confusion. There must be with us strong buttresses to counterbalance the thrust which would bring all to ruin. O Malthus, Malthus! you saw the source of mischief—who sees the remedy?

I thank you much for your address to the Franklin Society. It has many very valuable remarks and suggestions, but I thought there was some vagueness, for want of more divisions of the subject. Ought not moral and intellectual culture to have been considered separately? In one place you observe that books are not necessary to culture; in another you eloquently expatiate on their value. Now this I regard as no real inconsistency, but I wanted some distinctions to take away the appearance of it. You in your country of easy circumstances may look to universal school education; here I neither expect, nor indeed desire, at present to see it attempted. What a mockery to offer learning to the English labourer at eight shillings a week, or to the Irish peasant with his insufficient quantity of the worst kind of potato! Will the spirit of the age, from which you expect such great things, bring any mitigation to the sufferings of our mass? I fear not much; but it is still a duty to do all that is possible; and in as much as a government practises rigid economy, promotes legal reforms, and renders justice accessible to the poor by its cheapness, and by a spirit of real impartiality in the ministers of it—in as much as it trims the balance skilfully between the conflicting claims of different classes and interests, it will discharge its highest duties. You will not dispute, I conceive, that *these* views of political measures involve moral, and if moral, religious considerations of the utmost importance. Therefore you may find even our political events matters fit for your concern—the more, as it cannot be disputed that, in the main, the Whig is the party of reformation of all kinds, the Tory that of corruption and abuse.

A project, of which I am much more in dread than the attempts of the Laudians, is one of which our busy Bishop of London* is the head. He has founded a society for the purpose of bringing education under ecclesiastical control. This body are visiting all the London schools; they inquire of the masters (I know not whether they yet take cognizance of schoolmistresses) whether they will adopt the methods of the society; especially whether they will engage to teach Church of England Catechism, and whether they will submit to be examined by the society as to their competence in learning. If they consent, they are patronized; if not, an opposition school is founded close by, and all means are adopted to ruin their business. The only comfort is, that this association, being maintained solely by private subscriptions, will perhaps die away by degrees for want of funds, and also that it savours too much of an inquisition to suit the feelings of the English public. The German divines are a thorn in the flesh of our University clergy. They dare not pretend to despise their learning; and how to prevent their heresies from spreading amongst the students of theology? Depend upon it, the hypocrisy is to the orthodoxy in our Church as 99 to 1 at the least. But can we rejoice in this? I cannot, unless it is to lead to some greater good than I can conceive. A learned but here-

* Bishop Blomfield.

tical Cambridge divine tells me, "this generation of us *think*, the next will *speak.*"

You cannot, I am sure, complain of this letter for want of length. I hope and think it has answered all your questions. I have *made* time to write it, for indeed I am very busily engaged in collecting materials for my "Addison." The writing of the work I have not begun, excepting in detached notes, therefore I cannot yet judge what kind of figure it will make. I am in pretty good spirits about it, however—chiefly, perhaps, because, my bodily health being stronger, my mind is more alert and more inclined to look on the bright side, at least of things depending on myself. I must now bid you farewell.

Ever yours very sincerely,
Lucy Aikin.

To Miss Aikin.

Boston, April 28, 1839.

My dear Miss Aikin,—I learn that you are quite unwell, and I would that it were in my power to say a cheering word to you. I recollect the pleasure you have often given me by your long letters, and should be glad to repay my obligations. The spring, I trust, is doing you good. This season was never more beautiful here than at the present moment. Vegetation is more forward than usual by two or three weeks; and we have had a succession of soft, balmy days, which help us to comprehend Milton's "vernal airs," and "gentle gales fanning their odorous wings." It is not true that as we advance in life the sense of pleasure fails us. I certainly enjoy fine weather as I did not in my youth. I did not need it then; but this difference does not explain my present sensations. There is a spiritual delight in these "vernal airs" and "gentle gales," of which I was wholly incapable in the tumults of youth. Did you ever read the Life of Henry More, the Platonist? I have always been interested in him, and can comprehend how he enjoyed a calm stream of bland air as an emblem and almost a means of the access of the Divine Spirit. I have taken much pleasure in the old Platonists of your country, Cudworth, John Smith, More, and, I may add, Norris, though inferior to the former—not that I have studied them—but occasional draughts of their mysterious wisdom have been refreshing to me. Mysticism is so vague a word, that one hardly knows what it means; but it is a glorious extravagance, and perhaps a necessary reaction against the general earthliness of men's minds. I pardon the man who loses himself in the clouds, if he will help me upwards.

I have been good for nothing for a week, and have been looking for amusement to a book which deserves serious study, Hallam's Literature of the Middle Ages. I am glad to find in it more unction than in his former writings—more to please as well as instruct. I am much pleased with his view of Luther, the hardest character, perhaps, to be understood in modern time, not from any inherent difficulty, but from the prejudices and passions awakened by his name. The Reformation has been identified with him too much. The Reformation was due not so much to Luther as to the times. He found the pear ripe. It is wonderful how little difficulty he found in carrying *the people* with him, and they proved his body-guard. He was too strong in the popular heart to be touched with safety. He found immense aid in what was an accident, and that was the gradual opening of his eyes to abuses. He kept but a few steps in advance of the people, and attacked every error with the zeal of new discovery. In this respect the difference between Luther and the Author of our faith is remarkable. The latter from the first moment told his whole truth, and was immeasurably separated from the universal mind around him. I was glad to learn from Hallam that Luther's doctrine of justification by faith preceded his work as a Reformer. I had imagined that he was unconsciously goaded to frame it as a good weapon for assault on the good works of the Catholics. It is interesting to observe how this gross error (for such it was as Luther held it) was used to beat down other errors, showing us that "things evil" have their commission. The more I know of Luther, the less I credit the Catholic stories against him. He was a man of impulse, not calculating; coarse, unrefined, impetuous, infinitely self-confident, kept in a fever not only by his own fiery temperature, but by the excitements of fierce conflicts. Such a man must have laid himself open to misrepresentation perpetually, and we can understand how prejudiced opponents justified themselves in charging on him all manner of crimes; but his faults were those of a generous spirit, and it is impossible to overlook in his correspondence the signs and natural bursts of a sincere, disinterested, heroic devotee to what he thought God's truth. I could not agree with Mr. Hallam in the analogies he traces between Luther's age and ours; the difference is immense.

I beg you not to feel the least obligation to answer this letter. I do not write to put you to the slightest labour, but in the hope that a line from a distant friend may cheer you. When you can write with pleasure to yourself, I shall welcome a letter. I earnestly hope that *entire repose* will set you up for the worthy tasks you have set yourself. Very truly your friend,

WM. E. CHANNING.

To Miss Aikin.

Boston, May 10, 1839.

My dear Miss Aikin,—I received yesterday your letter of March 23, and it was most welcome. My last, if it has reached you, will show that I had no expectation of hearing from you. I had been told that you were too much indisposed and exhausted for any exertion. It seems that rumour grows by traversing seas as well as land. My accounts of your health made me unwilling to send you two tracts which I have lately published, one on Slavery, one on War. I now forward them. They were called forth by local circumstances; but I should have no heart to write on the local, if it gave me no chance of bringing out what I esteem universal and eternal, truth. I know you have no taste for discussions of slavery, but I hope you will read my letter, because it goes into no shocking details, because it is an exposition of principles to a certain extent, and because I should like to know whether the style is not more unexceptionable, freer, more natural and idiomatic, than what you have met in my other writings. Not that I have made the style an object; but I am ready to believe that an improved taste and purer conceptions have insensibly moulded the expression of my thoughts. Very possibly I err; and my pretensions on this subject are so humble, that you will not pain me by speaking the truth. "So all vain people say," perhaps you may be ready to reply. But among all my infirmities, I do not plead guilty to vanity; and the manner in which I have received severe criticism assures me that this is not my tender side. I hope that I have now done "the work given me to do" on the subject of Slavery. All my feelings, and, I may add, my interest, dictated to me silence. But I could not, I dared not, be still. This subject had got into the hands of our professed Abolitionists, a noble set of men on the whole, but so unwise and intemperate as to prejudice the cause in the minds of our most intelligent and influential people; and nobody out of their ranks would speak. The topic was most unpopular. In preparing my work on Slavery, I named it but to two or three friends; for had my project been known, I should have had to encounter the dissuasives, disapprobation and frowns of all around me. This motive for writing has very much ceased, and I now hope for strength to apply myself without distraction to the great objects to which my life has been devoted. Not that my occasional tracts have demanded much time. I have an impatience when engaged in such labours which carries me through them in a short time. My sensibility to slavery has been and is great, not only on the general grounds of justice and humanity, but from its particular relation to my country. I talk about my country with great freedom in my writings, and blame it more than all others, but I do so from the depth of my love to it. When I look at its unrivalled freedom and energy, and at the diffusion of means of culture among the people, I feel as if it had a higher work to do, a higher destiny to fulfil, than any nation on earth; and my heart beats indignantly or sorrowfully when I see this bright prospect darkened by slavery, that cloud from hell, which, if not scattered, *ought* to overwhelm and destroy. I do not know that I ever spoke to you so strongly of my country before. I am little anxious to recommend it to favour abroad. I feel that it cannot be understood. Travellers come here, and mix with our rich merchants, who alone are able to show hospitality on a large scale, and think they know America. The American people is hardly seen; but no matter. I never felt the slightest uneasiness at the reports such people carry home. I *know* what the country is, and knowing this, solicit flatteries for it no more than for my family. It will speak for itself in time, and with this faith I heed not what is said now. Nothing said about it, good or bad, can have any influence on it, so impetuous are the impulses which are speeding it on, whether to weal or woe. I have indeed solicitudes about it; but slavery is the only imminent danger. I am kept more and more in peace by my deeper, more reverential conviction of the mysteriousness of Providence. Once I presumed to be a prophet. Now I hope and submit. I still cling to the anticipation of the progress of the world by gradual, gentle, peaceful processes; but the lessons of history and my own observation make me more doubtful whether a worn-out, corrupt state of things is to be transformed by a quiet transition into a fresh and healthy one. Your own account of your National Church makes me fear that, like Catholicism, this mixture of tradition and tyranny will need a storm to sweep it away. There are elements of good in all societies, but often so overpowered by evil growth of centuries, that convulsions are necessary to set them free. I do hope that destruction is not required to renovation; but if they to whom society has a right to look for beneficent renovation, concentrate all their powers to resist, the same awful Providence which has in past times shaken the social state, will again heave it from its foundations. Had I nothing to rest on but political foresight, I should have gloomy seasons. My religious faith in human nature, in God's purposes towards His spiritual family, never fails me.

I thank you for your interesting account of the movements in your Church. Perhaps we differ in this, that I see in these more of fanaticism, you more of intrigue and ambition, and perhaps we are both not far from the truth. I have been learning somewhat slowly how possible it is for intrigue and fanaticism to meet in the same men. Once I could not comprehend this union of vehement impulse and selfish calculation. But is it wonderful that fanaticism which disorders the reason should prey on the conscience, that our moral as well as intellectual perceptions should be clouded by it? A morbid bigot naturally winks at and approves the worst means which favour his end. I find as I grow older that I am less indulgent to diseased actions of the mind, however generous their tendency. I distrust more, not only scowling fanaticism, but that kindlier and more cheerful form of insanity, enthusiasm. I reverence more the *calm reason*, using this word in its broad sense as comprehending all universal truths, consequently the great moral principles. Its essence being impartiality, it is the antithesis of selfish, worldly calculation, and it issues in more enduring as well as nobler sensibility than belongs to enthusiasm. Since I wrote you, we have been troubled with "rumours of war" between the two countries. *Can* we fight? Is the wild beast still so strong in us? For myself, there seems something unnatural in war between England and America. Are we not one family? Do I not feel the blood of my old mother in my veins? I cannot look on you as a foreign country, though I fear you do not return the kindness. I want the good people in both countries to say, "We will not fight;" and I am satisfied that we, the good, are strong enough to keep the peace. I beg you to feel no obligation to write to me unless you can do it with perfect ease. Consult your health. I rejoice to learn that you feel yourself able to work again. To both of us, no play is so refreshing as the healthy action of our faculties in such work as our consciences and hearts approve. May you have strength for your own happiness and for the good of others!

Your sincere friend,
W. E. CHANNING.

P.S. Dr. Carpenter sent me an admirable tract by Rev. Mr. Powell, of Oxford, on "Tradition." Writings like this and Archbishop Whately's make me hope there is a redeeming spirit in the Church. I am just looking over a book which has a degree of point and pungency in thought and expression, called "Guesses at Truth." There is a tone of spiritual conservatism in it which I can bear very well. Do you know whence it comes? I have this moment heard that the Quarterly Review has come out in favour of the Oxford party, and that Lord Brougham has assailed or disparaged me in the Edinburgh. If this be true, his Lordship might have found some worthier prey. I dare say he finds enough to blame, as do I with my inferior sagacity. Happily, I have lived too long to be in fear of reviewers. My writings have made their way, as far as they have gone, with very little help from this tribe, and, still more, without any efforts of friends or any patronage whatever. This is very cheering to me, as showing sympathy with what I think important truth, but not as a sign of any endeavours or wide-spread fame. I see far higher reputations fading away, and who am I that I should live? Providence is to raise up brighter lights to obscure not only my humble ray, but the long-acknowledged teachers of the world. What better can we ask?

I am almost ashamed to send this unconscionably long letter. How it has grown under my hands I know not. I have written it almost too fast for thought, and therefore it has overrun reasonable bounds.

To Dr. Channing.

Hampstead, June 19, 1839.

My dear Friend,—Your very kind letter has just reached me, and I cannot be easy without sitting down immediately to thank you for it most cordially, and to give you a few particulars of myself, which I know you will read with some interest. I have indeed been long a very poor feeble creature, and during our long winter and chilly spring (the very opposite of yours, for it has been unusually backward) I was almost a complete prisoner, and a solitary one; for the unhealthy season similarly affected many of my best friends, and kept them from visiting me. My spirits were severely tried in consequence. At length April arrived, and I was looking for better times, when I *caught*, I believe, the influenza, which speedily increased from a feverish cold to an inflammation of the throat and lungs, which brought my life into imminent peril. For my own part, I had not the slightest expectation, nor, I may add, wish of recovery. The love of life, as I may have mentioned to you, has always been feeble in me. Under the influence of sickness and dejection it was at this time quite extinguished, and I was not only calm, but happy, in the prospect of a speedy solution of that mystery of existence which had often weighed heavily indeed upon my spirit. I called to mind all things and persons interesting to me, whether near or distant, and did not omit to direct a long message of friendship to be conveyed to you. But the Great Disposer had not decreed my immediate release. I am still here speculating and reasoning; and the affectionate expressions of my friends, joined to the natural influence of returning strength, now dispose me to receive less ungraciously the boon of lengthened life—useless creature as I feel myself to be, or useful only as affording an object to the kind affections of relations and a few friends. I *live* in my sad domestic solitude and inutility, and I have the grief to see the young and amiable wife of one of my nephews sinking under a mortal disease, to leave behind her a heart-broken husband and motherless babe! Mystery, all mystery!

Much have I to say to you, besides returning you my thanks for your two pieces on "War" and on "Slavery." The last I hold to be the very best work that you have yet given us. I agree with you throughout, or very nearly so, and I much admire the manner in which you have treated the exceedingly delicate topic of the abolitionists. You have dealt out exemplary justice between them and their persecutors. Your commemoration of Darwin's slave gave me a thrill of delight. From the days of my childhood, when I was among the abstainers from sugar, till now, that kneeling figure has been the type of his race to my imagination. Let me add, that in this piece your style is more than ever to my taste. It is your true epistolary style, which I may well love best of all.

The lecture on War gives more hold to remark, and, perhaps, controversy. Yet there is very much in which I cordially concur. The preliminary observations, and more especially the remarks on the causes of the present long peace, and the summary of those which may again stir up war, the warning of the little reliance to be placed on commerce and prosperity as pacific, on account of the selfish and evil passions engendered by both, appeared to me not only just, but profound, and often original, and worthy to be widely diffused and deeply pondered. Your discussion, too, of the right in governments to declare war has much powerful argument and irresistible appeals to the heart and to the conscience. But your exhortations to Christians to submit to martyrdom rather than obey their governments in cases of unjust war, will, I conceive, be a good deal disapproved, both in your pure democracy, where " vox populi " stands pretty generally, I suppose, for " vox Dei," and in our mixed constitution, which freely admits of public meetings, petitions to the crown or the legislature, and instructions to representatives. It may be thought, perhaps justly, to tend to anarchy, and thus to war itself —civil war. You take new, and I think strong ground, in holding out a just acknowledgment of the rights of man as the firmest bulwark against war, that thousand-headed monster of wrong; this idea of the claims of man as such, you derive from the New Testament, which certainly does inculcate that equality among mankind on which rights are based. Yet, on other points, are there not considerable difficulties attending the religious view of the subject ? Our old Puritans found it hard to reconcile the spirit of Christianity with the armed assertion of civil liberty, and discovered no other means of accomplishing it than by giving more authority to the maxims and examples of the Old Testament than the precepts of the New. In fact, although wars of revenge and ambition are crushed in the germ by the Gospel denunciations against the passions themselves, it does so happen that even these are not so *directly* prohibited as self-defence—as any thought of resistance to tyranny, violence and wrong, exercised against ourselves. I do not see how any Christian can stop short of Quakerism on this point without allowing himself to regard these non-resisting principles as local or temporary in their intention. You, I suppose, take this view, as you permit self-defence. But in many cases this is permitting all. Practically, the line dividing offence from defence is very often evanescent. Once allow war not to be utterly unlawful, and we may listen to considerations of state expediency, utility. " Necessity, the tyrant's plea," comes in; and I own I see not on what other ground—certainly not that of justice—you yourself hold it *right* that your free states should be bound to supply troops to put down slave insurrections in the South. Thus each case of hostilities comes to be discussed on its own merits or demerits, and the applicability of the religious scruple comes to be matter of opinion. In the end, the decision is left to the moral feelings or moral principles of men—antagonists how unequal to their passions, prejudices and interests! No cause, however, can be more worthy of the zealous efforts of good men than that of peace. Your lecture is eminently adapted to awaken conscience and reflection to the enormous guilt of war, and it will be reckoned to you amongst your best services to the interests of human nature. Meantime, let us be thankful that our two governments have shown too much wisdom, whether of the best kind or not, to make enemies of two kindred nations. The Borderers may go on jangling, but there is evidently nothing else to fear.

You, who do not love our utilitarian philosophy, will rejoice, I suppose, to learn that no less men than Messrs. Whewell and Sedgwick are doing their utmost to get the works of Paley put out of the course of reading for Cambridge undergraduates; but I fear this step is not taken in favour of the beautiful mysteries of your Platonists, but of others more gainful to our State-church. Our clergy are desperately active at present, and proportionally mischievous. They will not allow us to have a normal school on terms of anything like fairness to Dissenters, and they everywhere talk very big of "the authority committed unto them" as the successors of the apostles. I have even heard of attempts amongst them to remind people of a monstrous old law, made against Popish recusants and still unrepealed, by which persons are liable to heavy penalties for not regularly attending their parish church. I apprehend, however, that this applies now only to Church people, the Toleration Act sheltering Dissenters. They have "all the plea" at present; the press seems as much their own as if they had an Inquisition at their command. But let them beware of what is gathering in silence. Men *think* very freely now and whisper; presently they will speak out and act, I trust. If you take up a list of new publications, it seems as if nothing scarcely was written or read amongst us except theology, and of the narrowest kind; but so it is, that a person might live in the midst of the best and most literary society for a year together, and never hear the slightest mention of any one new book on these subjects. I know not exactly who are the readers, but I suspect scarcely any laymen of the smallest note. The clergy often write *at* the bishop or the patron, not the public, and there are a number of women who write theology for little children, which some mammas encourage. The Tory party are in strict alliance with the Church; but I suspect they look more to the increase of their political power through this union than to any objects of a religious nature. You may perhaps have read in our debates, on what pretexts these high allies have defeated, for the present at least, the ministerial project in favour of a normal school, in which the Church would not have been permitted to impose her own dogmas on the children of Dissenters; and I think you will scarcely give such a man as Lord Stanley credit for honest bigotry on the occasion. I suppose that good is to come out of these conflicts between freedom and mental thraldom in the end, but the immediate effect is miserably depressing and irritating. One can scarcely witness with composure even the temporary success of arrogant priestly claims, supported by fashion, self-interest, or narrow-mindedness. You speak of Luther: have you read a selection from his "Table-Talk," translated into English, which appeared about ten years since? It is very entertaining, and helps one to understand him. I respect him much.

Mr. Rogers pointed out a passage in your "Texas," beginning, "England is a privileged country," as one of the finest in our language.

Have I not given you full measure this time? and yet I feel as if I had more to say.

Ever most sincerely yours,
L. AIKIN.

To Miss Aikin.

September 11, 1839.

My dear Miss Aikin,—Your letter of July was truly a relief and a gratification. I had heard of your indisposition from others as well as yourself, and could not but be solicitous about you. And now you are better, and I trust can begin to work again. You must not wait till you can accomplish much. If you can apply yourself to your task but an hour or even half an hour a day, and can write but a few lines or gather a few authorities, no matter; there is a pleasure in the consciousness of progress, however slow. To see something growing under our hands is a solace even in great weakness. During this summer I have been able to give little more than an hour a day to my work, but I have been all the happier for my pains. I am sorry that the renewed gift of life does not seem a greater good to you.

There we differ. I love life, perhaps too much—perhaps I cling to it too strongly for a Christian and philosopher. I welcome every new day with new gratitude. I almost wonder at myself when I think of the pleasure which the dawn gives me, after having witnessed it so many years. This blessed light of heaven, how dear it is to me! and this earth which I have trodden so long, with what affection I look at it! I have but a moment ago cast my eyes over the lawn in front of my house, and the sight of it gemmed with dew, and heightening by its brilliancy the shadow of the trees which fall on it, awakened emotions perhaps more vivid than I experienced in youth. I do not, like the ancients, call the earth, *mother;* she is so fresh, youthful, living and rejoicing. I do, indeed, anticipate a more glorious world than this, but still my first familiar home is very precious to me; nor can I think of leaving its sun and sky and fields and ocean without regret; and not only my interest in outward nature, but my interest in human nature, in its destinies, in the progress of science, in the struggles of freedom and religion, in works of genius, and especially in great subjects of inquiry, has increased up to this moment, and I am now in my sixtieth year. Indeed, life has been an improving gift from my youth; and one reason I believe to be, that my youth was not a happy one. I look back to no bright dawn of life which gradually "faded into common day." The light which I now live in rose at a later period. A rigid domestic discipline, sanctioned by the times—gloomy views of religion—the selfish passions—collisions with companions perhaps worse than myself—these and other things darkened my boyhood. Then came altered circumstances—dependence, unwise and excessive labour for independence, and the symptoms of the weakness and disease which have followed me through life. Amidst this darkness, it pleased God that the light should rise. The work of spiritual regeneration, the discovery of the supreme good, of the great and glorious end of life, aspirations after truth and virtue which are pledges and beginnings of immortality, the consciousness of something divine within me—these began, faintly indeed, and through many struggles and sufferings have gone on.

Since beginning this letter I have visited a beach, the favourite haunt of my boyhood. There I saw the same unchanged beauty and grandeur which moved my youthful soul, but I could look back only to be conscious of beholding them now with a deeper, purer joy. So much for what would be called an unhappy youth. Perhaps I owe to it much of my present happiness. I know not that in indulgence, prosperity and buoyant health, I should have heeded the inward revelations or engaged in the inward conflicts to which I owe so much. Will you pardon this egotism? I am almost unwilling to send it, but we may learn something from one another's experience, and I have thought that this internal history might be interesting and perhaps useful to you.

Your letter gives me another personal topic. You say Lord Brougham was my reviewer. I am sorry for it; not that I apprehend anything from the attack, but as a fellow-labourer in the cause of freedom I should have been left to do what little good I can undisturbed. The motive ascribed by Mr. Rogers can hardly be the true one. Lord B. and myself have too little in common for envy. Our paths are too distinct to let us jostle one another. Then he must be conscious that his gifts, by their *kind*, to say nothing of their extent, have given him a conspicuousness before which my reputation makes little show. Is he not given to *freaks?* We need not, then, study his motives. I still feel kindly towards him, for I have connected him with that joyful moment when

I heard of the accession of the Whigs to power. I have supposed him a chief worker in that triumph, and it is no mean praise to have stood by Liberal principles in the day of their depression, and to have carried them victoriously through the conflict. True, when he got power, he did not know how to use or keep it; but how common is this with men called great! How few are like our Washington, who, after fighting the battle of Liberty, have won fresher laurels in peace! One laurel suffices most men, and a man who renders one good service must not be forgotten. I suppose Lord B.'s chief merit to be in debate, and that his vehemence and sarcasm has not been surpassed since Lord Chatham. As a writer, I have always thought him somewhat clumsy; more remarkable for rude force than refinement, and very deficient in the ear. Did he ever write a musical sentence? I began his first book on Natural Theology, but finding that I should gain little, I laid it aside. I hear good accounts of his second, and I certainly respect him for this use of his powers. Has he taken sides with the clergy on the subject of education? I trust the Dissenters will suffer or sacrifice anything rather than suffer the established priesthood to get any control of the faith of their children. How stands this matter? But enough.

Your sincere friend,
W. E. CHANNING.

TO DR. CHANNING.

Hampstead, March 2, 1840.

You think, my good friend, supposing you have given yourself the trouble of thinking on the subject, that it is an unconscionable length of time since I have written to you—in which you are much mistaken. I wrote you a long letter very lately, and it was safely conveyed to the post; but by the egregious blundering of the Hampstead post-mistress (I have a great opinion of my sex and certainly think a woman fit to govern a kingdom, but defend me from she-governors of post-offices!)—by her egregious blundering in our new postage law my unfortunate epistle got to the dead-letter office, whence it was returned to me, opened, creased, dirty, and unfit to send you. Ah! you will never know what a loss you had there. Such a letter! And poor I must be at the trouble to write another. Well, I submit with a good grace to any temporary inconvenience by this new law, which reduces our heavy postage to a single penny from one extremity of our island to the other. The moral tendency of the measure seems to me of greater value than figures can express. In the humbler classes it restores parents and children, brothers and sisters, to one another, who had grown strangers by long discontinuance of all intercourse; it will give a stronger impetus to national education than all the arguments yet advanced, and will redeem many an hour from idleness or worse, for the usually innocent, often amiable and useful, employment of letter-writing. In Scotland, where families are often so widely scattered by the impulse of necessity or ambition, which carries their active youth to the farthest ends of the earth, family attachments are nevertheless kept up with remarkable zeal and constancy; with us, I am sorry to confess that this is not the case, at least in the lower classes. A boy or girl coming to London from a remote county to seek service, seems often to forget entirely the native village and the parent's roof, and with them all the moral restraints imposed by such ties. How stands this case, I should like to hear, with your New-Englanders who rush into the wilds of the *far West?* With them communication must often be difficult and tedious.

You expressed to me in your last an anxiety lest our clergy should be permitted to exert the control over national education which they have ventured to claim by right of their office. Never fear; it will not be submitted to. Notwithstanding the bluster of the Church party, nothing would so much surprise me as to see the Establishment winning, or winning back, a single inch of ground. That spirit of power, the genius of the nineteenth century, says *No.* I daily more and more perceive the sagacity of those who applied to the epoch of the passing of the Reform Bill Talleyrand's expression, " Le commencement de la fin." We have been striding on towards essential democracy and religious equality ever since; and nothing seems to me capable of arresting this progress, unless some such absurd and furious movements of a Chartist mob as might cause in the better classes the reaction of alarm. In spite of my *aristocratic letter* —written when I, too, was suffering something of a reaction from deep disgust at the interference of your border states in behalf of our Canada rebels, and their insolent and ignorant defiance of the laws of nations— in spite of feelings which the better behaviour of your executive has since mitigated—I view our domestic state with hope, and much, though not unmingled, satisfaction. The pacification of Ireland is a moral triumph which warms my heart with admiration, reverence and gratitude towards the true statesmen who have compassed it; and after this achievement I know not what task of reformation can be found too difficult.

No; we *will* not quarrel for a petty boundary question —it is not to be thought of. " What is that between me and thee?" May our rulers on both sides treat it as friend with friend, brother with brother. Believe me, the tie *is* felt on our side as strongly as it well can be on yours. By all the Liberal party, at least, it is strongly felt; and I cannot but regard it as the most favourable of all circumstances that this question should fall to be decided under a Whig ministry on our side.

You have, I hope, found time to read Professor Smyth's "Lectures on Modern History;" and if you have, I feel sure of your finding in them much to approve and admire. The writer, a *young* and lively man of seventy-six, is an old and dear friend of mine; he is also an admirer of yours, and he was just sending me a copy of his work to send to you when he learned that Mr. Rathbone had anticipated him: but I said I would let you know his intentions. The merit of the counsels of peace, of tolerance, of mild government, with which they abound, can only be appreciated by recollecting that these lectures were delivered by a *Regius* Professor to the sons, for the most part, of aristocratic, Tory and Churchly families, in those evil days when Cambridge had nearly lost all memory of her former honourable distinction as the Whig University. The ruling powers always regarded them with jealousy, and, as far as they decently could, discouraged the young men from attending them. They found, however, large and attentive and gratified audiences. The style appears to me a model for the purpose—lively, easy, extremely colloquial, but rising to eloquence and brilliancy where the subject prompts; and there is over all that charm of perfect sincerity and simplicity of heart, which I think must be felt even by those who know not how much it is the characteristic of the man. You will own that he has done thorough justice to the merits of all parties in your War of Independence, and that he knows how to estimate Washington.

It warmed and cheered my heart to read your *confes-*

sions of happiness; few have such to make. For myself, I think life has become dearer to me since I was last in danger of losing it; and this, strange to tell, in the face of a grievous anxiety, which is even now preying upon my heart. The health of my brother Charles, than whom I have no nearer and no dearer object of affection in the world, has long been in a very precarious state. His sufferings at this very time are exceedingly severe—and I tremble to think what may be the result. So dearly do I love him—so much has his life-long affection become a part of my very self—that I can think of one circumstance only which could render it tolerable to me to live after him—the prospect of being in some manner useful to his dear children.

Your friends the Farrars are just at present my neighbours. I fear he is still a great sufferer by sleeplessness, and the train of miserable ideas which attend it. A severe trial for his excellent wife, but in which there is no fear of her failing. I was glad to see her look in bodily health and vigour.

I am not now in spirits to add more.

Yours truly ever,
L. AIKIN.

To Dr. Channing.

Hampstead, May 16, 1840.

My dear Friend,—Accept my cordial thanks for your two new pieces, both of which I have read with deep interest and high approbation. That on the "Elevation of the Working Classes" embodies much that I have often felt and thought, without being able to bring it out; in fact, it applies to all classes; and when I have seen, as I often have, families of young persons, diligent, docile, willing and able to acquire rudiments of many sciences, many languages, considerably skilled in various accomplishments, but without one original thought, one lofty sentiment, I have murmured to myself in sorrow—To what avail? Hannah More had the merit of raising her voice against mere "finger accomplishments" in female education; and I regard her as the setter of the fashion of domiciliary visits of ladies to the poor—a fashion which can only be followed to advantage by such among them as are capable of elevating the minds, not merely administering to the desire of temporal goods, in those with whom they converse. The kind of elevation you describe is certainly very rare at present, and perhaps will always be so, but it is nevertheless the point to be aimed at, and I rejoice that you have taken up the cause.

I was much struck and touched with your sermon, and I agree very much with your views on the great and dark question of the origin of evil; but there is one passage in which, as I feel it a duty to inform you, you have laid yourself open to severe, and, I fear I must say, just censure. "They never can be fair," exclaimed a candid and excellent friend of mine, and your great admirer in general, on finishing your sermon—"They never can be fair, these divines—not even Dr. Channing. Here is a passage which is an absolute slander—an aspersion which he had no right to make, and which is not true;" and he read the passage: "Such scepticism is a moral disease, the growth of some open or lurking depravity." "What business," he continued, "has any one to impute such motives? What has the view which a mind takes of arguments on a difficult subject to do with depravity? The spirit of this judgment is precisely the same with that of a Catholic priest, who says 'you must be very wicked if you do not believe transubstantiation.'" I sat petrified with amazement at this burst

of indignation, and I endeavoured to mitigate my friend
—one of the mildest of men on common occasions; but
it was to no purpose. I could only plead that the offensive passage had probably escaped you by inadvertence.
"But," I said, "I will mention it to him, and we shall
hear what he says." "Pray do," exclaimed my friend;
"he ought to be told of it." I have now kept my word.
I own that, for my own part, I cannot comprehend a
doubt of the goodness of the Deity. We all feel that He
has bestowed on us much *intentional* good: to believe
that He has also inflicted upon us *designed*, that is *pur-
poseless* evil, would be to conceive of Him as a Being
weak, inconsistent, infirm of purpose, more than any wise
and good man—an idea at which reason revolts. At the
same time, all that I have known of the characters of
men who speculate freely, boldly, and of course sometimes absurdly, on these abstruse questions, convinces
me that moral character stands quite apart from theories
of this nature. If divines were admitted to know the
real sentiments of men of cultivated and reflecting minds
on religious topics, they would often be surprised, and
even shocked, to find how many, and what kind of persons, they stab in the dark. By general reflections of
this nature, they might even be alarmed at the deep,
silent hatred of their whole order which these insults
cause to rankle in the bosoms of a class possessed of so
much real, though usually latent power. This particular
doubt of the goodness of Providence I have often heard
discussed among wise and excellent men; and the conclusion has usually been, that perfect wisdom and goodness, combined with that absolutely unlimited power for
which divines contend, are inconsistent with the evil
which we see in the world; that you must limit one, at
least, of the attributes; and that power was, on the whole,
that which seemed most susceptible of such limitation.

To me, neither this nor any other solution of the problem appears entirely satisfactory. I believe it to be one which we have not at present the means of solving; but I believe that it will be solved, so as entirely to "vindicate the ways of God to man." At the same time, I know those who take a darker view of the subject, to whom you, if you knew them, would be as far as any one from imputing depravity, however secret.

Enough, however, of this. You will, I know, rejoice with me that the anxiety respecting the health of my brother Charles, which tormented me when I last wrote, has now subsided. He is now very nearly restored to health, and I have great pleasure in knowing that his frequent visits to me at Hampstead have been a principal means of his recovery. The breezes of this fresh hill-top are often the best of cordials to the dwellers in our overgrown metropolis. This great and busy hive is at present in its busiest and fullest season—in full hum—but I know not that there is any great object of general attention much deserving your notice. One book, indeed, there is which would interest you by the character of the writer, although many of the topics treated in it are probably too exclusively English for you to enter into. This is the "Life of Sir Samuel Romilly," published by his sons, and composed of his own diaries and letters. A more pure and perfectly disinterested public character has never been recorded; in these qualities he might be compared with your own Washington. No man in memory had so much personal weight in the House of Commons; and it was this alone which enabled him, in those bad times when the very name of Reform was hooted down by a corrupt administration and its sycophants, to force upon the legislature some of those mitigations of our sanguinary penal code which opened the way for the extensive improvements which have since been demanded by public opinion, and carried through by our best and ablest statesmen. In many other causes, also, he stood forth the undaunted, and also the skilful, champion of humanity, justice, and sound policy. His private life was that of the most virtuous, tender and amiable of men. If the book comes into your hands, read at least his own brief memoir of his early days. You will find it one of the most beautiful pieces of autobiography imaginable. It is remarkable that poetry should have been his first love, the object of his earliest aspirations—a grand confirmation of what I have always suspected, that the heights of virtue will scarcely be reached but by those who behold them clothed in the "hues unbounded of the sun"— hues lent them by a warm and bright imagination!

The Puseyites, or Newmaniacs, as I believe they are more generally called, are certainly making progress. We have clergy who refuse to dine out on Wednesdays and Fridays, being the fasts ordained by the English Church. The other day a curate published a manifesto against a Bible Society, headed by two clergymen, for presuming to meet and to distribute the Scriptures in his parish. He declares it to be *heresy* for any one to give away Bibles, excepting the person deputed by the bishop to do so—namely, the officiating parish priest. A bold step towards Popery! What is far more extraordinary, there are two laymen, members of the House of Commons, who think fit to scourge themselves! It is in vain to talk of the illumination of the age: at all times there have been, and I believe at all times there will be, *born* fanatics, whose destiny is to make, if they do not find, absurdities to believe and to propagate. I see no more probability that this distortion of understanding should become obsolete, than that squinting eyes or hump-backs should cease to be found. At the same time, I think that this exaggerated notion of Church power is less likely than any form of superstition to find favour in the sight of the English people at large. There is a constant and natural hostility between High-churchism and Whig, still more Radical, principles in government. Under our present Liberal administration, nothing is done by the State to strengthen the hands of the Church. The Chief Justice has just pronounced an important decision (that parish vestries cannot by law be *compelled* to vote money for Church-rates), which is likely ultimately to liberate Dissenters from this unjust burden; and which strikes also at the pride and assumption of the Establishment a blow which will be deeply felt.

And so the French have set their hearts on having back the relics of their Emperor from his prison-isle, that they may make them the object of a grand show and ceremony! It was right, I think, in our government to grant the request, since they regard it as an obligation, but I think it a mournful sign of the temper and spirit of that people. Military glory, it seems, is still their idol. To their restless temper, peace is insipid, freedom is indifferent; they must have *excitement*, and *that* nothing can yield so largely as war. I tremble for the results. To their king, this worship of the memory of Bonaparte must be exceedingly offensive. Nothing, certainly, but fear of the consequences of refusal, can have induced him to concur in their wish, and the same fear may soon compel him to seize some pretext for going to war with one or other of his neighbours; and so the flame would be rekindled throughout Europe. Horrible anticipation! The mind cannot entertain it without shuddering. What, alas! in such a case, would become of all our hopes for the improvement of man and his destiny?

Our rumours of war seem blowing over. The King of Naples is wise enough to submit. We shall settle our dispute amicably with you. China, indeed, we shall apparently be obliged to take some hostile measures with—but we still hope matters may soon admit of arrangement.

At home, I think we are going on well in almost all respects. The Tories seem further from power than ever, and many quiet reforms, which do much unostentatious good, are in progress. I know of nothing in our political state to excite apprehension, except it be the perpetual turbulence and restlessness of O'Connell, urging on his countrymen to arrogant claims and absurd enterprizes, and the violence and folly of our own Radicals. These absurd people may go on to produce some reaction in favour of Toryism—but that is all, I think, that is to be feared. Even with these men, I hope that a wise and liberal government will know how to deal.

Believe me ever yours, with true regard,

L. AIKIN.

To Miss Aikin.

July 18, 1840.

My dear Miss Aikin,—How good you are! The day before yesterday I received your letter of May, whilst that of March is unanswered. I am glad to learn that my lectures on the Elevation of the Labouring Class gave you any satisfaction. I have the subject much at heart, but I wrote the lectures in a state of exhaustion, which made me fear that they would do little good. I was glad, too, that you gave me the criticism of your "candid and excellent friend" on a passage in my sermon on Dr. Follen. To be sure, "slander" was a strong word; but no matter; I like to know precisely how I affect others. Your friend wronged me in thinking that I spoke as a *theologian*. No; I spoke from a moral impulse, a deep moral instinct, from as genuine and native a feeling as your friend's indignation. I spoke without sufficient care; I meant to say, as the whole passage shows, that *fixed doubts* of God's goodness, which the soul *rests in*, indicate something wrong within; and I cannot get over the conviction. In truth, this state of mind is almost incomprehensible. Atheism I comprehend, and I shall not be quick to set it down to depravity; but that a man believing in an intelligent Author of the universe, should question His benevolent purpose, and even ascribe malignity, amazes me; that his own soul should not teach him better, amazes me. There is something horrible in the thought. All the guilt of the human race combined would be a light matter compared with the wickedness of the Creator bringing us into life to torture us or to abandon us to the play of merciless elements. This is no matter of theology with me, but of moral feeling. I am indeed jealous on the subject of God's goodness. Your language on the subject is too measured and cold. What have we been living for, if we have not come to a generous trust in our Maker? I can forgive your friend everything but the ascription of a *priestly* spirit to me. If I know my own heart, I have not a particle of the spirit of "*the order*" within me. I see nothing peculiar in the relation of the religious teacher to God—no other relation than every man sustains; and I claim no rights but such as I extend to all. However, I will not wax warm about language which was not weighed very carefully. I am sorry to have wounded a good man, and I will modify my language, so that my real thought may be brought out.

I was truly rejoiced at your account of your brother's health. One cloud is scattered in your sky, and I hope you will enjoy the brightness. Your whole letter, indeed, breathes a freedom of spirit, an animation, which I have missed in some preceding ones. You are well enough, I suppose, *to work;* and what a happiness is this! I am a poor labourer myself; to-day I have written two hours only; and yet this effort, not wholly unsuccessful, will light up the day. The thought that I may live to give out my mind is full of exhilaration. Perhaps my case is singular: I am sixty years old, and yet have only begun the work which I have had in view a large part of my life. My friend Tuckerman used almost to be angry at my postponing my task; but I told him I must bide my time and see my way clear before me; and now that the time has come, I have little strength for the toil. Yet I do not faint; I feel, indeed, that I may be deluded as to the importance of what I have undertaken. Many men, far my superiors, have laid out their strength in a work which the world has refused to read, and their names are perpetuated by writings to which they attached no importance. I feel the uncertainty of all that I am to do; but it seems to me I have something worth saying, and I shall be grateful for the opportunity. If men should think differently, I shall not quarrel with them. That my own spiritual education will go on by trying to bring forth what is deepest in my own soul, I am sure, and I shall do the more for the effort, if not here, yet hereafter. I sometimes have a fear, and that is that my enthusiasm may be somewhat chilled by time. My memory I know will decline, and my capacity of labour; but the *chill* of the *heart,* this I do not like to think of. But I hope. My heart has kept its warmth under two severe trials; that is, the freest inquiry and a growing knowledge of the world. I think, too, that it has never been a superficial warmth. May I go on *loving* more and more fervently to the last! I have little fear that the intellect will be wanting to my next work, if the heart will but live and soar. I did not mean to give you so much of myself; but it so happens that my mind just now has taken this direction, and my letters are very apt to be tinged by what I think about at the time.

I see no need of thinking that some are "born fanatics," that the intellect has a "squint" from nature, &c. The social nature of man and his consciousness of weakness explain the importance into which the idea of "the Church" has swelled. How natural is it that men whose spiritual lethargy has been roused by coming together, by sympathy, by joint rites, by the priest's appeal to the multitude, should come to think that grace flows through the Church and the priest! As to your self-scourging member of Parliament, this is a natural consequence of a religion in which terrible punishment is the grand feature. It encourages me to see so much consequentness in these delusions. There is a method in this spiritual madness, and a degree of rationality amidst the wrecks of reason. Reason must then triumph at last.

You write more encouragingly about public affairs. I have more and more confidence in your ministry; but how can they stand if they are worsted in almost every new election? Conservatism seems to triumph at the polls, and is not this a sign of public opinion? I promise myself much from Sir S. Romilly's Life. I am reading now with delight Professor Smyth's Lectures. What a whole-hearted man! as we Yankees say. The love of liberty seems his very life-blood; and with this noble enthusiasm, how calm, how wise he is! We declaimers may take a lesson from him. On one point I should like his opinion and Mr. Hallam's. What was the relation of Isabella of Castile to the Inquisition? Was she merely carried on by the spirit of the age, or did her religion make her a forwarder of that abominable institution? Did she go beyond her time? I have read much of Mr. Hallam's "History of the Literature," &c., with great pleasure. It is a luxury to read works of this character, in which accurate and profound research is united with broad views, fine taste and lofty feeling. The capacity of labour implied in such a work fills me with admiration. I feel as if I had been an idler all my life. Will you tell me what place Carlyle holds among you, whether he influences opinion? We have some signs among us of a "transcendental" school, as it is called, i.e. we have some noble-minded men, chiefly young, who are dissatisfied with the present, have thrown off all tradition, and talk of deriving all truth from their own souls. They have some great truths at bottom, but of course wanting the modification which always comes from looking over the whole ground and seeing what is due to other truths. One discussion has risen out of this movement, respecting the place which miracles hold in Christianity. This school rest the religion wholly on internal evidence. A greater question will be, What was the inspiration of Christ? whether it was different in kind or only in degree from the inspiration granted to all? This begins to be agitated. In all these things I see aspiration after something better, not always wise—how can it be?—but a presage of good, whether near or distant. I hope to hear that your health continues to improve.

Wishing you every blessing,
I remain very truly your friend,
WM. E. CHANNING.

To Dr. Channing.

Hampstead, October 11, 1840.

My dear Friend,—Your last letter was very peculiarly welcome to me on many accounts. I felt that in giving you the "*ipsissima verba*" of my vehement friend, I had put your forbearance to a severe trial; but it has stood it, as I thought it would, nobly; and my friend begs to apologize for the word "slander," and is quite satisfied that he was more slanderous in imputing to you a priestly spirit. In short, your candour has quite turned his heart, and it is a heart worth turning. You are quite right in saying that my language on the subject was " too cold " and measured; it was indeed purposely kept down, for I wished to see the argument taken up by you alone, and was only desirous to show that *I* was not one of those touched by your censure. In fact, the goodness of God is what I have never doubted, amid all my doubts, more than just enough to make me look into the proofs. I believe, rather I feel it, just as I feel my own existence; I have, like you, a difficulty in conceiving the horror and the absurdity of an opposite opinion; and far rather would I endure any possible earthly misery, than lose my trust in Him who is *all*. Could there ever have been a good man without a Maker of man infinitely superior in goodness? One of Hume's Essays, in which he affirms that we might infer from the world around us an intelligent, but not a moral cause, struck me, on re-reading it a few years since, as so utterly illogical, so truly absurd, that I could only account for it, from a writer of his acuteness, by supposing that he thought it prudent to throw this cloak over his Atheism. Yet it is, indeed, worse than Atheism—as bad as ultra-Calvinism.

You ask if Carlyle makes any progress amongst us. Not with the thoroughly-read or the thorough thinkers, the intellectual leaders of society; but he finds audiences, and some readers and admirers (I can scarcely say disciples, for I believe nobody pretends to make out his system), amongst the half-read and half-thinkers. You will not admit, with me, that some men are born fanatics, but perhaps you will allow to Coleridge that some are born Platonists and others Aristotelians—in other words, that some minds have a bent towards the mystical, others towards the experimental in philosophy—that this difference is innate, and is ever reproducing itself under different shapes and names. In this country the experimental has long borne sway, with Locke for its leader; of late there has been somewhat a spirit of revolt; transcendentalism has some considerable advocates, and I think I can perceive that the general tone on these subjects is, in degree, modified. The High-church dearly love a system which draws a distinction between the reason and the understanding, and affirms that doctrines which appear to the latter a contradiction in terms may be all the more conformable to the dictates of the former—the higher and nobler faculty—this, you may know, is the language held by Coleridge concerning the Trinity. I think, with you, that some great truths may lie at the root of these speculations, but many processes are to be gone through before they can be brought into daylight and fitted for use. In the meantime, I both dislike and distrust the jargon—the cant of which Carlyle has such a quantity. You would see in the "Edinburgh Review" an article on his history, which appears to me to be an able exposure of his quackery, and at the same time a candid estimate of his merits and talents. The article is by a friend of mine, a man of immense reading, for his age, and a paragon among reviewers for downright honesty and impartiality—the rarest of all qualities when the writer lies screened under the irresponsible *we*.

The grand field for activity amongst us at this time is that of general education. A prodigious impulse has been given by the apparently insignificant grant which our Liberal government has extorted from the public purse, in spite of Tory opposition. The Established priesthood having been baffled, and by the ministry also, in its attempt to assume the control of public instruction, and force its own creeds and catechisms on the children of Dissenters, we may now hope that a free, large, and truly national system of instruction will be adopted. Little as I am disposed to sanguine views of human improvement, I own I do look with ardent hope to a general amelioration of manners and principles as the ultimate result of this exorcism of ignorance and brutality.

I trust we are in no present danger of the return of the Tories to power. This ministry has been well compared to the logging-stone, which one right arm can set shaking, but a hundred could not throw down. It seems to gain strength by the tempests which it weathers. There is great dissension, too, in the Tory camp, and some important desertions have taken place. But, oh! where will be all our hopes, should we see ourselves again plunged in the misery and wickedness of war? There is no wish for it, but, on the contrary, the greatest horror of it, as I sincerely believe, both in the government and the nation at large; but I fear that the spirit of the French people is the very reverse. They long to revenge themselves on their conquerors, to gain territory, plunder and glory—they abound in turbulent spirits, for whom peace offers no prospects, no career. I believe, indeed, that their king and all their best statesmen are pacifically disposed, but the awful doubt is whether they may not be compelled to yield to the torrent. Perhaps, after all, the heavy national debt of both countries is the best security for their peaceful behaviour.

You inquire about Isabella of Castile and her relation to the Inquisition, and I conclude, from what you say, that you have not read Prescott's life of her. He is her decided eulogist, and insists on our thinking her one of the most amiable of women; at the same time, he distinctly states that she directly violated the laws of her country in instituting that new tribunal—that no provocation whatever had been given her by the unhappy Moors or the Jews, the joint objects of her relentless and atrocious tyranny. In short, her persecutions appear to be amongst the most completely wicked—the most utterly inexcusable, on record. She had not even the apology of bad example; her Inquisition was an absolute novelty in the world. It is true that it was the invention and suggestion of an execrable monk, her father-confessor; but neither had Isabella the excuse of a weak and pliant character; she effectually withstood, on many occasions, the influence of a husband whom she is said to have loved; and I do not believe that she would have complied with her confessor in this matter, had she not expected to strengthen her royal authority by the destruction or banishment of her misbelieving subjects. Her bigotry, like that of Louis XIV., was little else than the spirit of despotism in disguise. The persecutions of our bloody Mary were venial, compared with those of her grandmother. *She* had great provocations.

Have you read Ranke's "History of the Popes of the Sixteenth and Seventeenth Centuries," translated by Mrs. Austin? If not, think that you have a treasure laid up in store. The writer has collected and studied his authorities with true German industry, and has poured a flood of new light on the most important period of modern history.; and I, for one, feel it a real misfortune to have groped through a large part of that period without his guiding lamp. The history of the Papacy is so closely intertwined with that of every European nation, that no one in future must presume to write of Tudors, or Stuarts, or Bourbons, without consulting Ranke; and to possess a true history of this wonderful line of monarch-priests, is a greater gain to philosophy than it is possible to estimate.

But why do I speak of books to read, to you who are so much better employed in writing? I cordially congratulate both you and the public on your task, and particularly on the ardent spirit with which you are pursuing it. I long to know *what* your work is to be, but, be it what it may, I am strongly persuaded that it will prove to be something that the world "will not easily let die." What you have been meditating half your life cannot but be something of importance, and worthy of general attention. You did well to "bide your time," and to wait till you were sure of having the ear of the public in right of your former publications. May health and strength be given you to complete all that is in your heart!

In my little, quiet way, I am jogging on comfortably enough. My spirits have lately had a *fillip* in the shape of a journey. Thanks to the railroad, I was able to convey myself, with little fatigue, to Southampton, where I found a kind friend in waiting to convey me eight miles further, to a beautiful mansion on the skirts of the New Forest. This is the largest sylvan tract remaining in Eng'and, and I was surprised to find how primitive a character it still preserves. A stone marks the spot where Rufus fell; his stirrup is kept as a relic at the royal hunting-lodge, where the forest courts are held; and, on the whole, it seemed to me that his name was quite as current in the mouths of men as that of George III., the last monarch who hunted here. The cottagers are devotedly attached to their native soil; they have continued on the same spot, from father to son, many of them from the Norman times, in fact; they enjoy many advantages from the neighbourhood of the forest, besides that delightful sense of liberty which waits upon the roamer of "the good green wood," and which he who has once tasted would scarcely exchange for a palace. The wood consists chiefly of noble oaks and stately beeches, and the undulations of the surface open a thousand picturesque glimpses of hill and vale, open glade and tangled wood, sprinkled with cottages embowered in flower-garden and orchard, and mansions standing proudly on their emerald lawns. From the higher eminences you command the Isle of Wight, with its bays and headlands, and the soft yet fresh sea-air breathes the very spirit of health. I was in a state of enchantment during my whole visit difficult to describe. Since I began this letter, I have been reading an article on all Carlyle's works in the "Quarterly Review." This author, who sets himself so vehemently against all "forms," ought to feel himself rebuked by the praise which he has extorted from the ultra High-church reviewer by his mystical use of the word *faith*, from which it is easy for such a reviewer to extract arguments favourable to ecclesiastical authority. Woe unto us if our philosophers are to be as hostile to the employment of reason in the investigation of truth as our high-priests!

I must at length put a period to my long letter. I must answer some other correspondents far more briefly.

Ever yours, with true respect and friendship,

L. AIKIN.

To Miss Aikin.

Boston, January 1, 1841.

My dear Miss Aikin,—I have no time to write a letter in reply to your last of October, but this was so acceptable that I ought not to let our steam-packet sail without some acknowledgment of it. You write under some fears of a war. Let us be grateful that the storm is blown over, or rather that its ravages are so confined. I confess I am shocked by your victories in Syria and your attack on China. My mind continually asks whether there is no relief from these terrible social evils, and I am continually driven back to the conviction that little outward melioration is to be hoped but from an inward one. At the same time, I see how outward evils obstruct the moral and intellectual advancement in which their remedy lies. In the course of the last few months, I have been more struck than ever with the terrible power conferred by our present social condition on individuals. A few men might have involved the civilized world in war—might have broken up the intercourse of nations, reduced millions to want, and made themselves felt in every human habitation over half the globe. I have asked, Ought a few statesmen thus to hold in their hands the destinies of the race? I ask, too, if this fearful concentration of power growing out of our union into communities ought to exist? Are any men, whether a ministry or legislature, worthy of such a trust? It is this vast dazzling power which has intoxicated, maddened the selfish great from the beginning; and history is little more than an unravelling of the complicated schemes and toils of men for winning it. Is not the prize too great to be set before men? Ought the vast energies of England to become a unity by political combinations which the ambitious may turn to their vile purposes? Cannot these vast masses of nations be broken up or modified? I merely state to you thoughts which have been rushing through my mind. I have been too busy in other ways to follow them out. That some great truth may come from pursuing them, I strongly suspect. The idea of making essential changes in these colossal accumulations of power which have lasted so many ages, must seem an extravagance, but the national bond is not what it once was. Men of different languages are beginning to understand a higher bond.

But I must stop dreaming. Your letter, as I said, gave me much pleasure, but I was sorry to read your severe strictures on Carlyle. Let us be tolerant. Let us be willing that men should talk in their own language, however *uncouth*—give us their extravagances, if they are earnest, strong-minded, generous men. Carlyle has often stirred up my spirit and opened to me noble fields of thought. I do not know that I owe him many new views, but he has made some great ones more real to me, and this is no small debt.

You must have discovered in me a touch of that malady called mysticism, and will therefore wonder the less at my German leanings. I am, however, no reader of German. I have caught this from nobody. It was born and bred in me, and therefore more hopeless. Accept this hasty expression of thought, if thought it may be called, as a testimony to the pleasure you give me by writing.

Very truly your friend,
W. E. CHANNING.

A happy new year to you! The best blessing descend on you from above! I rejoice in your better health.

The last "Quarterly Review," in the review of Carlyle, speaks of a new conservative school in France. Do you know anything of it?

To Dr. Channing.

Hampstead, Feb. 7, 1841.

My dear Friend,—Thank you much for your letter, and thank you for your "Emancipation," which I have received since. This last has much matter for reflection and remark. It is most important not to give any handle to the supporters of slavery by the adoption of flattering views which may prove delusive. I am by no means so indifferent as you to the diminished produce of sugar; and this not solely, nor chiefly, for the sake of the planters—though their interests deserve to be considered, especially now that they are no longer slave-holders—but for the sake of the great cause of emancipation itself. The effect of the scarcity and dearness of sugar in our market has been to cause a vehement effort to legalize the importation of *slave-grown* sugar from Brazil or Cuba; and though this has been resisted by the virtue of our ministry, it is said that some has been smuggled in; and I see in newspapers earnest pleadings in favour of applying the principles of free-trade to this case. If sufficient sugar is not made by the free blacks, it certainly will be procured elsewhere, and much to the detriment either of their brethren in fetters or of themselves; for it is now proposed to encourage, by lowering duties, the importation of sugar from our East-Indian possessions, which are capable of supplying an unlimited quantity. What will be the effect of this? Perhaps ultimately to reduce the *whole* population of the sugar islands to poverty and distress. The new luxuries which

the blacks have learned to relish—their schools, their
chapels too—all depend on their raising valuable exports;
and Mr. Gurney has been sharply enough attacked for
advising protective duties to be laid on to secure the
West-Indian monopoly, which will certainly be broken
up very shortly either by South American or Indian
competition. I never wrote such a page of political economy in my life; nor should have written this, but for
the higher interests connected with it. I entirely approve the spirit of all you say on the Slave question in
your own country. By the way, *our* India, which I have
just mentioned, is an immense field for the speculations
of the merchant, manufacturer, politician, legislator, philanthropist and missionary, to say nothing of the naturalist and poet. It has been making immense progress
since it has been thrown open to private enterprize. I
am never weary of reading the fresh accounts which are
continually reaching us. The advance making by the
natives in letters, in arts, in enlightened views and in
political importance, is *grand*. Our government is pursuing a noble policy with them—gradually raising them
to a level with *other* British subjects by admitting them
to public offices, and associating their leading men in all
liberal and benevolent institutions. If the enlightened,
philanthropic spirit of Rammohun Roy is permitted to
hover over the native country which he loved so ardently,
I trust it rejoices in the view. Australia, too, and New
Zealand! How many "embryo Englands," as one of our
travellers calls them, are rising up in the ends of the
earth! You will not, I hope, rebuke the nationality
which glories in the thought.—It is, indeed, as you say,
an awful power, and too great to be trusted to any man,
to decide on the question of peace and war. But also,
it can only be exercised by any one when nations are
disposed to suffer it. In the most important countries

of Europe, it is plain that this is no longer the case. Even in France it was only by the aid of a great War party that Thiers hoped to compass his wicked purpose of re-embarking his country on the troubled sea of ambition and conquest; and his project has been disconcerted by the energetic *No* of all the sounder portion of the French people and of total England; also in some measure, it must be allowed, by the formidable attitude assumed by the other great powers, and the unwilling conviction, even of his own faction, that France could not fight them all single-handed. I trust that peace now rests on a firmer foundation than before this alarm, and before our little war in Syria, which our politicians say was absolutely necessary for reducing France to reason, and which we may believe to have been so, considering the thorough repugnance of our present government to a warlike policy. The China question I do not profess to understand; but I hope the dispute is well settled before now. All is prosperous again with our commerce and manufacturers, and we, like you, have perhaps little to fear but from the results of a state of things which opens such a boundless field to the indulgence of sensuality and luxury.

I have got a problem for you. Years ago it exercised my thoughts, and I wrote a few pages on it; lately I learned from a note in Milman's History of Christianity that it had also suggested itself to him and to Archbishop Whately, and I am proud to find that we all incline to the same solution. It is this: Ought we to regard the lowest state in which man is found now as the true state of nature? or is the savage the true representative of the primitive man, or a deterioration of him? It was the general theory formerly that man was first hunter, then shepherd, then tiller of the soil, and by degrees became a builder of cities and inventor of arts and letters. But history is far from supporting this system. The oldest records we have, the Jewish Scriptures, nowhere afford the slightest glimpse of savage life or of a hunter state; and I have been told by a great student that there is no knowledge or record of any hunter tribe throughout the continent of Asia. In ancient Europe, in America, in New Holland, there have been or are tribes in the lowest state of man; but in your continent there are manifest traces remaining of nations in a much higher state of civilization; and even in Australia, the inland peoples are far superior to the wretched beings who were found existing on the seacoast; without boats, without nets or hooks, making their miserable meals of shell-fish. Herodotus describes the frontiers of civilization as everywhere occupied by small tribes or peoples, often differing totally in language, manners, occupations, from their next neighbours on every side; and bearing much the appearance of wrecks and relics of nations driven up into corners by successive floods of invaders poured forth at intervals, like the barbarians over the Roman provinces. It is plain that under such circumstances of national ruin and personal privation, men considerably advanced might sink into the state of savages; indeed, they could scarcely avoid it. On the other hand, we have not a single fact in all history to show the possibility of savages rising into civilization spontaneously, without the agency, that is, of some people in a superior condition. Whatever notions people may entertain of the origin of man, this is plain, that the progenitors of the race could not have supported life unless more instincts or more knowledge were vouchsafed to them than are now the portion of an infant; and I know not what obliges us to suppose that nothing more than the indispensable was bestowed. On the whole, then, I hope we may regard the savage state as an infliction brought upon certain tribes by untoward accidents—wars, famines, floods, pestilence—not the original or general condition of primeval man. Let me have your thoughts upon it. Also, pray tell me whether you have read Milman's History of Christianity, and what you think of it. Our High-churchmen are shocked at so free and fearless a book from a dignitary, and judiciously enough, instead of abusing, they try to smother it. Their Reviews do not choose to have heard of the work. It shows immense reading and a storehouse of curious and interesting facts; but I cannot say that it makes upon my mind any single, strong, definite impression; nor perhaps could one well expect this from what may be called a *civil* history of the religion from its origin to the suppression of paganism in the Roman empire. He seems to intend a continuation.—I suppose you have had, before now, Professor Smyth's second set of lectures on the French Revolution. They seem to me excellent, excepting a few supplementary ones written, under the influence of panic, since the passing of the Reform Bill. It hurts me, I confess, that he should hold out as a warning to England the frenzied acts of French slaves on first breaking their chains. We have lived to little purpose under a free government for centuries, if we now require such lessons to be read us; and I grieve that my dear old friend, whose intentions are always good, should thus have suffered himself to be scared out of his old Whig principles. Just now I think of him with peculiar sympathy, for we are fellow-mourners for our excellent and long-tried friend Mr. Whishaw. I know I have at some time mentioned him to you as eminent for his wisdom, his knowledge and his wit. If he had been followed by a Boswell, his recorded conversation would have outshone Johnson's. Between the men there was the immeasurable distance which lifts the philosopher above the bigot; and his virtue was as distinguished as his understanding. To have known, admired and revered him from my childhood, was among my highest privileges; and in losing him I feel as if I had now only *quite* lost my father. He was one of the Auditors of public accounts; and you will wonder to be told that he struggled in vain to carry the reform of keeping those accounts in Arabic numerals and in the English language, instead of Roman numerals and bad Latin. But Lord Grenville, then minister, would hear of nothing so revolutionary as writing "Hair-powder duty," instead of "Debitum super pulverem crinalem." So much for following the "wisdom of our ancestors"! I may also mention that Mr. W., originally designed for the Church, was obliged to change his destination, because the loss of a leg, while he was at college, rendered him canonically ineligible to the service of the altar. Are we not a sage people?—I have an extraordinary curiosity to know what is the nature of the great work on which you have been so long engaged, and what progress you make. Give me at least a glimpse when you write, that I may have the pleasure of speculating about it. You condescend to call yourself a mystic; but so clear a writer has, in my opinion, no just claim to the title. The "Lives of the Queens of England," by Miss Strickland, is a work of great diligence and merit, full of new facts from authentic records, which throw strong light on the manners of our Plantagenet times, full both of interest and amusement. There are indeed some mistakes, and the writer labours under the usual female misfortune, a want of sound and solid literature; but she merits great commendation for doing so much and so well as she has.

Believe me ever yours most truly,
Lucy Aikin.

To Miss Aikin.

Boston, April 14, 1841.

My dear Miss Aikin,—I always begin with thanking you for your last letter, and I beg you not to think that I do so from habit or courtesy. You sometimes make an effort to write, I know; and I want you to know that your kindness is not lost. I wish I could repay it; but the spring, while it revives all nature, has rather a withering influence on my frame. The mind, indeed, is alive to the genial season, and gives as warm a welcome as ever to the green blade and bud and flower. But the mild breezes make me very languid, and these breezes are blown away by chilly, freezing east winds, which form the only real objection to our climate. I am half tempted to let the steamer go without a letter, but I shall be better satisfied with myself, though you may not be, if I give you a few lines.

I feel as strongly as you can the difficulties of the sugar question in England, and I have not the wisdom to offer a solution. You are now paying the penalties of the unnatural restrictive system, and I wish you and we and all nations were rid of it. Your late periodicals make me hope that the Free-trade principles are spreading among you, though I feel that their application is to be modified by the claims or expectations which have grown out of old abuses. How great a benefactor England might prove to the world by adopting as her cause the abolition of all restrictions, the extension of the freest intercourse among all nations! Is not this the law of nature, of humanity, of society? What is plainer than that mutual dependence, mutual services, free exchange of products, is the end of Providence in the infinite variety of conditions, climates, &c.? England, I doubt not, will propose this object as far as her own advantage is concerned. Will a nation never think of the advantage of the human race? We will not complain, however, if nations will learn that their own interest is one with that of all men, and with the reign of the most enlarged justice and love. As to your problem respecting the primitive condition of the human race, I wish I could aid you. We grope in the dusk in those early ages. I cannot doubt, however, that agriculture was the first human pursuit. If we regard the first chapters of Genesis as traditions, they still retain their value on this point. The first man was a "tiller of the ground," and almost the first command given him was to "subdue the earth." Our first parents undoubtedly received peculiar communications from God, but I see no reason for supposing that these were more than were necessary to give an impulse and carry forward the race. It seems the grand design of the Creator that man shall work out his own good, be the framer of his own destiny. Agriculture was the grand art on which human progress depended. The hunter and pastoral states necessarily make man stationary in lot, by keeping him in perpetual motion. All great improvements of condition are fixtures. Architecture, which supposes settled residence, is a grand moral art. All the other arts, useful and ornamental, gather round it. Without a fixed home, one generation can transmit little to another. Without property in land, there will be no steady productive industry. Accordingly, agriculture holds a place in our earliest histories. In truth, no nations but the most savage have been found without it. Our Indians cultivate maize, and the first signs our fathers had of the natives at Plymouth were their corn-fields. Nothing is easier than to explain the origin of hunting and pastoral life. Agriculture is laborious, monotonous. At this day, the Yankee flies from the plough, not for the chase, but for trade, and delights to roam about, not with flocks, but goods for the market. Wild beasts made the first hunters, and an Englishman will not wonder that they who began to hunt from necessity, made it a trade. As to the rumours of a golden age, they are easily explained. The first inhabitants of the earth—few in number, without luxuries, and with a boundless world around them—lived simply, had few quarrels, practised few crimes. How could they do otherwise? Domestic ties alone bound them together. Government had not begun to scourge them. Later ages, more "improved," and therefore more licentious and rapacious, must have looked back on these earlier times with a deep consciousness of loss, and imagination found in them materials of a paradise. You see I have no faith as yet in any great civilization at first. Did you ever see the work of Bailly the astronomer, President of the National Assembly and Mayor of Paris, in which he endeavours to prove the existence in remote antiquity of a more highly civilized race than Greece, Rome and modern Europe? I have only heard of it. I think it would entertain you. The idea of primitive *savageness* shocks me. Many lean to it from a deep distrust of human nature. They think the tiger, after all, lies deepest in humanity, and that it has taken ages to tame him. I suspect the "taming" has made the tiger.

I have no time for other topics. I hope you have not been troubled by rumours of war between the two countries. One thing is plain—you and I will not fight. Boston and Hampstead shall, if possible, be excepted in the declaration of war. Which predominates in nations, folly or madness? Wishing you all good,

I am very truly your friend,

WM. E. CHANNING.

To Dr. Channing.

Hampstead, June 12, 1841.

My dear Friend,—You cannot thank me more sincerely for my letters than I thank you for yours. They are a true refreshment to my spirit, which often suffers a famine from the extreme and increasing scarcity in this country of such liberal and enlightened sentiment as forms the only food on which it can exist. I allow, freely allow, that some useful truths—practical ones—have been powerfully argued, successfully promulgated among us, of late years. The cause of Free-trade, which I, like you, believe to be that of true and just and virtuous policy, has gained and is gaining. Our Corn-laws are at the last gasp, and in timber and sugar, I believe, we are going right. But, alas! what avails all this if free speculation is taxed to prohibition—if religious liberty lies oppressed, stifled, down-trodden—if no man dares to say in the face of the world that all opinions have equal rights—that no one ought to believe himself entitled to put another to silence because his doctrines are not those of the majority, those that the State has endowed? We have in this country many evils—what country is without? What a sign of the times is it that so eminent a natural philosopher as Whewell, in his "Life of Galileo," labours to defend the proceedings of the Inquisition against him—calls them lenient—seems to suppose that the *Church* has a right to stop the promulgation of any truth which it regards as dangerous! Oh! I am sick at heart when I think upon these things.

You will see that we are threatened, too, with a Tory administration, but this is yet uncertain; it will depend on the new Parliament. Some think we shall see the fulfilment of the Duke of Wellington's prediction—that, if the Reform Bill were carried, parties would be so balanced, that it would be impossible to carry on any government at all. In France this seems to be almost the case.

I apprehend that the prodigious increase of zeal and activity, consequently of rancour, on the part of the Established Church, is mainly the result of Catholic emancipation, and the strength and courage it has lent to the Romanists, which Protestantism feels itself called upon to resist with all its might and by all its means, Puseyism being one. Such unlooked-for, and often opposite, effects flow from great public measures. The men who have spent their lives in bringing them about often live to rue in vain their own success. A consideration which, joined to several others, convinces me that *fluctuation*, much more than *progress*, is the great law of human affairs. But this you will be loth to admit.

I was struck with your idea of agriculture being the great civilizer of recent man, and I think that it has been so in some climates; but how this great affair of climate acts upon every other element of human life and society —how it *complicates* this whole subject! I know of nothing but the book of Genesis which can be adduced in favour of the notion that the whole race sprang from a single pair. Probably there were many original races adapted to different portions of the earth. "But why go on guessing where we cannot know?" Why? because we are guessing and speculating animals! I am ever speculating and guessing, because my mind is active and my body idle. This whole winter and spring I have been nearly a prisoner to the house; latterly I have been really ill, but matters seem now mending with me a little. I grieve that you should have been so much a sufferer. Perhaps we both feel that it is drawing towards evening with us. Well, so be it.

As for my book, it is still among the future conditionals. I am no longer the diligent labourer I once was. Your task proceeds, I hope. Great or small, it will be of the kind of books that we want, the offspring of *thought*, not of mere reading. Original writers, I believe, are always benefactors towards mankind; either themselves or their answerers are sure to bring out some new truths, or set some old ones in a stronger light. Whether Carlyle deserves at all to be put in the list of original thinkers, I am yet in doubt; to me he still appears little more than a jargonist. He makes his way a little in society, however—aye, and very genteel and very correct society—notwithstanding the tone of his work on the French Revolution, which is surely radicalism combined with the most odious and mischievous moral fatalism. According to him, all crimes and enormities are "by divine putting on." You do not love the doctrines of necessity in any shape: but surely you will admit that between the vulgar fatalist and the philosophic necessarian there is this essential difference, that the first talks as if *any* man may be destined to commit a crime, as any man may be destined to die of a fever; the second firmly holds that none but a *bad* man can ever be destined to commit a crime, since no man can do anything but what he *wills* to do; his will, indeed, is actuated by motives, but in the mind of a virtuous man those which prompt to crime will never gain the preponderance. In fact, do we not *feel* that there are many actions which it is impossible, so long as we possess our senses, that we should ever find any temptation to commit; so fixed is our conviction that nothing could ever make it worth our while? Fatalism is certainly not original in Carlyle, nor in the French school of writers from whom he borrowed it, but I fear they may have done something towards rendering it popular. There is a circumstance respecting the French people at this time which I think remarkable, and am in doubt how to interpret. During their revolution, never was there such contempt for human life; blood was poured out like water; a man was crushed with as little regard as a beetle: now the feeling is so changed that they can scarcely bear the idea of capital punishment; their juries find "extenuating circumstances" even in the horrid act of a parricide, in order to save him from death. I should like to ascribe this scruple to none but good motives or causes; but when I consider how strong is the sentiment of moral indignation in every pure and virtuous and noble breast—how uniformly all nations, where morals have been strict and manners unsophisticated, have marked their horror of great crimes by taking away the offender from the midst of them, and compare this with the acknowledged profligacy and wickedness of Paris, and the assertion of those who know its society best, that the only inexpiable fault there is evil-speaking—I hesitate. My father has somewhere observed that universal indulgence is near akin to universal profligacy, and I confess that I do not see with satisfaction the anxiety manifested in France, and in some degree here also, to abolish capital punishments, while crimes are rather on the increase. The "godly watch" set upon one another by your Puritans was one extreme, and an odious one; but the total disregard of the conduct of others, where it does not immediately affect ourselves, so inculcated at Paris, and perhaps in high life generally, is still more fatal to all the lofty sentiments and heroic virtues, and certainly favourable to all the vices.

The completion of this long letter has been accidentally delayed for a few days. In the meantime our good ministry has been out-voted. All now depends upon the spirit of the people. If they please they can return a majority against the Tories—but *will* they? since it cannot be done without risk to the worldly interests of many. The crisis may be called awful, when Ireland is taken into the account. I incline, however, to the hoping side; so far as this, let who will be in power, public opinion must be respected, and, sooner or later, all really salutary measures must be carried; the question is one of this year or next with regard to several of the more important. But no such calm language as this will be held on the hustings, and the evils of party virulence will abound. Alas for those who speak or write as the servants of truth and posterity in the midst of party discord! You, I trust, are safe from its influence. May you only be favoured with health and strength for the completion of your work! I long to see it.

Pray believe me ever your affectionate friend,

LUCY AIKIN.

To Dr. Channing.

Hampstead, June 30, 1841.

My dear Friend,—Many thanks for your "Memoirs of Dr. Tuckerman" and the accompanying Journal. I believe they will cause me to send you almost a pamphlet in return; but you, who enjoin me sometimes to write fearlessly what I think, will not, perhaps, be impatient under this result. Your character of your friend appears to me exceedingly candid and discriminating, as well as affectionate. It is unfortunately true, that with all his heroism of benevolence, he did not make an agreeable impression here in general society. This was partly because, like all men of one idea, especially such as are eloquent, he could neither speak, nor suffer others to speak, of anything else in his presence—which wore out the patience even of the best-disposed; partly because, for want of knowledge either of the state of the poor with us, or of the plans adopted for their benefit, he, in the words of a very benevolent friend of mine, to whom I introduced him, "recommended as novelties the very things we had all been practising for thirty years."

It might well have been supposed, even by those ignorant of the fact, that in an old and densely-peopled land like ours, where great inequality of conditions had always prevailed, and where, as we are apt to flatter ourselves, humanity had always been a striking feature of the national character, many schemes must have been put to the proof for the relief of such destitution, physical and moral, as our great system of parish support could not reach. But well might Dr. Tuckerman have failed to be led by this consideration to acquaint himself fully with the facts, when an unworthy Englishman goes so far in ignorance or ill-will as to calumniate his country on this very head. I refer to the very offensive speech of one Mr. Giles, of Liverpool, reported in the Journal you have sent me. It has pleased this person, after *judiciously* pointing out the efforts of pastor Oberlin as a kind of compensation for the horrors of the French Revolution, to advert generally to the exertions making in favour of the poor and indigent young, "through the diffusion of an education adapted to raise the soul more and more from earth, and point it heavenward." He professes, however, to speak on this subject with "horror and shame," as a native of England, the only country "wanting in her duty" on this head. While "the proud despotism of Prussia," as he says, "trains up her youth, from the cradle to manhood, in a knowledge of themselves and the world around them, free-born England casts them off as orphans." And he goes on to represent our agricultural and our manufacturing population as alike existing in a state of sordid, almost savage ignorance, and the last, as abandoned to all the excesses of the worst passions of mankind, utterly " neglected by those whose wealth and power they secure."

In England, misrepresentation like this would not deserve refutation; but it may not be labour lost to offer to you and to your fellow-philanthropists beyond the Atlantic, a slight sketch capable of showing both what has actually been done here in this great cause, and the circumstances which have rendered it impracticable to do more, or more speedily, or in a different manner.

After the establishment and wide diffusion of Sunday-schools, the first comprehensive scheme for popular instruction was that of Joseph Lancaster, schools on whose system forthwith arose by hundreds on every side. It is indeed true that the clergy, and other enemies to the diffusion of education among the lower classes, especially if independent of the control of the Church, opposed the poor Quaker with disgraceful virulence, and nothing could have upheld him but the protecting hand of George III., and the energy of his pious wish " that every poor child in his dominions should be enabled to read its Bible." A kind of compromise at length took place; Dr. Bell and the Church Catechism were introduced into the system, and, under the name of National schools, we have still all over the country multitudes of establishments, supported by voluntary subscription, which afford to thousands the rudiments of common knowledge, and some acquaintance, it is to be presumed, with their duties to God and man.

A system of national education at the public expense was next projected and moved in the House of Commons by Mr. Brougham. It was rejected—and why?

Because the necessity of neutralizing the hostility of the clergy had compelled him, by the provisions of his Bill, to subject the whole to their superintendence and authority. All classes of Dissenters rose as one man against such stipulations, and by their wise jealousy, or just indignation, the measure was thrown out. In a country enjoying less either of civil or religious liberty this could not have occurred—not, for example, "in the proud despotism of Prussia." Without the command of the sovereign, no such project could there have been brought forward; and had he commanded, it must have been carried into execution, whoever was jealous or indignant. This attempt, however, drew great attention to the subject, and was by no means unproductive of good. "Let us alone," exclaimed the "*free-born*" English, "and we will do it ourselves." Infant schools, perhaps the most effective of all the means yet adopted for the prevention of early corruption of morals, were devised, and, with the rapidity of an epidemic, overspread the whole face of the land. An active rivalry between the sects on one hand, and the Church, which had now found it needful to buckle in earnest to the unwelcome task, on the other, effectually prevented the zeal on either part from flagging. The small aid from the public purse since obtained by a Whig ministry, on terms as equitable as the bench of bishops would allow, has given a fresh stimulus, by the conditions annexed to all grants, to the exertions of voluntary subscribers. The difficulty has been to find fit teachers in sufficient numbers. Institutions, however, have been founded for the supply of this demand, and should the prosperity of the people keep pace with their generous ardour, the English people may soon contemplate their own plans for popular education with a glow of satisfaction, to which the Prussian vassal, for whom "drill obligation" and "school obligation" stand on the same ground of compulsion, guarded by the same legal penalties, must for ever remain a stranger.

All that a free government could properly do by positive enactment it has done. It is now compulsory on the owners of factories, on the managers of workhouses, the superintendents of prisons and penitentiaries, the captains of ships of war, to provide for the children and youth under their charge the means or opportunities both of school learning and religious instruction—and is this little? If, after all, it must be confessed that there is still a great and lamentable deficiency in the means of carrying civilization, by which I understand a just and influential sense of the true interests of human nature, throughout our vast population, it would be equitable at least to weigh more deliberately than some censurers seem to have done the magnitude of the task, and the difficulties to be surmounted in its execution. Clusters of factories, mills and warehouses, rise among us like exhalations; much within the memory of man, our principal seats of manufacture have swelled from moderate country towns, sometimes from nameless hamlets, into aggregates of human dwellings, exceeding in population most of the capital cities of Europe. What provision could exist in these places for gratuitous education, or who was there to supply the want? What orphan-schools, almshouses, hospitals, established charities of any kind, could be looked for? All was to be created, and by whom? The few older families fled, one after another, from the din and smoke of machinery and the elbowing of the newly rich, to calmer retreats. The master manufacturers, men for the most part of scanty, often of no education, narrow therefore in their views and frequently sordid, were slow in learning the claims of those whom they regarded chiefly as a part of the apparatus employed in producing their wealth. This was to be expected; and when it is considered that the periods of the greatest distress to the workmen were precisely those of difficulty and failure to themselves, from temporary obstruction of demand, it will be confessed that much destitution, physical and moral, was inevitable.

By degrees, public opinion began to bear on this mighty mass of evil, and the eyes and hearts of men to open both to the claims of these lower classes, and to the frightful dangers of disregarding them; but even then the efforts of benevolence were encountered among many obstacles, by one in particular, which there were no obvious means of overcoming. This was the wholesale employment of children, almost infants, in various branches of manufacture, particularly in that vast one of cotton twist. To attempt to give instruction to these little victims would have been absurd, and even inhuman. Not a moment could be spared from their too short hours of rest for any other purpose; and by necessity they were left to grow up to the stature of human maturity with scarcely any other evidences of humanity about them. But has no remedy been sought or applied to this giant mischief? What are all those long deliberations of Parliament which matured at length the Factory Law, but the most touching evidence of the parental care of the State over those who had no one else to care for them? Under this law, the hours of working are strictly limited, and by its provisions the children will receive education—as far as it consists in giving the rudiments of literature. Those moral influences, which are indeed of infinitely more value, the State cannot give, or can give but very imperfectly. If parents be without all sense of their own duties, who can avert the dreadful consequences from their unfortunate offspring? Besides their setting to their children examples which too frequently counteract all the influence of the precepts of religion and virtue, it has been found in all parts of our country much less difficult to raise funds for the maintenance of schools, than to persuade parents to enforce the regular attendance of the pupils. Ignorance too gross to form any estimate of the value of what was rejected—false indulgence—but far more frequently a selfish reluctance to give up during school hours any profit or convenience derived from the labour of the child, have largely operated in counteraction of all plans of this nature. The case is the same, I perceive, with you. Three-fifths appear from the Journal to be the highest average attendance on the schools of the Home Mission. In like manner church-building, the progress of which among us exceeds anything ever dreamt of by our ancestors, but yet perhaps no more than equal pace with the increase of our population, is often found easier to accomplish than church attendance. And do not your own ministers at large in effect confess a failure, when they broadly state that it is an error to suppose that their services are attended by the lowest class? Either there will always remain at the bottom of society a sediment which will refuse to be incorporated with the clearer liquor, or at least it can be but very slowly and gradually taken up. Establish, either in our country or yours, a Prussian compulsion, drive the children to school, and all ages to church, by the terror of fine and imprisonment, and what will be gained to compensate the loss of that spirit of independence, which has probably been the most important element of all in the greatness and progress both of England and her noblest offspring? No valuable end can be attained but by means of a congenial character, therefore not the diffusion of moral feeling and virtuous conduct, or of devotion, by arbitrary force. Better a slow, better a partial progress, than one which, under the show of universality, is delusive, and must fail in the full trial.

With regard to that visiting of the poor at their own houses, to which the agency of Dr. Tuckerman was at first confined, there is little reason to impute negligence to our middle and higher classes, whatever faults may often be found in their manner of performing the office. It had always been the practice of the better kind of country ladies to distribute benefactions among the cottagers, and often to carry, as well as to send them, aids in sickness. In towns of moderate size the same things were done; but Hannah More, in her "Cœlebs," by representing her *pattern* young lady as regularly devoting two evenings in a week to making her rounds among the village poor, unfortunately made it a fashion and a rage. I say unfortunately, because nothing is ever done well and wisely which is taken up in this manner. Judicious people saw that it was neither an expedient, nor indeed a safe employment, for the inexperienced girls who undertook it. They objected that young ladies would be exposed to injury, both in temper and taste, by the quantity of vulgar and interested flattery and vulgar and spiteful gossip which would be forced upon them; that their ears would continually be assailed by grossness of expression, and their minds either sullied or saddened by too close and unveiled a view of human vices in their coarsest forms. While we guarded them with unceasing solicitude against the approach of even doubtful society of their own class, it seemed strangely inconsistent to permit them to come into habitual contact with what was positively bad in a lower class.

I have no doubt that these and other objections urged in the beginning were found to be just, to a certain extent. The impulse was given, however, and nothing could stop it. It acted at first chiefly within the Evangelical party; but that party became, at length, great enough to give the tone to society at large; and the practice of thus superintending the poor has become so general, that I know no one circumstance by which the manners, studies and occupations of Englishwomen have been so extensively modified, or so strikingly contradistinguished from those of a former generation. By these female missionaries numberless experiments have been made and projects started. Some have addressed themselves to the bodies of the poor, others to their souls, and there has been much quackery in both departments. Some have distributed Calvinistic tracts, others bread and soup tickets. Some have applied themselves to clothing the children, others to teaching them, others to reading to the sick and infirm. One of the results of this system, and which will not have your entire approbation, has been the formation of a prodigious number of associations for the accomplishment of objects to which the efforts of single persons were unequal. Women in this country have seldom enough of habits of business, and especially of that habit of the world which enables men, by conciliation and compromise, to pursue their objects with almost any associates, to be good members of committees. I fear theirs are not always schools of forbearance or good manners; but practice may improve them. It is a decided advantage that the new accession of zeal among the clergy has urged them to take almost entirely out of the hands of the ladies the theological department, in which their bitterest dissensions had of course occurred.

Good and evil have arisen out of this great movement, as out of all others. The good I need not particularize. It is enough to say that much aid, much comfort, much instruction of many kinds, and, it may be hoped, some improvement in decorum, in piety, and in morals generally, may have been effected. On the other hand; I think that it has given rise among the ladies to much spiritual pride and self-inflation; much of an imperious, pragmatical, meddling habit, which has rendered many both odious to the poor, to whom they took credit for being the greatest of benefactresses, and troublesome and unamiable to their equals. It has diverted the minds of numbers, not from dissipation only, but from literature, from the arts, from all the graces and amenities of polished life, and rendered many a home intolerable to husbands, fathers and brothers, thereby causing more moral mischief than all their exertions could eradicate among the poor. But the wise and the foolish, the gentle and the ungentle, will ever throw their own characters into all their occupations and pursuits. With regard to the poor, the benefits they have derived have been counterbalanced by a vast increase among them of hypocrisy, and a disgusting cant of piety, assumed to flatter the ladies; of fraud and imposture generally, and of a fawning, dependent, servile spirit, unworthy of free men. Idleness and helplessness have, in many wealthy and *well-visited* neighbourhoods, become more profitable than activity and a manly resistance of the evils of life. Intemperance has been fostered among the men, by an assurance that if *they* did not provide necessaries for their families, the ladies would.

I apprehend that more good, and certainly fewer evils, have attended the exertions of some excellent men who among us have followed in the footsteps of Dr. Tuckerman; they alone ought to attempt indiscriminate visiting of the lowest of the low in great and vicious cities. Ladies might act more usefully under their directions.

I fear I must have wearied you by this long account; but I wished, besides refuting a most injurious imputation on my own country, to make you acquainted with the results of our experience in attempts to benefit the poor, the ignorant and the vicious. Your country is still young in the arts of dealing with human misery on a great scale. The essential differences between an aristocratic and a democratic social system which penetrate into every part, must vary the working of every plan and modify every result; but, after all, it is common human nature which is to be dealt with, and the great principles must be the same.

You naturally wish that the increase of your city should not proceed, if it is to be followed by the moral evils which have accompanied, in all times and countries, a similar aggregation of men and dwellings. In vain!—gregarious man will ever go on joining house to house, and street to street, and vice and misery will ever find abodes among them. But will not virtue dwell there also, and domestic happiness—warm hearts and enlightened minds? Will there not be there, as everywhere, more good than evil, more enjoyment than suffering? There will; for all is in His hands who loves the creatures He has made. This, after all, is the true balm for the wounded bosom of philanthropy, when, after many trials and much experience, she discovers how hard a task it is to do even a little good—unalloyed, how impracticable! I will now release you.

Believe me ever most sincerely yours,
LUCY AIKIN.

To Miss Aikin.

July 10, 1841.

My dear Miss Aikin,—And so you are waking up at last to see your dangers from the Church! It has seemed to me that your sagacity has been at fault in this particular. My deep interest in your country as the European stronghold of freedom has often turned my thoughts to this subject. Perhaps I have given you my views of it partially. I will now do it more freely, but with the distrust which I have in my judgments on a distant country. I write *immediately*, because your letter has filled my mind with thoughts which may evaporate if not seized at once. In assigning the causes of the decline of Dissent, I should give a prominent place to Methodism. This from the beginning stood quite apart from Nonconformity. Wesley leaned more to the Church, and gave that leaning to his disciples. The consequence was that the large body of the people absorbed by Methodism, among whom were some of the most pious, and who belonged properly to Dissent, were weaned from it. Methodism reaped largely in the field from which Nonconformity used to gather a harvest, and thus the latter was sensibly weakened. Methodism in another way harmed Dissent greatly. It awakened a kindred spirit within the Establishment. Methodism in the Church was regarded very suspiciously among High-churchmen, but it was destined to labour in their cause. It created within the Establishment the *very preaching* which devout people had sought among the Dissenters; and of course the strong attraction of the Church, no longer counteracted, but aided by and joined with this, grew more and more irresistible. When "serious" clergymen and "serious" professors were found springing up and multiplying within the imposing edifices where the State worshipped, the reason for deserting them and congregating in obscure meeting-houses ceased; and it ceased at a moment when from other causes the attachment to the meeting-house had declined. Thus Methodism has served the Church.

Dissent has laboured under many difficulties. With all its nobleness, it wanted from the beginning a broad foundation. It did not plant itself on grand, immutable principles. It did not commit itself fully to the cause of religious freedom. It was very willing that the Church should decree the Thirty-nine Articles and St. Athanasius' Creed. It went beyond the Church in excommunicating for opinion. It quarrelled with the Church for decreeing rites and forms, and for not taking the *shape* which was presented in the New Testament. Of consequence—when, in the progress of intelligence, forms, rites, copes, surplices and outward arrangements, lost their importance—Nonconformity lost its dignity, because less respectable in its own eyes and that of others. Its sphere was narrowed. Men found less to fight against in the Church. Meanwhile, Dissent did not rise to higher views of religious liberty. Within the last hundred years it has become even more intolerant than in the days of Watts and Doddridge. The Unitarians alone rise to the apprehension of spiritual freedom, and the unpopularity of their theology has been extended to their liberality. Thus Dissent, which in the days of Laud fought the battle of religious liberty, has in this more advanced age fallen away, and become a prop of spiritual tyranny. One sad effect you witness—the free minds in literature and among the common people do not take refuge in Dissent. Generally speaking, what is there to carry enlightened, independent men to the meeting-house?

What is there in Dissent to attract the strong master-spirits of the age? The multitude, rising up indignantly against the Church, are rather driven into infidelity. Thus intolerance not only brings down punishment on itself, but dishonour on the sacred cause of religion.

I must hasten to that which is the strength of the Church, and contributes to the decline of Dissent. I refer to the aristocratical spirit of your country. This is your master-evil, and one which you cannot fully comprehend, for you live and move in it all the time; it is the air you breathe; and, like all familiar things, fails to be distinctly recognized. It is very strong yet. An intelligent friend writes me, that the spirit of caste seems stronger than ever in England, that he sees no tendency to the fusion of people into one sympathizing community, that society seems to be more broken into distinct and mutually repulsive classes. Be this as it may, the higher ranks are worshipped among you, and they do, must, and will give all their weight to the Established Church; so much so, that were the Church to cease to be formally established, it would lose little or nothing of its power. The higher classes are its pillars. But you will say, Have not these sustained it always as well as now, and why then is Dissent more endangered now by this cause? I answer, The middle classes, in which lay the strength of Dissent, have prospered, have grown rich and luxurious and aspiring, have caught the spirit of fashion, the desire to press upward, the passion for assimilation to those above them, and in this way have been brought more and more under the power of the upper classes in all concerns where opinion and fashion operate. The more the Dissenters have become "respectable," in the worldly sense, the weaker the spirit of Dissent. Even the Quakers have felt this influence.

England needs now a new spirit of "Nonconformity," far deeper, nobler, more searching, than anything which has existed. Do I not see the signs of it?

Shall I name one more cause of the power of the Church?

At this moment there is everywhere a reaction in favour of authority—a very natural one, growing chiefly out of the anxiety of the moneyed interests. The middle classes, which favoured liberty by their growing wealth, begin now to fear the invasion of their wealth from those below, and are more willing to strike a league with those above. They grow fearful of free opinions in all departments, and favour an Established Church as establishing everything else. All selfishness is shortsighted, or these men would see that their interest and duty and dignity all lie in one line,—i.e. in making common cause with the mass of their fellow-creatures, and sparing no efforts to lighten their burdens, and to elevate them intellectually, morally and socially. There can be no peace to the modern world till this truth is understood. A fire is kindled in the "lower classes," as they are called, which is smouldering when it seems quenched, which cannot die. How we ought to rejoice to lift up our depressed brethren! But no; we hate and fear them the more because they have caught the idea of some better, higher lot. We strengthen State authorities, Church authorities, to keep them down. We make religion hateful to them by using it for their subjugation. But all in vain. The revolution, which we might make a pure blessing, will come in storm, if in no other way, and will punish terribly and justly those who choose to keep their brethren in the dust.

You see what a long letter you have called out. Your notice of the Church produced a rush of thought which I have poured out as rapidly almost as it came. The question is, Am I right? I feel more and more how at a distance we err about other countries. I think much about England and France, and less about my own country, because this is secure. We have nothing to fear here. Our moneyed interest, which you alone hear in England, is given to croaking, but among the people there is no alarm. We may, do, and should, suffer from our passions and follies, but the two great free countries of Europe have serious difficulties. Still I hope much for them. The mass of the people, who have my chief sympathy, are struggling into light in your country, and this makes all sure in the end. I can add nothing on the other topics of your letter.

Very truly your friend,
WM. E. CHANNING.

To Dr. Channing.

Hampstead, August 6, 1841.

My dear Friend,—It delights me to think how far our correspondence is from languishing. I trust you have ere now received a long letter from me, occasioned by your Home Mission Report, and I yesterday was gratified by your letter on our Church. I answer it while fresh in my mind. I am not able to say whether Methodism, meaning strictly the sect founded by Wesley and that division of it which followed Whitfield, has been injurious to Dissent or not. I believe the converts were chiefly either members of the Establishment, or persons who had previously known nothing or cared nothing for religion in any shape. It seems as if the spread of the evangelical spirit in the Church had checked in some degree that of Methodism, which scarcely, I think, keeps up its proportion to the population. But when I lamented the decline of Dissent, I had in my mind that of Presbyterianism chiefly— that is, of the only sect which could boast of learned ministers, and which once included in its bosom a very considerable body of wealthy and well-educated and enlightened families.

As for the other old denominations, the Independents and the Baptists, they are by no means declining in numbers. Formerly their congregations were seldom found but in towns and among the trading classes, but I am now told that there is scarcely a rural village throughout the country in which either they or the Methodists, under some of their subdivisions, have not some humble place of worship. They reckon, I believe, by hundreds of thousands. But in this aristocratic country, as you truly call it, numbers *alone* stand for little or nothing. These Dissenters have no political power or weight whatever, as their ministers have confessed or complained. They have not even a single member of Parliament belonging to them, while the little Unitarian aristocracy has about fifteen. Their opinions are, I believe, Calvinistic to a high degree, and it is only as persons asserting practically the right of private judgment in religion, that it is possible to prefer them to the members of the Establishment. I know not at all what their political bent may be: this only we may rely on, that any administration which should strongly favour the Church would be certain of their enmity—a consideration which may come to be worth the attention of Sir Robert Peel. At periods of crisis every right aim tells. The Church-rate question has served in very many parishes throughout England as a muster-roll of the rated householders, and in a majority, I think, of these, the dissidents altogether have carried it against Mother Church. Observe that rating, i.e. to the poor, goes lower than the elective franchise, at least comprises much greater numbers. It may a little illustrate this matter to you if I mention that full half the maid-servants I have had were either some kind of Methodists or regular Dissenters; and I believe this to be general. You see from this, that there is no apparent tendency to what you would call pure Christianity in our lower classes—except, indeed, that among the Baptists there are, or were, some Unitarians. The sect of Socialists, the growth of which seems connected or coincident with that of Chartism, is not a Christian sect, it seems, but a Deistic one, which has exposed itself to just disgrace by condemning the institution of marriage. I know not at all to what extent it has spread, or whether it still increases. The public at large scarcely know it but through the invectives of the Bishop of Exeter in the House of Lords, in which there is probably both exaggeration and misrepresentation. Still I have heard, apparently on good authority, that there is scarcely a town in England without a Socialist congregation—an ugly fact, if it be one. A comparison of the religious state of our country now and a hundred years ago, will not, I conceive, support your theory of the progress of mankind. Then we had Low-church principles in the Establishment; the Dissenters learned, respected and steady; the Deists, what there were of them, learned also, moral, and too prudent to promulgate their opinions among the vulgar.

No; I cannot go all the length you have done in your late address, though I admire it very much, and cordially thank you for it; and if it be an exact delineation of the *present* state of opinion with you, especially of the tolerant, rather the enlarged, enlightened state of Christian feeling, I must say that we might take a lesson from you with great advantage. But I have often wished to ask you on what special ground you fix your confidence in the constant progress of the race? You reckon much, I know, on the influences of Christianity; but in this there is nothing new; and why should this power over the human heart be continually augmenting? If the world could be considered as an individual, we might readily suppose it a design of Providence that all its experiences of every kind should be tending to increase its knowledge and improve its virtue. But when two things remain always the same—the nature of God and the nature of man—when every human creature is born into the world with the same ignorance, and, what is more, with the same appetites and passions, as his earliest and rudest progenitors—when the necessity for the existence of evil, whatever may make that necessity, cannot be supposed likely to cease—can we reasonably expect more, than that in some countries the progress of the arts of life may redress some outward inconveniences, and obtain for a portion of society some outward comforts and luxuries, and that great crimes of violence may become more rare, and vice in the higher classes less gross? Men may grow more skilful in adapting means to ends, but may we hope that their ends will be wiser or better? The very diffusion of knowledge may prove little more than the beating out of the ingot into gold-leaf. In this country at least, literature in its higher sense is certainly not advancing; books must be made so rapidly, that even industry, labour, cannot be bestowed on the manufacture. For the interests of good taste and the effectual cultivation of the mind, it would be far better if we had not above one-tenth of the new books that are published; and so in science, the sciolists may amuse themselves, but assuredly they do nothing for the advance of any branch of study.

Your new people may be making progress, and I

hope they are; but in these old countries population increases upon us so frightfully, that it will be very well indeed if in any respect we can hold our own. Such are my more gloomy speculations; but it is impossible to concur more entirely than I do in what you point out as the *improvement* to be made of the present state and tendencies of society, or in the warnings which you think required.

No more will I add at present. I doubt if you will thank me for so much on the discouraging side. But you seek the truth, and it should be told you.

Ever most sincerely yours,
LUCY AIKIN.

To Miss Aikin.

Boston, December 15, 1841.

My dear Miss Aikin,—Thanks for your two unanswered letters—unanswered so long, not for want of will, but strength. I have been ill, a prisoner to my chamber for a month, and I am still so exhausted after six weeks' release from my chamber, that I take but short walks, and find even letter-writing wearisome. I can give you but a few lines, for I began this morning with a letter to Mrs. Baillie, which grew under my hands, and I have not much power left for other correspondents. Had you come first, I should have treated you more generously.

Your letter, giving an account of the interest taken in the education of the poorer classes by those above them, opens too great a field for me now; and I must say the same of your remarks on my faith in social progress. How little of our minds we can crowd into a few pages, even when we have most command of thought and utterance! I owe you a pleasure which I ought to acknowledge. I had postponed the reading of Milman's "History of Christianity," as I do of many good books, but your favourable mention of it determined me to take it in hand; and as soon as I began to convalesce after my late illness, I applied myself to the pleasant task. Sometimes, indeed, my weak head was strained to take in his long, complicated sentences, and I wished that he had added the charm of a simple style to his other merits, but I was too much interested to be discouraged. I have been truly delighted as well as instructed by the work. What amazes me is, that it should have come from the hands of an Episcopalian clergyman. Am I wrong in seeing in it true moral courage? Are there many in that Church to sympathize with such large, liberal views? To me, that Church seems at the moment very much fallen; indeed, never so degraded before. In the days of her Butlers, Berkeleys, Sherlocks, &c., she wanted life and efficacy; but there was something venerable in her grave, calm, large wisdom. Now, Methodism and Oxfordism have brought her low indeed.

If I did not respect your sex as highly as I do, I should say that this Church is passing through the stage of "old-womanism;" but I have seen and revered so many excellent old ladies, that my conscience and, I may add, my heart will not allow me to use this unfeeling phrase. I may say that the Church seems falling into spiritual dotage. Her chief faculty is memory of the old, and of much which is best forgotten. To wipe the dust from old customs, old costumes, old phrases—to revive decayed authority, and substitute these for fresh, living thought —such seems to be her task. To be sure, she has zeal, but it is of a *shrewish* cast, and manifests itself very much in scolding and denouncing such as will not come under her rod. The Methodistic element is incomparably more respectable than the High-church element, and it

T

seems as if the latter were getting the predominance in your Church.

It is truly comforting to find so free and generous a spirit as Milman's in such a community. He makes me doubt whether my view of the Church may not be exaggerated—whether she may not have more youthful blood in her veins than I had supposed. I may seem to speak sportively, but it affects me that the true grandeur of Christianity should be so overlooked by great communities bearing the Christian name.

During my convalescence, I read a considerable part of Miss Mitford's "Village," perhaps for the third time. Her short sketches, overflowing with life and beauty, refresh me when I am too weak for long stories, and she has often been a cheering friend in my sick room. My children also read to me " Charles O'Malley," a book full of action and graphical power; the work of a fresh, ever-observant and inventive mind, not going far into human nature, but giving the surface of life very vividly; a book to intoxicate adventurous, daring young men, by sketches of war, in its strange mixture of gay conviviality, recklessness and bloodshed. I read such books with much interest, as they give me human experiences in strong and strange contrast with my own, and help my insight into that mysterious thing, the human soul.

I could tell you more of my amusements, but can only add, that I am very faithfully your friend,

W. E. CHANNING.

P.S. You ask about my "great work." I beg you not to use the phrase again. I have nothing great about me but the *undeveloped* within. My wish is to throw in a little light on some great problems relating to human nature—and, I may say, the divine—by giving my views in connection with metaphysics, ethics, politics and theology. I hope to escape a large work, for my aim is to give only *my own* views, the fruits of my own thinking. I am a little discouraged, for the winter is gone, and I have brought very little to pass. How do you go on? I want you to write a free, courageous book, not to stand in awe of critics. Speak out in your own strong style.

To Dr. Channing.

Hampstead, January 10, 1842.

My dear Friend,—It grieves me much to find that illness was the cause of that long silence which I had been wondering at and lamenting. This cause did not suggest itself to me, because I had received from you a sermon delivered far from your home, and, as I thought, recently, which certainly bore no marks of feebleness. This, I think, is almost all I shall say to you about it, for a good reason—that I know nothing of the subject. Your discourse goes entirely on the ground of religion being a social, an uniting principle; and such indeed I know it to be usually. To me, however, it has never been so; on the contrary, I have always felt it as a matter more strictly personal than any other; and the very last office I could bear to commit to any human being would be that of speaking to my Maker for me, or in my name. I mention this only as what is, not what ought to be: at least it is a matter in which every one must do as suits best with his temper and circumstances. I can imagine that if it had ever been my fortune in youth to attend upon any minister who could either have satisfied my judgment or moved my heart, I too might have known devotion as a bond of friendship, a social pleasure. Your charity is very large, and certainly no man ever had less of the *priest.*

I am glad my mention of it led you to read Milman's work; and I made him very happy two days since by telling him that he had cheered your convalescence. It was very many years since we had met before, and that but once, yet we had each a strong remembrance of the other, and met like friends. I found him cheerful, animated, quite without pomp or pretension, and full of agreeable conversation. I agree with you, however, that his style in writing is by no means so easy or simple. His close study of Gibbon seems to have injured him in this point. There is no writer whose faults are more infectious than Gibbon's—condemn them as you will, you cannot contemplate them long without a strange propensity to repeat them. In fact, though certainly faults, they are seldom gratuitous ones. Most of his ambiguities prove, on examination, devices to comprise much matter in few words : this is seldom the case with those of his imitators. You ask if our Church has many Milmans. Very few, I conceive; and the clergy are so far from being proud of his learned and courageous work, that they and their reviews have preserved a studied silence respecting it. I know not which way Mother Church is setting her face. Oxford, indeed, casts a longing eye towards Rome, but with the powerful evangelical anti-Popery party to watch her, she durst not what she would. Then Scotland is almost in a flame on the old ground of the superiority of the Church authorities to the civil power and the laws of the land. In that country the Sabbatarian fanaticism burns still fiercer than among our Evangelicals. What think you of a provincial presbytery's excommunicating a man and his wife also for burying their child on the Sunday —the general custom here, at least with the working classes ? I fear indeed *we* grow no wiser.

How far, I wonder, have I brought down my own

small particular story in my letters to you? I doubt if I have told you that I went, in the middle of September, to that deserted seat of fashion and gaiety, Bath. The railroad brought the journey within my strength, and I had the reward of my effort by leaving in those warm waters a very troublesome gouty affection, which had kept me long in a state of suffering and languor. Since my return I have been labouring upon Addison with vigour, and am not quite without hope of bringing it out before the end of our London spring, lasting till August. Mr. Hallam says it is time the public should be put in mind of him, for we have had no such writer since, and I find the same is the faith of all our high literati. One thing strikes me as quite unique in him. He was a great reformer of manners, yet never drew upon him the anger either of the high or the low—he improved mankind, and they did not persecute him. But perhaps I say wrongly *mankind*. His chief aim was to improve *womankind*, as the first step to amending society, and *we* were so good and so docile as to thank him even when he took the liberty of laughing at us. Had he begun with *you*——

Pray, had your Miss Sedgwick the like benevolent design in all the elaborate disparagement that she bestows on the outsides and insides of us unhappy women of England, with our Queen at our head? The hardest morsel is her choosing to record, and thus to sanction, the sentence of one of the girls of her party, that a woman gentle and lovely *could not* be an Englishwoman. Such stuff is not worth talking about, but American women visiting England will certainly be sufferers by these demonstrations of national hatred. Your niece did not look like a hater: I should be glad to be remembered to her.

You and I have our own private treaty of amity,

but this slave-trading is likely, I fear, to make ill-blood between our governments.

I have been lately led to think of one of the greatest differences between education among us now and half a century ago—consisting in the introduction of German literature. The study of this language is now become so nearly universal in good- society, that twenty years hence young people will be saying with wonder, " I do really suspect that neither that old Mr. Such-a-one nor his wife know German." Just as *we* used to say of some of our elders regarding French. I have made some young people stare by telling them that, in my childhood, Mr. William Taylor, of Norwich, whose translation of Bürger's Leonora was the spark which fired the muse of Scott, was quite as much wondered at for knowing German, as a person would now be for a profound acquaintance with Russ. What are to be the effects of this new ingredient on the flavour of our lighter literature, I cannot clearly perceive; certainly, if Carlyle be made the example of its influence on taste and style, nothing can be fancied more detestable. Mrs. Austin, on the contrary, is able to render a vast variety of German styles all into pure and flowing English, preserving at the same time something quite foreign in the subject-matter and turn of thought. There seems to be something more profoundly sentimental — more cordially affectionate—in the expressions of the Germans than is the tone with us, and all our travellers hold their demonstrations to be sincere and trustworthy. On this account we certainly love them better than any other foreign people (it is to be considered that we have no national rivalries with them); yet a want of polish, tact, refinement, is remarked, which often gives a tinge of burlesque both to their sublime and pathetic. Mr. Taylor has somewhere said that " there is a *too-muchness* in almost all German writers." It seems as if the lightness of touch and perfection of taste of a Voltaire were gifts denied to their national mind. In one study their writers show a quite original spirit, combined with their well-known laboriousness—that of biblical criticism; and it is in this that I apprehend they are producing the strongest effects on other nations. Their most startling paradoxes seem to have found a welcome among your divines, and they certainly have not been universally rejected here. At our universities, "German Theology" is a word of fear and reproach; but those who, like Milman, would dive into Christian antiquities, well know that their main reliance must be on the guidance of German *down-diggers*. Are they destined once more to produce a revolution in religion? Will new blood be poured into the old churches of Christendom from their veins? Alas! neither of us can expect to live long enough to see these questions solved by the event. How I long sometimes to peep into the yet unopened leaves of the book of fate, to read the destinies of nations in their moral relations! It is not the doom of dynasties that I would learn.

We have nothing new in literature, and in politics we are mutely awaiting the meeting of the new ministry's new Parliament. The grand trials of strength will be on the corn-laws and protective duties—momentous questions, no doubt, but on which, if all who are unqualified to judge would be silent, there could be no popular cry. Every year there is more or less of distress in our manufacturing towns, because such are the productive powers of our gigantic machinery, that every year some markets are overstocked, and the mill-owners are obliged to hold their hands. But this simple explanation never satisfies the sufferers; false or partial causes are sought out: it is now the fault of your banking system, now of our own. Once it was the decrees of Bonaparte; now it is our corn-laws. All Europe seems to be over-peopled, and the wages and condition of the working classes sink in consequence—sink without help or hope of restoration. Sad truths, which in your new country you will know nothing of for many ages. Our magnificent colonies afford us, indeed, considerable relief; and I cannot repress some swellings of national pride, as I spread before me the map of the world and realize it to myself, that the British empire is the widest ever known to history. It is a proud feeling to dismiss an English MS. to the press, and think in how many zones and regions your thoughts will be read—the more reason they should be worthy and noble ones.

I must not spare more time from my Addison, even to chat with you, but I could not bear to let your last lie a day longer unacknowledged. I grieve that you have been so long a sufferer, and shall be very anxious to hear that your strength returns completely. Be not too impatient to resume your literary labours, notwithstanding our impatience for the work you have in preparation. It is in vain to urge, while the body refuses to second the eagerness of the mind. I now feel that a week of the application of health performs more than months of languor. Do you recollect Mrs. Carter's pretty dialogue in verse between Body and Soul, and their mutual reproaches? I always thought poor Body was the ill-used party.

Adieu. May all good attend you!

Ever your sincere friend,

LUCY AIKIN.

To Miss Aikin.

June 12, 1842.

My dear Miss Aikin,—Your letter of January 10th has been by me a long time unanswered, but you will not misinterpret my silence. I have done to you as to others. I had a pressure of engagements in the winter, with no great strength to meet them. Three months ago I left my home to find an earlier and milder spring in the middle States, and began too early to travel in Pennsylvania. There I had a renewal of the disease from which I suffered towards the end of the autumn— inflammation of the lungs, and passed through an illness in an inn, confined to my bed a week or more, and about three weeks to my chamber. Having lived in a most comfortable home, I should have looked forward to sickness under such circumstances with not much pleasure; but I learned that I could dispense with many customary indulgences, and on the whole recovered as fast as if I had been under my own roof. Happily, I was imprisoned in the beautiful valley of Wyoming, to which Campbell has given a European reputation; and as soon as I could bear a strong light, I seated myself at the window, beneath which flowed the Sasquehannah, and beyond swelled the gentle hills or mountains, with forests at their summits and the freshest verdure of cultivation below. All manner of fine things have been said about Nature; but I do not know that she has been called a physician or found a place in the Materia Medica, but I can testify to her healing virtues. Love within doors and beauty without divided with the doctor the credit of my recovery. Were I to set up for physician, I should give myself to the study of the influence of mental and spiritual agents on disease. Who knows but that I should do much to banish the odious drugs which so often inflict worse diseases or pains than they cure! We have some religious physicians who pray occasionally with their patients, and I suspect the prayer often does more good than the medicine. The diseases of civilization are nervous to a great degree,—the very ones to be reached by spiritual agencies.

For many years past I have spent my summers in the most beautiful island of our country, Rhode Island. This summer I have determined to try inland air, and have retreated to the mountainous district of Massachusetts, where I am to settle which I enjoy most, mountains or my dear native ocean. One of my great pleasures is that my friend Miss Sedgwick lives a door or two from me. I wish you could see her in her family, almost worshipped, not for her genius, but her loveliness of character, and shedding blessed influences through perhaps the most united family I have ever known, and I am sure you would forgive her severe remarks on English women. I do not know what these are but through your letter; for so little relish have I for travels, especially for journals, that I do not hold myself bound to read them, even from the pens of my dearest friends. Let me say, however, that there are extenuations of Miss S.'s offence which you can hardly understand. National tastes are formed very much by circumstances, and our taste is educated under influences which unfit us for an impartial estimate of English women. You know, I suppose, that we have much more beauty in our country than there is in yours, and this beauty differs much in character. One of your intelligent countrymen said to me recently, "The beauty of American women is more sylph-like; that of English women, stronger, more masculine." And so it is. Hardly anything can exceed the delicacy and loveliness of our young women.

The sight of them is one of my pleasures as I walk in the streets. Unhappily, these sweet flowers are very frail. Whether from climate or wrong modes of living, or from the burden of toil which motherhood in this country lays on your sex, our young women fade at an early age. Still the character of their beauty at the age when woman acts most on the heart has great influence on our taste, and in some degree injures it. Our distinguished painter Mr. Allston has sometimes been blamed here for giving so much embonpoint to his women, and for giving them feet and ancles stout enough to stand on. We incline somewhat to the Chinese taste. Now it is not strange that the English woman does not satisfy us. She has more embonpoint, a stouter frame, more pronounced features, stronger manners, gestures, movements. She has a more elastic step, but takes strides, as we say. She seems less feminine, less refined. She, too, has somewhat freer manners. She talks on subjects which would call up the colour in an American woman's cheeks. Strange that a colony, sent from England into a wilderness and a bleaker climate, should arrive at the distinction which I have stated! The nervous temperament predominates here more than in England, I believe, and may explain some of our peculiarities, though in itself a strange thing. Southey has said we are growing into Indians, and yet the Indian has no nerves. He does not know what consumption is, and we most of us die of it, and suffer much from nervous fever. This constitution of ours gives us some signal advantages, on which I should like to dwell in another letter. It promises us perhaps superiority in the fine arts, as well as in person and manners. One of your very keen-eyed countrywomen observed that the profiles of the American gentlemen were of a higher order than yours. But I have a great deal to say on the point, and have given you now as much as an English lady can take in at once. I have shown you my confidence in your patience and kind feelings.

Very truly your friend,
WM. E. CHANNING.

I rejoice to learn from Mrs. Baillie that you are going on bravely with your Addison, and promise myself a great deal of pleasure from it.

To Dr. Channing.

Hampstead, August 9, 1842.

My dear Friend,—It grieves me to learn that illness has been the cause of your long silence; but it is past, I hope, and if your summer be bright and balmy like ours, it will give you strength to support the rigours of the coming winter. But O that you would come to recruit in our milder climate! We should then soon exorcise that strange phantom of a petticoated man which your imagination has conjured up during your illness, and some demon has whispered you to call an Englishwoman. I am well persuaded that you could have formed no such notion of us when you were here, although I believe you then saw but little society, and that of an inferior kind.

As to the very delicate subject of comparative beauty, our travellers attest that you have many very pretty girls; so have we: and even Miss Sedgwick pronounces that "the Englishwoman is magnificent from twenty to five-and-forty." We are satisfied; so let it rest.

With respect to our *step*, or *stride*, as you say, I have a little history to give you. Down to five-and-forty or fifty years ago, our ladies, tight-laced and "propped on French heels," had a short mincing step, pinched figures, pale faces, weak nerves, much affectation, a delicate helplessness and miserable health. Physicians prescribed exercise, but to little purpose. Then came that event which is the beginning or end of everything—the French Revolution. The Parisian women, amongst other restraints, salutary or the contrary, emancipated themselves from their stays, and kicked off their *petits talons*. We followed the example, and, by way of improving upon it, learned to march of the drill-sergeant, mounted boots, and bid defiance to dirt and foul weather. We have now well-developed figures, blooming cheeks, active habits, firm nerves, natural and easy manners, a scorn of affectation, and vigorous constitutions. If your fair daughters would also learn to *step out*, their bloom would be less transient, and fewer would fill untimely graves. I admit, indeed, *some* unnecessary inelegance in the step of our pedestrian fair ones; but this does not extend to ladies of quality, or *real* gentlewomen, who take the air chiefly in carriages or on horseback. They walk with the same quiet grace that pervades all their deportment, and to which you have seen nothing similar or comparable. When you mention our "stronger gestures," I know not what you mean. All Europe declares that we have *no* gesture. Madame de Staël ridiculed us as mere pieces of still-life; and of *untravelled* gentlewomen this is certainly true in general. All governesses proscribe it. Where it exists, it arises from personal character. I have seen it engaging when the offspring of a lively imagination and warm feelings, repulsive when the result of a keen temper or dictatorial assumption. Again, your charge of want of delicacy I cannot understand. The women of every other European nation charge us with prudery, and I really cannot conceive of a human being more unassailable by just reproach on this head than a well-conducted Englishwoman. We have, indeed, heard some whimsical stories of American damsels who would not for the world speak of the *leg* even of a table, or the *back* even of a chair; and I do confess that we are not delicate or indelicate to this point. But if you mean to allude to the enormities of Frances Wright, or even to some of the discussions of —— ——, I can only answer, we blush too. Be pleased to consider that you have yet seen in your country none of our ladies of high rank; and few of your people, excepting diplomatic characters, have had more than very transient glimpses of them here, while we have had the heads of your society with us. Now I must frankly tell you, in reference to your very unexpected claim for your countrywomen of superior refinement, that although I have seen several of them whose manners were too quiet and retiring to give the least offence, I have neither seen nor heard of any who, even in the society of our middle classes, were thought entitled to more than this negative commendation—any who have become prominent without betraying gross ignorance of more than conventional good-breeding. The very tone of voice, the accent and the choice of phrase, give us the impression of extreme inelegance. Patriot and stanch republican as you are, I think you must admit the à-priori probability that the metropolis of the British Empire, the first city in the world for size, for opulence, for diffusion of the comforts, accommodations and luxuries of life, as well as for all the appliances of science, literature and taste—the seat of a court unexcelled in splendour, and of an aristocracy absolutely unrivalled in wealth, in substantial power and dignity, and especially in mental cultivation of the most solid and most elegant kind—would afford such a standard of graceful and finished manners as your State capitals can have no chance of coming up to. Further: it has been most truly observed that in every country it is the *mothers* who give the tone both to morals and manners; but with you the mothers are by your own account the *toilers*. Oppressed with the cares of house and children, they either retire from society into the bosom of their family, or leave at least the active and prominent parts in it to mere girls: and can you suppose that the *art and science* of good-breeding, for such it is, will be likely to advance towards perfection when all who have attained such proficiency as experience can give resign the sway to giddy novices? With us it is quite different. Young ladies do not *come out* till eighteen, and then their part is a very subordinate one. It is the matron who does the honours of her house and supports conversation; and her daughters pay their visits beneath her wing. Under wholesome restraint like this, the young best learn self-government. "Sir," said Dr. Parr, when provoked by the ill-manners of a rich man who had been a spoiled child, "it is discipline that makes the scholar, discipline that makes the gentleman, and it is the want of discipline that makes you what you are."

One of your young women showed her taste and breeding by asking an English lady if she had seen "Victoria;" and I must mention that Miss Sedgwick has thought proper to describe the first and *greatest lady in the world* as "a plain little *body*," adding, "ordinary is the word for her." It was no woman luckily, but your Mr. D., who had the superlative conceit and impertinence to express his *surprise* to a friend of mine at finding so much good society *in London*. Now I think I have given you enough for one letter.

Let me thank you very gratefully for your "Duty of the Free States." We ought all to be grateful to you as one of the most earnest and powerful pleaders for peace between our two countries. I trust there is now good hope of the settlement of all our disputes. But your man-owners may as well give up all hope of our lending our hands to the recovery of their chattels; we shall go to war sooner, I can tell them. Your piece gave me much new information respecting the obligations of the free states in connection with slavery; they are more onerous than I thought. You *must* carry your point as to the district of Columbia at *all* risks, and I apprehend you will do so as soon as your people can be brought earnestly to *will* it—a state of public feeling which seems to be advancing. After our victory over slave-trade and slavery, no good cause is ever to be despaired of, not even although many of its champions may show themselves rash, uncharitable, violent. Reason, justice and humanity, must condescend to own that they need the service of the passions to lead the forlorn hope in their holiest crusades. Your lively delineations of the Southerns and the Northerns struck me very forcibly. The contrast is just what we should draw between English and Irish. Difference of climate may in great degree account for this in your case, but it can have no part in ours. We should ascribe it to difference of race, had not the original English settlers in Ireland grown into such a likeness of the old Celtic stock. Nothing more inscrutable than the causes of national character. Climate certainly modifies the original type. Thus the picture which you draw of American women in your letter bore much resemblance, I thought, to the Creoles of our islands. But surely the same character cannot apply to the women of both North and South any more than to the men; for, independently of all other causes, the presence or absence of domestic slaves must modify every detail of domestic, and of course of feminine, life.

We have a new book which, if it fall in your way, will surely interest you. It is the "Life of Oliver Heywood," composed chiefly from his own journals by the Rev. Joseph Hunter. He was one of the two thousand ejected Presbyterian ministers of Charles II.'s time. After he was *silenced*, so far from holding his tongue, he passed the rest of his life, more than thirty years, in assiduous, almost incessant preaching, as a kind of missionary. His sphere of action was the wild mountainous tract along the borders of Lancashire and the West Riding of Yorkshire, then thinly sprinkled with pastoral villages, small towns engaged in woollen manufacture, and seats of rustic gentry—now a region of factories and steam-engines, mostly deserted by its hereditary gentry, but swarming with population. Oliver Heywood founded many congregations, and was indeed one of the chief fathers of Protestant Dissent in all that country; it was a productive soil, and the seed sown by him has brought forth abundantly. The wealthy descendants of the poor and rude people whom he penetrated with his own profound sense of practical religion, his own stern hostility to the claims of *power* in the concerns of conscience, and his defiance, his scorn of persecution, have not yet quite lost the spirit of their forefathers, although they have mitigated their gloomy austerity and Calvinistic faith. Many of them are at this time the zealous and liberal supporters of the Unitarian congregations in Bolton, Manchester, Leeds, Halifax, &c. The picture of manners is very striking. I doubt if anything has been published which brings so close those rigid men whose lives might be called one long religious service—with whom to fast and pray appeared the great *ends* for which mankind were created. The intensity of their bigotry was frightful, and it was chiefly exerted against their brother sectaries. When they are themselves under persecution, one is disposed to respect and admire them; but yet it is impossible to forget that they are quite ready to do as much, and more also, to all who differ from them if ever their own turn should come round again. You must see the book. I will try to beg you a copy of my friend James Heywood, one of two wealthy and most worthy brothers, at whose desire and cost this life of their ancient kinsman has been written. Mr. Hunter is in every part thorough master of his subject, and his own portion is full of curious and valuable matter.

This reminds me of *your* Mr. Savage, with whom I had an interesting conference. The spirit of "Old Mortality" seems to have migrated into his form. There is something in what Carlyle keeps repeating about *real* men, *earnest* men. It is they alone who stamp their image into coming ages. *They!* I should have said *you.*

My "Addison," a theme on which there is no room for anything very *earnest*, though I am *real* as far as I go, proceeds at a very leisurely pace, but I hope to be ready for the next book season. I have been fortunate in obtaining much new matter, especially some very agreeable unpublished letters from the lineal representative of his executor, Tickell.

Ever your sincere friend,
LUCY AIKIN.

Dr. CHANNING, born 7th April, 1780, died on the 2nd October, 1842. Miss AIKIN, who was born 6th November, 1781, survived till the 29th January, 1864.

www.ingramcontent.com/pod-product-compliance
Lightning Source LLC
Chambersburg PA
CBHW020524300426
44111CB00008B/540